Also by Christopher Hitchens

BLOOD, CLASS AND EMPIRE

The Enduring Anglo-American Relationship

CHRISTOPHER HITCHENS

NATION BOOKS
NEW YORK

BLOOD, CLASS AND EMPIRE: *The Enduring Anglo-American Relationship*

Copyright © Christopher Hitchens 1990, 2004

Originally published as *Blood, Class and Nostalgia: Anglo-American Ironies* by Farrar, Straus and Giroux, 1990

Published by
Nation Books
An Imprint of Avalon Publishing Group
245 West 17th Street, 11th Floor
New York, NY 10011

Nation Books is a co-publishing venture of the Nation Institute and Avalon Publishing Group Incorporated.

Library of Congress Cataloging-in-Publication Data is available.

ISBN 1-56025-592-7

9 8 7 6 5 4 3 2 1

Printed in the United States of America
Distributed by Publishers Group West

For Carol Blue

Acknowledgments

I used to wonder why there was no attempt at a general discussion, in book form, of the related phenomena of Anglophilia, Anglophobia, Anglo-Americanism, and Anglo-Saxondom. I now wonder less. The subject is so vast and extensive that any attempt at synthesis will disappoint somebody. The following pages are neither a narrative history, nor a cultural survey, nor a full-dress political analysis. But they are offered as incisions, made at selected crucial points, into the hide of the intriguing animal. Some parts of the anatomy will, I hope, have become clearer to view.

I have more people to thank than it is decent or possible to mention. Andrew Wylie, my literary agent, and Steve Wasserman and David Rieff, my editors, were present at the very first conversation which led to this book, and had the grace to keep up their interest until the very end. Authors who moan with praise for their editors always seem to reek slightly of the Stockholm syndrome, but authors who do not thank their friends are being remiss. Without these friendships, and the stern duties which came with them, I would have written an infinitely poorer book.

Leonard and Rhoda Dreyfus offered a true refuge for writer and editor in the closing stages, lending us the flawless English and colonial (and revolutionary) ambience of their beloved Virginia while rescuing me from the Carnaby Shoppe, the Piccadilly Pub, and the Royal Burgers of the neighboring mock-Tudor "English

Inn." I hope that some of the happiness of this outcome is reflected in what follows.

CHRISTOPHER HITCHENS
Charlottesville, Virginia
October 1989

Contents

Preface

To open a paper at the overseas news pages during the year of grace 2003 was to be confronted by a fairly predictable menu of crisis, if not an exactly measurable standard of crisis management. An American foreign-policy "expert," whether headquartered in Langley, Virginia or Foggy Bottom, Washington, or at one of the nation's proliferating think-tanks and institutes, could be expected to have something to say about many or all of the following:

- Along the so-called "green line" that has divided Israelis from Palestinians in an informal manner for many years, a physical wall was being constructed, partly for "security" reasons and partly for annexationist ones.
- The frontiers of Iraq were becoming heavily porous, with the postinvasion nation-state open to unlicensed entry from Syria, Saudi Arabia, Kuwait and Turkey.
- The expansion of NATO and the European Union was being jeopardized by a petrified intransigence on the part of the Turkish occupiers of Cyprus. Realpolitik appeared to demand an accommodation with Turkey, while law and precept and the resolutions of the United Nations all told against the grabbing and settling of Cypriot soil by Turkish forces.
- In Northern Ireland, repeated attempts to square the circle of

Republican and Unionist attrition were foundering on embedded reefs of distrust, as the demography of the Six Counties moved slowly towards a Catholic demographic majority and as Sinn Fein emerged as the largest Republican party.

- Along the borders of India and Pakistan, and the borders of Pakistan and Afghanistan, and within the disputed state of Kashmir, a toxic combination of Hindu-Muslim rivalry, "holy war" infiltration, and thermonuclear weapons offered the most appalling likelihood of what is no less appallingly euphemized as a nuclear "exchange."
- In Zimbabwe, the prosperity so urgently needed for a respite in the woes of Southern Africa was being squandered by the kleptocratic autocracy of Robert Mugabe.

On most days, the news was fairly sporadic as between Tamils and Sinhala in Sri Lanka, or as between the United Kingdom and Argentina on the Falklands/Malvinas question. But the plain fact remains that the main duty of an American foreign-service officer was to master the legacy of partition and postcolonialism that has been bequeathed to the United States by the United Kingdom. Every one of the frontiers cited above, from the Durand Line in Afghanistan to the Iraq-Kuwait demarcation made by Sir Percy Cox in 1921, was drawn by British diplomats. Sometimes the spirit of their activity could be summarized in the title of Sir Penderel Moon's celebrated memoir of the scuttle from India: "Divide and Quit." America has inherited, not to say assumed and annexed, responsibilities from other European powers as well: It is the superpower arbiter in formerly Dutch Indonesia as well as the formerly Belgian Congo (as it had been, also, so memorably and calamitously, in French Indochina). But it is the relationship with Britain above all that conditions its present posture, and furnishes the ethnopolitical boundaries that it patrols. Even in the case of former Yugoslavia, which was not previously part of the British imperial dominion, American policy in the 1990s was to a near-fatal extent determined by a historic British friendship with Serbia, and by the partitionist tradition—one could almost say fanaticism—of the British Foreign Office, as exemplified by Lords Carrington and Owen.

I completed this book just as the long Cold War was drawing to a close, and I am grateful now that its main intention was retrospective. I had not imagined—in my chapter on Kipling, say—that within a decade or so there would again be British soldiers, let alone American ones, on the North West Frontier between Afghanistan and Pakistan. Nor would I have thought that an Anglo-American expedition to occupy Mesopotamia was a very strong probability. If it comes to that, I had not expected that the ominous place-name Sarajevo would become vivid and actual for an entire new generation. Yet I have since spent, or had to spend, a good bit of time in these locations, as the unraveling of a pseudo-stable superpower standoff has released or encouraged primeval forces, and perforce reconstituted one of the most durable alliances of the twentieth century in an improvised attempt at confronting a new set of antagonists.

The best I can claim for this work is that anybody reading it for the first time might still be able to trace the filiating threads that make that same alliance so intelligible historically. It was no great shock to me, either, to witness British and American forces acting in concert in Kurdistan in 1991, in Bosnia and in Kosovo later in the decade, and in Basra in 2003. They both had a self-conscious sense of a tradition: one that could be readily resumed both rhetorically and politically. Of the chapters of this book, I could most easily update the one on the cult of Winston Churchill. American official speech after September 11, 2001 was more rife than ever with Churchillian tropes, whether uttered by Rudolph Giuliani or Donald Rumsfeld, and once again a British ambassador to Washington was able to donate a bust of "The Last Lion" to a war-minded administration. (During later hostilities in Iraq, however, no further use was made of Churchill's famous recommendation that truth in wartime must be protected by "a bodyguard of lies." One wonders why this remark was not deployed on the one occasion where it might have done some good.)

Most Americans and a large but probably diminishing number of British people tend to take it for granted that an Anglo-American partnership is in the natural order of things, and another conceivable merit of this book is to have argued that such an assumption is historically unsound.

There have been notable fluctuations in the level of amity and mutuality that supposedly bind London to Washington and, surprisingly to some, these fluctuations are more apt to occur under a Conservative government than a Labour one. I vividly remember standing on an American diplomat's private lawn in Aspen, Colorado in early August of 1990, watching Margaret Thatcher and George Bush respond to the news that Saddam Hussein had invaded Kuwait. (The period of post–Berlin Wall "peace dividend," now so hard to remember but then so eagerly anticipated, had thus lasted for perhaps nine whole months.) President Bush gave off an impression, which I have never been able to dispel in my mind, that the news had not come as a complete surprise to him. He spoke with complacency and understatement. When it came time for Mrs. Thatcher to seize the microphone, however, the entire tone of things underwent a dramatic change. She spoke of aggression and invoked defiance. I always believed the story that has since been confirmed officially—that she instructed Bush in private that " this is no time to go wobbly." Be that as it may, on the following day the President himself was reaching for Churchillian language and saying that the Iraqi occupation "would not stand." (This in itself is consistent, by the way, with the suspicion that a partial Iraqi intervention in Kuwait would not have been a *casus belli,* whereas the full-scale annexation that soon disclosed itself was more than had been foreseen. The then American ambassador to Baghdad, Ms. April Glaspie, had on the occasion of her last meeting with Saddam informed him that the United States took no view of the border dispute between Iraq and Kuwait: a border drawn by the abovementioned Sir Percy Cox some seven decades previously. She had even gone so far as to tell him that Americans were prepared to be understanding about this, having had their own problems "with British colonialism.")

At the time of the Aspen summit, it was an open secret in Washington that the Bush administration now looked to Chancellor

Helmut Kohl's freshly reunited Germany as America's best friend-to-be in Europe. As Sir Robin Renwick, a distinguished British envoy to Washington, phrases it in his book *Fighting with Allies*:

> Margaret Thatcher breathed a sigh of relief when George Bush defeated the Democratic contender in the 1988 presidential election. But with the new team's arrival in the White House she found herself dealing with an administration that saw Germany as its leading European partner, that proclaimed its support for European integration, and also disagreed with her about nuclear defense. "I felt I could not always rely as before on American cooperation."

Bereft of her once-mighty admirer Ronald Reagan and almost pathologically hostile to Herr Kohl, Prime Minister Thatcher saw an advantage at once. Did Germany have any traditional friends among the emirs and sheikhs of the Gulf? Any useful bases and intelligence connections? Any experience of fighting in the region? No. But Britain did, and could make itself highly serviceable to any American effort. The first "coalition of the willing" was forged that very day, though of course—and given the fact that Saddam had abolished the very existence of a UN member state—it was very much easier for this coalition to secure the assent of the Security Council and General Assembly.

Mrs. Thatcher did not remain Prime Minister for long enough to hail the eventual triumph of allied arms in Kuwait, having been deposed by her own party while attending a summit in Paris and having been replaced by John Major. And President Bush's victory in the Gulf was not enough to insulate him against the Clintonian challenge in the summer and fall of 1992. The accession of Clinton was, in some superficial ways, the advent of the most Anglophile administration imaginable. The new President and a whole clutch of his inner circle—Strobe Talbot, Robert Reich, Ira Magaziner, George Stephanopoulos—had been Rhodes Scholars at Oxford. Yet, by a most odd and ironic chance, Bill Clinton had himself previously been a student at Georgetown of Professor Carroll Quigley, author of *The Anglo-American Establishment*. This book, which was not able to find a publisher in the good professor's lifetime, is an exposé of a secret plan, formulated by Cecil Rhodes and his successors, for a covert Anglo-Saxon "New World Order." It is still to be found by way of certain conspiracy-minded book clubs, and contains some absorbing information about the role played by the empire-minded Milner group or "Round Table," and by successor cliques such as the pro-appeasement Cliveden set. One cannot know the precise effect of this teaching upon the impressionable young Clinton—who did cite Quigley as a formative teacher during his presidential campaign—but one can be certain that for other reasons the "special relationship" went into a decline during the Clinton-Major years.

Those in the United States who wished to prevent the obliteration of Bosnia-Herzegovina by Greater Serbia, this being the ostensible if vacillating policy of the Clinton administration, were met with consistent discouragement from the British Tories. In an especially cynical twist, the Major government denied the right of the Americans even to pronounce on the ongoing atrocity since there were no American "troops on the ground." (The British ones, it seemed for most of the time, were there only to protect themselves or to guarantee Serbian gains.) The Republican Party in the United States, for its part, held fast to the idea, so tellingly phrased by one of its spokesmen, that America had "no dog in this fight." This had also been the view of the Bush-Baker-Eagleburger administration.

In the result, the American military rescue of Sarajevo by a brief aerial bombardment was the outcome of another coalition, not so much of the "willing" as of the internationalist left-liberals and the neoconservatives. Barely recalled today but highly significant, this alliance was to be reconstituted for the war in Kosovo, which finally put an end not just to the "Greater Serbia" fantasy but to the regime of Slobodan Milosevic himself. My categories are not precise: Many left-liberal internationalists opposed the intervention and some neoconservative types (Henry Kissinger prominent among them) did so likewise. However, an agreement between elements of both such forces was for the first time thinkable. And by that point, Tony Blair had replaced John Major in Downing Street.

Comment on the Clinton-Blair relationship was at first confined to the production of an immensity of lazy prose concerning the so-called "Third Way" between traditional social democracy and globalized transnational corporate capitalism. As might have been predicted, this relationship turned out to be self-managing. What was not so predictable was the emergence of what one of Tony Blair's later nemeses was to term "ethical foreign policy." While Robin Cook was still his loyal Foreign Secretary, in April 1999, Blair made a speech at the Chicago Council on Foreign Relations in which he declared that coexistence with acquisitive and aggressive dictatorships was both unwise and immoral as well as ultimately impossible. It was Blair who urged a faltering Clinton into a full-scale engagement in Kosovo, and who resolved to send British forces on a rescue mission to defend the government of Sierra Leone against a bloody tribalist aggression supported from neighboring Liberia. And all this while, half-hidden from view and memory, British and American aircraft were taking to the skies every morning and evening, and patrolling over northern and southern Iraq to enforce the "no-fly" zones. This ten-year joint enterprise for the protection of the Kurds and the Shi'ites, which had also involved French planes for the early part of its existence, was the unexpired portion of the first Gulf War and the unacknowledged portent of the war to come.

It is now a commonplace to say that the assault on American civil society of September 11, 2001 "changed everything." It did not so much change as confirm the preexisting Anglo-American understanding; an understanding which had been somewhat indistinct since the advent of George Bush to the presidency. Bush was by nature a provincial isolationist and had campaigned as a foe of "nation-building" and other internationalist schemes. He was for lifting sanctions where possible and dubious of the role of American forces in the Balkans. No doubt most of Blair's entourage would have preferred the election of Albert Gore. However, the engulfing flame of the twin towers in lower Manhattan, in which British citizens were

"London-Washington axis"

the second-largest group of victims, was to rekindle (if the term may be allowed) a much more traditional version of the London-Washington axis. Many Americans were heard to say that they wished it had been Mr. Blair rather than Mr. Bush or even Mr. Giuliani who spoke for them that dreadful week: Moments of emotion and crisis even now seeming to require someone to whom the heritage of Shakespeare and Churchill was somehow in the genes.

Not only that, but there were British special forces, and British cruise-missile submarines, ready, able and willing to go to battle stations in and around Afghanistan. Indeed, and as in the case of former Yugoslavia if diametrically reversed, there were British advisors who counseled the immediate insertion of ground troops as against the American overreliance on high-altitude bombing. Moreover, there was residual British influence in both India and Pakistan, and expertise, too.

Neither was British influence in NATO or the European Union to be despised. The Tories, who had often spoken too glibly about a Britain that could "punch above its weight" (while using their own weight to prolong the reign of Slobodan Milosevic) could only envy this signal example of bravura statecraft. It sometimes seemed that, if Bush would not remove the Taliban from power, Blair was willing to try it on his own.

In his 1999 Chicago speech, Tony Blair had in fact mentioned Saddam Hussein as a once and future threat and as a man with whom a reckoning could not be indefinitely postponed. He can thus be acquitted on the vulgar charge that he only turned his own attention to Iraq when a faction of the Bush administration decided to carry the war into Saddam's camp. He was also wont to stress the record of Ba'athist genocide and aggression, and not to confine himself to allegations about terrorism and the threat of weapons of mass destruction. However, the confrontation with Iraq was to become, for him, the obverse of the relative triumphs in Kosovo and Kabul. And we have it on his own authority, and that of many of his advisors, that he felt that America should not go into Iraq alone. Or, to put it another way, that British support would almost by definition cancel the charge of American "unilateralism." He seems also to have felt that British endorsement would permit "leverage" on other issues of concern, such as the Palestine question and the precarious state of Africa.

The United Nations is, of course, a product of a "coalition of the willing"—to be exact, of an Anglo-American coalition. Its name comes from Franklin Roosevelt out of conversations with Winston Churchill (who borrowed the actual two words from a poem by Lord Byron) and its very existence is predicated on the idea that war is a first resort and diplomacy a second resort. (To qualify for membership, nation-states had to have declared war on the Axis powers by a certain date in 1945; those who declined were excluded for many years.) One might also mention some other considerations, such as the strong suggestion that member states should sign away some of their sovereignty by subscribing to Eleanor Roosevelt's "Universal Declaration of Human Rights." (The USSR and Saudi Arabia were the main countries to refuse this invitation when it was first proffered.) However that may be, by the spring of 2003 the majority of the UN membership believed themselves to be in a postcolonial and multilateral universe, and were well practiced when pressed in invoking the highest ideals of law and procedure rather than pick a fight with one of their most delinquent states.

The Blair government attempted to split this difference, arguing both for an American-sponsored resolution that threatened the Saddam regime with penalties for noncompliance, and for a second resolution specifying the penalties. Underestimating the politicized intransigence of the Chirac government in particular, this policy had the effect of making London seem abjectly subordinate to Washington, while simultaneously obliging the United States to mount an enormous propaganda effort for which it felt no enthusiasm. Colin Powell and George Tenet, envoys of the two American ministries that were most viscerally hostile to the "regime-change" policy in Iraq, were put to the trouble of mounting an unconvincing presentation about Ba'athist weaponry and Ba'athist support for terrorism. The neoconservatives in Washington were privately furious with Blair, and much of the British press publicly so. The first faction knew that he was by no means their "poodle," while the second could not let go of this facile and memorable coinage.

It was once said (by the Reverend Ian Paisley as a matter of fact) that "bridge builders" are doomed, because bridges—like traitors— "go over to the other side." Blair as bridge builder is anticipated—if not predicted—in this book: It was obvious that someday the United Kingdom would have a Prime Minister who saw, or rather felt, no contradiction between the Atlantic and the European dimension. In retrospect, the bizarre reflection is that such a politician took so long to emerge. How can one describe Churchill as a man of global vision when he refused even to participate in the early building-blocks of the then "Common Market"? How can a man like Sir Anthony Eden have risen to be Prime Minister and then decided to fight Eisenhower, Dulles, Krushchev, Nasser and the United Nations all at the same time? How could Harold Macmillan have put himself in the position of a wretched supplicant for membership of Europe who could be loftily vetoed by General de Gaulle? How could Harold Wilson have botched both Britain's application to Europe and been Lyndon Johnson's boot-boy in Vietnam? One's sense, as a reasonable English person, of having been ruled largely by provincial morons does not diminish in retrospect when it comes to the scrutiny of Edward Heath (too fixated on Brussels to bother with Washington) or James Callaghan (too insular and chauvinistic to take Europeans seriously, yet a credulous ditto to the doctrines of Henry Kissinger) or Margaret Thatcher. The latter, at least, displayed some scope and grandeur when it came to the resolutions of Irish and Rhodesian questions at Hillsborough and Lancaster House, and was prescient about Mikhail Gorbachev, but soon collapsed into a phobic relationship with Europe and a clientelistic one with Ronald Reagan.

Blair's very formation as a person, as distinct from a politician, was highly congruent with the educated majority of his generation, to whom a sojourn in Manhattan or San Francisco, and an easy familiarity with American style, was noncontradictory as regards a trip on the Eurostar for a lunch in Paris, or a vacation in Tuscany or Catalonia. It is a vast condemnation of the British political class to have failed to produce, until almost the end of the twentieth century, a notable leader of whom this could be said. It is an even more considerable condemnation, when one reflects that most actual or potential leaders of the major British parties still do not quite match this unexceptional standard.

In one way, Blair's historic role in persuasively eliciting and confirming American interventionism is a vindication of my chapter on "Greece to their Rome." Knowing that the United States under Bush was likely to settle Saddam Hussein's hash in any case, the Prime Minister decided to try and civilize, or at any rate temper, the inevitable. In undertaking this, he clearly overestimated his ability to carry other European governments with him, and also his capacity—strongly manifest in Bosnia and Kosovo—to persuade his party and his voters that a matter of Gladstonian principle was at stake. I dwell this long on the Iraq war because, whatever its implications may turn out to be, it has obviously remade American and European politics in a manner not seen since the era of Vietnam. Once again, there are celebrations or denigrations of the "Anglo-Saxon" or "Anglo-American" global axis. While, almost fifteen years after this book was first published, and almost a decade of "New Labour" governance, British life is still dominated by a stalemate between European institutions and American connections.

Eclipsing this, in a new but unplanned synthesis, is the unprecedented alliance between British social democrats and American conservatives in a worldwide conflict with delinquent states and their non-state nihilist proxies. It's easy enough to point out that this alliance is both ad hoc and inconsistent—Pakistani generals and Saudi princes do not feel the weight of it in the same way as Iraqi generals and Afghan fundamentalists have done, and there is a narrow but deep division between London and Washington when it comes to the long misery of the Palestinians. Nonetheless, and on the credit side of those like myself who are in general support of the war aims of the Coalition, it can be argued that the British and American governments were quicker to realise that the world really had altered with the revival of jihadism, while other equally conservative European and

Asian regimes tried to act as if only a few uneasy adjustments were necessary. The most unreformedly and unapologetic colonial regime in Europe—the France of Jacques Chirac—was salient in trying to make a separate peace with every outlaw from Saddam Hussein to Robert Mugabe. Powers that at least attempted a new world order are not necessarily to be judged in the same way as those who seek to profit from chaos and cynicism.

This moment happened to coincide with a revisionist episode among Anglo-American historians and intellectuals. Sometime between the confrontations with Afghanistan and Iraq, Niall Ferguson's history of the British Empire began to enjoy a considerable vogue among American scholars, who were not displeased at an accounting of imperialism which presented it in the light—a more Scottish than English light, as few detected—of a civilizing and modernizing process. Professor Ferguson's work was more than nostalgic: It seemed to explain why it was that so many former colonies were now beseeching their former masters for aid and succor. It was in this period of opportunity, also, that an American publisher was found ready to publish—or rather to republish—David Gilmour's magnificent biography of Lord Curzon, the most grandiose and most Orientalist of the viceroys of India. Lord Curzon had doubtless, if only because of his celebrated conceit, had an unfairly bad press heretofore. One still stirred with unease at the idea that direct rule of entire subcontinents was being discovered to have retrospective merit. I return the inquisitive reader to the same set of postcolonial calamities with which I began. The dull term "exit strategy" barely serves to cover such a retreat.

At the same moment, an enormous audience was found for Professor Bernard Lewis's panoptic explanation of disorder within the Islamic world, and his book *What Went Wrong?*, which was serialized in the *New Yorker*, went through several fast-selling editions and was cited in almost every learned discourse. Taking as his starting point the same date proposed by Osama bin Laden—the collapse of the Ottoman caliphate and the arrival of British imperial soldiers in the streets of Jerusalem and Constantinople in 1917/18—Lewis showed that there was a pervasive and ultimately reactionary yearning for a return of the lost world of Muslim dominion.

This point was valuable on its own. (Few Western "anti-imperialists" paused to notice, in their denunciations of Bush and Blair, that bin Laden was calling for the restoration of an empire far more authoritarian and theocratic than the British one: an empire, moreover, that had foundered in an alliance with the Kaiser's Germany and that had proclaimed a *jihad* that utterly failed, as all jihads do.) I turned Professor Lewis's pages with some impatience, all the same, as I waited for his pronouncements on the Sykes-Picot Agreement and the Balfour Declaration. After all, that secret Anglo-French carve-up of Syria and Palestine and Iraq, and that more open British official promise to allow both a Jewish "national home" in Palestine *and* self-determination for its "non-Jewish" population, were also quite contemporary with the other earthshaking events in the Levant of the period. Bernard Lewis, I was rather disappointed to discover, dealt with these two developments by omitting them entirely from his account. In his story, Arab nostalgia and resentment was chiefly atavistic and had no genuine historic grievance with which to sustain itself. How odd, then, that so many of the founding Arab nationalist leaders and intellectuals were Christians, who had no desire to see the restoration of Ottoman rule. . . .

In the same time-frame, Max Boot (a man with a name almost perfectly crafted for his metaphorical purpose) produced a volume titled *Savage Wars of Peace*. This title is a line from Rudyard Kipling's poem "The White Man's Burden" (discussed at some length on pages 64–68 of this book) and Mr. Boot, a writer for the *Wall Street Journal* and a fellow at the American Enterprise Institute, took an unapologetic view of the wars of colonial counterinsurgency from the Philippines onward. In time, he argued, the Western way of war would prevail and the sort of resolve that the British had lost would replenish itself anew. (I couldn't help but notice that the Muslim Moro Islanders in the Philippines, whose massacre was protested so strongly by Mark Twain during his disagreement with Kipling and Churchill, had again emerged as a population willing to shelter the surrogates of al-Qaeda.)

Similar arguments were made, drawing on more classical Greek precedents, by the military scholar Victor Davis Hanson and by Philip Bobbitt, nephew to Lyndon Baines Johnson and onetime member of Clinton's National Security Council. Most especially in Mr. Boot's work, the intention was to rescue the word "empire," when attached to American policy, from any kind of pejorative connotation.

As I was completing this introduction, I was invited by the hawkish *Washington Times* to contribute an article about the Hollywood version of Patrick O'Brian's twenty-volume seafaring masterpiece, put on celluloid under the title *Master and Commander*. Surely, said the commissioning editor, I would admit that the pluck and grit of Captain Jack Aubrey were somewhere in my makeup, and that now was the time for the Nelson touch to be brought to bear to vanquish the foe. I replied that I had been born in Portsmouth, brought up on naval bases, schooled to the "Hornblower" tales, and had thus been unaware until relatively late in life that Horatio Nelson had supported the slave trade and had hanged the leaders of the Neapolitan Republic after they had surrendered under a flag of truce and safe-conduct. Stephen Maturin, the cosmopolitan freethinker who was at Aubrey's elbow, was more my type, but wasn't going to be played by Russell Crowe. . . .

Another notable historian actually underwent second thoughts in the opposite direction at about the same time. Professor Paul Kennedy of Harvard had attracted enormous attention a decade or so previously, with his work, *The Rise and Fall of the Great Powers*. This was an essentially simplistic and projectionist text, which argued for a general historic principle of "imperial over-stretch." Whether Roman or British, all great centers of power would sooner or later discover that their legions and commitments were too far-flung and too costly. No throne or dominion was exempt from this cycle, and the American one was fast becoming too-much extended in debt and strain. I gave the book as bad a review as I could when it came out, for its sheer banal determinism, but never expected a Canossa on the scale that Professor Kennedy later offered to his critics. He had occupied some the intervening time studying the evolution of the modern American "carrier group," any one of which (a gigantic carrier bearing an airforce the size *describing military industrial complex in a nutshell)*

of Italy's and a cruise-missile arsenal capable of making war on a super-power; each carrier shadowed by a flotilla of smaller but more agile ships, and escorted by nuclear submarines the size of dreadnoughts beneath the waves, and highly sophisticated airplanes invisible in the skies above) was the equal of any fleet ever to take to the seas. And the United States had more than a dozen such "carrier groups," and was outfitting more of them.

Astonishingly, this titanic investment represented barely a statistical point in the national budget, and might indeed have a more than Keynesian effect in providing both highly paid employment and technological spin-off. This was not naval and military and aerial "superiority" as earlier powers had conceived it. It was absolute global military mastery, outdoing all potential rivals combined and doubled, on a scale that no other power in history had even been able to conceive.

if only we'd lived (drone strikes) to see

There was also a political or perhaps near-ideological point that did not disclose itself so immediately in the *Tendenzwende* (as Germans historians call a shift of scholarly opinion) of so many experts. The United States Department of Defense had partly invested in such technological and cybernetic superiority in order to obviate the need to leave punctured American bodies on the battlefield. It could pound and destroy almost all potential enemies from mobile positions that were invulnerably over the horizon. General Wesley Clark's celebrated dispute with his political masters during the Kosovo war had largely to do with his conviction that ground action rather than high-altitude bombardment would be more efficient as well as more humane: a conviction that violated the late-1990s dogma that war should be casualty-free, at least on the American side. The immolation of thousands of American and other civilians in their places of work on September 11, 2001 has clearly altered the national attitude towards body bags, though it remains to be seen by quite how much it has done so. The situation in postvictory Afghanistan, for example, would obviously have been more decided if American forces had been willing to deploy farther "in country." This point was made with particular force by many British officers, whose experience of close-order and low-intensity fighting is one asset in which they are not surpassed by their senior partner.

It was in reaction to British and French perfidy in such instances as the Sykes-Picot Agreement, which clearly revealed the First World War to be an imperialist war, that President Woodrow Wilson was compelled to announce his "Fourteen Points" concerning national self-determination. It was actually the Bolshevik Revolution that caused the publication of these "secret treaties" and which dispelled forever the aura of lofty and disinterested diplomacy. The Wilsonian moment, and its successor moments in the campaign for the League of Nations, the Atlantic Charter, and the UN Declaration of Human Rights, has long attracted the scorn of those—beginning with Rudyard Kipling (see pages 78–80)—who see a pharisaic veil being draped over the ugly figure of superpower ambition. Not just the element of hypocrisy, but also the element of hubris, is obviously present at these deliberations. Great powers are not altruists, to begin with. And even Professor Kennedy might wonder if he had overstated his revised case, at a time when even official circles in Washington are wondering aloud if the forces of the American empire are not being stretched too tightly and too thin, in lands where they have more military than cultural influence. Has it not also become obvious that thermonuclear weapons, once a central pillar of the "special relationship," are more than ever obsolete as well as hateful, while the "war on drugs" is merely another name for the colonialism that once waged Opium Wars? Now more than ever is a time to be selective and discriminating about resources as well as methods.

I closed the original version of this book, at a time when I hoped the long Cold War might also be closing, with the pious thought of "a world without conquerors." I was aware even then that this was a slightly sanctimonious ending. Anglo-Americanism has some attainments to its credit. The English language has become a lingua franca, in India and Africa and elsewhere, not because of its association with empire, but because of its flexibility and capacity for assimilation (and because of the extraordinary literature, more and more of it written by Asians and other former "subjects," with which it is associated). It is the tongue

[handwritten annotation: only ideals of American revolution remain relevant]

both of the Internet and of air-traffic control. One of Nelson Mandela's first actions as President of a liberated South Africa was to reattach his martyred country to the British Commonwealth. English is also the language of the English Revolution and of its descendant, the American Revolution of Thomas Paine and Thomas Jefferson and of the documents in which the doctrine of human rights has become, at least on paper, universalized. After the collapse of the Soviet Union, and the atrophy or discredit of the Chinese and Cuban ones, the ideas of this revolution are the only valid ones remaining. In other words, one aspires to conquests made by ideas and values, not nations. The fight to make these ideas and values symmetrical with the demands of combat, in a clash not of civilizations but about civilization, will be the great task of those who hope to learn anything from history.

CHRISTOPHER HITCHENS
Washington, D.C.
October 21, 2003 (Trafalgar Day)

[handwritten annotation: celebrates victory over French + Spanish during Napoleonic War at battle of trafalgar (in Andalusia)]

BLOOD, CLASS
AND EMPIRE

Introduction

In the United States, it is considered extremely insulting to say of somebody that he or she is "history." To be told "You're history" is to be condemned as a has-been. I know of no other country that has this everyday dismissal in its idiom. But then, I know of no other country that has such a great weakness for things that originate in England—the has-been country par excellence. (A British person, seeking to be extremely self-deprecating about something in his or her own past, might say modestly and dismissively, "But that's all ancient history." I trust the distinction is plain.)

In fact, no nation can quite do without a stock of historical and mythical and semi-literary reference, and the United States is anything but an exception. It has a powerful need for evocations of *grandeur*, which makes it the more noticeable that, when reaching for such necessary evocations, it so often ignores its own past and letters. On a surprising number of occasions, the preferred imagery is derived from England, and from the British Empire. Often, those who deal in this rhetoric are public figures who dare not risk an obscure or a confusing allusion, and who presumably have reason to think (if only because their advisers tell them so) that these points of reference are familiar and customary. Even as I was writing this book, on these themes, my attention was caught by a bizarre little exchange in front of the House Foreign Affairs Committee in Washington. On December 9, 1986, I was following the first public appearance made by Lieutenant Colonel Oliver North, who was in the process of igniting a huge national debate about secret government, overseas intervention, American will, and—descending abruptly to bathos—his own decision to plead the Fifth Amendment. Two California congressmen, Robert Dornan and Mervyn Dymally, had a verbal exchange as North was completing his bombastic and contradictory testimony. His own voice almost as gravid with emotion as North's had been, Congressman Dornan hailed the errant soldier:

> Then I have just one observation. Almost a century ago, Rudyard Kipling wrote a rather tragic poem about the ingratitude of all peoples toward their military forces in time of peacetime, and I will just paraphrase the first of six lines: "He is Ollie this and he is Ollie that. Get him out of here, the brute. But he is the savior of his country when the guns begin to shoot." Thank you for your service, Colonel North.
> MR. DYMALLY: Will the gentleman yield?
> MR. DORNAN: I will be glad to yield.
> MR. DYMALLY: There is another line: "To thine own self be true, and it must follow the night, the day thou canst be false to any man."

The fascinating thing about both these impromptu West Coast interjections (Representative Dornan, a farouche Orange County right-winger, may have polished his a little beforehand) was not the mangling of the quotations but the relative accuracy with which they were rendered. True, Kipling's "Tommy"—though no tragedy—is one of his better-known doggerels, and not even Allan Bloom would claim that Polonius is no longer taught in schools. But it seemed automatic for these two legislators to reach for these tags when debating about matters of empire, war, and destiny. This is a supreme, if oblique, compliment to the depth at which the so-called special relationship between the two countries and cultures operates and obtains.

Although it is expressed in idealistic terms and based upon a carefully cleansed reading of "history," this relationship is really at bottom a transmission belt by which British conservative ideas have infected America, the better to be retransmitted to England. The process of transmission has been made easier, admittedly, by those Americans who are themselves receptive to the temptations of thinking with the blood, or the temptations of empire, or the temptations of class and caste superiority. But it was always in the British mind to press these ideas upon them. If you want to know what, and how, people really think, then catch them talking in private during wartime. Here is what British Security Coordination, the special organ of Winston Churchill and Sir William Stephenson ("The Man Called Intrepid"), wrote in its secret history of the campaign to mold American thinking between 1939 and 1945:

> In planning its campaign, it was necessary for BSC to remember the simple truth that the United States, a sovereign entity of comparatively recent birth, is inhabited by people of many conflicting races, interests and creeds. These people, though fully conscious of their wealth and power in the aggregate, are still unsure of themselves individually, still basically on the defensive and still striving, as yet unavailingly but very defiantly, after national unity and indeed after some logical grounds for considering themselves a nation in the racial sense.

British self-confidence about American vulnerability on these scores was based on a careful appreciation of "history" and upon the old and trusted verities of blood—the very tie they had been exploiting since Kipling. With the advantage of ethnic solidarity and homogeneity, and with an instinct for social hierarchy and "the right people," the British Establishment was enabled to fight at far beyond its own weight, and to behave for some time as if it controlled a much larger country than it really did.

But, having inculcated imperial habits and disciplines into their larger, clumsier cousin, the British had in time to accept that they, too, could be manipulated. The self-congratulatory tone of BSC in the 1940s is matched if not surpassed by another secret memorandum, this one from the 1960s. It is Richard Neustadt's report to President Lyndon Johnson, written in July 1964, about the possibility of taming and domesticating an incoming British Labor government. Neustadt had been talking to the right people in London, and knew his Harold Wilson. He proposed some intensive ego-stroking on a forthcoming Washington visit that Wilson was to pay: *→ play to their arrogance as they play to American insecurity*

> Numbers of things can be done on the cheap to avoid shocking his sensibilities. For one, the President might ask for his advice on a short list of replacements for David Bruce. For another, Averell Harriman might figure prominently among his hosts. . . . It will be worth our while to ease the path for Wilson, pay him a good price.

It is amusing and ironic to see an American plan to use the embrace of American aristocracy—the Bruce-Harriman Georgetown network—to captivate an untutored British politician. But such is the nature of the special relationship. Nor was this all. Emulating the British tactic with America, Neustadt proposed to his President that use be made of domestic British sympathizers. As he boasted:

> What follows has been drawn from conversations with *politicians* (mainly Wilson, Gordon Walker, Healey, Brown, Mulley, Jenkins—and Heath), with *officials* (mainly Hardman, Cary, Palliser, Armstrong, Bligh) and with *spectators* (mainly Gwynne-Jones, Buchan, Beedham, Duchene). Before I left,

I swapped appraisals at our Embassy with Bruce, Irving and Newman.

Neustadt here demonstrated a very shrewd knowledge of the inside track that runs between the Foreign Office, *The Economist*, the stately home think-tank at Ditchley Park, and Grosvenor Square. Since the central matter was the securing of continued British conformity with American nuclear policy, it was essential for Neustadt to be exact. In fact, he was well equipped by these conversations to be prescient. Noting that Wilson wanted to be viewed in his own Cabinet as "first brains-truster on the model, he says, of JFK," he minuted:

> When officials get their hands on the new Ministers, Foreign Office briefs presumably will urge affirmative response to us (assuming we stand firm) and then hard bargaining about terms and conditions. Assuming Gordon Walker is the Foreign Secretary (he almost certainly will be) I expect he will submit with little struggle. . . . Assuming Denis Healey is Defense Secretary (he seems confident he will be), his own interest in a mission East of Suez (and in sales of British aircraft), his mistrust of continentals, his disdain for MLF, comport well with the bulk of these official views.

Seeking to massage British pride over the loss of sovereignty in nuclear matters, Neustadt first stressed the main point, which was that there could be talk of Atlantic consultation on strategy and policy "up to the final decision on the trigger, which is yours and must remain so." Having thus reassured LBJ, he suggested some easy reassurance to the Brits: "some symbols both for public satisfaction and for Gordon Walker's *amour propre* (to say nothing of Wilson's). Symbolically, if there are British colonels now at Omaha, could we have them ostentatiously replaced by generals?"

At one level, this is ordinary Washington "bottom line" talk. At another, though, it is the distilled essence of a "special relationship" that has been built up in an ad hoc fashion to suit the needs—sometimes contrasting, sometimes harmonious—of two elites. The hypocrisies of this marriage of convenience have often been occluded, at least partially, by an apparent cultural and linguistic familiarity. (Even Neustadt employed Kipling's famous phrase "East of Suez" as if it were natural to him.) This is evident whether one is considering—as I shall be—the relationship in its thermonuclear, its racial, its imperial, its espionage, or its poetic aspects. The rituals of Anglo-Americanism and Anglo-Saxondom, so often unexamined, reveal the subtext of this mutual manipulation, and suggest that the English connection has been used to seduce and corrupt America, the better to suborn itself. This is "history," and not all that ancient either.

[handwritten margin note: 1) seduce, bribe, manipulate]

On a smoggy evening in the spring of 1989, I found myself standing under the palms of Wilshire Boulevard in Los Angeles, outside the ornate ugliness of the Beverly Hilton Hotel. This was one of many incongruous locations where I had pondered the question: What is it that explains the special place occupied by Englishness in the American imagination? That evening, Ronald Reagan was due to receive the Winston Churchill Award at the hands of Prince Philip, Duke of Edinburgh and the consort to Her Majesty Queen Elizabeth II. The master of ceremonies was to be Bob Hope, assisted by Rosemary Clooney. In this labyrinth of clashing images, I hoped to find a few intelligible threads.

The Beverly Hilton is owned by Merv Griffin, and its ballroom was for years the setting of the Academy Awards dinner. At first, the evening looks like any other tuxedoed rally of California show biz, with the paparazzi shouting questions at celebrities from behind a police line. But tonight, when these celebrities reply automatically that they are "excited," they are replying to a different question. Here comes Marvin Davis, head of 20th Century-Fox and, if not a big noise in the oil industry, certainly a very loud report. When he tells the boys he's "wild about it," it's because they have asked him: "How does it feel to be dining with Royalty?"

Of course, by "Royalty" the celebrity-hardened Los Angeles reporters *could* mean Princess Caroline of Monaco, or some princeling of the Gulf whose tankers bear the American flag, or King Juan Carlos of Spain. But there is an unspoken capital R which comes with British Royalty; the cachet of the real thing. Combine this with the evergreen and potent name of Churchill, and you have blue-chip Anglo-Americanism on its highest deportment.

There is a deal of received wisdom about this blue-chip status, which derives itself from solemn and sound observations about the common blood, common language, shared history, and recognizably similar institutions that span the Atlantic and the years. This, preeminently, is to be an evening of reaffirmed speechifying along such well-established lines. The Churchill Foundation, a coalition of American businessmen which is hosting this weighty soirée, is only one part of a nexus of scholarships, trusts, foundations, and institutions devoted to the care and feeding of what the British—but no longer the Americans—are still given to calling the "special relationship." An educated American knows, when prompted, that his country's "oldest ally" is France. Many Americans, if given a word-association test for "special relationship," would probably reply "Israel." Yet there is something to the texture of mixed affections and impressions, summarized in the frequent use of the phrase "the Old Country," or even, in sentimental moments, "the Mother Country," that reserves the British a singular place.

For one of the many mutations of this Anglo-Americanism, one need search no further than the Beverly Hilton's bar. On a ground floor, only a few yards from the neon and deco of Wilshire Boulevard, and wisely screened from all natural light, one discovers the Red Lion. Here, the simulacrum of an English country pub or "snug" has been lovingly faked. In the bogus grate burns a phony, heatless log fire. Beer pumps draw up franchised, tasteless American lagers with German names. Unconvincing paneling combines with rounded and "aged" wooden tables and chairs to sham the dingy atmosphere of a "Dickensian" alehouse as shown off to willing

American tourists. (Eight time-zone hours ahead, in London, any pub with a trace of Sam Weller or Mr. Pickwick is being hurriedly converted into an L.A.-style cocktail bar.)

There are pubs like this, often in airport terminals for some reason, that demonstrate the strength of British traditional imagery all over America. The word "tradition" is in fact the key to an appreciation of Brit kitsch. Evelyn Waugh, on an earlier exploration of the special relationship and its Los Angeles dimension, did very well with the Church of St. Peter-Without-the-Walls, created by the visionary Dr. Kenworthy to lend tone to his Whispering Glades burial plaza:

> For this is more than a replica, it is a reconstruction. A building-again of what those old craftsmen sought to do with their rude implements of by-gone ages. Time has worked its mischief on the beautiful original. Here you see it as the first builders dreamed of it long ago.

Later dreamers have improved on Dr. Kenworthy, by importing the *Queen Mary* and London Bridge to American climes.

Quitting the Red Lion for the ballroom is exchanging a poor microcosm of Anglo-American fellowship for the full-dress reproduction of all its most distinctive features. The ceremonial part of the dinner begins with Walter Annenberg, former Ambassador to the Court of St. James's and formerly indicted newspaper tycoon, giving the toast to the House of Windsor. With unusual unction and deference, he insists on giving it the full title of "The Loyal Toast"; a mark of etiquette which would make him appear ostentatious even among English royalists. In reply, Prince Philip proposes the health of the President of the United States.

Then come the national anthems, played by a smart Marine band. "God Save the Queen" commends itself, as usual, for its brevity and is, after all, the selfsame tune as the American standby "My Country 'Tis of Thee." "The Star-Spangled Banner" takes longer. Written in 1814 after its author, Francis Scott Key, had watched the British bombard Fort McHenry in Baltimore on their way to burn Washington, it has a third verse which is increasingly omitted from official printings. Referring to the British, it declares: "Their blood has wash'd out their foul footsteps' pollution." It goes on to say:

> *No refuge could save the hireling and slave*
> *From the terror of flight or the gloom of the grave.*

As a slight salve to British honor in the squalid matter of 1814, the music to the national anthem was composed by an Englishman named John Stafford Smith, who lived between 1750 and 1836. We have, alas, lost his original words, though the song was called "To Anacreon in Heaven" and was meant as a ditty for a young men's drinking club, in a tavern as unlike the Beverly Hilton's Red Lion as it is possible to imagine.

Since Ronald Wilson Reagan is no longer President, we are spared a rendition of "Hail to the Chief," the words of which were taken from a ballad by Sir Walter Scott in *The Lady of the Lake*, and set to music by the Englishman James Sanderson. But we do get the Marine Hymn, one of the few official American ditties to which English people seem to know the words. Expressing as it does the first American ambition to be as far-flung as the coast of Libya and the heart of Mexico, it answers to some chord in the British breast; perhaps confirming that the errant former colony could still recognize the right colonial and martial stuff when it saw it.

The ex-Chief, Ronald Reagan, is only the fourth person to be honored by the Churchill Foundation. Previous recipients have been W. Averell Harriman (a mandarin among foreign service mandarins and a special confidant of the Atlanticist class as well as a relation by marriage of the Churchill family), H. Ross Perot, and Margaret Thatcher. Perot, who is usually described by nervous subeditors as "the eccentric Texas billionaire," has run a foreign policy all his own on the gross revenues of innumerable corpora-

tions, and could by a stretch be said to have that odd word "swash-
buckling" in common with Sir Winston. ✓ Both mavericks

Prince Philip, the social centerpiece of the night's events, is in
fact following in his son's footsteps as a bridge builder of the "special
relationship." Prince Charles was the one who put the Churchill
medallion around the neck of H. Ross Perot in 1986, and he also
can claim to have bestowed the royal warrant upon Mr. and Mrs.
Walter Annenberg. In their protracted struggle to acquire the patina of "class" for their operations and for their many charities and
promotions, they have found the patronage of the Prince of Wales
to be essential and continuous. When she was Ronald Reagan's
chief of protocol, Mrs. Annenberg once so far forgot herself as to
curtsy publicly to Charles when greeting him at Andrews Air Force
Base; an impromptu gesture of fealty that did minor damage to the
stipulations of the American Constitution and which led to some
growling from those who still remember the United States as a
republic.

In Los Angeles at any rate, visiting British crowned heads get,
as it were, two bites at the cherry. They can appear in the vestments
of former British glory and pageantry, much as they do elsewhere,
and represent the astonishing historic continuity of the United
Kingdom. But they also constitute a uniquely appetizing morsel
for those who live by the codes of stardom and who hunger for a
star with "class" and magic. I found this out for myself by making
an appearance on *Sonia Live*, the upbeat bicoastal chat show hosted
by Sonia Friedman and transmitted on the Cable News Network
with the Hollywood logo in the background. In front of a prime-
time audience of daytime viewers, I was asked to comment on the
Charles and Diana marriage, and the rumors of its impending
breakup. When I said that I thought the whole thing was a press
bonanza, and that the obsession with monarchy was beginning to
bore even the British, the tempestuous Sonia was appalled. "*Mister*
Hitchens," she intoned in reproof, "how can you sit there with that
lovely English accent and say such a thing? That wedding was a
fairy tale for all of us here." It was as if I had offended a specifically

American striving
for stability

Californian household god. Which in a way, I had. In 1988 it was announced that Princess Diana had been, by a large margin, the woman most often featured on the covers of American magazines in the course of that year. One could scarcely enter a supermarket without seeing her photograph on the rack, or barely utter a sentence in an English accent without inviting friendly inquiries about her. Across a swath of the imagination of America, it seemed, England was understood principally as the home of the Windsors; a sort of theme park for royal activities and romances. Without the monarchy, ran the unstated question, what would be the *point* of the old country?

This attitude, to which the British embassy defers as a matter of course, was amply catered for in November 1985, when Prince Charles and his bride paid an official visit to Washington. The much-hyped joint appearance was timed to coincide with an immense exhibition, "Treasure Houses of Britain," at the National Gallery of Art. Taken together, the Prince and Princess and the country-house trove could have been designed to reinforce the impression of Britain as a museum run by people of a certain faint breeding, a museum, moreover, uniquely accessible to monied Americans. I can still recall the half-embarrassed frenzy which seized the nation's capital in the days before the momentous opening; the pseudo-debutante flurry of "coveted invitations," protocol crises, and etiquette hysteria. → fear of being judged

Republican values were the loser in this carnival. The British by Tourist Authority inserted a special supplement, consisting of one country hundred and sixteen pages, into *The Washington Post*, in which the first paragraph misidentified John Adams as the third President of the United States. This did nothing to quell the general enthusiasm. The "Style" section of the *Post* forgot itself completely at the reception for the country-house owners, writing: "With guests like the Duke of Bedford and Lord Montagu of Beaulieu, the wave of Anglophilia continued to wash over the town. After all, laughed Chinese ambassador Han Xu, 'they were here before.' 'I think Washington has always been Anglophile—since Churchill,' said

Gospel of Capitalism over class

Clare Boothe Luce. 'I think we're all Anglophiles,' noted Librarian of Congress Daniel Boorstin. 'How can we fail to be Anglophiles? Unless we hate ourselves.' " (In 1961, Mr. Boorstin published a celebrated book called *The Image: A Guide to Pseudo-Events in America*.)

John Adams (the *second* President of the United States) wrote to Thomas Jefferson in July 1813: "I read in Greek a couplet, the sense of which was 'Nobility in men is worth as much as it is in horses, asses or rams; but the meanest blooded puppy in the world, if he gets a little money, is as good a man as the best of them.' "

In reply Jefferson, the third President of the United States, wrote: "The passage you quote . . . has an ethical rather than a political object. I agree with you that there is a natural aristocracy among men. The grounds of this are virtue and talents. . . . There is also an artificial aristocracy, founded on wealth and birth, without either virtue or talents."✓

This correspondence might as well never have been written for all that Georgetown could have cared during that week. Gushed the *Post* in still another special spread: "Susan Mary Alsop, Senator Jay Rockefeller, Katharine Graham, Evangeline Bruce, philanthropist Ethel Garrett and Washington doyenne Polly Fritchey—there may not be titles before these names, but they are Washington's social nobility, the kind of people who don't pay a couple of pounds to visit the Treasure Houses; they stay there as guests. It will be old money, old power, old china and lots of familiar faces." The echo of "social mobility" in the tautology "social nobility" is very, very distant.

But note, again, the latent connection between British "style" and American "class." The existing Georgetown aristocracy, already heavily inflected with Anglophilia, so to speak recertifies itself as aristocratic by its ease of access, not to an exhibition about stately homes but to the homes themselves. Thus, between the cult of vulgar celebrity and the cult of wellborn good taste, the English have the rather maddening ability to score twice. They can produce genuine dukes and real lineages to set against *Dynasty*, that most

[handwritten margin note at top: "I wonder if he'll talk → about east-coast as england within america"]

[handwritten margin note left side, vertical: "California presidency / will always connote nouveau (history only 1800s) P"]

[handwritten margin note left: "disagree" / "mystic"]

suggestively named soap opera. They can also produce a princess who eats lunch with John Travolta and Donald Trump, and a presenter named Robin Leach for that great yearning, fawning, televised exercise *Life Styles of the Rich and Famous.*

It may be no coincidence, then, that the era of Ronald Reagan was at once a celebration of the nouveau riche and a stage in the evolution toward a monarchic and ceremonial presidency. The ground for this had admittedly been manured well before, with the slightly risible term "Camelot" being coined to give a tinge of mystic English Arthurian splendor to the rather tacky and modern court arrangements of the Kennedy clan. Indeed, one of the more startling journalistic conventions, on the accession of a new American President, is the publication of his bloodline as it relates to the English monarchy. There is even an ornate appendix to Burke's *Presidential Families of the United States*, entitled "Presidents of Royal Descent." Starting with George Washington, who devoted most of his life not only to expelling the British monarchy but to ensuring that it could never return to America in mutated form, the tireless Burke "credits" him with a descent from Edmund Crouchback, John of Gaunt, and Henry III, with a collateral line tracing itself to Edward I, King of Scotland.

Thomas Jefferson is by various byways connected to David I, King of Scots. President Monroe is argued to have had the blood of Edward III and John of Gaunt coursing in his veins, while both William Henry and Benjamin Harrison descend from Henry III, and John Quincy Adams from Edward I. President Buchanan could be traced to the loins of Robert II, King of Scots. Even Abraham Lincoln is depicted as descending from Edward I through a rather tortuous Welsh byway, and President Grant could also count David I, King of Scots, as an ancestor. With a little creativity, President Garfield can be connected to Rhys ap Tewdr, founder of the Tudor dynasty, and Theodore Roosevelt to Robert III, King of Scots. Of all the nineteenth-century American Presidents, none were of other than English descent save the unassuming Dutchman Martin van Buren, who was also the first to be born an American citizen and one of the few to be elected President having been Vice President. The next Vice President to succeed directly to the White House was George Herbert Walker Bush, and the day after his election in 1988, Mr. Harold Brooks-Baker, publishing director of *Burke's Peerage*, was widely quoted in the American press as disclosing that the President-elect was a distant relation of Britain's reigning Queen Elizabeth II. Mary Tudor, said Brooks-Baker, had become an ancestor of the Bushes by her marriage to the Duke of Suffolk. "Most great American Presidents were of royal descent," he purred, "but none as royal as George Bush."

In lesser, cottage-industry ways, this obsession with tradition and kinship is replicated by the Edinburgh shops that will offer to trace the clan tartan of any American tourist, and by the many English parish churches down on their luck that turn a shilling by tracing the rural and feudal "roots" of credulous visitors. As Alexis de Tocqueville put it: "Aristocracy has made a chain of all the members of the community, from the peasant to the king." As he also put it, perhaps prematurely: "Democracy breaks that chain, and severs every link of it."

On this night in the Beverly Hilton, Ronald Reagan is not so much forging links as reinforcing them. The persona of Churchill, the presence of the royal family, the idea of the Atlantic alliance— these are powerful totems with which to work, set in the context of the sort of gala ceremony in which he excelled for eight years. In deference to the essential imagery of the Churchill-Roosevelt wartime alliance, the British consul's handout for the evening politely repeats one of Reagan's favorite fabrications: "His film career, interrupted by three years of service in the Army Air Corps during World War II, encompassed fifty-three feature-length motion pictures." Reagan's former agent Lew Wasserman is one of the many people in the audience who know this to be an artful fiction, but tonight Reagan is to receive at least the touch of the potent Churchill mantle, so a finest hour is mandated for him too and nobody will be so churlish as to note the missing prefix "un-" before the surreptitious word "interrupted." It may be true that Reagan *does Reagan have a military record?*

played an RAF hero in one of his movies, but he stayed firmly on the studio back lot until the conclusion of hostilities.

From this podium, Reagan will be led home and later conducted to the airport to fly to London, where he will be dubbed a Knight by Queen Elizabeth. Unmentioned in Burke because of his ancestry in the loam and sod of Ireland, he will therefore not be able to say, as Churchill once said in his address to both houses of Congress, that, other things being equal, he might have made it there on his own. Unless to the House of Lords.

The evening, in part a run-up to the Reagan knighthood, is doubly laden with the mythology of monarchy and Churchillism; the two most commanding elements of the postwar British influence on America, with a close third being Margaret Thatcher (already honored by this same Foundation) and the remainder being Liverpudlian and London entertainers, for whom Hollywood had already established a steady pattern of annexation and assimilation.

The Churchill Foundation, to judge by its letterhead and personnel, comprises various layers in the *mille-feuille* of Anglo-American sentimentality. At one end, there is Bob Hope, who was born Leslie Townes Hope in Eltham, Kent, in 1903 and who left England when he was four. Arch-comedian of the middlebrow, and golfing friend of the mafia of mediocrity that surrounded Eisenhower, Nixon, and Ford, he is the sort of sports-check Republican cliché-monger whom Pamela Harriman would not have in any of her houses. Yet the old-line Georgetown Democratic grande dames are also here, either in the flesh or in the spirit. Pamela Harriman graces a prominent table, and is quite possibly the only person present not to have voted with enthusiasm for the royally descended George Bush. Marietta Tree, former chatelaine of Ditchley Park and another widow of a wartime "special relationship" hero, is on the board. In between are more recent opportunists like Robert E. Wycoff, president of Atlantic Richfield, who served as chairman of the dinner and who split the tab with Robert Maxwell, a newspaper tycoon who can sympathize from experience with Walter Annenberg's brush with the ethics police, and a man

Ghislaine's father!

whose newspapers are devoted to the conservative version of the Atlanticist ideal. In a revealing speech, Mr. Wycoff's deputy, John Loeb, describes the purpose of the gathering and of the Churchill Foundation as the recovery of American technological and scientific primacy: "Something we urgently need in these times when we are being outstripped by others in scientific education and achievement." Churchill himself, who was repeatedly forced to give ground in the face of superior American scientific and technological firepower, might have permitted himself a scowl here. The Foundation, which like many others tends to reckon success in terms of Nobel Prizes, endows a scholarship at Churchill College, Cambridge—continuing a tradition of American business interest in that university which, although it does not match the Rhodes scholarships, goes back at least as far as the acquisition of the *Encyclopaedia Britannica* in the early years of this century.

Perhaps unaware of these gradations of Anglo-Saxondom and Anglo-Americanism, there is the winner of the annual Winston Churchill essay competition, sponsored by the *Los Angeles Times*. The boy comes from El Toro High School, which is in the catchment area of the Naval Air Station, and the subject of his essay is Churchill's fondness for the idea of historic compromise. Who knows where he got the idea—the absorbing thing is the image of an El Toro High School senior, bent over the composition of a Winston Churchill prize essay in the year of grace 1989. This testifies to an impressive persistence not just in the iconography of Churchill but in the approved perception of the special relationship that goes with it.

The apotheosis of the approved version was expressed by Prince Philip as he prepared to invest the old entertainer with the silver medallion and chain of the award. He told Reagan that he "exemplified the spirit of that illustrious man in whose name we pay this tribute." Reagan was regaled with praise for his "outstanding gifts of leadership, which helped the nation to regain its confidence, vigor, and sense of purpose and to recapture the respect of foreign friend and adversary alike." He was exalted in his own favorite terms for his unswerving advocacy of "peace through strength."

Prince Philip went on, in his speech to the gathering, to recall a moment in 1951 when he had visited Washington with his new wife, then still the Princess Elizabeth. The old King was still on the throne, and Sir Winston had just been elected Prime Minister again. A member of the Truman administration, eager to say the right thing, had congratulated the Prince on the reelection of his wife's father. This joke is better than it sounds. The subliminal association between the various items that make up the inventory of Englishness is, as the Red Lion shows, an indispensable part of its appeal. And there is actual utility to this subliminal awareness. Ronald Reagan, the master of suggestion, is reckoned by experts to have turned in his best performance on the Normandy beaches on the anniversary of D-Day, neatly appropriating the Churchillian style in the process. As long ago as 1952, the Republican Party had sensed the potential of television in politics. As the historians of political advertising put it in their book *The Spot*, here is how the Eisenhower-Nixon campaign designed its pathbreaking election-eve TV pitch in 1952: "Film clips of Korea, Alger Hiss and Julius and Ethel Rosenberg—the convicted "atomic spies"—depicted the Democratic record; clips of Eisenhower with soldiers, with his family and with Winston Churchill suggested the Republican alternative." Thus Churchill, who was in many ways a radical and an iconoclast as well as a Tory and an imperialist, and who fought tooth and nail against the rise of the American Empire, can somehow be made to "belong" to the Republican patriots who make up tonight's audience, just as the House of Windsor can be claimed as part of the family by what the social pages call "L.A. royalty."

These extend, according to the breathless report in the *Los Angeles Herald Examiner*, from Betsy Bloomingdale to Walter Annenberg. They sit, this evening, around a vast orange bombe, made in the shape of a crown. Some way east of the city, near the junction of Bob Hope and Frank Sinatra Drives in Rancho Mirage, Mr. Annenberg keeps his unrivaled collection of oil paintings and displays them to selected visitors in a naïve, unsorted fashion, turning from a canvas to show off his Christmas cards from the Queen Mother. ("They come special delivery, insured," he boasted to the art critic Paul Richard.) The mutual reinforcement of tycoonery and aristocracy, economic royalists and monarchists, requires some rough-and-ready manipulation in the cultural field, but it can be done, and those who can do it regard it as money well spent.

How else, after all, could the Reagan entourage hope, after eight years of scandal and deficit and unanswered questions, to be invested with the pomp and glory and honor that Prince Philip has been dispensing? When Reagan claimed the moral authority of the Founding Fathers for his Nicaragua policy, he made one of his few miscalculations of the public mood. There were murmurs of distaste at this too promiscuous borrowing of America's dearest idols. The comparison with Churchill is no less grotesque, of course, but if Prince Philip makes it, then who can complain? A vicarious legitimation is offered by a respected, traditional ally.

The occasion draws to a surreal close with the singing of Rosemary Clooney, whose evocations of Killarney and Cloghamore have reduced many a St. Patrick's night to maudlin and lachrymose demonstrations. The Irish-American community has been the slowest to succumb to the general insipid Anglophilia (being one of the few ethnic American groups polled, for instance, that did not instinctively side with Britain in the Falklands conflict). But tonight Ms. Clooney eschews the green in favor of what looks like a jacaranda tent, and when she does sing of Cloghamore there is nothing in her rendition to discompose the Crown. Faced by an alliance between "the quality" from both sides of the Atlantic, even Fenianism succumbs to sentimentality.

That very morning, the newspapers had been full of a high-level disagreement within the NATO alliance. The ostensible disagreement concerned the deployment of nuclear weapons, but this in turn posed the question of differing responses to political change in the Warsaw Pact states. In the dispute, only Downing Street had taken the American side. In briefings and interviews, West German and French spokesmen referred quite unironically to "the

Anglo-Saxon bloc"; the alliance within the alliance. If these spokes-men had been present at the Beverly Hilton they would have had no cause to think of their shorthand as a simplification.

Introductions ought to state a purpose frankly. My purpose has been to see what underlies this kinship, and to see if any sense can be made of the widely different ways in which "England" informs the mind of America. The "special relationship" is some-thing that is *supposed* to elude definition; *supposed* to be protean and vague. It was not even given a name until Winston Churchill sought to encapsulate it, for now forgotten short-term reasons, in 1946. It is neither a political alliance, a strategic consensus, an ethnic coalition, nor a cultural and linguistic condominium—yet it is all of these.

Its real roots and character are to be sought in the grand triad of race, class, and empire—the trivium upon which the relationship rests. These are the three words which, still, evoke the most ner-vousness and denial and equivocation in everyday American dis-course. If you dig for the roots of this ambiguity, you will come repeatedly across the traces of a small archipelago that was once a great maritime empire. No, I do not mean Greece—though the comparison has been attempted.

[1]

Greece to Their Rome

Much can be divined about any individual, however outwardly complex, from his or her explanation of the decline of the Roman Empire. A thousand schools of thought contend, and those who attribute the eclipse of ancient glories to lead poisoning, homosexuality, polytheism, monotheism, incest, the appeasement of barbarism by mercenarism, or the malign influence of steam baths upon testicles are all, in the final result, revealing their own peculiar and general theories of history and evolution.

Those who wish to avoid these critical judgments usually take refuge in theories of transition, whereby one age simply melts slowly into another, and whereby chance does little, in sapient retrospect, that was not prepared beforehand. An undoubted fact— the replacement of the British Empire by American power—can thus be presented very much according to taste. It may have been the happy result of a common heritage. It may have been the outcome of a grand design by one party or another. It may have been determined by forces of which both parties were only gropingly aware. Still, the resulting synthesis—the "special relationship"—is an important modern fact.

Seeking, however arbitrarily, to assign some point in time when this fact, not yet accomplished, became visible and palpable, one is continually returned to a moment in North Africa in 1943. Harold

Macmillan, son of an English father and an American mother, was then serving as Winston Churchill's personal emissary to General Eisenhower. British dependencies were being wrested back from German occupation, but only with the aid of enormous American subventions. Macmillan, who had the fondness of his class for classical allusion, was discoursing with Richard Crossman. Crossman, a leading British social democrat and wartime propagandist who was later to be the co-editor with Arthur Koestler of *The God That Failed*, made a note of Macmillan's *pensée*:

> We, my dear Crossman, are Greeks in this American Empire. You will find the Americans much as the Greeks found the Romans—great big, vulgar, bustling people, more vigorous than we are and also more idle, with more unspoiled virtues but also more corrupt. We must run Allied Forces Headquarters as the Greek slaves ran the operations of the Emperor Claudius.

On its own, the remark might have been no more than an occasional pleasantry. Crossman had already made a small name for himself at Oxford with the publication of *Plato Today*, a book which had traced the Athenian roots of the authoritarian state. What more natural than an exchange of tags between cultivated Englishmen abroad, surrounded as they were by boisterous American advisers and dependent as they grudgingly were on masses of American war materials? Yet the thought seemed to have occurred to Macmillan with regularity and continuity. On another occasion, addressing his staff, he said: "These Americans represent the new Roman Empire and we Britons, like the Greeks of old, must teach them how to make it go."

Very much later in his life, after the British Empire had been humbled in North Africa by the Suez calamity of 1956, and after he had come to power as Prime Minister with undisguised American backing, Macmillan was to return to the theme again and again. According to Enoch Powell, a member of his Cabinet and a fervent opponent of the cession of British influence to the vulgarity of America, Macmillan had been much preoccupied with the idea that the "special relationship" would somehow allow the English ghost to pass into a new and vigorous body: " 'We are,' he reiterated in a series of monologues late in 1956 and early in 1957, 'the Greeks of the Hellenistic age: the power has passed from us to Rome's equivalent, the United States of America, and we can at most aspire to civilise and occasionally to influence them.' "

Macmillan's analogy is open to every kind of objection. For one thing, it was obviously not intended for American ears. For another, there were still British ears upon which it would have fallen very awkwardly. But it expressed, and still expresses, a metaphorical truth. Post-imperial Britain, during the arduous and sometimes embarrassing process of becoming post-imperial, leaned very decidedly toward the United States. Not without rancor, it appointed the United States its successor. Not without quibbling and reservation, the United States took up the succession. There had been, in both countries, those who saw a version of this accommodation when it was still a long way off. Their premonitions are part of the subject of this book.

How does it come about that the British still employ the words "class" and "empire," while in the United States these are facts but not concepts? How is it that the image of an English princess graces the cover of every American celebrity and sensation magazine? Why should it be that, as the rest of the world absorbs mass-produced American television output, the educated class in America itself prefers the diversion offered by the English country-house drama on its otherwise scantily financed Public Broadcasting System? Why is Winston Churchill the most quoted politician in American national life? Is it coincidence that, in repeated tests of American style and taste, the words "English" and "British" are synonymous with a certain elusive sense of the sophisticated? Is it of interest that the terms "East Coast," "Establishment," and "Anglophile" have been, at certain crucial points, effectively interchangeable?

This is only to brush the surface of the relationship, and to reconnoiter some of the apparent texture. Yet this very texture may be the direct and indirect result of a history so entwined, imbricated, and intimate as to form, in both cases, a version of the second identity. Like many apparently close kinships, this superficial sympathy may conceal as much as it discloses. In his third *Satire*, Juvenal reacted quite ungenerously to the Greeks who had made a cultural but not a political conquest of Rome:

> Here's one from Sicyon,
> Another from Macedonia, two from Aegean islands—
> Andros, say, or Samos—two more from Caria,
> All of them lighting out for the City's classiest districts
> And burrowing into great houses, with a long-term plan
> For taking them over. Quick wit, unlimited nerve, a gift
> Of the gab that outsmarts a professional public speaker—
> These are their characteristics.

This, of course, is by no means what Harold Macmillan meant the Americans to understand by his remarks. But it contains an unmistakable element of what he meant the English to understand. Why not, in exchange for the pains and humiliations of being superseded, at least exert the influence that the effete may always bring to bear upon the brash? Macmillan was the most opportunist British politician since Lloyd George, and would probably have made no great claim to originality. But it is amusing and instructive to read his observations, and catch his tone, and measure both against reality. In Rome, Greeks became very influential, but Greekness in the sense of Hellenism did not. In modern America, very few English or British figures achieved influential standing except in their role as expatriates, with strong roots in an existent country. But certain British ambitions, precedents, designs, habits, and political patterns made, however metamorphosed, an extremely deep impress upon American life.

The literary mirror is often the most precise. Juvenal saw the Greeks as subtle and devious elements of corruption in a staunch Republic that embodied the manlier virtues, or that at least affected to do so. In our own time, English and American satiric writers have found themselves elaborating the same point from differing perspectives. Here is Evelyn Waugh, describing the exiled members of the Hollywood Cricket Club in his 1948 novella *The Loved One* (whose subtitle is *An Anglo-American Tragedy*):

> For these the club was the symbol of their Englishry. Here they collected subscriptions for the Red Cross and talked at their ease, out of the hearing of their alien employers and protectors.

As if in answer, here is Tom Wolfe, wise in the ways of the Brits but resentful of their unearned cachet, in *The Bonfire of the Vanities*:

> One had the sense of a very rich and suave secret legion that had insinuated itself into the cooperative apartment houses of Park Avenue and Fifth Avenue, from there to pounce at will upon the Yankees' fat fowl, to devour at leisure the last plump white meat on the bones of capitalism. . . . They were comrades in arms, in the service of Great Britain's wounded chauvinism.

Exactly forty years separate the publication of these two fictions. On the face of it, this seems a tribute to the way that cliché and stereotype outlive the events that formed them. During those four decades, however, the wheel turned in such a way as to confirm Evelyn Waugh's prefiguration, and to leave the English with only the sorts of consolation rather cruelly delineated by Wolfe.

The reason for this, surely, is the masochistic inversion that made nonsense of Macmillan's analogy even as it was being first uttered. England, Great Britain, the United Kingdom, or what you will, had never been Greece to America's Rome. It had always been *Rome* to America's—what? The hesitation is a pregnant one. The original American revolutionaries, many of them drawn from an essentially English class of gentlemen, took the Roman ideal as the model of republican virtue, and tended to stress those Romans, such as Cicero and Plutarch, who had been most inflected by Hellenism. The example of Cincinnatus was continually contrasted with the gross monarchism and corruption identified with "the royal brute" George III. Addison's *Cato* was performed for the troops during the extremities of Valley Forge. Indeed, the play has been argued by Garry Wills to have inspired, by its frequent performance throughout the Revolution, two of that Revolution's most famous sayings:

> What pity is it
> That we can die but once to serve our country.

And:

> It is not now a time to talk of aught,
> But chains or conquest, liberty or death.

Not only did the play give tone to the courage of Nathan Hale and Patrick Henry, but it also contained a graphic series of warnings against the young Republic's chief enemy—Caesarism:

monarchism = having an emperor

> What is a Roman that is Caesar's foe?
> Greater than Caesar, he's the friend of virtue.

plutocrats

The greatest insult that could be hurled at a political backslider such as Aaron Burr was "Caesar." Franklin Roosevelt only softened this image in his famous assault on the "economic royalists." *oligarchs*

Thomas Jefferson's design for the new republic and its federal city was indebted to Hellenism in the Doric, Ionic, and Corinthian proportions of his house at Monticello, but to Republican Rome in

the case of Washington itself. Thomas Moore, who visited the
capital during Jefferson's presidency, wrote lightheartedly:

> In fancy now beneath the twilight gloom,
> Come, let me lead thee o'er this second Rome,
> Where tribunes rule, where dusky Davi bow,
> And what was Goose Creek once is Tiber now.

Slavery as exception

("Davus" was the typical name for a slave in Roman antiquity, and
the reference to "dusky Davi" is yet another reminder of the great
exception to the lofty principles of the Revolution.)

Rome, then, is present in the American idea from the very start.
But the Rome cited by Macmillan is a very different one—the
Rome of conquest and booty and purple, not the Rome of Cincinnatus leaving his plow. And the Britain he represented had few
traces of the Greek in it, though perhaps some of the Byzantine.
What he seems to have intended was the self-conscious subordination of British to American power, as a simple concession to the
new global reality, and a corresponding or perhaps compensating
adoption by the United States of British customs or mores.

If that is what he wanted, then that is what he seems to have
got. But the ambiguities of this Graeco-Roman synthesis are more
interesting than a mere political and diplomatic compromise might
suggest. Long before Macmillan, in fact, the British were striving
to limit the extent of American republicanism, which they saw as
a threat and a rival. Throughout the nineteenth century, as I will
argue and show, they tried to prevent the emergence of a continental United States. Thwarted in this effort, they turned to making
common cause with a new "expansionist" America in 1898. Seeking
thereafter to engage America on the British side in European quarrels, they stimulated and helped aggrandize what might be termed
the superpower spirit among American elites. In the titanic battle
against Hitler, they were forced to acknowledge that the proportions of the relationship had changed, and that Britain could now
survive only as a junior partner. But along the way, huge alterations

had been made in the American system. The United States found itself committed in far-off places with which it had no common history, it found itself a nuclear power, it found itself involved as an arbiter in the politics of old Europe, and it found itself engaged along the widest front in history against the Soviet Union. In the origination of all these historic changes, it had been the British connection that was seminal.

And with this connection, which was in so many ironic and unexpected ways to come at Britain's expense, came a series of cultural influences. At certain crucial times, the old atavistic themes of blood and language were reinstated, with a stress on Anglo-Saxondom which would have horrified the young men who thrilled to Addison's *Cato*. Elements even of British monarchy and aristocracy recovered their credit in American life. At particular points, American statesmen made it their business to uphold and guarantee the British Empire—though in general they never lost sight of the overarching ambition not to abolish but to supplant it.

The cultural cross-fertilizations bear an oblique but definite relationship to the political and imperial ones. At a time when the United States seemed to many English people to be a young country, free of Old World restraints and pretensions, W. H. Auden hymned its freshness and modernism in his "New Year Letter" making a virtue of:

> That culture that had worshipped no
> Virgin before the dynamo,
> Held no Nicea or Canossa,
> *Hat keine verfallenen Schlösser,*
> *Keine Basalte,** the great Rome
> To all who lost or hated home.

new york
within america

Auden and Isherwood and Aldous Huxley and many others, even the dubious and seedy characters symbolized by the cynical Dennis

*Has no ruined castles,/No marble columns. The lines are taken from a poem by Goethe which opens: *Amerika, du hast es besser.*

Barlow in *The Loved One*, could interpret the idea of Rome as "the big city"; a grand site for the pursuit of hedonism and modernist experiment. Sexual freedom, vast spaces, an escape from the class system and from the idea of military and imperial education, an encounter with the melting pot—these were the mixtures of impulse summed up in the old phrase "New World." Conversely, those like T. S. Eliot who felt a reverence for the organic, ordered, Burkean, hierarchical principle were moved not merely to admire England's persistent attachment to an *ancien régime* but actually to involve themselves with it. Analogues of this emotional diagram—conservative Anglophile Americans and transplanted liberal and radical Englishmen—persist to this day, though with different overlaps and several contradictions.

The complicating factor has been empire: the special contribution of the English example to American life and institutions. Acquisition of empire meant both collusion with and rivalry with the British Establishment. Which of the audience of Addison's *Cato* could have imagined that in the hinge year of 1898 the most trumpeted poet in America would be Rudyard Kipling, who had written with scorn and contempt of the Revolution of 1776?

Yet it was empire, and the emulation of the former master, that eroded republican virtues and institutions. As Charles Beard wrote in his classic *The Rise of American Civilization*, in the chapter "Imperial America," by the year 1898:

No philosophy of Empire was worked up to systematic perfection and fused with the Constitution into the current system of ethics. Either on account of logic or Christian training, American thinkers shrank from an overt application of the Darwinian law to the struggle of nations for trade and territory. They were of course not unaware of the ancient creed, for they had heard about the theory and practice of Rome. In their schoolbooks they had read *Pro Lege Manilia*, the panegyric by Cicero, which summed up in a single sentence the old doctrine of might: "*Do not hesitate for a moment in pros-*

ecuting with all your energies a war to preserve the glory of the Roman name, the safety of our allies, our rich revenue, and the fortunes of innumerable private citizens." They had before them also the voluminous writings of European imperialists who scorned the more tender sentiments of liberals and frankly advocated war and expansion for glory and emoluments. [Italics mine.]

There is a distinctly modern ring to Cicero's injunction in the age of "credibility" and "peace through strength." It shows, at any rate, that the idea, not of becoming Roman, but of becoming a different kind of Rome, had occurred to people long before Macmillan. And in 1898, too, it had been with English encouragement that this connection was made. The results of the imperial transformation were not confined to politics and foreign affairs. Beard noted the emergence of a national style that might be called the American grandiose:

At last the measureless energy of American life had been discovered and accepted, save by a few artists who hoped that time and tide might be turned back and that the spirit of Chicago might yet be bodied forth in the delicate refinements of Renaissance Gothic. In 1914, an English critic, Clive Bell, declared that American architecture seemed on the verge of a revival worthy of Florence but after the World War he began to think it was to be more like Augustan Rome. . . . Possibly the steel frames and towering domes of business enterprise triumphant might grovel in the dust with the baths of Caracalla and the palaces of the Caesars.

Of course, 1914 was another Anglo-American hinge year. There is a permanent debate in the United States about a strange phenomenon called "the loss of American innocence." Some have dated this defloration or awakening as late as the Indochina war. But others have seen an almost Jamesian irony in the seduction, by the corrupted and ruthless British statesmen of the Great War, of the naïve Anglophile Woodrow Wilson. (This irony is scarcely tempered by the knowledge that Henry James himself played a small part in the seduction.)

In his poem "Not Like This," Czeslaw Milosz refers beautifully to irony as "the glory of slaves." In the evaluation of the ironic (suppose there to be such a process) some weight ought to be given to the ancient question: "Who whom?" (or as some iconoclastic modern grammarians would have it: "Who who?"). At whose expense is the irony of the Anglo-American transition, where the historic colonial power has become, in practice, the political and military colony? Is it at the expense of the United States, which has abandoned its affectation of anticolonialism and been invaded repeatedly by English manners and English taste? Or is it at the expense of the British, who called in the New World to redress the balance of the Old and then found that it was the New World doing the calling?

Elaborated and refracted through different episodes and processes, that is the question this book hopes to answer. There is an irony at the core of Macmillan's apparently modest but actually rather conceited ambition, which sorts well with the history and argument which led up to it and which occurred after it. And it may turn out that the irony of Juvenal—the irony of usurped and displaced Britannia enjoying a posthumous revenge in the fleshpots of Manhattan and Georgetown and Hollywood—is the apposite one.

These ironies are present as much in the late twentieth century as they were in the late nineteenth. They seem always to have been waiting to be pointed out. It was in the high noon of late Victorian imperialism that the equestrian statue of Boadicea was raised on the banks of the Thames at Westminster, with lines from William Cowper's notorious diatribe poem inscribed on the plinth. Recalling the British warrior queen's defiance of the Roman invader, Cowper had been superbly confident in his reading of destiny:

Rome, for empire far renowned,
Tramples on a thousand states;
Soon her pride shall kiss the ground—
Hark! The Gaul is at her gates!

as Cowper had the Druidic prophecy continue, for Boadicea:

Regions Caesar never knew
Thy posterity shall sway,
Where his eagles never flew,
None invincible as they.

And finally, as if the British were immune to the Greek admonition
to avoid hubris:

Ruffians, pitiless as proud,
Heaven awards the vengeance due;
Empire is on us bestowed,
Shame and ruin wait for you.

In the 1980s two controversies recalled this imagery to mind. The
first was the publication of Professor Paul Kennedy's book *The Rise
and Fall of the Great Powers*, which argued that the United States
was not and would not be immune to a cyclical law that condemned
all great systems to perish by "overstretch." Not strikingly original,
the argument exploded like a bomb in the context of widespread
angst over the American deficit. Professor Kennedy employed the
line: "Rome fell, Carthage fell, Scarsdale's turn will come," which
he had adapted from George Bernard Shaw's play *Captain Brass-
bound's Conversion*. (In the original, which was true to the vision
of complacent suburban stockjobbing, the suburb marked out for
eclipse had been "Hindhead.") The entire vexed question of "Number One" and "Top Nation" had been borrowed whole cloth from
the English precedent.

Yet even as the finally uninteresting argument about "Number

One" was going on, there were British minds prepared to squabble over who had the most influence at the Roman court. In the course of a parochial power struggle over the future of the Westland Helicopter Company, which at one stage was held to threaten the survival and "credibility" of Mrs. Thatcher's government, it became important to the Prime Minister's faction to blacken all criticism as "anti-American." The matter in question, which was the undue advantage given to the U.S.-based Sikorsky consortium in a bid which also involved potential European tenders, was essentially secondary. The real dispute was over Britain's place in an acknowledged American imperium. There were those, even in the Conservative Establishment, who found all this a trifle unsettling. They muttered, as indeed they had muttered against Macmillan, about American "imperial power" and the reduction of the United Kingdom to "dependency" and "a client state."

There was a prompt intervention by Roger Scruton, normally considered a convenor of the "race and nation" element in the Tory Party, and editor of the (normally *völkisch*) *Salisbury Review*. Employing his regular column in *The Times*, he argued in imperial terms for colonial subordination. Did the critics of the multinationals not realize, he inquired, that "the British Empire lives on in America, just as the Roman Empire lived on in Byzantium, although in a form more vital, more industrious and more generous." This elegant glaze of variation on an old theme showed how powerful the vicarious instinct remains in British circles; powerful enough in this instance to risk the payment of a compliment which could only embarrass those to whom it was offered. It didn't really seem to matter, to Scruton at least, which empire lived on in which, as long as the idea of empire could draw moral and historic sustenance from some simulacrum of a "special relationship."

Somewhere in the subtext of all this is the ticklish question of race and the awkward matter of class. Ethnic hierarchy in America actually confuses the two things in a revealing minor way, since the word WASP, which denotes a racial and religious group, is only ever applied to a certain social layer of it. (George Bush is a

WASP. George Wallace may have been a white Protestant of Anglo-Saxon descent, and even rather vocal on all three points, but a WASP he was not.) Anglo-Saxondom, however, has always played a large role, sometimes spoken of and sometimes not, in the ordering of American society by caste and color. Once again, it was Evelyn Waugh who hit off the observation most deftly in *The Loved One*:

> "I presume the Loved One was Caucasian?"
> "No, why did you think that? He was purely English."
> "English are purely Caucasian, Mr. Barlow. This is a restricted park . . ."
> "I think I understand. Well, let me assure you Sir Francis was quite white."

Dennis Barlow, exploiting his advantages as an amoral Greek in the Californian Rome, also lets slip another trick of the trade when discussing his crude, naïve employer with a fellow expatriate:

> "My manner is congenial. He told me so yesterday. The man they had before caused offense by his gusto. They find me reverent. It is my combination of melancholy with the English accent. Several of our clientele have commented favorably upon it."

Thus the fully debased version of "the glory of slaves."

It was, of all people, the late James Burnham who made one of the shrewdest plays upon the "Greece to their Rome" allegory. Himself of English parentage and Oxford-educated, Burnham became one of the foremost advocates of an "American World Empire" (his phrasing) and of the necessary "receivership" (also his phrasing) into which the United States would have to take the British dominions. Burnham persuaded some crucial American statesmen of the correctness of this view (see pages 243–50). But he argued that the thing should be done with due regard to British sensitivity. The British could be induced to fall in with the plan, he wrote, because with some part of themselves they desired the security of a larger and stronger system:

> A similar longing, similarly expressed, was widespread throughout the Hellenic world during the century preceding the foundation of the Roman Empire. It is like a bachelor who begins to prepare himself for the restrictions of matrimony by discoursing on the beauties of "true love."

In both Britain and America today, both the Roman and the Athenian complexes can be found in recurrent forms. Perhaps the reason for this is that the implied relationship, however it may differ from any real or imagined Greece or Rome or Byzantium, contains enough to flatter both parties. As Plutarch put it in his *Precepts of Government* (here adumbrated by Sir Ronald Syme in his *Greeks Invading the Roman Government*):

> Plutarch . . . confined his advice to the ruling class in the cities. They must cease from strife and ambition, forget the glories of a distant past and abide in contentment under a superior power. Furthermore, the rule of Rome (he reminded them) was not a product of chance or violence. Virtue and Fortune had collaborated.
>
> The signal contribution that Plutarch made was less obtrusive. He hit upon a genial device, the sequence of parallel biographies, from legendary heroes down to generals and statesmen. The two nations were thereby recognized as standing on parity.

"Parallel biographies" is a potentially telling phrase, which might go some distance to explaining the ease with which Americans and British exist in each other's imaginations. Winston Churchill may be, and is, quoted endlessly by American politicians, to the mutual satisfaction of two traditions. Princess Diana can painlessly become an American star or celebrity. In the world of literature and entertainment, the common language and mutual history make for alternating waves of fashion, with Liverpool intelligible in Los Angeles and vice versa. Moreover, while the larger and richer relation can bask in its quite recent but definite preeminence, the poorer and smaller one can privately boast of having a more polished and civilized tradition. As Sir Ronald Syme puts it: "Hadrian, more a Greek than a Roman, paid honor and deference to the exponents of Hellenic eloquence." What did that cost him?

Returning to Macmillan's original formulation after these reflections, it is clearer than ever that he intended the "special relationship" to be a relationship between conservative forces. The Americans were to supply the capital, and the British were to provide the class. This would give the British imperial manner a fresh lease, and lend some much-needed tone to the grandiosity of the American century. These are the unspoken conventions which have, in variant form, governed the relationship since its inception.

[2]

Brit Kitsch

In January 1946, Mr. Edmund Wilson wrote a pained review of *Brideshead Revisited* for *The New Yorker*. Evelyn Waugh, he lamented, had disappointed him. There had been the fizz and wallop of *Vile Bodies*, the venturesome innovations of *Black Mischief*, and the sinister, strangely modern energy of *A Handful of Dust*, which even took its title from *The Waste Land*. And now this . . . this *harlequinade*, as Wilson eventually settled upon calling it:

> The reader has an uncomfortable feeling that what has caused Mr. Waugh's hero to plump on his knees is not, perhaps, the sign of the cross but the prestige, in the person of Lord Marchmain, of one of the oldest families in England.
>
> For Waugh's snobbery, hitherto held in check by his satirical point of view, has here emerged shameless and rampant. His admiration for the qualities of the older British families, as contrasted with modern upstarts, had its value in his earlier novels, where the standards of morals and taste are kept in the background and merely implied. But here the upstarts are rather crudely overdone and the aristocrats become terribly trashy . . .

Wilson was a decided Anglophobe at least as far as the ticklish questions of class and empire went, and was to spend much of that year of 1946 wondering aloud and in print at how little the British seemed to have learned from the experience of war. His acidulated description of their sahiblike behavior in Rome and Athens and their chilly demeanor at home had elements of love-hate in it, but the exasperation certainly predominated. In this, for once, Wilson was in a fairly safe American majority. The famous "Open Letter to the People of England," printed by *Life* magazine in October 1942, had come close to summarizing the view of most Americans who were not consumed by Anglophilia, and certainly expressed the private opinions of the Roosevelt administration as well as the Luces:

> One thing we are sure we are *not* fighting for is to hold the British Empire together. We don't like to put the matter so bluntly, but we don't want you to have any illusions. If your strategists are planning a war to hold the British Empire together they will sooner or later find themselves strategizing all alone.

Wilson would never have said "strategize," any more than Evelyn Waugh would have, but he would have approved the sentiment. The Americans of the 1940s admired the British for qualities of democracy, solidarity, and courage. They did not intend, as had happened in 1914–18, to let their general admiration and generosity be parlayed into a rescue operation for the British Establishment, the British class system, and the British Empire.

Edmund Wilson was slow to see the point in his *Europe Without Baedeker*, but in the real world the British were giving ground very fast to a nascent American empire which in later life he was to recognize and to find highly unpalatable. It was only when the Britain of great prewar dominions had become a memory that nostalgia for it became possible. This nostalgia was nowhere more lusciously indulged than in America, which developed an unslakable thirst for the high style of the country house, the hunt, the brittle drawing-room repartee, and the other supposed strengths of the English manner.

Some of this was merely coincidental with the recrudescence of conservatism as a force in American life, but some was directly connected to it. On the cusp of the seventies and the eighties, there was an efflorescence of mannered, extreme, conservative journalism on the campuses of many of the more "traditional" American universities. The most celebrated example was that of *The Dartmouth Review*, which fought to restore "standards" to a college much altered by the liberal race-and-class buffetings of the preceding decade. One of its founding editors was Benjamin Hart, who was born within a few years of Edmund Wilson's death. He is the son of Jeffrey Hart, who is professor of English at Dartmouth and also a veteran co-editor of William F. Buckley's *National Review*.

Benjamin Hart directed the "Third Generation" project for the Heritage Foundation, which was the major think-tank resource for the soi-disant Reagan revolution. In 1984 he published a book, *Poisoned Ivy*, which became the manual of the eager young conservatives then migrating from college to Washington. Inescapably, the book was compared to Buckley's earlier classic *God and Man at Yale*, and Mr. Buckley himself did little to discourage this comparison by contributing an introduction.

After Mr. Hart gave me an inscribed copy of this book in the summer of 1987, I turned its pages with interest. My interest was undiminished when I realized that I had read parts of the work before. For example, at the opening of the fourth chapter Hart gave an account of a conversation with one of his *Dartmouth Review* colleagues, a man named Keeney:

"The problem with modern education is that you never know how ignorant some people are," Keeney said. "It's not that students are stupid. In fact, many have a worldly surface. But suddenly the crust breaks and you find yourself in a bottomless pit of chaos."

In *Brideshead Revisited,* Evelyn Waugh has the old Farm Street confessor Father Mowbray observe wearily:

The trouble with modern education is you never know how ignorant people are. These young people have such an intelligent, knowledgeable surface and then the crust breaks and you look down into depths of confusion you didn't know existed.

As I reviewed the pages further, I found more echoes of the same work. Still describing the embattlement of his young conservative co-thinkers, Hart recalled a certain Jones:

Jones and I often went to Mass together. Jones seemed to spend an awful lot of time in the confessional. Whatever he said to Monsignor Nolan through the grille, his confessions must have been memorable, as the silver-haired priest always emerged from the booth afterward with an amused look on his face.

Or as Anthony Blanche had put it so well in *Brideshead,* remembering the boyhood of Sebastian Flyte at Eton:

We used to go to Mass together. He used to spend *such* a time in the confessional, I used to wonder what he had to say, because he never did anything wrong; never quite; at least he never got punished. Perhaps he was just being charming through the grille.

I was rather touched by Hart's reaction when I teased him about this source of inspiration. *"Brideshead Revisited,"* he said with some gravity, "was the stylebook upon which my generation modeled itself." Under further teasing, he conceded that some of his generation were going less by the novel than by the celebrated television series shown on the Public Broadcasting System (PBS) in 1981, at the dawn of the Reagan era.

The *Masterpiece Theatre* Sunday evening debauch of English-ness is one of the standbys and continual referents for students of Anglophilia and its American mystique. When Alistair Cooke as-sumes the leather armchair, the free association begins and En-glishness takes on its varied guises and incarnations: the civilized country house; the strained but decent colonial civil servant; the regimental mess; the back-to-the-wall wartime coolness under fire; the stratified but considerate social system; the eccentric but above all literate milieu of London in assorted moods and epochs.

As the cameras roam the room before discovering Mr. Cooke, they linger upon marble busts, oil paintings, carefully bound first editions, and sporting and military prints. As an additional touch for the transmission of John le Carré's *The Perfect Spy*, with its boarding schools, racecourses, and fog-sodden country scenes, a portrait of Her Majesty the Queen was placed on the wall behind Mr. Cooke's perennially reassuring features. Tom Wolfe, whose satirical attitude toward the cult of England is well known, once drew attention to the fact that *Masterpiece Theatre* is subsidized by Mobil Oil. He could have emphasized the irony of a giant corporation which had grown fat on the eclipse of Britain's position in the Middle East, but as an archconservative and nativist he chose rather to dub PBS "Petroleum's British Subsidiary."

On the occasion of the showing of *Brideshead Revisited*, Mr. Cooke ceded the leather armchair to William F. Buckley. There was more irony in this than might have been thought—more irony even than in Benjamin Hart and his cohort of moralistic young "family values" warriors, modeling themselves on the doings of a fictional group of English upper-crust bisexual alcoholics at the close of the First World War.

Shortly before the showing of *Brideshead*, Mr. Buckley had printed a defense of his own close relations with Evelyn Waugh, and a reply to the detractors and mockers of those relations, in the *National Review* of November 14, 1980. His indignation had been aroused by a review of Evelyn Waugh's *Letters* written by John Kenneth Galbraith. Galbraith had made much of the fact that in 1960 Waugh wrote to his old schoolmate and friend Tom Driberg as follows:

> Can you tell me: did you in your researches come across the name of Wm F. Buckley Jr., editor of a New York, neo-McCarthy magazine named *National Review?* He has been showing me great and unsought attention lately and your article made me curious. Has he been supernaturally "guided" to bore me? It would explain him.

As Edmund Wilson had noted in his favorable review of *Scoop,* the word "bore" is one of the deadliest in the English lexicon, and one reserved by Waugh as an ultimate deterrent. ("The story of William Boot comes to its climax when the grown-up public-school boy faces down the Communist boss of Ishmaelia, who is trying to get him off the scene while a revolution takes place. 'Look here, Dr Benito,' said William. 'You're being a bore. I'm not going.' ") Stung by its employment in connection with himself, Mr. Buckley ransacked the correspondence. He had written to Waugh in 1960, inviting him to reconsider some published criticism of Senator Joseph McCarthy and to think about contributing to *National Review* at "a guarantee of $5,000 a year for a piece every few weeks, of two thousand words. That is higher pay by far than we have given before, higher than what we have paid to Max Eastman, John Dos Passos, Whittaker Chambers . . ."

Waugh's reply to this enticing offer (more money than Whittaker Chambers, he may not have appreciated, was the highest favor the magazine could bestow) was rather churlish. "Until you get much richer (which I hope will be soon) or I get much poorer (which I fear may be sooner) I am unable to accept." Buckley persisted, sending Waugh a free copy of his book *McCarthy and His Enemies* and enclosing a review of Waugh's latest novel. The review was by Joan Didion, who in those days wrote for *National Review*. Waugh's reply was even more *de haut en bas*:

> Thank you for sending me the proof of the preface to the new edition of your book on Senator McCarthy.
>
> The only correction I would suggest is that it is improper to call Bertrand Russell "Lord Bertrand Russell," a style only used by the younger sons of Dukes and Marquesses. He is properly called either Earl Russell or Lord Russell.

Having delivered this piece of what his admirers would rather tiresomely call "vintage Waugh," he closed with another two sentences of near-pure condescension:

> Please thank Miss Didion for her kind review. I could not understand the opening, but the rest of her article showed her to be a most agreeable young lady.

In later exchanges with an indefatigable Buckley, Waugh said things that one is surprised to see Buckley reprinting. "At your best you remind me of Belloc; at your second best of Randolph Churchill." This is better than being called a bore, but not by nearly enough. Yet Buckley was so determined to show the increase in the warmth of the correspondence that he omitted no detail. And Waugh did finally contribute a piece to the *National Review*, at a rate of payment not disclosed. It was a review of Garry Wills's book on Chesterton. ("Mr. Wills's literary style . . . is not uniformly bad. Indeed, again and again he shows himself capable of constructing a grammatical, even an elegant, sentence.")

In 1958, Harold Isaacs—who had, incidentally, been one of the few Americans to witness the British restoration of the French Empire in Vietnam in 1945—published an extremely influential book called *Scratches on Our Minds*. His ostensible subject was

India and China, but his theme was the subliminal mastery that is exerted on consciousness by certain literary, historical, cultural, and emotional images. Isaacs found that images of this sort, at once inchoate and durable, were important at the level of decision making in government, as well as among elites in journalism, business, and the academy. They formed part of the common stock of allusion and reference—one might call it the unacknowledged legislation—which underlay the ways in which people thought and responded, and the ways in which they made up their minds.

The English connection to America—the "special relationship"—and the competing strains of Anglophobia and Anglophilia are at bottom a matter of "scratches on the mind." The scratches are more numerous and wider and deeper than in any comparable case, and educated persons can debate them with some background. Thus a writer like Evelyn Waugh can be a matter for some disputation and analysis, and a figure of some importance, for two such widely separated commentators and essayists as Edmund Wilson and William Buckley. He can also provide a kind of guidance and suasion to a generation that never knew him, and which heroically fails to get his point.

Mr. Wilson was in very many ways the product of an English education, as that term is classically understood, and Mr. Buckley actually underwent a brief incarceration in an English boarding school (from which he wrote a pompous letter to King George V reminding him of the obligation of the British Crown to repay its war debt to America). Mr. Buckley's style, whether in print or on the small screen, is regularly described by both admirers and critics as "Anglicized," a description which most English residents in America find mildly risible but which testifies to a definite "scratch on the mind" in the association of certain manners with a certain grammar and vocabulary. Mr. George Will, one of the products of the Buckley forcing house, takes care to have himself photographed for publicity purposes with a neatly folded copy of the London *Times* on a breakfast tray beside his desk, which is a scratch of a kind also.

The scratch on the mind is of its nature hard to identify or to classify, but there seems very little doubt that it has to do, in this case, with different definitions of the word "class." In America, class means style, presence, heft, glamour, taste, charm, wealth, poise, moxie, ambition, achievement, and what you will. In England, where to "have class" may also mean all or at any rate most of those things, it carries the further implication of anything that may be envied, or that cannot be faked, or that can be recognized more easily than defined. But it also means, famously, something that *can* be defined: hierarchy, snobbery, discrimination, stratification, and the hereditary principle.

(To go back a paragraph or two, this is why Mr. Buckley was entirely wasting his time in trying to interest Evelyn Waugh in the cause of Senator McCarthy. Waugh may have been sympathetic to Franco, and may have derided Auden and Isherwood as "Parsnip and Pimpernel" when they exchanged their modish Communism for exile in the United States in 1940, but to him Joe McCarthy was an ignoble demagogue, attempting to incite the vulgar against the East Coast Establishment and not incidentally trading on Anglophobia to do so.)

Waugh took the trouble to make this sort of unspoken "scratchy" connection tolerably explicit in *The Loved One*. The cynical hero Dennis Barlow is at the mercy of his crude boss at the pets' funeral parlor, but still finds that servitude has its consolations:

"Through no wish of my own I have become the protagonist of a Jamesian problem. Do you ever read any Henry James, Mr. Schultz?"

"You know I don't have the time for reading."

"You don't have to read much of him. All his stories are about the same thing—American innocence and European experience."

"Thinks he can outsmart us, does he?"

"James was the innocent American."

"Well, I've no time for guys running down their own folks."

"Oh, he doesn't run them down. The stories are all tragedies one way or another."

"Well, I ain't got the time for tragedies neither. Take an end of this casket. We've only half an hour before the pastor arrives."

Barlow behaves in this deplorable way in spite of the tribal admonitions of Sir Ambrose Abercrombie, the deliberate stage Englishman who has guessed the link between "class" English style and "class" American, and who sees it as part of a personal and national survival kit:

> We limeys have a peculiar position to keep up, you know, Barlow. They may laugh at us a bit—the way we talk and the way we dress; our monocles—they may think us cliquey and stand-offish, but, by God, they respect us. . . . I often feel like an ambassador, Barlow. It's a responsibility, I can tell you, and in various degrees every Englishman out here shares it. . . . You never find an Englishman among the under-dogs— except in England of course.

Sir Ambrose here touches lightly on the critical question of mutation. An Englishman, he is saying, need only cross the Atlantic in order to acquire a cachet that would by no means belong to him automatically if he remained at home.

Why should this be? Clearly, some part of it has to do with the matter of race (or tribe, or genealogy if you prefer). An Englishman in America is so to speak an axiomatic WASP; a member of that large and strange minority that needs no national day parade on Fifth Avenue to make itself felt, and which might be met with weird oaths if it did choose to stage such a procession. But as I've argued elsewhere, the word WASP has an ambivalent relationship to ethnicity and usually denotes a certain *tone* as much as a certain shade or confession.

Clearly, the thing that makes America so penetrable to "class" as defined in the English sense is this. As defined in the English sense, America is not supposed to have any sense of class *at all*. "Class," says Paul Blumberg in his book *Inequality in an Age of Decline*, is "America's forbidden thought." Status, yes. Income, yes. Even "mobility"—yes, yes, yes. Class—no.

The English presence in American life, however, allows the mutation of class as "class" into class as "style." The world of fashion and glossy journalism, as well as the world of television and advertising, provides continual evidence of this process. To choose only at random from my reading while writing this chapter:

- An article in the New York smart set magazine *Seven Days* asks why S. I. Newhouse prefers British editors for his Condé Nast magazine empire. " 'Si likes the U.K. accent,' said a designer. Others say these editors are also adept at analyzing American society as a class system. Tina Brown has nearly created her own for *Vanity Fair*." As well as *Vanity Fair*, Newhouse's *Vogue*, *Traveler*, and *Self* were at this period edited by English immigrants.

- In the May 1989 issue of *Esquire*, the "Man at His Best" feature opens with the words: "Carl Reiner once said that he didn't believe Englishmen really had accents, they just all got together and agreed to talk that way to make the rest of us feel bad." Three pages later is an article on the great American zip fastener and the struggle that this innovation had to become accepted over the fly button. "A zipper added a dollar to the cost of a pair of trousers; buttons cost only two cents. That's where matters stood until 1934, when the Prince of Wales, the Duke of York and their second cousin 'Dickie' Mountbatten suddenly started wearing zippered flies. It wasn't something they flaunted, obviously, but word got around anyhow. The zippered fly was finally respectable."

- As the Bush era began, the much-consulted *New York Times* culture critic Paul Goldberger advanced the opinion that Ralph

Lauren, *né* Lipschitz, was "the real design symbol," "the one-man Bauhaus" of our age. The Lauren style, given a substantial exposure by the Bush weekend manner at Kennebunkport, Maine, is based on the real expense and the supposed gentility of sports like polo and sculling; the assumed Edwardianism of dress and the WASP aesthetic in general. One of Lauren's admirers, Hugh Barnard of *Retail Marketing Report*, anatomized the secrets of snob appeal as follows: "Steamer trunks, antique armoires, life-size paintings of military officers of long-ago wars, upholstered chairs by tables laden with books." In principle these status artifacts can be found in the inventory of any culture; in practice they are the props department of *Masterpiece Theatre*.

Examples of this sort could be multiplied by any casual reader of the American press. Especially in the advertising of certain kinds of car, tweed, scotch, and hotel, and in the advertising industry itself, a version of the English accent seems to be de rigueur. The British pander to this taste even at the official level, with the national airline advertised by the likes of Robert Morley and the Tourist Board presenting England as a hellhole of thatched roofs, Dickensian pubs, and haunted castles. These pubs, and these county affiliations, can of course be mutated for transatlantic purposes. In order to reach the exclusive suburban town of Somerset, outside Washington, D.C., you turn left on Warwick, right on Windsor, and so forth. In his book *Class*, Paul Fussell gives a list of the tract suburbs surrounding Houston, Texas: Nottingham Oaks, Afton Oaks, Inverness Forest, Sherwood Forest, Braes Manor, Meredith Manor, and so on. Somewhere in Middle America there is a suburb entirely fitted out by Fussell, who was asked by a developer to supply an alphabetical list of British-sounding street names that would raise the neighborhood in the esteem of potential middle-class house buyers. Fussell was then living in Knightsbridge, and furnished a list beginning Albemarle, Berkeley, and so on, until "I couldn't resist Windsor for W, and today there's some poor puzzled fellow wondering why success is so slow in arriving, since for years he's been residing at 221 Windsor Close instead of living on West Broad Street."

In one of the terminals at John F. Kennedy Airport, I recently came across an American public telephone housed in a red London telephone box, or booth. A notice inside informed me that this was a gift of the British Tourist Board, to convey a little of the flavor of England in a faraway land. Red telephone boxes, for so long so characteristic of the English scene and as reliable an "establishing shot" in movies about London as the uniformed bobby or Nelson's column, are of course being uprooted and replaced by more American, streamlined, colorless models. In other words, the condition for the appearance of this artifact at JFK was its failure to represent even a hint or taste of the actual England. This was as good a working definition of English kitsch as I could have hoped to find— with the arguable exception of the "English muffin," a confection so grim that it could not have been sold in England even in wartime.

It is of the essence of Anglophilia that the object of its desire is unattainable. The cult of something at once vanished and super-seded is secure against any too abrupt swing in fashion. It is reliable and time-tested. It also avoids the awkwardness that used to bedevil Anglophilia, especially Anglophilia of the political kind, in that no question of "dual loyalty" or "servility" is any longer involved. When the British fleet patrolled the oceans and upheld Imperial Preference, and the King was the Emperor of India, an overfond-ness for things English could expose the American addict to ridicule and even contempt. As Paul Fussell puts it:

> It is in part because Britain has seen better days that An-glophilia is so indispensable an element in upper-class taste, in clothes, literature, allusion, manners and ceremony. The current irony of the Anglophilic class motif will not escape us. . . . To acquire and display British goods shows how archaic you are, and so validates upper- and upper-middle-class standing.

"Literature, allusion, manners and ceremony." On the turn of the year in 1988, *The Washington Post* recommended books in all categories in its weekly book review supplement. Under the section headed "Great Britain," the titles were, in order: *The English Country House, The Book of the Royal Year, The English Season, Mary Stuart's Scotland,* and *Gloriana: The Portraits of Queen Elizabeth I.* In the American mind, an indissoluble connection now seems to exist between the idea of England and the ideas of heritage, tradition, royalty, pageantry, and good taste.

This is odd, in view of the fact that the two most obvious English mutations to have occurred in America in the last decade go by the names "punk" and "skinhead." In their imported form, true, they are simulacra of authentic tendencies among British youth, and it is difficult to imagine the regalia and conduct of, say, a West German or Italian football fan commanding such attention. Perhaps even at the allegedly "classless" level, an English model is felt to be instructive. There was certainly a period in the 1960s when British rock music sold itself as a new social and democratic phenomenon—the Liverpudlian foursome, the determinedly flat vowels of Mick Jagger. But even that benefited from a preexisting contrast; one that could be reasserted when the children of those who watched *The Ed Sullivan Show* had ripened into *Brideshead* fans. Of course, this happens the other way around. In 1946, Wilson was already noting of the English that when it came to mass-produced American taste, "our Hollywood stars are already their stars, our best-sellers their best-sellers." That would be an uncontroversial observation today.

In America, it is, in the end, always the England of the past that reasserts itself. Here, the mutation can operate in the other direction. When T. S. Eliot said in 1928 that he was a classicist, a royalist, and an Anglo-Catholic, he may have been echoing what Charles Maurras had said of himself (*"classique, catholique, monarchique"*) more than a decade earlier. But whatever the inspiration, it could apparently be materialized only in England. Fleeing the Boston of Henry Adams, he took some time to acquire the confidence to say "we" while in the company of Englishmen, and would more than once sign himself with the pseudonym *metoikos*: the Greek word for "resident alien" and thus perfectly apposite for a convert to both kinds of Rome. Becoming a British citizen in 1927 ("I don't like being a squatter. I might as well take the full responsibility") he was seen by Virginia Woolf shortly before the event sporting a white tie and waistcoat. Other friends noted other affectations. Richard Aldington was embarrassed when in the course of a stroll Eliot lifted his hat to a sentry outside Marlborough House. On the anniversary of the Battle of Bosworth he would wear a white flower and attend Mass in memory of the Yorkists and of Richard III. As Hope Mirrlees put it in her lecture "The Mysterious Mr. Eliot," these and other poses made her conclude that "he wasn't a bit like an Englishman." But he was like an *idea* of an Englishman, and possessed the zeal of the convert, and identified England with history and faith and hierarchy, and could see the point of Evelyn Waugh.

It was these "scratches on the mind" that were so artfully enlisted by the British in their incomparably skillful war for American opinion during the Second World War. In 1941 the Museum of Modern Art in New York City mounted an exhibition entitled "Britain at War." The catalogue of this show, which was produced in collaboration with the British Ministry of Information, is still redolent with the ideas and conceptions that have underpinned Anglophilia before and since. It opens with a poem by T. S. Eliot, written for the occasion, called "Defence of the Islands":

> Let the memorials of built stone—music's
> enduring instrument, of many centuries of
> patient cultivation of the earth, of English
> verse
> be joined with the memory of this defence of
> the islands.

This reached the right note of evocation, especially skillful when one recalls Eliot's misgivings about the war and his ambiguity about the cause in which it was fought. Herbert Read contributed the introductory notes, forgoing his own preference for the aesthetic and anarchic in favor of praise for the Imperial War Museum and the Ministry of Information. He praised the new "realism" of Graham Sutherland's paintings of air-raid damage, and wrote, as if calling on an effortless reserve of national confidence:

> It must then be remembered that though the English are energetic in action, they are restrained in expression. Our typical poetry is lyrical, not epical or even tragic. Our typical music is the madrigal and the song, not the opera and the symphony. Our typical painting is the landscape. In all these respects war cannot change us; and we are fighting this war precisely because in these respects we refuse to be changed.

This beautifully rendered paragraph, with its tender emphasis on the pastoral, could easily induce forgetfulness of the world's first industrial revolution and the world's first and greatest modern empire. Henry Moore's drawings of Londoners in bomb shelters, and the still photographs of cavalry patrols waiting under trees for mechanized Nazi invaders, also helped to reinforce a picture of England as a vulnerable miniature, populated by gentle but durable people. The caption to one photograph reads: "Tanks on a country road. Once more, the contrast of tragic mechanism and the famous old-fashioned loveliness of Britain." Again, one would barely have remembered that the tank was a British invention. Even the photograph of a "Nelson class" warship, showing the serried "pom-pom" guns, captioned them as "a Chicago piano," as if the very vernacular of modern weaponry were somehow antithetical to the English character. Under a two-page display of "ordinary people" going about their duties as fireman, nurse, pilot, and sailor there appears the caption: "Since the start of this war the virtuosity of news photographers has shown to all the world the unfamiliar beauty of the British race."

A few pages later comes an arresting photograph of the high altar at St. Paul's Cathedral, the dome pierced by a Nazi bomb but the memorials to faraway proconsuls standing unscathed to either side of the great screen. With an adroit use of the restraint and understatement of which Herbert Read had written, the picture is otherwise untitled. Studies of dogs, horses, and children, some wearing gas masks, succeed it. Then comes another bomb-damage photograph, this time showing "Burlington Arcade: A shopping center familiar to all American visitors."

The catalogue is completed by a selection of cartoons, chosen by Sir Kenneth Clark. Here, Osbert Lancaster and Heath Robinson display every variety of British phlegm and sangfroid. As a final practical hint, "because we in the United States shall soon be seeing strange new examples of camouflage," the endpapers give some tips on concealment in modern warfare.

The Anglophobes, whose influence was still very great, were powerless to combat this mild yet convincing appeal, elsewhere expressed in books and films like *Mrs. Miniver* (George Bush's favorite movie) which reinforced the idea of a civilized kindred people, slow to anger but resolute when roused. The phrase "love-hate relations" is often used in connection with Anglo-American emotions and entanglements, and the distance between admiration and envy has never been a difficult one to traverse. It is the abolition of the *need* for envy that has secured Anglophilia in the place it now occupies in America. Two anecdotal histories may illustrate the relation.

Few people now bother to read Owen Wister, whose 1902 novel *The Virginian* invented the romantic discourse of the cowboy and the Western, and was read with avidity on both American seaboards as well as across the Atlantic. Of partially English descent, having the English actress Fanny Kemble as his grandmother, Wister was a lifelong friend of Theodore Roosevelt and wrote an adoring account of their relationship. He also composed two popular historical and moral books in defense of the idea of Englishness, published during and after the First World War. The first, *The Pentecost of*

Calamity, was an early call to arms against the Kaiser, issued in 1915 and covering the entire German nation and character with atrabilious abuse. The second and the more significant and by far the longer is called *The Straight Deal* and subtitled *The Ancient Grudge*. It is a frontal engagement with Anglophobia, which Lister locates in the American inferiority complex. He identified the three foundations of "the ancient grudge" as patriotic American schoolbooks which stressed the villainy of the redcoats and the perfidy of the King, "various controversies from the Revolution to the Alaskan boundary dispute," and "certain differences in customs and manners."

In a chapter entitled "Rude Britannia, Crude Columbia," he admitted that the British could be arrogant and superior but argued that they had much to be arrogant and superior about. Whereas, he said, he blushed at the lack of polish and sophistication displayed by Americans overseas and at home. He recorded with pleasure, for the instruction of his readers, a conversation with a gentleman in London who, elaborating the delights of the season, added: "And if there's nothing at the theatres and everything else fails, you can always go to one of the restaurants and hear the Americans eat."

In his final chapter, significantly entitled "Lion and Cub," Wister hymned the glories of the British Empire's performance in the just concluded Great War, argued that Britain had always been the protector of America "from Bonaparte to the Kaiser," and wrote: "We are her cub. . . . She has seen clearly and ever more clearly that our good will was to her advantage."

The publication of this book drew upon Wister a reply of such sustained and brilliant fury that the windows still rattle when it is read aloud. Daniel T. O'Connell, a barrister and the director of the American Friends of Irish Freedom, issued a pamphlet called *Owen Wister: Advocate of Racial Hatred*, which certainly started as it meant to go on by describing Wister as follows: "Parasite himself, he conceives of America as a parasite, living on from decade to decade by the favor and under the protecting wing of

England." Repudiating Wister's praise for England's broad and generous attitude toward Empire, O'Connell wrote:

> There is not in the history of any country, nor in criminal annals anywhere a record of crimes so shameful, so callous, so vile as England's opium war or England's present opium trade, or the rape of the Boer Republics, of the crimes in India and in Persia and in Ireland and in Egypt, of Amritsar and of Cairo.

As if to show that his objection to imperialism was a patriotic rather than a radical one, O'Connell went on to derogate Wister for his attacks on the crudeness of American manners and said: "If a passage like this should occur in a book by a 'Red' he would be locked up." After some indignant defenses of the American revolutionary tradition, at the expense of which Wister had had some ponderous fun, the pamphlet went on: "What he says leaves the impression that he is a frank sycophant. He is always in awe of persons and things English . . . he should know that the gorge of anybody, *even an Englishman*, will rise at cringing servility and flattery." O'Connell was especially angry at Wister's lack of respect for Ireland's old ally, France, saying bitterly: "How foolish Pershing appears now with his 'Lafayette, we are here.' " He closed with a deadly burst about "the man who is allowed to pick up the gossip of the Junker class in England," adding that Wister would "not succeed in making this Republic a nest for the spurious Anglomaniac breed."

This recalls an almost forgotten epoch, when Fenianism was a serious force in American life and when real hatred of the Crown and the Union Jack was a potent political element. This, too, has declined along with the power of Britain and the natural erosion of the generation that kept the spirit of Sinn Fein alive. Still, even the attenuated Irish National Caucus mobilized as late as 1986 against a treaty which would have allowed extradition of wanted Republicans to British courts. They had enough congressional votes pledged in advance to abort the provision, and were only overborne by the sudden sentiment on the Hill which followed Mrs. Thatcher's decision, alone among European heads of government, to endorse the highly popular American bombing of Libya.

The second instance concerns Anglophilia in its post-imperial, mannerist phase. In 1969, Richard Nixon sent gales of mirth through the Protestant and prep school establishment of the State Department and Georgetown by appointing Walter Annenberg to be his ambassador in London. There were, from that natural establishment's point of view, several things about this gazetting that threatened to make it a *bêtise*. For one thing, Walter's father, Moe, had been accurately described by Drew Pearson as running a publishing empire "built up on the gang wars of Chicago and the illegal race wire." For another, Walter himself had only avoided indictment for massive tax evasion because his father agreed to take the rap for both of them. For still another, the senior Annenberg's business associates had names like Lucky Luciano, Meyer Lansky, and Johnny Rosselli; men who continued William Randolph Hearst's keen interest in Cuba but in a radically different vernacular.

All of this, and Annenberg's association with railroad interests in Pennsylvania which his own newspapers were not shy to promote, made him seem an impossible choice for the London embassy. People began to speak as if Joseph Kennedy, the bootlegger and Nazi sympathizer, had never had the job. "Walter Annenberg, of all *people*, to be Ambassador to London of all *places*," groaned James "Scotty" Reston, one of the all-time "special relationship" apparatchiks. Senator William Fulbright, emulator of Rhodes in the Anglophile scholarship business, said that Annenberg was "simply not up to the standards we expect of our premier diplomatic post." Worst of all, the Annenbergs were not replacing just anybody. They were replacing David and Evangeline Bruce. This couple came as close to an incarnation of the ruling class of the "special relationship" as any two individuals could.

After a thin time during his confirmation hearings, where it was openly suggested that he had bought the job by campaign contributions and by his loud support for an unpopular war in Vietnam, Annenberg arrived in London for an even thinner time. Winfield House needed extensive repair after the departure of the suave and accomplished Bruces, and temporary quarters had to be found for Walter and Lee. Worse still, the day of Walter's accreditation at Buckingham Palace was the day when a rare BBC film of the Queen at work was being made. As Her Majesty graciously inquired how the Annenbergs were settling down, the cameras caught a figure hideously ill attired in court costume saying: "We're in the embassy residence subject, of course, to some of the discomfiture as a result of a need for, uh, elements of refurbishment and rehabilitation." In a cruel review of the show, Gore Vidal wrote that the Queen looked as if a cigar had just exploded in her face. Certainly she was momentarily at a loss for words.

Annenberg seemed able to do nothing right. He was openly laughed at in White's Club for making fatuous remarks about the weather ("The rain," he had said to break a silence, "is pouring down with determined resolution.") He was lampooned for the lavish party he threw for Richard Nixon's mediocre daughter Tricia and sniggered at by Joseph Kraft and other American columnists for his lack of savoir faire. But very slowly and doggedly he began to outlast his critics.

The breakthrough came, as breakthroughs will in England, with money well spent. The million-dollar "refurbishment" of Winfield House, paid for by Annenberg himself, made the Bruces look dowdy without making the Annenbergs look ostentatious. The same was said when the ambassador loaned his extraordinary collection of pictures to the Tate Gallery. Opinion began to turn when the Annenbergs threw a party for the seventy-year-old Earl Mountbatten of Burma and remembered to decorate the main reception room in the colors of the Burma Star.

Indeed, it was through assiduous attention to royalty that the gauche and unpromising man trumped the minor snobs who had joined in deriding him. The Queen and the Queen Mother became frequent visitors to Winfield House, and word was soon passed that Her Majesty felt the ambassador had been ill used. He began to bloom under the signs of her favor. He kept a portrait of Winston Churchill on his desk at all times. He commissioned a coffee-table book on the splendors of Westminster Abbey, soliciting contributions from traditionalist figures like John Betjeman and A. L. Rowse. Ranked low by art critics, the book still received royal approval and was thus much cooed over in the better circles. Most extraordinary of all, Annenberg became so obsessed with the Nixon crisis and the defeat in Vietnam that he decided to commission a book. Its subject was the parallel between the fall of the Roman Empire and the circumscription of American power. He engaged Michael Grant, an English historian, to work on the project, and the result, *The Fall of the Roman Empire: A Reappraisal*, was published by the Annenberg School Press. Grant purported to find thirteen "fissures" in the Roman Empire, and concluded obediently that "we have to look no further than our own fragmented British and American communities to find the very same phenomena in more or less developed forms."

The impending disgrace of his chief and patron, Richard Nixon, did not diminish the loyalty of the British royal family to Annenberg. In March 1974 he was able to welcome Prince Charles to his California estate, felicitously named Sunnylands, and to introduce Frank Sinatra, Bob Hope, and Governor and Mrs. Reagan to him. The heir to the throne has never since made a visit to California without calling on the Annenbergs or doing some slight service to the Annenberg Foundation. When the Queen visited Philadelphia in 1976, Lee Annenberg was asked to make all the arrangements for her sojourn. All of this effort was requited when in 1981 Ronald Reagan asked her to be chief of protocol. It was in that capacity that she received Prince Charles on an official visit in 1981, and dropped the curtsy I mentioned earlier. There were some democratic mutterings at this departure from custom, and some Republican ones, too, from Fenians like Jimmy Breslin, who fumed about the British record in Ulster. The row was over in a day. The alliance of British royalty and new Reaganite money was an unstoppable combination, whatever Evangeline Bruce might say to her more ironically disposed Georgetown friends. And the Annenbergs were invited to Charles and Diana's wedding, which Mrs. Bruce was not.

As an envoi, it might be noted that in late 1988 Walter Annenberg sold his massively circulated *TV Guide* to Rupert Murdoch. In 1972, Annenberg had offered to place this great resource at the disposal of Nixon's "misunderstood" Vietnam policy. Rupert Murdoch, meanwhile, had become an American citizen and had asked Richard Nixon to become a columnist for his London *Sunday Times*. Between them, the two arrivistes had acquired a share in the prestige of the royal family and the *Times* newspaper—no light matter in the status business, especially for men with direct memories of how their own fortunes had been gained in the first place.

In the case of Wister, Anglophilia took the form of admiring a country and a culture because it was strong. In the case of Annenberg, Anglophilia took the form of an annexation of prestige, made possible because Britain was now weak. The scratches on the mind remain intact: a hoard of imagery and potential cachet made more accessible by the relegation of the United Kingdom to the second class. This consideration has even mellowed the once irreconcilable Fenians. To take an amusing case in point, the Irish Republican sympathizer Peter Maas wrote, in *The Nation* of March 28, 1987, that there was insufficient American protest at London's policy of repression in the Six Counties of Ulster. Among the reasons he cited for this betrayal was:

> Our love affair, from jurisprudence to Princess Di, with Ireland's conquerors—the Brits. It makes you wonder why Adams, Jefferson and Washington went to all that bother.

Broadening the attack to take in the so-called liberals, Maas went for Anthony Lewis of *The New York Times*, who had once rather grandly written that a policy of "enlightened colonialism" would be best for Northern Ireland:

> I can only think that Tony Lewis, whom I otherwise admire, is infinitely more at home lunching in the gracious surroundings of an exclusive London club than he would be, say, knocking down a Guinness in a Gaelic Athletic Association hangout in West Belfast.

Mr. Maas is a writer of best-sellers, and finds no difficulty in summoning the trusty images of effete Englishness to the keyboard. One year later, though, I chanced to notice a letter from the same Mr. Maas in the rather different pages of the Condé Nast *Traveler*, a magazine for the well-heeled cosmopolitan. This letter, too, was a protest:

> How could you run a piece on Jermyn Street and not mention Foster and Son? The first time I peered at its window display I went in and asked how long it would take for a pair of boots, and they said four months. I said that was a little long for me.

However, Mr. Maas tells us, his promotion of *Serpico* and *The Valachi Papers* took him back to London and indeed back to Jermyn Street, and one day he nerved himself to enter Foster and Son once again:

> "I not only want boots in the style of those in the window, but the same leather with its marvelous patina." They protested. "But, sir, these boots have been there for one hundred fifty years, and they have been polished every day . . ."
> Of course, I've been getting all my boots there ever since. I recently stopped in, not having been in London for at least

three years. "Good morning, Mr. Maas," they said, as if I'd been in just a few days before. Wonderful!

Immunity to "class" temptations is evidently hard to acquire, even for those who know how to deplore the temptation in others. Not for nothing is hypocrisy known as an English vice.

[3]

The Bard of Empires

I n her celebrated essay "Imperialism," Hannah Arendt had some words of reproof for Rudyard Kipling's best-known poem, or at least for the best-known single phrase of his poetry, which is "The White Man's Burden." As if determined not to give any impression of approval, she confined herself to the most obvious and familiar judgment, which was to say:

> The fact that the "White Man's burden" is either hypocrisy or racism has not prevented a few of the best Englishmen from shouldering the burden in earnest and making themselves the tragic and quixotic fools of imperialism.

In America, as Joan Didion once pointed out, there is always a danger that when people say, "No man is an island," they think they are quoting from Ernest Hemingway. Yet the difficulty in Kipling's case—his famous verses are still almost universally assumed to apply to Colonel Blimp and the Union Jack—does not arise from any confusion between the original author and the later employment of a memorable line. "The White Man's Burden" was finished on November 22, 1898, in Rottingdean, Sussex, and sent straight off across the Atlantic to Theodore Roosevelt. It was, in every sense, addressed to the United States. Its explicit purpose was to nerve Roosevelt in particular, and American opinion in general, to take an unabashed advantage of the conquest of the Philippines.

"Teddy" had just been thrust into power as governor of New York State after a showy and successful performance in Cuba—the local counterpart to the Filipino triumph. Like a number of President McKinley's supporters, he thought that what was worth fighting for was worth holding on to. But he did not have the language in which to express this imperial yearning. It was one thing to deliver two bully knockout punches to the decrepit edifice of the odious Spanish Empire, and quite another to seize control of its territories and their inhabitants. The stanzas, therefore, came to him at the right place and the right time:

THE WHITE MAN'S BURDEN
The United States and the Philippine Islands

Take up the White Man's burden—
    Send forth the best ye breed—
Go bind your sons to exile
    To serve your captives' need;
To wait in heavy harness
    On fluttered folk and wild—
Your new-caught, sullen peoples,
    Half devil and half child.

Take up the White Man's burden—
    In patience to abide,
To veil the threat of terror
    And check the show of pride;
By open speech and simple,
    An hundred times made plain.
To seek another's profit,
    And work another's gain.

Take up the White Man's burden—
    The savage wars of peace—

Fill full the mouth of Famine
  And bid the sickness cease;
And when your goal is nearest
  The end for others sought,
Watch Sloth and heathen Folly
  Bring all your hope to nought.

Take up the White Man's burden—
  No tawdry rule of kings,
But toil of serf and sweeper—
  The tale of common things.
The ports ye shall not enter,
  The roads ye shall not tread,
Go make them with your living,
  And mark them with your dead!

Take up the White Man's burden—
  And reap his old reward:
The blame of those ye better,
  The hate of those ye guard—
The cry of hosts ye humour
  (Ah, slowly!) toward the light:—
"Why brought ye us from bondage,
  "Our loved Egyptian night?"

Take up the White Man's burden—
  Ye dare not stoop to less—
Nor call too loud on Freedom
  To cloak your weariness;
By all ye cry or whisper,
  By all ye leave or do,
The silent, sullen peoples
  Shall weigh your Gods and you.

Take up the White Man's burden—
  Have done with childish days—
The lightly proffered laurel,
  The easy, ungrudged praise.

[66]

> Comes now, to search your manhood
> Through all the thankless years,
> Cold-edged with dear-bought wisdom,
> The judgment of your peers!

It was proposed to publish the poem in order to influence the Senate debate on a treaty that would take over the governance of the Philippines. This treaty was meeting with halfhearted objection from William Jennings Bryan, and with more decided misgivings from those who feared the high cost of empire or who dreaded the word itself. On January 12, 1899, Roosevelt forwarded "The White Man's Burden" to Henry Cabot Lodge, with a covering note: "I send you an advance copy of a poem by Kipling which is rather poor poetry, but good sense from the expansionist viewpoint." Roosevelt had found an ingenious word for it. "Expansionist" did not then carry its later aggressive connotations. It signified the idea of an America unwilling to endure indefinite confinement and restriction, surrounded as it was by open seas and the vacant possessions of declining European empires. After all, it need have meant no more than "outward-looking." "Expansive"—a term altogether generous in its implications, just as Kipling himself strove to be in his. Cabot Lodge also found himself stirred by the prevailing generosity of spirit. He replied: "Thanks for the advance copy of Kipling's poem. I like it. I think it is better poetry than you say, apart from the sense of the verses."

Neither Lodge nor Roosevelt, then, mistook the poem for a paean to British imperialism. Indeed, apart from going to the trouble of subtitling it "The United States and the Philippine Islands," Kipling had taken other precautions to make his meaning plain. For one thing, the injunction at the head of each stanza would by 1898 have been supererogatory in the case of a British audience. For another, despite his presumable distaste for the Spanish monarchy, it is unlikely in the extreme that he would have written "No tawdry rule of kings" if his intended audience had been the London *Times*. In point of fact, and with Roosevelt's help, "The White Man's

Burden" was first printed in the New York *Sun* on February 5, 1899, the day before the Senate yielded to McKinley's urgings about the treaty which took the archipelago under American protection. Kipling's lines were often used by Cabot Lodge and Roosevelt in articles and addresses favoring the "expansionist" cause. Roosevelt, who was already friendly with other young British imperialists like Cecil Spring-Rice, kept up a correspondence with Kipling on military and diplomatic and colonial matters for the rest of his life and was rewarded at his death with a valedictory poem entitled "Great-Heart." Elected President at least partly on the credit he had won in Cuba by the "storming" of San Juan Hill, and succeeding to a McKinley who had been slain by a distinctly "foreign" type of anarchist whose name nobody could pronounce, he wrote to Kipling at the close of his first term on November 1, 1904:

I have done a good many things in the past three years. . . . It is natural that some people should have been alienated by each thing I did, and the aggregate of all that have been alienated may be more than sufficient to overthrow me. Thus, in dealing with the Philippines I have first the jack-fools who seriously think that any group of pirates and head-hunters needs nothing but independence in order that it may be turned into a dark-hued New England town-meeting, and then the entirely practical creatures who join with these extremists because I do not intend that the islands shall be exploited for corrupt purposes.

I have accomplished certain definite things. I would consider myself a hundred times over repaid if I had nothing more to my credit than Panama and the coaling stations in Cuba. So that you see my frame of mind is a good deal like that of your old Viceroy when he addressed the new Viceroy.

This letter is more or less a prose version of stanzas five and six of "The White Man's Burden." It seizes the sense of thankless responsibility that is so gratifying to the colonial mind, and couples it with that sense of pride in selfish achievement that is likewise inseparable from the enterprise of conquest. Note, in particular, that whether or not Roosevelt realized that the word "viceroy" meant "deputy king," he already quite liked the sound of it.

There were three distinct peculiarities in Kipling's approach to the United States. The first was that, unlike every other visiting English writer of the nineteenth century, he landed on the West Coast and made his way east. The second is that he felt hostile to, and wrote against, the principles of the American Revolution and the principles of democracy. The third is that, British super-patriot though he undoubtedly was, he liked the United States more and more as it decided to move outside its own borders. Some combination of these experiences and attitudes gave him a powerful apprehension of the strength of the country, and an intense feeling that it must be enlisted on the British side.

In 1889, Kipling took ship from India and landed at San Francisco. He had promised to send back dispatches to that distinguished British-Indian journal *The Allahabad Pioneer*, and the result is a sketchbook travelogue entitled "From Sea to Sea." It is a racy, semi-serious narrative, full of commingled admiration for, and reservations about, the size and vitality of the United States. Already a devotee of Bret Harte, he was slightly discouraged to learn that his fellow San Franciscans thought him to be too Anglicized:

A reporter asked me what I thought of the city, and I made answer suavely that it was hallowed ground to me because of Bret Harte. That was true. "Well," said the reporter, "Bret Harte claims California, but California doesn't claim Bret Harte. He's been so long in England that he's quite English. Have you seen our cracker-factories and the new offices of the *Examiner*?"

Matters did not improve with any speed on the journey eastward. Like Martin Chuzzlewit and Mark Tapley, who began to roll their eyes at each other whenever an American introduced one of his fellows as "one of the most remarkable men in the country" or (an irritating variant) "perhaps as remarkable a man as any in our country," and who had to endure the baiting of the British lion at the imperishable dinner of the Watertoast Association, Kipling was easily roused to scorn. Whether or not he had read *Martin Chuzzlewit*, he observed sarcastically of an acquaintance made at a Fourth of July festivity that "he trampled upon the British Lion generally." At the same occasion he recorded drily that an American introduced his fellows by saying: "They include very many prominent and representative citizens from seven states of the union, and most of them are wealthy. Yes, *sir*. Representative and prominent." And, like Martin and Mark, he had a low threshold for being bored while traveling:

> Some of the persons in the coach remarked that the scenery was "elegant." Wherefore, even at the risk of my own life, I did urgently desire an accident and the massacre of some of the more prominent citizens.

Kipling was writing for an audience in the Raj that was quite prepared to consider the idea of America a joke in itself. But his condescension masked a certain unease. Americans might be laughable, but they could be treacherous and even threatening. As he put it in his poem "The American Rebellion (1776)," even the title of which was intended to debase:

> 'Twas not while England's sword unsheathed
>   Put half a world to flight,
> Nor while their new-built cities breathed
>   Secure behind her might;
> Not while she poured from Pole to Line
>   Treasure and ships and men—

> These worshippers at Freedom's shrine,
>   They did not quit her then!
>
> Not till their foes were driven forth
>   By England o'er the main—
> Not till the Frenchman from the North
>   Had gone with shattered Spain;
> Not till the clean-swept oceans showed
>   No hostile flag unrolled,
> Did they remember what they owed
>   To Freedom—and were bold!

Lexington and Concord appear, in this cosmology, as a stab in the back, of the sort a silky Pathan or cruel Afghan might have delivered. But Kipling had a saving shrewdness about the value of his own propaganda and the appeal of his own emotions. Back in the United States in the mid-1890s, and considering long residence, and married to an American woman as well as possibly infatuated with an American man, he began to take a more considered view. It was a great shock to him to see the blaze of animosity that arose in 1895, when Britain and the United States almost went to war over the Venezuelan border dispute. President Grover Cleveland was under attack for being in the pay of British interests (a common gibe in those times) and had responded with extremely minatory speeches and promises. Cecil Spring-Rice took Kipling to hear some of the debates in Congress during a visit to Washington, and the effect was a shaking one. A critic, Louis Cornell, has speculated:

> Without the soothing influence of a common enemy, America and the British Empire maintained a friendliness that was at least precarious. If Kipling's occasional trumpet calls on behalf of Anglo-Saxon unity now seem a bit shrill, we must remember that they sounded above the rumblings of Anglo-American rivalry. "So far as I was concerned," Kipling wrote

forty years later, "I felt the atmosphere was to some extent hostile."

There was not immediately a common enemy in sight, though Kipling dropped a broad hint about this when Venezuela came up again and in a poem he alluded to the impossibility of cooperating "with the Goth and the shameless Hun." Still, there could be a common cause. Before the outbreak of the Spanish-American War, but when the idea of a "shattered Spain" had ceased to be a British historic monopoly, he wrote, in early 1898, "The Song of the White Men":

> Now, this is the cup the White Men drink
>   When they go to right a wrong,
> And that is the cup of the old world's hate—
>   Cruel and strained and strong.
> We have drunk that cup—and a bitter, bitter cup—
>   And tossed the dregs away.
> But well for the world when the White Men drink
>   To the dawn of the White Man's day!
>
> Now, this is the road that the White Men tread
>   When they go to clean a land—
> Iron underfoot and levin overhead
>   And the deep on either hand.
> We have trod that road—and a wet and windy road—
>   Our chosen star for guide.
> Oh, well for the world when the White Men tread
>   Their highway side by side!
>
> Now, this is the faith that the White Men hold
>   When they build their homes afar—
> "Freedom for ourselves and freedom for our sons
>   And, failing freedom, War."
> We have proved our faith—bear witness to our faith,

> Dear souls of freemen slain!
> Oh, well for the world when the White Men join
> To prove their faith again!

Rather as the Northern and Southern states had composed their differences by combining in the "expansionist" cause, so Kipling hoped that the growing strength of the United States could be harnessed to the existing British Empire. Race was the natural cement, and the idea of "their highway side by side" was an increasingly popular one in the speeches of Senator Albert Beveridge and others, such as Andrew Carnegie.

This brave new style involved the Kipling faction in America in a direct confrontation with a man Kipling himself professed to admire above all others. During the course of his "From Sea to Sea" expedition, Kipling had endured the longueurs of the trip by consoling himself with the thought of Mark Twain. At length he ran him to earth in Elmira, New York, and was almost too fulsome in his approbation. To the readers in Allahabad he wrote back:

> You are a contemptible lot, over yonder, Some of you are Commissioners, and some Lieutenant-Governors, and some have the V.C., and a few are privileged to walk about the Mall arm in arm with the Viceroy; but I have seen Mark Twain this golden morning, have shaken his hand, and smoked a cigar—no, two cigars—with him, and talked with him for more than two hours!

Much of the talk concerned international copyright, in which both men were very much interested because of the lack of an agreement between London and New York, but Kipling was evidently afraid of being a bore. He heard Twain out while the latter explained that he never really read any fiction. He asked the inescapable question "whether Tom Sawyer married Judge Thatcher's daughter and whether we were ever going to hear of Tom Sawyer as a man." And he strained somewhat for effect when he depicted the growth of intimacy between them: "Once, indeed, he put his hand on my shoulder. It was an investiture of the Star of India, blue silk, trumpets, and diamond-studded jewels, all complete." When Kipling aimed for the sublime, he always stuck at the imperial. This was a form of temptation which Twain, as it turned out, was well able to resist. When, a decade or so later, Kipling became the semi-official laureate of the Roosevelt-Lodge set, with his verses urging white solidarity and the conquest of the Philippines, Twain emerged as the greatest and most scornful opponent of the new imperialism. Striking at the very point that Kipling had made his own—the emulation by Americans of the trailblazing British—he wrote witheringly that his fellow countrymen should "let go our obsequious hold on the rear-skirts of the sceptered land-thieves of Europe."

Twain was very quick to identify a connection that had also occurred to Kipling—the collusion between British and American war aims in the colonial world. Unlike other European states, Britain had taken a benign view of the Philippine war. In return, the United States government resisted pressure, particularly but not exclusively pressure from Irish- and German-Americans, to disown British policy in South Africa. In his essay "To the Person Sitting in Darkness," Twain ridiculed the imperialist Joseph Chamberlain, who married May Endicott, the daughter of President Cleveland, and who was very fond of making speeches about "the Union Jack and the Stars and Stripes":

> Mr. Chamberlain manufactures a war out of materials so inadequate and so fanciful that they make the foxes grieve and the gallery laugh, and he tries hard to persuade himself that it isn't a purely private raid for cash, but has a sort of dim, vague respectability about it somewhere. . . . And by and by comes America, and our master of the game plays it badly— plays it as Mr. Chamberlain was playing it in South Africa.

Even Kipling in the end was to give up the Boer War as a bad job, and to write "No End of a Lesson." But by then the tacit understanding between London and Washington was well devel-

oped. One area of its development in particular, as also noticed by
Twain, was China. Nothing made him laugh more than the Anglo-
American scramble for that country, combined as it was with a
simultaneous campaign against Chinese immigration. In the *New
York Herald* for December 30, 1900, he published "A Greeting
from the Nineteenth to the Twentieth Century":

> I bring you the stately nation named Christendom, return-
> ing, bedraggled, besmirched and dishonest, from pirate raids
> in Kiao-Chou, Manchuria, South Africa and the Philippines,
> with her soul full of meanness, her pocket full of boodle and
> her mouth full of hypocrisies. Give her soap and towel, but
> hide the looking-glass.

In other and later comments, when it was announced that American
troops in the Philippines would adopt "Kitchener" tactics against
the stubborn rebels, Twain was mordant about the imitation of the
British style. In a letter to Frank Doubleday in 1903, Kipling still
wrote that "I love to think of the great and godlike Clemens."
Perhaps he had not heard of Twain's activity in the Anti-Imperialist
League, or perhaps he could afford to be magnanimous. The sorts
of attitudes embodied by Kipling were by then in the ascendant
over the sorts of attitudes symbolized by Twain. When Admiral
Alfred Thayer Mahan published his book *Lessons of the War with
Spain*, he argued that the American empire ought to proceed *à
l'anglaise*, with a concern for native welfare uppermost. But he
could have been quoting directly from "The White Man's Burden"
when he warned that "the inhabitants may not return love for their
benefits—comprehension or gratitude may fail them." This entirely
unironic observation is followed by what *must* be a semi-conscious
quotation, when Mahan speaks of "alien subjects, still in race-
childhood" (see lines 6–8).

There is evidence that Kipling's self-pitying interpretation of the
race question was not lost on those whose main concern was the
domestic front. D. W. Griffith's sinister film masterpiece *Birth of*

a Nation was based on a racist novel by Griffith's friend Thomas Dixon, a Baptist ranter from North Carolina whose tale *The Leopard's Spots* was published in 1902. Its subtitle was *A Romance of the White Man's Burden.* Evidently, the apple did not fall very far from the tree.

I began by describing "The White Man's Burden" as Kipling's most celebrated poem, and I did so in spite of the claim of "Recessional" to that high eminence. As so often, Kipling is accused of the most reflexive racialism when he is innocent of it, and treated leniently when he is guilty. Those who regard him as a jingo thug are thus many times more likely to cite "lesser breeds" than any of the "White Man" poems, and to be indifferent in any case to what Kipling meant by "burden." To him, quite explicitly, the lines of "Recessional" were an admonition against hubris and almost a satire upon imperial self-regard. With at least a part of himself, Kipling saw that there was a term set to the dominion of the English, if not to that of the "White Men" *tout court.* So there is a useful irony in the letter that Kipling received shortly after the publication of "Recessional" in the London *Times* on July 17, 1897, for the edition marking Queen Victoria's Jubilee:

> I thank you for the high pleasure we all had in reading your noble "Recessional." It has touched everybody—not merely the critical people—as the one utterance of the year worth while.

The writer was John Hay, ambassador of the United States to the Court of St. James's. It is difficult at this distance to be certain of his motives and feelings, but it is certain that in the premonitory period before the actual outbreak of the Spanish-American War, Hay had been enlisting actual and potential sympathy for an American "expansionist" program. He may simply, as an admirer of English letters, have responded to the fierce modesty of Kipling's verse, which celebrated empire even as it warned against its demise. He may have caught the edge of the lines:

> Far-called, our navies melt away,
> On dune and headland sinks the fire . . .

Or he may, like other American envoys to London before and since, have felt the need to have a foothold in the literary camp. But the sheer fact that Kipling's first major poem after the world-weariness of "Recessional" should have been addressed to Americans, and should have begun every verse with the injunction "Take up," would not escape a man like Hay, who had dined long and often with Henry Adams and Theodore Roosevelt and who, in 1898, was taken by Kipling to dinner at the Savoy in order to be introduced to Cecil Rhodes. Kipling was, in this sense, John the Baptist to the age of American empire.

Reasonably satisfied as he was that the United States had found an alternative to republican and democratic illusions, and fairly sure as he became that no American fleet was ever likely to challenge a British one, Kipling still did not like the Anglo-Saxon cousins all that much. His appeal to them had a purely instrumental aspect, which was the making of a common cause against imperial Wilhelmine Germany. His most energetic hour therefore struck when Britain and Germany went to war.

Within a few weeks of the conflict's inauguration, Kipling was writing fervently to Theodore Roosevelt. The tone of the correspondence tends to give the lie to those who argue that Kipling became unhinged about the Germans only after he lost his son John (no body ever being recovered) at the battle for Mons in 1915. He appears to have been in a state of racial and national excitement from the start. As he put it to Roosevelt (who was also to lose a son in the carnage) on September 15, 1914:

> I wish you could spend half a day with the Belgian refugees as they come into Folkestone. The look on their faces is enough, without having to hear their stories which are like tales from Hell. When people congratulate each other that So

and So's womenfolk were shot outright one realises a bit about German culture.

Nothing, not even the propaganda horror fiction about Prussian factories for making corpses into soap, was beneath Kipling's contempt or hatred. Yet he remembered his political manners when addressing "Teddy" and did not forget to couch the appeal in seductive terms:

> For once I agree with the advanced Germans (they have left the Pan-German school behind) who say that with England out of it, Germany holds the US in the hollow of her hand. I needn't point out to you that the Monroe Doctrine would become a scrap of paper not worth tearing up.

Roosevelt was pressing the British case in speeches and articles, and Kipling urged him to be even tougher in his attacks on neutrality. "As I see it, the US, for existing Teutonic purposes, is practically English. . . . The Allies are shedding their blood (and the butcher's bill is a long one) for every ideal that the United States stands for by the mere fact of her Constitution, not to mention her literature, press and daily life." In 1916 Kipling made one of his more sonorous efforts at short-term influence with his poem "The Question," which sought to prick the American conscience:

> Brethren, how shall it fare with me
> When the war is laid aside,
> If it be proven that I am he
> For whom a world has died?

> If it be proven that all my good,
> And the greater good I will make,
> Were purchased me by a multitude
> Who suffered for my sake?

That I was delivered by mere mankind
Vowed to one sacrifice,
And not, as I hold them, battle-blind,
But dying with open eyes?

That they did not ask me to draw the sword
When they stood to endure their lot—
That they only looked to me for a word,
And I answered I knew them not?

If it be found, when the battle clears,
Their death has set me free,
Then how shall I live with myself through the years
Which they have bought for me?

Brethren, how must it fare with me,
Or how am I justified,
If it be proven that I am he
For whom mankind has died—
If it be proven that I am he
Who, being questioned, denied?

He and his American wife had little but contempt for Wilson,
whom Kipling termed "the Schoolmaster." After Wilson's equivocal
response to the *Lusitania* (he had asked Germany for guarantees
against a repetition), Caroline Kipling wrote to her mother: "This
morning we have the news that Germany has had her note accepted
by America about the *Lusitania*, and all Americans of our generation and upbringing, undiluted by European dregs, must feel
bitterly and lastingly ashamed." When Frank Doubleday wrote to
Kipling in encouraging tones in May 1916, suggesting that an "important person should be sent out to the USA on a mission of
friendship and goodwill," Kipling replied with contempt: "That is
the talk of the old world which died on August 4, 1914. Men do
not prove their friendship and goodwill now by their mouth but

by their lives. You chose, after due thought, to commit moral suicide."

A little later, he wrote to another friend that "I almost begin to hope that when we have done with him there will be very little Hun left." Some of this sort of enthusiasm seems to have communicated itself to Roosevelt. In the summer following the sinking of the *Lusitania*, he began to speak demonstratively about "hyphenated Americans." This extremely base appeal, which at least stopped short of suggesting that Germans were racially inferior, seemed to be a direct response to a letter from Kipling in which he had asked:

> Has it ever struck you that if the game goes our way, the largest block of existing Germans may perhaps be the eight million within your Borders? And precisely because, to please this Contingent and to justify his hereditary temperament, Wilson did not protest against the invasion and absorption of Belgium, Wilson will not be able to save for them the sentimental satisfaction of having a Fatherland to look back upon from behind the safety of the United States frontier. It seems a high price to pay for "domestic politics."

Though Wilson duly joined in the Roosevelt-inspired "hyphenation" campaign, and played his part in the "preparedness" hysteria, and eventually took the United States into war with Germany, Kipling never felt Wilson had done the right thing for the right reasons. He had nothing but cold contempt for Wilson's famous Fourteen Points for a peace settlement, and shortly before the Armistice wrote to "Teddy," sulfurously:

> To put it bluntly the USA which has grown up and thriven for 142 years under the lee of the British Fleet would have gone down with the rest of us into oblivion two years ago.
> An ape looking down under the palm tree on which he sits is reasonable compared to—but I needn't tell you. Simulta-

neous as to indemnities. The 14 Ps have no word about those.
All earth, it seems, must bear the cost of the war that was
forced upon it, or if begun would have ended in a few weeks
if the US had entered with the rest after the *Lusitania* was
sunk.

The cadence of the last sentence echoes a frightening line in Kipling's poem *The Children*: "Not since her birth has our earth seen
such worth loosed upon her." But it was a bit much for Roosevelt,
combining as it did a slightly raving syntax and a distinct tone of
ingratitude. He wrote back with a combination of reassurance and
reproof, reminding Kipling that, after all, there had been German
and Irish-Americans among the crews of *Captains Courageous* and
saying:

I am stronger than ever for a working agreement between
the British Empire and the United States; indeed I am now
content to call it an Alliance.

Granted this, proportion should not be lost:

But now, friend, do not overstate your case. It is strong,
and it needs no overstatement. You say that "the United States
existed for 142 years under the protection of the British Navy."
As a matter of fact for the first ninety years the British Navy,
when, as was ordinarily the case, the British government was
more or less hostile to us, was our greatest danger. I am not
condemning Great Britain. In those good old days the policies
of the United States and Great Britain toward one another,
and toward much of the outside world, were sufficiently alike
to give a touch of humor to *the virtuous horror expressed by
each at the kind of conduct of the other which most closely
resembled its own.* [Italics mine.]

Roosevelt understood this reciprocal self-righteousness exceedingly well, having often turned it to his own account. As late as the last decade of the nineteenth century, he had himself called for a greater American navy in order to counter the threat of the British fleet. Now he was calling for a greater American navy in order to counter the threat of the German Grand Fleet. Soon the United States would propose to Britain that there be an international naval treaty in which for the first time in history the size of the British fleet be limited. It would also be mentioning (to Kipling's cousin Stanley Baldwin among others, in his capacity as Chancellor of the Exchequer) the outstanding matter of Britain's gigantic war debt and the obligations imposed by same. There was, therefore, nothing to be gained by sentimentality.

By the time of the Armistice, the Russian Revolution had triumphed. Kipling was not among those who viewed this with indifference. In his poem "Russia to the Pacifists" he declared against Bolshevism, and put heart into the Winston Churchill faction in the British government who favored armed intervention. The cause of anti-Soviet crusading was another opportunity for the British to enlist the United States in a front of common interest, and Wilson was persuaded, not without misgivings, to send an American Expeditionary Force to Russia. This was not a happy or fruitful collaboration. The American troops, and their officers, considered themselves used and subordinated by the British and made repeated complaints to Washington about the fact. Their commander, Major General William S. Groves, wrote a very bitter memoir of the campaign, which helped decide a future generation of American military men that second fiddle to the British was not a noble or desirable position. (General Pershing had come to a similar conclusion on the Western Front.) Another illuminating book on the intervention came from Ralph Albertson, who coordinated the relief efforts of the American YMCA and was the last U.S. citizen to leave Archangel when the campaign was abandoned. His book *Fighting Without a War* recounts numerous telling examples of British arrogance and high-handedness. The chapter in which these are laid out is entitled "The White Man's Burden."

In spite of the general reaction against English guile and condescension that set in, particularly among writers and intellectuals but also among politicians and businessmen, in America between the wars, Kipling himself did uncharacteristically well. The irony is that he did well as an unintended result of the battle over Imperial Preference. The United States was seeking to penetrate the British and colonial markets but was meeting with stiff resistance. A special area of contestation was the world of film. Acts of Parliament were passed insisting on arbitrarily high levels of "domestic content" in films to be screened in England. Tory ministers and backbenchers inveighed regularly against screen-borne "American rubbish" and worried about the effects of Hollywood fantasy upon the sturdy British public. They also wondered how to retaliate. Kipling was consulted by the Empire Marketing Board in 1926, and urged the idea of propaganda films, in documentary and dramatic form.

The idea didn't catch on with the staid and unimaginative Empire Marketing Board, but in Hollywood the image of England and the Empire became a popular staple, and a considerable colony of well-spoken and suave Englishmen found, like Dennis Barlow at the Happier Hunting Ground, that the "combination of melancholy with the English accent" was a serviceable recipe for success. Cary Grant, Ronald Colman, David Niven, Basil Rathbone, and Errol Flynn all mastered this recipe to varying degrees, as did Charles Laughton and Herbert Marshall. The better studios all saw their point, and adopted the formula. Bertolt Brecht, sitting in a movie theater near Times Square, was both impressed and appalled to see American audiences cheering the heroics of English redcoats, as if the imperial soldier was interchangeable with the cowboy or the wagon-train pioneer. As Philip French has put it:

> Not many of these performers could be plausibly cast in Westerns; on the other hand American actors could quite easily be placed on the North West Frontier with the right explanation. In *Lives of a Bengal Lancer*, for example, Richard

Cromwell was introduced as the American-reared son of the regiment's commanding officer (Sir Guy Standing) and Gary Cooper established as a Scots-Canadian. In these roles, the American actor would invariably be presented as an insubordinate rebel who eventually came to appreciate, in the final reel, the unwritten code of the regiment and the demands of the Empire.

"How is the Empire?" George V is loyally supposed to have said on his deathbed. The two variants muttered by disloyal courtiers are that he said, "What's on at the Empire?" or that he inquired, "How's the vampire?" in a malign reference to Mrs. Wallis Simpson. The confusion is a pardonable one, given the speedup and blurring of imagery. The original "vamp," Theda Bara, got her eponym by playing a man-eater in the screen version of *The Vampire*, by Rudyard Kipling. American cinemagoers also had the opportunity to see *Gunga Din, Elephant Boy, Captains Courageous, Wee Willie Winkie*, and *The Light That Failed*.

Without Kipling's popularity, it is inconceivable that the genre of lesser imperial writers would have been translated to the screen, with A. E. W. Mason and Percival Christopher Wren to the fore, and such memorable successes as *The Four Feathers* and John Ford's *The Black Watch*, to say nothing of *Clive of India, The Charge of the Light Brigade*, and Korda's *Sanders of the River*.

The political and cultural consequences of this were not slight. When the British embassy and its propaganda division sought to combat the influence of Charles Lindbergh's America First and other isolationist or pro-Nazi organizations, they turned at once to Douglas Fairbanks, Jr. He was prepared to make public appearances and speeches even in the "hot" areas of Anglophobia like Chicago. Neatly leapfrogging over the massed ranks of anti-imperialist intellectuals and academics, as he had over so many bulwarks and balconies, Fairbanks used his standing in the new medium to appeal to the public directly. Of the small number of

Americans to be knighted, Fairbanks probably did the most to earn his "K."

The importance of all this is attested by Sir John Wheeler-Bennett, who before and during the Second World War was charged by the British ambassador with finding and wringing the nerve of Anglophilia in American life. He made a friend of Ted Roosevelt, Jr. (whom he met "by chance at a dinner at the Century"), and found they had a love of Kipling in common. He also noted with approbation that young Roosevelt had been "Governor-General of the Philippines and Governor of Puerto Rico, America's only two colonial possessions." In his book *Special Relationships*, Wheeler-Bennett described meeting Lindbergh at the Roosevelt mansion Sagamore Hill in Oyster Bay. He went on to describe the strenuous British contest with Lindbergh over the German threat (intriguingly adding of Lindbergh that "in the later years of his life we found a comradeship as Cold Warriors").

Imperial film was Wheeler-Bennett's entrée into Hollywood, via the friendship of Alex Korda:

His British naturalisation was an honor he cherished greatly. Winston Churchill was his hero and there existed a great friendship between the two men, which Winston crowned with a knighthood. This act, though it caused some raised eyebrows, he defended fiercely and loyally, for no-one had done more for the British cause, whether by financial contributions or by such excellent films for export as *Fire Over England* and *Henry VIII*. Robert Vansittart [head of the German section of the British Foreign Office] was another friend who always praised him. (A little known fact is that "Van" also wrote the words of Sabu's song in *The Thief of Baghdad*.) This confidence in him was justified in every respect. He extolled Britain and Britain's cause on every possible occasion, in fair weather and foul. I have been privileged to listen to a debate on the British way of life conducted in the fiercest of broken English between Alex and David Selznick to my silent delight and satisfaction.

Once the Second World War had actually begun, and there was the sticky business of American neutrality to be got over again, Wheeler-Bennett was sent back to Hollywood by Lord Lothian "to discuss with certain well-disposed movie moguls, of whom Walter Wanger was one, the making of such non-documentary films as *Mrs. Miniver* and *Eagle Squadron*." Introduced around Bel-Air by Korda and his wife, Merle Oberon, Wheeler-Bennett got the chance to lobby Sam Goldwyn and to co-direct a picture, entitled *The Hitler Gang*, with Mia Farrow's father, John.

Thus the ground so well watered by Kipling bore fruit after his death, in the decisive battle for American opinion. Wheeler-Bennett makes plain that nothing in his propaganda career gave him more satisfaction—not even helping the young John Fitzgerald Kennedy to write *Why England Slept*, and seeing copies of the result sent by the boy's corrupt and anti-British father to the King and members of the Court of St. James's, with the vulgar admonition from father to son: "You would be surprised how a book that really makes the grade with high-class people stands you in good stead for years to come."

This was all preface to an extraordinary moment in October 1943 when Winston Churchill wrote a short note to Franklin Roosevelt. The correspondence between the two men was voluminous, and especially on Churchill's side took the form of several letters, cables, or memos each week. He had at the beginning of the war evolved with Roosevelt a style of address, calling himself "Former Naval Person" in order to recall the period of the First World War when each had served in his country's naval establishment, Churchill in the Admiralty and Roosevelt in the Navy Department. "Former Naval Person to President" was the accustomed, indeed routine, opening of his messages, with Roosevelt replying in kind. The October 17, 1943, communication, however, reads more like a personal letter and is presented formally:

My dear Mr. President,

I am sending you with this letter two small unpublished works of Rudyard Kipling which I think I mentioned to you. Similar copies were given to me by the President of the Royal College of Surgeons of England on the occasion of my admission as an Honorary Fellow of the College, and I thought that you would like to have both books for your library.

I understand that Mrs. Kipling decided not to publish them in case they should lead to controversy and it is therefore important that their existence should not become known and that there should be no public reference to this gift.

Yours sincerely,
Winston S. Churchill

Neither of the poems—"The Burden of Jerusalem" and "A Chapter of Proverbs"—has yet appeared in any anthology of Kipling's work. Both are reproduced below:

But Abram said unto Sarai, "Behold the maid is in thy hand. Do to her as it pleaseth thee." And when Sarai dealt hardly with her she fled from her face.

Genesis 16:6

The Burden of Jerusalem

In ancient days and deserts wild
There rose a feud—still unsubdued—
Twixt Sarah's son and Hagar's child
That centred round Jerusalem

(While underneath the timeless boughs
Of Mamre's oak 'mid stranger-folk
The Patriarch slumbered and his spouse
Nor dreamed about Jerusalem.)

But Ishmael lived where he was born.
And pastured there in tents of hair
Among the Camel and the Thorn—
Beersheba, South Jerusalem

But Israel sought employ and food
At Pharaoh's knees, till Rameses
Dismissed his plaguey multitude,
With curses, toward Jerusalem.

Across the wilderness they came
And launched their horde o'er Jordan's ford,
And blazed the road by sack and flame
To Jebusite Jerusalem.

Then Kings and Judges ruled the land,
And did not well by Israel,
Till Babylonia took a hand
And drove them from Jerusalem.

And Cyrus sent them back anew,
To carry on as they had done,
Till angry Titus overthrew
The fabric of Jerusalem.

Then they were scattered North and West,
While each Crusade more certain made
That Hagar's vengeful son possessed
Mohammedan Jerusalem.

Where Ishmael held his desert state
And framed a creed to serve his need—
"Allah-hu-Akbar! God is Great!"
He preached it in Jerusalem.

And every realm they wandered through
Rose, far or near, in hate and fear,

And robbed and tortured, chased and slew,
The outcasts of Jerusalem.

So ran their doom—half seer, half slave—
And ages passed, and at the last
They stood beside each tyrant's grave,
And whispered of Jerusalem.

We do not know what God attends
The Unloved Race in every place
Where they amass their dividends
From Riga to Jerusalem.

But all the course of Time makes clear
To everyone (except the Hun)
It does not pay to interfere
With Cohen from Jerusalem.

For 'neath the Rabbi's curls and fur
(Or scents and rings of movie-kings)
The aloof, unleavened blood of Ur,
Broods steadfast on Jerusalem.

Where Ishmael bides in his own place—
A robber hold, as was foretold,
To stand before his brother's face—
The wolf without Jerusalem.

And burdened Gentile o'er the main,
Must bear the weight of Israel's hate
Because he is not brought again
In triumph to Jerusalem.

Yet he who bred the unending strife,
And was not brave enough to save
The Bondsmaid from the furious wife,
He wrought thy woe, Jerusalem.

A CHAPTER OF PROVERBS

1. The wind bloweth where it
   listeth, and after the same
   manner in every country.
   Be not puffed up with a
   breath (of it)

2. Of a portion set aside a
   portion or ever the days
   come when thou shalt see
   there is no work in them

3. For he that hath not must
   serve him that hath; even
   to the peril of the soul

4. Take the wage for thy work
   in silver and (*it may be*)
   gold; but accept not honours
   nor any great gifts

5. Is ye ox yoked till men have
   need of him; or the camel
   belled while yet she is free?
   And wouldst thou be eved
   with these?

6. Pledge no writing till it is
   written; and seek not
   payment on (any) account
   the matter shall be
   remembered against thee.

7. There is a generation which
   selleth dung in the street
   and saith: "To the pure all
   things are pure."

8. But count (thou) on the one
   hand how may be so minded;
   and after write according
   to thy knowledge.

9. Because not all evil beareth
   fruit in a day; and it may
   be some shall curse thy
   grave for the iniquity of
   thy works in their youth

10. The fool brayeth in his
    heart there is no God;
    therefore his imaginings
    are terribly returned on
    him; and that without interpreter

11. Get skill, and when thou
    has it, forget; lest the
    bird on her nest mock thee,
    and He that is Highest
    look down

12. Get knowledge; it shall
    not burst thee; and amass
    under thy hand a peculiar
    treasure of words:

13. As a King heapeth him
    jewels to bestow or cast
    aside; or being alone in
    his palace, fortifieth
    himself beholding (*them*).

14. So near as thou canst, open
    not thy whole mind to
    any man.

15. The bounds of his craft are
    appointed to each from of
    old; they shall not be known
    to the cup-mates or the
    companions

16. For three things my heart
    is disquieted; and for four
    that I cannot bear:

17. For a woman who esteemeth
    herself a man; and a man
    that delighteth in her
    company;

18. For people whose young
    men are cut off by the
    sword; and for the soul
    that regardeth not these
    things.

19. In three things, yea and
    in four, is the metal of
    the workman made plain:

20. In excessive labour; in
    continual sloth; in long
    waiting; and in the day
    of triumph.

21. There is one glory of the
    sun and another of the
    moon and a third of the
    stars: yet are all these
    appointed for the glory
    of the earth which alone
    hath no light.

22. Hold not back (*any*) part
of a price.

23. Despise no man even in thy
heart; for the custom of
it shall make thy works of
none effect

24. Use not overmuch to
frequent the schools of
the scribes; for idols are
there and (*all*) the paths
return upon themselves.

25. Envy no man's work nor
deliver judgement upon
it in the gate, for the end
is bitterness.

26. Consider now those blind
worms of the deep which
fence themselves about as
it were with stone against
their fellows;

27. And reaching the
intolerable light of the
sun straightway perish
leaving but their tombs;

28. By those whose mere multitude
the sea is presently stayed;
the tide itself divideth
at that place.

29. Small waves after storm
laying there seeds, nuts
and the bodies of fish,

(*at last*) an island ariseth
crowned with palms; thither
the sea-birds repair.

30. Till man coming taketh
all to his use and hath no
memory of aught below
(*his feet*)

31. Out of the dust which
had life come all things
and shalt thou be other
than they?

32. Nevertheless, my son, dare
thou greatly to believe.

This is practically the only communication from Churchill, in an entire file of correspondence which extends in print over three volumes, to which Roosevelt made no reply or acknowledgment of any sort. The poems themselves do not form part of the published archive, but Roosevelt did keep them in their handsome privately bound blue-and-gold covers. They still repose in the Roosevelt Library at Hyde Park, New York, where I unearthed them one April day in 1988.

The poems, and the circumstances of their donation, possess all sorts of potential and actual interest. First, it is interesting to note that October 17, 1943, the day of Churchill's covering letter, was the day before Lionel Trilling's famous attack on T. S. Eliot's edition of Kipling was published in *The Nation*. Trilling went for Kipling on the grounds of "the snippy, *persecuted* anti-Semitism of ironic good manners." In his response, Eliot tried to maintain civility by a good-humored pretense that Kipling was more anti-"Hun" than anti-Jew.

If either could have seen the unpublished poems, they might have hit upon verses twelve and thirteen of "The Burden of Jerusalem" (what a chap Kipling was for burdens, to be sure). Written after a visit to Palestine under the British Mandate, which was to bequeath that burden to the United States as it had and would so many others, the poem shows a tension between Kipling's unease with Jews and his dislike of anti-Semitism when it came from non-English sources. (This is not the place for this argument, but many people who don't much care for "Cohen from Jerusalem" may still express outrage when he is roughly handled by their rivals or enemies.) As for "burdened Gentile o'er the main," the addiction of Kipling to the idea that dominion was something thrust on an unwilling island race is here shown to be incurable. (It also copies the second line of the third verse of "The American Rebellion," where the "burden" is the thirteen colonies.) Balfour appears by implication as the only sufferer from his Declaration, which slyly promised Palestine to both nationalisms. Kipling had witnessed some of the rioting occasioned by Balfour's legacy.

In other respects, the poem might easily be termed Zionist in tone. But that raises an unsuspected difficulty. What about verse fourteen?

> For 'neath the Rabbi's curls and fur
> (Or scents and rings of movie-kings)
> The aloof, unleavened blood of Ur,
> Broods steadfast on Jerusalem.

Up until then, true, the lines are German-hating rather than Jew-hating, and recall Kipling's sanguinary letters to Teddy Roosevelt in 1914–18, as well as Eliot's posthumous 1943 defense. (Remember Kipling writing to Roosevelt that he often hoped that, by the end of the Great War business, "there will be very little Hun left.") But what a poor return for the solicitude of Hollywood is contained in line two! It is possible that Churchill asked Roosevelt to keep the whole poem to himself out of consideration for Sam Goldwyn and Alex Korda, both of whom had certainly heard worse but neither of whom might have cared for this line of talk from the foremost British imperial rhymer at a time when they were being teased for being uncritical about the Brits.*

Another possibility occurs to me. Throughout the preceding year, Churchill had been fending off suggestions from Roosevelt, some of them couched in rather definite language, that Britain should give point to the agreed terms of the Atlantic Charter by liberating India from colonialism. In August 1942, Churchill had replied to these promptings with some asperity, writing from Cairo that any such concession would be a highly dangerous precedent:

> Here in the Middle East, the Arabs might claim by majority they could expel the Jews from Palestine, or at any time forbid all further immigration. I am strongly wedded to the Zionist policy, of which I was one of the authors. This is only one of the many unforeseen cases which will arise from new and further declarations.

Roosevelt did not reply to this letter either, but he did drop the subject of Indian independence for quite some time. Is it then thinkable that Churchill sent him some minatory Kipling in order to remind him that anti-imperial gestures did not come cost-free? Was *he*, in other words, prepared to shoulder the burden and accept the bizarre ingratitude of the natives?

"A Chapter of Proverbs," however, contains no warnings against light-mindedness where imperialism is concerned. Indeed, though Churchill obviously meant it to resonate with warnings to nations, it is intended by Kipling as an admonition to individuals along the lines of "If" or "Something of Myself." Verses three and six might conceivably possess a certain irony in view of Churchill's poorly concealed bitterness and sarcasm about the terms of Lend-Lease. And verse twenty-four appears to be a conscious echo of the *Rubaiyat* of Omar Khayyam, itself mildly fatalistic about the great

---

* It might have reminded them of Kipling's venomously anti-Jewish poem "Gehazi" (1912), in which he excoriated Attorney General Sir Rufus Isaacs for holding shares in an American company named Marconi.

schemes and doings of potentates. Otherwise, the poem is a skillful exercise in the deceptively difficult enterprise of emulating Biblical English. Churchill did have a tendency to send Roosevelt cryptic messages from the Bible, or hortatory extracts from Shakespeare. In fact, in the month after he sent the secret Kipling poems, he cabled the White House with the one line: "See St. John, chapter 14, verses 1 to 4." These verses contain a (presumably unintended) blasphemy: "Ye believe in God, believe also in me," before going on to make the famous reassurance about "In my Father's house there are many mansions." In the context, the message seems to refer to security and other arrangements for the Churchill-Roosevelt summit in Cairo. But in more general terms, it conforms to Churchill's taste for impressing America with his literary and rhetorical command.

If one could decide on a hinge moment, when power and decision passed finally from British to American hands, the fall of 1943, when Macmillan made his "Greece to their Rome" remark in North Africa, would probably be the date assigned by any objective historian. Ironic, then, that Churchill's confused and emotional last stand should have involved the invocation of Kipling. Conceivably, he was not even sure of his own motives; was, perhaps, looking for some talisman with which to impress Roosevelt and with which to make a claim of English right and duty. If so, he fell short of the mark.

Ironic, too, that it should have been Kipling for whom he reached in an extremity. More than most Englishmen, Kipling had worked to inculcate the idea of empire in the American mind. He had written and spoken in such a way as to stifle misgiving about conquest, and to replace misgiving with a sense of mission—of "burdens" solemnly shouldered. He had done so in order to prevent Britain from being shorn of her possessions either by those who inhabited them or by imperial Germany. When the time came for those colonies to be disburdened, they were mostly taken into the trusteeship of the United States. This was not the outcome Kipling had anticipated, unless you count "The Roman Centurion's Song," in which an old soldier begs the imperial Legate not to recall him. His last duty to Rome, he says beseechingly, is that of "staying on":

> Let me work here for Britain's sake—at any task you will—
> A marsh to drain, a road to make or native troops to drill.
> Some Western camp (I know the Pict) or granite Border keep,
> Mid seas of heather derelict, where our old messmates sleep.

For Kipling, at least, Britain had been Roman, not Greek. While he thought of torches being passed or burdens laid down, he could still imagine the island race somewhere in the game. Perhaps, given the transmission of British imperial notions to the Legates of the new Rome, he was not so quixotic a figure as Churchill's gesture makes him seem.

[4]

Blood Relations

In 1858, as British and French "expeditionary forces" were trying to push their way to Peking, they met with a doughty rebuff from Chinese coastal defenses at the Barrier Forts. A number of British vessels were disabled by the fire of the defenders, and owed their survival to the action of Josiah Tattnall, commander of the supposedly neutral American squadron that was on hand. He intervened boldly both to shield the British ships from Chinese gunnery and to tow them to a place of safety out of range. When asked to account for his abandonment of neutrality, Tattnall replied simply: "Blood is thicker than water."

This famous and rather mysterious saying, which combines elements of cliché with elements of mixed metaphor, has been a standby throughout the "special relationship." It was, in this place and time, a premonitory slogan for the events of 1898 and the rhetoric and poetry of Rudyard Kipling. The American penetration of China, which was a classic case of the Bible and the trading post in tandem, could never declare itself as explicitly colonial if only because America was explicitly anticolonial. But it did not scorn to follow the far more openly imperial path blazed by London, after the overthrow of the Canton system in what we crudely remember as "the Opium Wars." As the coast of China became permeable to Westerners, so American residents and businessmen began to expect more in the way of support from Washington. In 1843 an American mission was appointed by Secretary of State Daniel Webster and instructed to take advantage of the gains procured by Britain in the "very important marts of commerce" that were becoming accessible. The mission was charged to uphold "the commercial and manufacturing, as well as the agricultural and mining interests of the United States."

There were American diplomats in the succeeding period, Humphrey Marshall and Peter Parker among them, who wanted an independent policy for the United States. This, they thought, would position Washington to take advantage of any shift in Britain's fortunes, and perhaps to supplant the cotton of Manchester with the commodity that was king in the American South. All such initiatives were overruled, and the United States continued to follow a course that became known, for obvious reasons, as "jackal diplomacy." The British would dictate terms to the Chinese and incur their detestation for the drug trade. The United States would act as the junior partner, at once more scrupulous and less implicated. Proposals like those of Commodore Perry, that the United States should seize Taiwan as a counterweight to the British presence, were (ironically in view of future events) thought to be too risky to this enterprise. After the Tattnall affair in 1858, the American envoy William Reed was well placed to follow the British and French all the way north, to wait for them to extort the right of foreign embassies to reside in Peking, to observe as they demanded free passage along the Yangtze, and to rejoice when they received a guarantee of the protection of missionaries and their converts. After Lord Elgin had accomplished all this (and had ordered the Imperial Palace at Peking to be obliterated by way of underlining his point) the new American chargé, S. Wells Williams, waited a month before calmly claiming the same rights and concessions for Americans.

It was this ad hoc but ingenious method that incubated the desires of the "Open Door" lobby, which pushed for free trade and an American share and which in early 1898 was rewarded, principally because the Chinese authorities hoped to play on divisions among their foreign predators, with the concession for the southern extension of the main Chinese railway line. Elaboration of the main policy was postponed until after the war with Spain, by which time McKinley and Roosevelt had Guam and Hawaii at their disposal—island possessions effectively pointless except as "stepping-stones" to China. (The epoch in which metaphors of conquest and threat, such as "stepping-stone," "ripe fruit," "dagger pointed at," and "strategic island," were commonplace was just dawning in American life.)

No sooner was the 1898 war over than John Hay, now Secretary of State after that instructive sojourn at the London embassy, began to review his Chinese options. Immediately before the conflict with Spain, Hay had doubted the wisdom of a formal British approach, which had called for an Anglo-American front against other Western powers who might seek exclusive rights in China. The administration was ever wary of the dormant but easily roused anti-British feeling in Congress; a reserve of emotion which always inclined Hay to the "informal alliance" preference that, ever since, has been a condition of the "special relationship." However, he continued to help thicken the layer of American missionaries and American men of enterprise that was growing by accretion under the Union Jack. In March 1899 he said solemnly that American opinion deplored "the great game of spoliation now going on," adding thoughtfully that the U.S. government had "great commercial interests" and (in a phrase he must have picked up along with Kipling's "the great game" while at the Court of St. James's) would not consider its "hands tied for future eventualities." By then, also, the United States had a Pacific navy, proved in combat if only at Manila Bay, and could do better than Josiah Tattnall had done at the Barrier Forts. "You may fire when you are ready, Gridley," Admiral Dewey had said to his subordinate as he found the Spanish fleet at his mercy in Manila. Parasitic on British power in the Pacific though they had been, other American admirals could recognize that they held an initiative, and that their own day was only a matter of time.

The extent of American sea power is perhaps second only to its nuclear capacity as a symbol of the country's world standing. Any study of the origins of either phenomenon shows the British influence to have been inescapable.

At Yorktown on October 19, 1781, General Cornwallis ordered his troops to pile their arms and sent his sword to George Washington. As the redcoats offered the formalities of surrender, an American revolutionary band played "The World Turned Upside Down," a song which originated in the English Puritan revolution.

On April 19, 1988, I flew to Patrick Henry Airport and went from there to Yorktown, at which highly appropriate embarkation point I joined the USS *Iowa*. This enormous Second World War battleship, named for America's most pacifist and isolationist state, had been recommissioned by the Reagan-Weinberger rearmament administration and was returning from a tour of duty in the Persian Gulf. The morning's newspapers gave a graphic account of a battle in those waters during which American naval vessels, supported by British ones, had destroyed two Iranian oil platforms and sent three Iranian ships to the bottom. Every man on board the *Iowa* was cursing the luck that had brought them home with their tremendous sixteen-inch guns unfired.

Amid the *Iowa*'s array of martial features is one incongruity. The admiral's quarters boast a large, luxurious sunken bath. This fitting, which is found on board no other ship, was installed for the comfort of the disabled Franklin Delano Roosevelt. In November 1943, he boarded the USS *Iowa* and steamed at top speed across the Atlantic and through the Mediterranean to meet Winston Churchill. Their first place of rendezvous, ironically enough, was Tehran. In those days, Persia was a semi-colony of the British, and in 1944 it became the site of a squabble between Churchill and Roosevelt over competing British and American oil concessions. Later, in the 1950s, it became the site of an Anglo-American cooperative covert operation to overthrow a nationalist government and secure the Pahlavi dynasty. It was to deal with the direct consequences of that folly that the USS *Iowa* and her sister ships had again been seen in Middle Eastern waters. The USS *New Jersey* had spent some days off the coast of Lebanon in 1984, tossing shells as heavy as Volkswagens from her sixteen-inch muzzles at the supposed positions of Iranian sympathizers. I wasn't the only person to be reminded, by this classic gunboat demonstration, of Joseph Conrad's bizarre evocation in *Heart of Darkness*:

> Once, I remember, we came across a man-of-war anchored off the coast. . . . In the empty immensity of earth, sky and water, there she was, incomprehensible, firing into a continent.

As if to quench any such misgivings, the USS *Iowa* calls itself "The Big Stick" and this Teddy Roosevelt phrase appears, with an appropriate silhouette, on its official papers and stationery. "Gunboat diplomacy," a phrase readily understood in the America of the 1980s, is a British term invented in the piping days of Lord Palmerston (who once remarked that Great Britain "has no permanent friends, only permanent interests"). I am myself what the Americans call a "navy brat," born in Portsmouth as the son of a long-serving officer and brought up in the environs of naval bases from Malta to Rosyth. I found this a natural advantage in conversations aboard the *Iowa*. The seaman who met me at the dock gates was named Burton, and he told me straightaway that he had made a pilgrimage to England, to see his ancestral town of Burton-on-Trent. The captain had a wooden blotter on his desk, made from the timber of HMS *Victory*, Nelson's flagship at Portsmouth. He spoke of Portsmouth as a "Mecca" for sailors of his generation, and called his colleagues to hear when I said that I had seen the last of the Royal Navy battleships, HMS *Vanguard*, being towed away for scrap in the early sixties. "She slipped her tugs and ran aground, didn't she? Like she was protesting." He knew the climax of the story before I could get to it. And his gunnery officer joined in, to say with considerable gravity that it was HMS *Warspite*, out of all British men-of-war, that he personally would have saved from the scrapyard. He seemed to know every engagement in which she had ever taken part.

It was affecting and impressive to see the place held by British naval lore. In the wardroom there was a photograph of Ronald Reagan, who had secretly sold weapons to the Iranian foe in order to finance his private war in Nicaragua. But there were also several prominent souvenir photographs of HMS *York* and HMS *Battleaxe*, which had kept the *Iowa* company in a passage through the Suez Canal: the same canal that had nearly had American and British ships firing on one another in 1956. (The British narrowly missed bombing American civilians as they were being evacuated from Cairo airport, and the U.S. Chief of Naval Operations, Admiral Arleigh Burke, told the State Department that his Sixth Fleet "can stop them [the British] but we will have to blast hell out of them. If we are going to threaten, if we're going to turn on them, then you've got to be ready to shoot. We can do that. We can defeat them.")

Nothing of that unpleasantness; Britain's last, mad resistance to the coming American hegemony, remained. On board the *Iowa*, the British were felt to be an exemplary study both in seafaring and in handling "hot spots" overseas. As the huge, beautiful ship cut its way through the water toward its new home port on Staten Island, I stood on the bridge to watch a few demonstration broadsides (saying a silent valediction to those faraway Druze villages, as the gigantic shells went screaming off toward the horizon) and talked with Seth Cropsey, Under Secretary of the Navy and an occasional defense essayist for *Commentary, The Public Interest,* and other organs of neoconservative reflection. "I think you'll find," he said, "that most of our people have studied and admired the British example. Once in a while someone like Eddie Luttwak says we should study the Germans instead. But that'd most probably be disastrous." (Luttwak's most famous text is, of course, *The Grand Strategy of the Roman Empire.*)

Secretary Cropsey's recently retired superior, Secretary of the Navy John Lehman, who brought the *Iowa* and others out of mothballs, once said that his job took him to London twelve times before it took him west of the Missouri. Even in a period when America was widely held to be turning to the Pacific and away from the Atlantic—the *Iowa* had taken part in three deployments off the coast of Central America since 1984—the values of the "special relationship" still obtained. The forty-eight cruise missiles she carried were blood kin to the ones emplaced under the control of the USAF at the deceptively bucolic-sounding English villages of Molesworth and Greenham Common.

A few weeks before I shipped out on the *Iowa*, a motorcycle messenger from the British embassy in Washington had come to my front door. He bore this notice, blazoned with the Union Jack:

The following announcement has been made in London today:
The Queen has been graciously pleased to approve a recommendation by the Secretary of State for Foreign and Commonwealth Affairs that the Honourable Caspar W. Weinberger be appointed an Honorary Knight Grand Cross in the Civil Division of the Most Excellent Order of the British Empire (GBE).

The message went on to say, departing from the language of the Gazette and the Court of St. James's, that "this is the first award of a GBE to an American citizen for eleven years. The award to Mr. Weinberger recognizes his outstanding and invaluable contribution to defense cooperation between Britain and the United States during his seven years as Secretary of Defense." It did not take very expert decoding to recognize in this a reference to Mr. Weinberger's fraternal role in the Falklands crisis, when a potentially quixotic British naval expedition had been protected by the superior supply and reconnaissance resources of a big brother as it made its way down to the South Atlantic. "Closet Brits," an exasperated Jeane Kirkpatrick had scoffed at her Reaganite colleagues, as they gradually moved to discard her own preferred allies on the Argentine General Staff, whose combat experience had been gained, until that point, chiefly against civilians.

Mr. Weinberger duly appeared with his wife at Buckingham Palace on February 23, 1988, and was solemnly invested with membership in the Most Excellent Order. There were no chirrups of republican protest in the United States, such as still occasionally arise when an American official is too ostentatiously attentive to the British Crown. Perhaps this was because Mr. Weinberger had recently retired. Perhaps it was because, as a United States citizen, he had forsworn the right to call himself "Sir Caspar." (That would have been very choice: Sir Caspar John, brother to the painter Augustus, had in his time been First Sea Lord.) But if he had to stay in the closet as a Brit, Mr. Weinberger could still "come out" as a Tory. Edwin M. Yoder of *The Washington Post* attended a breakfast meeting with him between his retirement and his knighthood, and in a little-remarked column brought us this glimpse:

> Someone asks the former Secretary whether all the U.S. borrowing of recent years might not someday restrain our freedom of action. Not at all, Weinberger says. Much of California, his home state, was developed by British and French and German capital. It's nothing new.
>
> But might the precarious indebtedness expose the United States to the sort of jam the British got into in 1956, when a run on sterling forced them to scrap the Suez operation? Nothing of the sort, Weinberger insists. "They withdrew—and they didn't really have to—because the Labor politicians wanted to go on winning elections." But, sir, someone says, the Conservatives, not Labor, were running things—Sir Anthony Eden himself. And everyone remembers the dangerous run on sterling. No, Weinberger insists. It was all Labor's doing.

Even if it *had* been "Labor's doing," it's surprising that Mr. Weinberger didn't possess enough institutional Washington memory to recall the day when Sir Anthony Eden's deputy, R. A. Butler, called U.S. Treasury Secretary George Humphrey to beg in person for a loan to save the pound. Humphrey offered a generous loan with interest deferred—on the condition that the British got out of Egypt. That sort of talk between London and Washington doesn't take place every day, and this was the hinge moment when the United States replaced Britain in the Middle East. Indeed, Humphrey had asked Eisenhower not to squeeze Eden's exchequer *too* hard, precisely because "if they throw him out then we have those socialists to lick."

But no matter. Weinberger may have got everything factually wrong, while still comprehending the deep grammar of the "special relationship."

The founding Clausewitz of this relationship was Admiral Alfred Thayer Mahan, who summarized in his own person the elements of love-hate, envy and emulation, admiration and calculation, that have always defined the military half of the "special relationship."

At first reading, Mahan's historic contribution to the study of sea power qualifies him for that overused and frequently misleading title "Anglophile." This was certainly the simplistic view taken of him by Duff Cooper, a protégé of Winston Churchill and leading Tory of his day, who contributed an introduction to a later Mahan biography that now reads like a hostage to fortune:

At a time when Anglo-American relations were by no means so established and so cordial as they are today, and when an American writer might easily have injured his own reputation by evincing pronouncedly pro-English sentiments, Mahan, though of Irish origin himself, never hesitated to express his admiration and affection for Great Britain. Deeply religious and high-principled to the point of austerity as he was, we can feel confident that it was not the welcome which his books received in this country nor yet the lionising to which he was subjected in London that won his heart; it was rather his profound study of English naval history and his intimate knowledge of our greatest Admirals which made him love Great Britain less only than the United States.

Cooper was, perhaps, laying it on a touch thicker than water. The condescension of the British Establishment is notorious, but what might have served in the 1890s was getting a bit thin by the time of Churchill. Mahan had his own "agenda," as people now say and as we shall see. Still, the British had had every reason to feel grateful and enthusiastic, as Cooper went on to stress. Mahan, in his short-term view,

> was so far from regarding the growth of the Royal Navy with any jealousy or ill-will that, on the contrary, his only fear was that it might prove inadequate to its great responsibilities. However that might be he felt strongly that the United States could not rely for their security on the naval forces of another power, and he was continually urging on his fellow-country-men the necessity of creating a navy of their own. In the last book that he wrote, published in the autumn of 1913, he urged the United States to "wake up betimes" and he warned them that neither the Monroe Doctrine nor the exclusion of Asiatics could "be sustained without the creation and maintenance of a preponderant navy."

(Cooper thus neatly made the then essential connection between foreign and immigration policy.)

Even as shrewd a critic as Richard Van Alstyne, in *The Rising American Empire*, says: "Unlike Strong, Beveridge and other lesser lights, Mahan never became effusive over the cults of race, religion and superior civilisation. He recognised that the United States was a member of the complex of national states, and he saw its survival in terms of sea power collaborating with the British Empire." Actually, the record shows that Mahan was a good deal swayed by considerations of blood. Indeed, it was not for nothing that the French edition of Mahan's writing, published in 1906, was entitled *Le Salut de la Race Blanche et l'Empire des Mers.* The editor and presenter of these papers was Professor Jean Izoulet of the Collège de France, who had also fathered such works as *La Croix et l'Epée en Occident* and *L'Expropriation des "Races Incompétentes."* He dearly wanted to claim Mahan for the French "civilizing mission" and even went so far as to remove Mahan's praise for Sir Garnet Wolseley from one of the translated chapters. Alas for Professor Izoulet, Mahan had chosen firmly in favor of Albion.

The Influence of Sea Power upon History, Mahan's masterpiece, begins with an evocation of "that English nation which more than any other has owed its greatness to the sea." Citing Arnold on Rome's victory over Hannibal, and Sir Edward Creasy on Britain's victory over Napoleon, Mahan, making the then uncontroversial assumption that Britain was most accurately to be compared to Rome, continued: "Neither of these Englishmen mentions the yet more striking coincidence, that in both cases the mastery of the sea rested with the victor."

Mahan had so thoroughly grasped this point, and had become so enamored of the nation that had put this point into practice and action, that he invariably gave England the benefit of every doubt. In his writings on the Navigation Acts and the War of 1812, he almost unconsciously sided with the British against the United States. The Navigation Acts, after all, stated peremptorily that all imports into or exports from the British Isles or their far-flung colonies had to be conveyed in English vessels. Aimed directly at any other nation which dared to act as carrier, and designed to put the Dutch out of business, these Acts were enforced with tremendous arrogance. As Mahan mildly put it:

> A century and a quarter later we find Nelson, before his famous career had begun, showing his zeal for the welfare of England's shipping by enforcing this same act in the West Indies against American merchant ships.

Nelson, of whom Mahan was to write glowingly in another book, called *Types of Naval Officers*, was above criticism: *sans peur et sans reproche*. But Mahan's admiration of the British naval tradition was so intense that it even allowed him to be pro-British concerning events that took place seven years after Lord Nelson's death. In his account of the War of 1812, Mahan showed a little of the hand that he was later to play so deftly and persuasively in his *Influence of Sea Power*. By setting up the British as examples, and by according them the right to be admired and understood, he also suggested that they should be emulated. Here is the method at work:

> That much of Great Britain's action [in 1812] was unjustifiable, and at times even monstrous, regarded in itself alone, must be admitted; but we shall ill comprehend the necessity of preparation for war, if we neglect to note the pressure of emergency, of deadly peril, upon a state, or if we fail to recognize that traditional habits of thought constitute with nations, as with individuals, a compulsive moral force which an opponent can control only by the display of adequate physical power. Such to the British people was the conviction of this right and need to compel the service of their native seamen, wherever found on the high seas.

Having taken it upon himself to present the British case for stopping American vessels and press-ganging their crews, Mahan argued that it was of no use for Americans to complain and strike heroic attitudes at such high-handedness:

> The conclusion of this writer is, that at a very early stage of the French Revolutionary Wars the United States should have obeyed Washington's warnings to prepare for war, and to build a navy.

Mahan, in other words, envied and admired the British but wanted to supplant them as much as to ally with them. In 1894 Andrew Carnegie began to propagandize for his idea that Britain and America should fuse or federate. Although this campaign was also designed to make America realize its "expansionist" potential, and was directed against isolationism, it did not meet with Mahan's entire approval. In fact, invited to comment by the editors of the *North American Review*, he had this to say:

> It is not then merely, nor even chiefly, a pledge of universal peace that may be seen in the United States becoming a naval power of serious import, with clearly defined external conditions dictated by the necessities of her interoceanic position; nor yet in the cordial cooperation, as of kindred peoples, that the future may have in store for her and Great Britain. Not in universal harmony, nor in fond dreams of unbroken peace, rest now the best hopes of the world, as involved in the fate of European civilization. Rather in the competition of interests, in that reviving sense of nationality, which is the true antidote to what is bad in socialism.

So, no utopian ideas of a reunified Anglo-Saxondom. But mutual alliance by all means. As Mahan went on to put it:

> Our Pacific slope, and the Pacific colonies of Great Britain, with an instinctive shudder have felt the threat, which able Europeans have seen in the teeming multitudes of central and northern Asia; while their overflow into the Pacific Islands shows that not only westward by land, but also eastward by sea, the flood may sweep.

Roosevelt's later letter to Kipling is anticipated rather well by another of Mahan's essays at about this time, in which he insisted:

It should be an inviolable resolution of our national policy, that no foreign state should henceforth acquire a coaling position within three thousand miles of San Francisco—a distance which includes the Hawaiian and Galapagos Islands and the coast of Central America. . . . In the Caribbean and the Atlantic we are confronted with many a foreign coal depot, bidding us stand to our arms, even as Carthage bade Rome.

Close your eyes and you could be listening to any British imperialist of the Joseph Chamberlain school. Except that such an orator would not have gone on to say, as did Mahan:

In conclusion, while Great Britain is undoubtedly the most formidable of our possible enemies, both by her great navy and by the strong position she holds near our coasts, it must be added that a cordial understanding with that country is one of the first of our external interests. Both nations doubtless, and properly, seek their own advantage; but both, also, are controlled by a sense of law and justice, drawn from the same sources, and deep-rooted in her instincts.

Beginning his naval service in the Civil War, Mahan took part in blockade duty in the western Gulf south of New Orleans. We do not know what view he formed of British support for the Confederacy, though he had been in London in July 1863 and noted an editorial in the London *Times* which carried on insufferably about the "sad condition to which the Republic of Bunker Hill and Yorktown was reduced; Grant held up at Vicksburg, Lee marching victorious into Pennsylvania." (*The Times* hoped this would teach contrition.) But he did gain some valuable comparative experience from the campaign. As his almost uncritical biographer W. D. Puleston said, he observed naval warfare

carried on in much the same manner as it had been under Nelson, Cornwallis and Collingwood off the coasts of France during the Napoleonic Wars. Late in life, when Mahan described the dreary monotony of the British blockade of Napoleon, and the weather-beaten ships of the British Navy, he could by simple recollection picture these ships and the conditions that they had endured.

He was to have other chances to indulge his fascination with the English at first hand. He paid a return visit to England on board the SS *Worcester* in 1871, and managed to see five of the great national cathedrals. At Exeter he attended Easter service and wrote in a letter of "the vast numbers of the faithful who during four centuries have worshipped under the same arches . . . the vague, awful mystery of great age which seems to people the building with the ghosts of the many generations gone to their rest."

Cruising around the world with the U.S. Navy, Mahan found himself generally approving British colonial policy, though he was a little disturbed by the misery and poverty he saw in Aden. But rank and ancestry came first with him. As he wrote in 1893 about Admiral Hawke ("closely connected by blood with the Maryland family of Bladen; that having been his mother's maiden name"), who died only three days before the British flag was struck at Yorktown:

In the great struggle for Anglo-Saxon predominance, which had begun under William III, but was now approaching its crisis and final decision in the Seven Years War, the determining factor was to be the maritime strength of Great Britain. . . . In this eminent particular, which involves real originality, no sea officer of the eighteenth century stands with him: in this respect only he and Nelson, who belongs rather to the nineteenth, are to be named together.

Mahan, in point of fact, counted North America as "civilized" to the extent that it had been the scene of English victories over the French and other comers. So it's hardly a wonder that his books on sea power, warmly and pointedly reviewed by Theodore Roosevelt in *The Atlantic Monthly*, were received with even more enthusiasm in England. In a letter to his friend Captain Bouverie Clarke of the Royal Navy, Mahan was to acknowledge "the recognition which your countrymen have obtained for me from my own." Certainly, the British were unstinting in their welcome for Mahan and his tomes when he visited England in 1894. The Royal United Service Institution had prepared the way by serializing and digesting Mahan's work as it came out. But when his ship, the USS *Chicago*, put in at Gravesend, the British began to excel themselves.

A banquet was given by the Lord Mayor for Mahan and his superior, Admiral Erben. Mutual toasts were exchanged, to the President and the Queen, to the United States and the United Kingdom, and to the respective fleets of the two nations. Admiral Erben, responding to the latter, toasted the visit of the British to New York a short while previous, when "the British Lion and the American Eagle marched down Broadway *together* in the only way they will go." A lion and an eagle parading *à deux* was the sort of symbolism in which the *Punch* of those times used to specialize, and in fact the magazine was equal to the occasion with some doggerel verses.

Mahan was taken to view the memorabilia of Lord Nelson at the Royal Naval College in Greenwich. He dined with Queen Victoria and was received cordially by the Prince of Wales, by Prime Minister Lord Rosebery, and by the Marquis of Salisbury at Hatfield House itself. He received honorary degrees from both Oxford and Cambridge in one week, was honored on Admiral Lord Howe's day by the Royal Naval Club, and in general received what Americans call "the whole nine yards" and British people used to refer to as "Foot, horse, and guns." Modest and religious as he was, Mahan could not forbear to boast a little to his wife about his British acclaim:

The London *Times* has been calling me Copernicus again. I find that their meaning is, Copernicus taught that the sun was the centre of the system—not the earth as was believed before

his time, and I have been the first to show that sea-power is
the centre around which all other events move. . . . In the
philosophy of the subject, we must all sit at the feet of the
eminent writer. My dear, do you know that it is your husband
they are talking about?

For Mahan, there was a special significance in the applause of
England. He seems to have been particularly moved by the toast
to him and his fellow officers proposed at the aforesaid Lord Mayor's
banquet by Lord Roberts, who was already the holder of the Victoria Cross for his efforts in the desperate subjugation of the Af-
ghans and was known almost universally as "Bobs." This great
veteran, who had one extraordinary campaign still before him,
expressed the hope that Mahan would one day write a book about
the army. This hope was to be requited in the most handsome
way.

Before quitting English waters, Mahan went to the Cowes re-
gatta, where he was again feted by royalty and the aristocracy. The
Queen's nephew, Kaiser Wilhelm of Germany, put in an appearance on his yacht, having just opened the Kiel Canal, and pronounced himself also to be a student of *The Influence of Sea Power*.
Nobody was ill bred enough to make anything of this coincidence,
and Mahan was able to repay some of the hospitality he had enjoyed
by receiving the Prince of Wales, the Duke of York, and Earl
Spencer (ancestor of the present Princess of Wales) aboard the USS
Chicago.

The year 1899 saw the various threads, spun with apparent independence by Mahan, Theodore Roosevelt, Henry Adams, John
Hay, Cecil Rhodes, and Kipling, drawn together in a web of "manifest destiny." It was the year of the consolidation of American
power in the former Spanish possessions of Cuba and the Philippines, gained in a near-bloodless conflict. It was also the year of
intense British difficulty with the Boer farmers in South Africa.
Mahan was equal to both emergencies, since he saw in them the
vindication of his theories of sea power, the common interest of

the two countries, and the opportunity for American ascendancy. The first precept had been easily demonstrated by Admiral Dewey's contemptuous rout of the Spanish fleet in Manila Bay and (with the exception of the loss of the legendary *Maine*) by events in Havana harbor also. So, quoting the second of these three precepts in support of the third, he turned to Sir William Wilson-Hunter, an English author and friend of Kipling's, who had written about the Philippine developments in the following terms:

> The Colonial empire of Spain crumbled to pieces at a touch from the youngest of the Christian governments. America starts upon her career of Asiatic rule with an amplitude of resources, and with a sense of moral responsibility which no previous state of Christendom brought to the work. Each western nation, as we shall find, has stamped on its eastern history the European ethics of the age when its supremacy was won. *In the splendid and difficult task which lies before our American kinsmen*, they will be trammelled by no Portuguese Inquisition of the Sixteenth Century, nor by the slave colonisation of Holland in the Seventeenth, nor by that cynical rule for the gain of rulers which for a time darkened the British acquisition of India in the Eighteenth. The United States, in the government of their dependencies, will represent the political conscience of the Nineteenth Century. I hail their advent in the East as a new power for good, not alone for the island races that come under their care, but also in that great settlement of European spheres of influence in Asia, which, if we could see aright, forms a world problem of our day.

(Sir William shared President McKinley's difficulty, which was that of not realizing that the Filipinos were Christian already.) Mahan, as his biographer put it, "rarely used other men's words to convey his own thoughts," but went so far as to reprint this piece of white man's enthusiasm in a published letter about the Philippines. He continued to present the American occupation of that archipelago as—what else?—a necessary hinterland to the American policy of an "open door" to China.

He did not confine his generalizations about the Philippines to the Far East. In the same year as his Kiplingesque defense of the Manila expedition, he embarked upon *The Story of the War in South Africa, 1899–1900.* Published as the century turned, this is perhaps the most eloquent apology for British empire and imperialism ever penned by a foreigner. It outran even the rather shamefaced defenses of their own actions that British patriots were able to devise. But it had in common with them a sense of calling and destiny, perhaps fresher and more naïve for being newly adopted:

> The naval battle of Manila Bay [wrote Mahan] will to the future appear one of the decisive events of history, for there the visions of the few, which had quickened unconsciously the conceptions of the many, materialized as suddenly and unexpectedly into an actuality that could be neither obviated nor undone. What Dewey's victory was to the over-sea expansion of the United States, what the bombardment of Fort Sumter in 1861 was to the sentiment of Union in the Northern States, that Paul Kruger's ultimatum was to Imperial Federation. A fruitful idea, which the unbeliever had sought to bury under scoffs, had taken root in the convictions of men, and passed as by a bound into vigorous life—perfect, if not yet mature.

This expression of the world-spirit, even if it tended to overlook the fact that at Fort Sumter the British Empire had been on the other side, was still very serviceable for the present as Mahan saw it, and for nascent American as well as Anglo-American ambitions.

"Perfect, if not yet mature." Mahan was perhaps overly impressed by the ability of the British to call upon, not colonial *troops*, but English-speaking *allies* as far apart as could be: "as far apart, geographically, as the British Islands, Canada and Australia." Mahan was sober in deciding the importance of this factor:

> After making allowance for mere racial sympathy, which in the present context has had even in the neutral United States so large a share in determining sympathies, the claim of an English newspaper is approximately correct, that the universal action of the colonies, where volunteering far exceeded the numbers first sent, "indicates what is the opinion of bodies of free men, widely separated by social and geographical condition, concerning the justice and necessity of the quarrel in which we are now engaged."

In seconding this emotional and self-justifying appeal to blood, and in slightly reprobating the British government's slowness to act upon it, Mahan pressed his case with almost reckless solidarity. When one reflects on the continued political survival of the Boers, and upon the avowed principles of the Union in the American Civil War, one wonders how prudent it was of him to write of

> the sentiment of the unity of the Empire, an ideal which under different conditions may well take to Imperial Federation the place that the Union occupied in American hearts and minds in 1861. Alike in breadth of view and in face of sentiment, nothing exceeds the power of such an ideal to lift men above narrow self-interest to the strenuous self-devotion demanded by great emergencies. Should this be so in the present case, and increase, *Imperial Federation and expansion of the United States are facts, which, whether taken singly or in correlation, are secondary in importance to nothing contemporaneous.* [Italics mine.]

This was putting it pretty high. Even though news of British bone-headedness in the field had reached him, as it had every newspaper

reader, and even though reports of British swinishness to the ci-
vilian population must have penetrated at least as rumors, Mahan
chose to ignore the second and say of the first:

> In so far, that element of stupidity which has been somewhat
> lavishly attributed to the British officers' too simple-minded
> attention to their end to the exclusion of care for their own
> persons and those of their men, has a military value not only
> great, but decisive. The quality needs direction and control,
> certainly; but having been reproached for now two centuries,
> the question is apt—where has it placed Great Britain among
> the nations of the earth?

This was Anglophilia with—for once the old phrasing has its point—
a vengeance. Mahan had so far committed himself to Lord Roberts
of Kandahar, soon to be immortalized again as "Roberts of Preto-
ria," as to repay, and more than repay, Roberts's desire in 1894
that Mahan should write a book about the British army. A few
years later, Lord Roberts was to join the Tory rebellion against
Home Rule for Mahan's Irish cousins. But all that, along with the
Somme, lay in the future. For the present, Mahan could find glory
even in British military and imperial folly. As for Lord Roberts,
Mahan found words that G. A. Henty himself could hardly have
penned without blushing:

> It is not by such affairs that contests are decided—on the
> playground or in strategy. Lord Roberts proceeded with his
> preparations undisturbed by the mosquito buzzings about his
> ears or on his trail.

But in spite of this part-vicarious and part-genuine enthusiasm
and comradeship, Mahan had a shrewd sense that the alliance could
only be temporary. To this day in the Operational Archives in the
Division of Naval History at the Washington Navy Yard, there
reposes a document, written by him, dated December 1890 and

entitled "Contingency Plan of Operations in Case of War with Great Britain." It is a generally pessimistic study, imbued with a wholesome respect for British maritime strength. In general, he thought, the best that the United States could hope to do was to fight a defensive war. However, in one instance there might be a chance for an initiative. "No attempt can be made to carry the war to the other side of the Atlantic, or against a *fortified* island in the West Indies. In the latter quarter, maritime raids may be attempted under favorable circumstances."

Ten years later, in 1900, he was to write with more confidence that "Great Britain's interests elsewhere are so great that she must now unload herself of responsibility for the Caribbean." A matter of a decade or so after *that*, Theodore Roosevelt was to warn Kipling about his too boastful attitude toward the United States and "the lee of the British Fleet." Not long after that, the United States was to limit the size of that fleet and to express displeasure at a British naval treaty with Japan. In 1940, Franklin Roosevelt, who was trained on Mahan during his years at the Navy Department, was to lend Britain some old destroyers in exchange for the cession of British colonial power in the Caribbean. The relationship of water to blood, in other words, was to prove rather more ambivalent than Commander Josiah Tattnall, or those who lauded his high spirit, could have supposed.

Neither Theodore Roosevelt nor Alfred Thayer Mahan was of sufficiently Anglo-Saxon "stock," as the saying goes, to make very much of the bloodline element in the new alliance between London and Washington that burgeoned from 1898. But racial kinship was a strong and continuous theme of that period, and steps were even taken to extend and deepen it by marriage and amalgamation.

In his book *The Protestant Establishment*, where the word WASP made its acronymous appearance in the American language, E. Digby Baltzell spoke of the year 1901 in slightly exaggerated tones:

In that year a British-American, White-Anglo-Saxon-Protes-
tant (WASP) establishment, consolidated through family alliances between Mayfair and Murray Hill, involving many
millions of dollars, authoritatively ran the world, as their
ancestors had done since Queen Elizabeth's time.

This might have been putting it high, though as Baltzell says, it
was the year when "the Protestant patrician Theodore Roosevelt
entered the White House and J. P. Morgan, leading layman of the
Protestant Episcopal Church and unrivalled czar of our business
civilization, formed the first billion-dollar trust, the United States
Steel Corporation." It was also true that at that period the Senate
was dominated by WASPs (or brahmins as they have sometimes
been known) of the sort typified by Henry Cabot Lodge and Nelson
W. Aldrich.

This might have happened anyway, without any great production
being made of Anglo-Saxon bloodlines, if it were not for "expansionism." The expansionist cause meant that there was no further
need to downplay an English connection, as sturdy Americans had
been wont to do during the middle decades of the century, especially during Britain's perfidious Civil War policy. Expansionism
had also helped to heal *that* wound in American life, by employing
the Southern-dominated officer corps in the glorious campaigns in
Cuba and the Philippines. Finally, a wave of Jewish and Catholic
immigration from Southern and Eastern Europe as well as Ireland
had contributed to a WASP self-consciousness in reaction. Faced
with what even quite tolerant figures described as "mongrelization," those who could claim a purer "stock" made haste to do so.
There were even nativist reasonings in which this could be dressed
up. There was the continuity with the first settlement of the country, sometimes known as the *Mayflower* complex. There was the
language. There was the ever-present yearning for an ancient and
honorable history. And for those who aspired to gentrify themselves
and to dignify the possession of land and property, there was a
natural model just across the ocean, which had (as Tocqueville

pointed out) avoided going the way of the French aristocracy by its genius for adaptation. This genius for adaptation now took the form of intermarriage with "American cousins."

When Henry James wrote *An International Episode* in 1878 (publishing it with *Daisy Miller*) he was able to make deliciously skillful use of the mutual incomprehension that obtained between the mansions of Rhode Island and the town houses of London—to say nothing of the castles of the Home Counties. But by the turn of the century, and in the years preceding the outbreak of the Great War, the familiarity gap had closed with hectic—some thought indecent—speed. On the boat to America, Henry James's Count Otto Vogelstein (admittedly not a conspicuous Englishman) was reflecting: "There appeared to be a constant danger of marrying the American girl; it was something one had to reckon with, like the railway, the telegraph, the discovery of dynamite, the Chassepot rifle, the Socialistic spirit; it was one of the complications of modern life." Later he wrote: "For a Bostonian nymph to reject an English duke is an adventure only less stirring, I should say, than for an English duke to be rejected by a Boston nymph." This was progress of a sort, and involved two commodities with a very different consistency from blood and water—capital and class.

Wealthy though many English aristocrats undoubtedly were, the flow of money in exchange for title could really go only one way. The two most famous and emblematic marital alliances—that of Jennie Jerome to Lord Randolph Churchill and of Consuelo Vanderbilt to the Duke of Marlborough, Jennie's nephew by marriage, illustrate the point. English primogeniture tribalism meant that money "settled" on a bride became the property of her husband. Self-made American tycoons were inclined to kick at this idea when it came to their own daughters. Leonard Jerome was compelled to write to Randolph's father in the most unsentimental terms:

In the settlement as finally arranged I have ignored American customs and waived all my American prejudices and have

conceded to your views and English custom on every point—
save one.

This one point was an allowance in her own name to his daughter.
And when another Marlborough sued for the hand of Consuelo
Vanderbilt, he received after laborious negotiations a block of
shares in the New York Central Railway Company with an income
guaranteed for life—happily for him in view of the brevity of the
marriage.

The Vanderbilt-Marlborough vows were solemnized by Bishop
Henry Codman Potter, the embodiment of white Protestantism
and sometimes dubbed "the First Citizen of New York." He represented a high synthesis of the Episcopal and the social, and was
proud of being on terms with J. P. Morgan as well as with more
roughly hewn elements such as Samuel Gompers. The relative
delicacy and restraint of the match between two great clans was
not always echoed in the rest of the marriage market. An adver-
tisement placed in the encrusted Tory pages of the London *Daily
Telegraph* in February 1901 read: "Will any dukes, marquesses,
earls or other noblemen desirous of meeting, for the purpose of
marriage, young, beautiful *and* rich American heiresses communicate with . . ." There followed the name and address of a broker
in New Orleans. A New York newspaper had earlier published a
marriage guide which explained the ropes to the aspiring American
noblewoman:

Dukes are the loftiest kind of noblemen in England. There
are only twenty-seven of them in the whole United Kingdom.
Of these there are only two available for matrimonial purposes. These are the Dukes of Manchester and Roxburghe.
The Duke of Hamilton is already spoken for, the Duke of
Norfolk is an old widower, and the Duke of Leinster only
eleven years old.

Viceroys, of course, were even rarer since there was only one at any given time. How clever, then, of Mary Leiter to land Lord Curzon, the great potentate of the British Indian Empire, and to add the fortunes of her father's partnership with Marshall Field to his broad acres. (Decades later, when Ian Fleming summarized the Cold War aspects of the "special relationship" in James Bond's warm male bonding with a CIA agent, the agent also bore the name of Leiter. Fleming was a terrible snob.)

There were more than a hundred such weddings between American money and British nobility in the period before the onset of the First World War, and one of them was to give birth to Winston Churchill, the most famous son the "special relationship" ever produced. The great chronicler of the period, George Dangerfield, has a masterly cameo moment in his book *The Strange Death of Liberal England*. The occasion was a ball given in fancy dress at the height of the 1911 House of Lords controversy. An embattled Liberal government had threatened to swamp an obdurate Tory upper house with the creation of five hundred new peers:

On Empire Day, Mr. F. E. Smith and Lord Winterton gave a fancy dress ball at Claridge's. In the middle of the ballroom floor among the Junos and Ceres' and the Cleopatras and the Louis Quinze duchesses and the pink tulle ballet girls and the young politicians in velvet with jewelled snuff boxes, stood Mr. Asquith and Mr. Balfour, dressed in ordinary evening clothes. At midnight a way was cleared through the room for the figure of a peer, wearing robes of state, and bearing on his coronet the legend "499: just one more vacancy." It was Mr. Waldorf Astor. This delicate allusion to the Royal Prerogative was greeted with rounds of applause from Mr. F. E. Smith in his eighteenth century white satin, and Mr. Winston Churchill in his scarlet domino . . .

From its inception in the new century, then, the Anglo-American relationship was an affair between military, diplomatic, and social elites. But this did not automatically limit its appeal. The ideology of "Anglo-Saxondom," based as it was on blood, could infuse the meanest in station with a sense of superiority. Admittedly, the *Anglo-Saxon Review*, popular at the time in the better circles, was managed by Jennie Jerome in her capacity as Lady Randolph Churchill. But in resistance to the melting pot and in anticipation of empire, there was a populist Anglo-Saxonism at work also. In a very widely circulated and influential book called *Our Country*, published in 1885, the Reverend Josiah Strong had intoned mightily. "It seems to me," he said, "that God, with infinite wisdom and skill, is training the Anglo-Saxon race for an hour sure to come . . . If I read not amiss, this powerful race will move down upon Mexico, down upon Central and South America, out upon the islands of the sea, over upon Africa and beyond." This prophecy was seconded by a leading pro-expansionist demagogue, Senator Albert J. Beveridge of Indiana, who cried, even as Congress was moving to annex Hawaii: "We are Anglo-Saxon and must obey our blood and occupy new markets and, if necessary, new lands." Discoursing about these "new lands," which were "shores hitherto bloody and benighted," he saw no option but "Anglo-Saxon solidarity . . . an English-speaking people's league of God for the permanent peace of this war-torn world."

In England, Joseph Chamberlain made speeches that were woven from the same rhetorical thread, while in South Africa Cecil Rhodes was also meditating on an Anglo-American world dominion. It was also at this time that elements of what might be called the WASP aesthetic began to take shape. The old established College of New Jersey took the opportunity, in the late 1890s, to change its name to Princeton, a title more in keeping with the culture of aspiration. The tortured Anglophile Woodrow Wilson, who inaugurated a faculty at the university, once wrote that everything rested upon the selection of men who were "companionable and clubbable . . . If their qualities as gentlemen and as scholars conflict, the former will win them the place."

There was a hunger for academic "tradition" and for a more ivy-infested context for the incubation of elites (which can still be seen in the hilarious quadrangles of Yale and the sherry parties of Charlottesville). In 1901, two Chicago entrepreneurs purchased that special treasury of English imperial and anthropological learning, the *Encyclopaedia Britannica*. As they sought to invest their new property with ever-greater prestige and respectability, they turned to two irreproachable Anglo-Saxon institutions—the London *Times* and Cambridge University. *The Times* was persuaded to take considerable advertising from the *Britannica* and to act as its sponsor. In 1910, Cambridge University was induced to become, for the look of the thing, the publisher of the eleventh edition. At a lavish dinner given in London to celebrate this new synthesis, the eleventh edition's editor, Hugh Chisholm, made a self-criticism. The *Britannica*, he said,

> put too narrowly the British point of view in a great number of subjects. You will often find in its articles the use of the phrase "in this country," meaning England; and the phrase really represents a certain mental attitude on the part of the contributors.

The intended scope of any broadening of this mental attitude was ringingly expounded by the next speaker, Ambassador Whitelaw Reid, who represented the United States at the Court of St. James's. He evoked

> the undivided and indivisible English-speaking race; that race which is united in its history, in its language, in its pride in the past, in its hopes and in its aspirations for the future, whose kindred flags engirdle the world . . .

The new edition was a distillate of colonial thinking, full of eugenics and optimism. It bore, on its title page, the following:

Dedicated by permission to His Majesty George V, King of Great Britain and Ireland, and of the British Dominions beyond the seas, Emperor of India. And to William Howard Taft, President of the United States of America.

The new harmony could not have been expressed with greater felicity, or to the greater satisfaction of the British end of the axis. For the moment, Chicago's new wealth was paying the price of deference to the dearly bought cachet of royalty and tradition. But an order of precedence based on the idealistic notion of blood was not to survive the shedding of that blood on the scale that in the boom year of 1910 was only four years away.

[5]

Vox Americana

In 1890, as the era of Anglo-Saxon revivalism was dawning in the United States, a whimsical little ceremony was enacted in Central Park. A group of American Shakespeare enthusiasts gathered, nets and cages in hand, and released a carefully taxonomized collection of birds. Their aim was to introduce to the continent all of the avian species mentioned by the bard that were not already native. There are more than fifty kinds of bird cited in Shakespeare, including ostriches and peacocks, so the aim of the enthusiasts was a decidedly quixotic one. Like many such enterprises, it had a chiefly banal result. Instead of an American boscage enlivened with skylarks, nightingales, and (remembering *Julius Caesar*) "the bird of night" sitting "even at noon day, upon the market-place," what the country got was the European starling. This bird, long the bane of London cornices, preys upon vermin while being a pest in its own right. It also displaces other birds with cuckoolike callousness, and in this instance lost little time in deposing the New York State bird, *Sialia sialis*, or Eastern bluebird, from its traditional tree-cavity nesting places.

Nobody in that epoch was keener on human and cultural imports from England than Woodrow Wilson, who had since boyhood been enthralled by the images of English and Scottish chivalry and custom. But when he wrote his chapter "The Swarming of the English" in his now neglected *History of the American People*, he meant to summon a much more healthful, bucolic, and replenishing image than that of the ravenous and proliferating starling.

Hymning the cheerful, thrifty, and staunch Anglo-Saxons who had peopled the Eastern seaboard, Wilson gave full rein to the never-absent dimension of sentiment in his personality:

> It was this self-helping race of Englishmen that matched their wits against French official schemes in America. We may see the stuff they were made of in the Devonshire seamen who first attempted the permanent settlement of the new continent. For a time all that was most characteristic of the adventurous and sea-loving England was centered in Devonshire. Devonshire lies in the midst of that group of counties in the southwest of England in which Saxon ancestry did least to destroy or drive out the old Celtic population. There is accordingly a strong strain of Celtic blood among its people to this day; and the land suits with the strain. Its abrupt and broken headlands, its free heaths and ancient growths of forests, its pure and genial air, freshened on either hand by the breath of the sea, its bold and sunny coasts . . .

All this, and Drake and Raleigh, too. Wilson was not even trying to write history. But when he later fell in with Theodore Roosevelt's idea of there being real Americans and "hyphenated Americans," he could claim to have praised and documented the first cause of this conceit. Italian-Americans there might be; Irish-Americans and Jewish-Americans, too. But there is something axiomatically absurd, in the hyphenate moral universe, about the idea of an English-American. Thus the later need for a term like WASP. The yeomen and bowmen of the downs and the dales and the hamlets of England had no need of a hyphen. They were, when it came to America, original. They were first.

Wilson's entire *History* was infused with an almost automatic response to the calling of race. It was evident when he wrote about

the "Peculiar Institution" set up by the Southern Christian Anglicized gentry for their special convenience:

> Domestic slaves were treated with affection and indulgence,
> cared for by the mistress of the household. The life of the
> southern planter's wife was a life of executive labor, devoted
> chiefly to the care and training of her slaves. Social privilege
> and the proud *esprit* of their class bred in southern masters
> a sense of the obligations of station; and the spirit of the better
> men ruled the conduct of the less noble.

Not even the hideous irruption of the Civil War into these chivalric
property relations was enough to shake Wilson's attachment to the
idyll:

> No rumor of the emancipation proclamation seemed to reach
> the southern country-sides. No sign of the revolution that was
> at hand showed itself upon the surface of southern life. Gentle-
> women presided still with unquestioned authority upon the
> secluded plantations. . . . Great gangs of cheery negroes
> worked in the fields, planted and reaped and garnered and
> did their lonely mistresses' bidding in all things without rest-
> lessness, with quiet industry, with show of faithful affection
> even. . . . There was, it seemed, no wrong they fretted under
> or wished to see righted. The smiling fields . . .

The future President's attachment to the manorial style was an
obvious consequence of his Anglophilia; his affection for the plant-
ers and their arrangements being at least as much a matter of class
feeling as of racial solidarity. But he was capable of deserting the
emollient and languorous style for something far more abrasive. In
the same year as the planned release of Shakespearean birds, 1890,
there was a national census which taxonomized the *human* population of the United States. Wilson studied this census and did not
care for what he found:

Immigrants poured steadily in as before, but with an alteration of stock which students of affairs marked with uneasiness. Throughout the century men of the sturdy stocks of the north of Europe had made up the main strain of foreign blood which was every year added to the vital working force of the country, or else men of the Latin-Gallic stocks of France and Northern Italy; but now there came multitudes of men of the lowest class from the South of Italy and men of the meaner sort out of Hungary and Poland, men out of the ranks where there was neither skill nor energy nor any initiative of quick intelligence; and they came in numbers which increased from year to year, as if the countries of the south of Europe were disburdening themselves of the more sordid and hapless elements of their population.

"Disburdening" here meant the assumption of another burden by—whom? It would not be precisely correct to say "the white man," however swarthy some Calabrians or even Hungarians might prove to be. In any case, Wilson had already been extolling the virtues of the dusky tenantry on the Southern slave plantations. No, the objection was to the dilution of Anglo-Saxondom. This confusion, between America's need for labor and the revulsion of the Protestant Establishment toward certain kinds of immigrant, has taken many forms down the years. But whether it is an objection to Jews, Catholics, Chinese, Japanese, lumpen elements, or fifth columnists, it has always had some bearing on the Anglo-American "special relationship."

Just as Kipling was to vanquish Mark Twain on the matter of the Philippines, so the nascent cooperation between Britain and America for the open door to China was to reflect itself (as Duff Cooper bluntly pointed out in his encomium to Admiral Mahan) in a campaign against Chinese immigration. Wilson viewed the Chinese incursion with special distaste, again drawing the satirical wrath of Twain, who, in a speech at the Waldorf-Astoria in New York in 1900, said: "Behold America, the refuge of the oppressed from everywhere—who can pay fifty dollars' admission—anyone except a Chinaman."

As Democratic nominee in the election of 1912, Wilson found that his published attitudes on immigration were brought up against him with some bitterness. He had encountered the dilemma of many an anti-immigrant politician—that of having to conciliate newly enfranchised Americans. In the course of the election, he made a number of promises and commitments to the foreign-born, including a pledge that literacy tests would never be used to determine citizenship. In 1915, he vetoed an attempt by Congress to impose quotas on immigration by this means. But by 1915, an entirely new avenue of attack on "un-Americans" and "hyphenated Americans" was opening up.

Prompted, as we saw, by Rudyard Kipling, Theodore Roosevelt had impugned the loyalty of German-Americans. After the *Lusitania* sinking, with meetings of the jingoistic Navy League starting to draw large crowds, Wilson began to feel the need to accommodate to his former rival's propaganda. In a number of addresses he called for "preparedness," a useful code word for suggesting the enemy without and the enemy within, while yet not quite defining it. In another speech, this time to the Daughters of the American Revolution, that ideal vessel of the *Mayflower* spirit, he cheerily suggested that critics and faint-hearts be subjected to the fine old college practice of "hazing." Who knows what Princetonian memories, or nostalgia for English public school stories, prompted this presidential endorsement of bullying and baiting? The speech was even more noteworthy for its coinage of a catchphrase or slogan. The question for the "hazers" to put to the doubters, said Wilson, was: "Is it America First or is it not?" Not for the last time in his career, Wilson was handing a weapon to those who detested everything he stood for. In later years the cry of "America First" was to become the combined cry of the chauvinists and the isolationists, and was to be directed principally at the Anglophiles and their allies. It's interesting and important to remember that it was coined in England's cause, at an ultra-WASP rally.

In his annual message to Congress at Christmas the same year, Wilson developed the theme of Americanism and nativism even more bluntly. "The gravest threats against our national peace and safety have been uttered within our own borders. There are citizens of the United States, I blush to admit, *born under other flags*, who have poured the poison of disloyalty into the very arteries of our national life." All this made his claim to "neutrality" in the Great War seem pharisaic. So did the intense profiteering in the name of the British war effort by J. P. Morgan and others of the Protestant elite, who treated the Neutrality Act with disdain and added considerably to the art and science of the dummy company in supplying the materials of war.

The British Establishment not only benefited from the wave of chauvinism, but made it its business to encourage and generalize it. Sir Gilbert Parker, who headed the British propaganda effort in the United States, was imprudent enough to write an article for *Harper's* magazine in March 1918 in which he simultaneously boasted of his achievement in the manipulation of American public opinion and reinforced the ethnic undergirding of the "special relationship":

I wonder how many Americans know that all German-Americans are still Germans by law; and if they do know it, how they must resent the iniquity of the nation that makes of the law of naturalization a scrap of paper; to be torn up, like the sacred compact for the neutrality of Belgium!

Seeking to relate this to the joint project of expansionism and empire, Sir Gilbert ingeniously reminded his audiences that George III had after all used "German mercenaries" against the heroes of the thirteen colonies, and rushed on from this revision to evoke the brave days of 1898:

What was accomplished at Manila toward making America a world power was exceeded infinitely there by the splendid

action of Admiral Chichester and Britain's navy in threatening
the German naval forces, which drew the two nations together
in a spirit of comradeship.

He added that "the British Empire" had been "the faithful friend
of President Monroe, whose doctrine could never have become
valid and continuous without the British navy."

Having stressed the aspects of race and empire, Sir Gilbert
moved serenely on to the matter of class. He made large claims
for the penetration of the American upper reaches by the British:

> I need hardly say that the scope of my department was very
> extensive and its activities widely ranged. Among the esti-
> mates was a weekly report to the British Cabinet on the state
> of American opinion, and constant touch with the permanent
> correspondents of American newspapers in England. I also
> frequently arranged for important public men in England to
> act for us by interviews in American newspapers . . . Among
> other things, we supplied three hundred and sixty newspapers
> in the smaller states of the United States with an English
> newspaper, which gives a weekly review and comment of the
> affairs of the war. We established connection with the man
> in the street through cinema pictures of the Army and Navy,
> as well as through interviews, articles, pamphlets, etc.; and
> by letters in reply to individual American critics . . . We
> advised and stimulated many people to write articles; we uti-
> lized the friendly services and assistance of confidential
> friends; we had reports from important Americans constantly,
> and established association, by personal correspondence, with
> influential and eminent people of every profession in the
> United States.

The reaction to this conceited article in many quarters, particularly Midwestern ones, might have been summarized in the words
"Thanks for telling us." But it was true that American organs of

mass and elite opinion had been uniquely permeable to the British approach, combining the affectation of patriotism with the invocation of anti-immigrant feeling and distilling both into a vague but palpable veneration of empire. A special symbol of the latter was the invention, by the American journalist Lowell Thomas, of the myth of "Lawrence of Arabia." Thomas had been dispatched to the Middle Eastern theater by the Creel Committee, a super-patriotic front organization sponsored by Wilson and subsidized by the British press tycoon Lord Northcliffe. In a rather apt deployment of disdainful "Greek to their Roman" rhetoric, Lawrence himself described Thomas as "the American who made my vulgar reputation; a well-intentioned, intensely crude and pushful fellow."

The precursors of Hollywood also made their mark, as they were to do thenceforward. D. W. Griffith made a film, very much in the spirit of his adaptation of *A Romance of the White Man's Burden*, called *Hearts of the World*. This matched footage from the Western Front with fearsome scenes of Lillian Gish being flogged and otherwise ill used by bestial German soldiery. Anti-Hun feeling was further inflamed by *Yellow Dog*, a film which promoted itself by saying: "The yellow dogs of the nation are the Americans with German souls who seek to sow dissatisfaction and distrust. The picture shows how the evil may be stamped out."

The "stamping out" took the form of a crusade against political dissent, which was to climax after the war with the Palmer Raids and the Abrams trial and deportation.

Woodrow Wilson himself was forward in the thickening of this atmosphere, taking a leading part in "Liberty Loan" rallies and attacking "slackers" in the argot of Tom Brown. But those, like Sir Gilbert Parker, who watched this with satisfaction were missing a point. It might be true that hysteria would extend even to the banning of a film called *The Spirit of '76*, on the finding that its portrayal of the redcoats was "calculated to make us a little bit slack in our loyalty to Britain in this great catastrophe." And it might equally be true that the once powerful Irish and German populations had been stymied or eclipsed. But what was actually in formation was an American, not an Anglo-Saxon, nationalism.

In a memo to the British War Cabinet in late 1917, Sir Robert Cecil kept up the great tradition of his family's arrogance by writing: "If America accepts our point of view . . . it will mean the dominance of that point of view in all international affairs." He added that "though the American people are very largely foreign, both in origin and in mode of thought, their rulers are almost exclusively Anglo-Saxons, and share our political ideals." It might seem unfair to make someone even as senior as Cecil into a representative figure (when cautioned by the American ambassador to remember the Boston Tea Party, he replied with composure that he had never been to Boston, nor graced a tea party in that fair city), but he was not unrepresentative either. In his regard for the trinity of blood, ruling class, and empire he took a standard Anglo-Saxon position.

Wilson had a due regard for the disillusionment that came with peace, even as he was helping to repress and deport those who gave political voice to that disillusionment. He had been stung by accusations of being England's pliant servant, and he had the experience of Pershing's armies and the weight of American credit with which to negotiate. Welcomed after victory at a banquet in Buckingham Palace in December 1918, he behaved with pronounced understatement and later warned King George V:

> You must not speak of us who come over here as cousins, still less as brothers; we are neither. Neither must you think of us as Anglo-Saxons, for that term can no longer be rightly applied to the people of the United States. Nor must too much importance in this connection be attached to the fact that English is our common language. No, there are only two things which can establish and maintain closer relations between your country and mine: they are community of ideals and of interests.

Compare this with "The Swarming of the English." By mutation through war and overseas commitment, the old Anglo-Saxondom had in fact turned into a whitish version of "America First," with a generally less sentimental attitude toward "the old country" except when rhetoric might by occasion demand otherwise. Even Senator Albert Beveridge, who had thundered about the tie of blood before the First World War, now began to stress the unique and distinctive Americanness of the white destiny.

Wilson, as ever, tried to be on both sides of the argument. He had with some misgiving allowed the Palmer Raids to go ahead and the criminalization of "foreign anarchists" to proceed apace. In 1919 the Ku Klux Klan revived, as Baltzell points out, "no longer as a White conspiracy to keep the Negro in his place, but as a Protestant crusade against the un-Americanism of Catholics and Jews." Though Wilson would have been far too fastidious to countenance any such scurrility, he did make an explicit connection between race theory and subversion in a conversation with his physician, Dr. Cary Grayson. Grayson records that Wilson was much exercised by news of socialist upheaval in Germany:

> He said the American negro returning from abroad would be our greatest medium in conveying Bolshevism to America. For example, a friend recently related the experience of a lady friend wanting to employ a negro laundress offering to pay the usual wage in that community. The negress demanded that she be given more money than was offered for the reason that "money is as much mine as it is yours."

If matters went on in this way, said Wilson, there would soon be workers on the boards of American businesses. Not even the "great gangs of cheery negroes" could be relied upon anymore.

However, when the newly Republican Congress proposed a quota bill which would have favored immigrants from Northern Europe only, Wilson discreetly withheld his support from anything so explicit. He allowed the bill to die by failing to sign it, though he never gave any explanation of his conduct and was by that time very near to death. Some biographers have speculated that he felt bound by the promises he had made to the immigrants in the 1912 election. However that may be, the bill was reintroduced after the inauguration of Harding and passed by an almost unanimous vote. Later legislation, introduced in 1924 by Senator Reed and Representative Johnson, established "national origins quotas" that were based on 2 percent of each foreign-born group in the United States and depended upon their proportion as of the 1890 census. This negation of the Emma Lazarus principle was, writes Baltzell with emphasis, *"the last surge of active nativism in this country to be led and strongly supported by the old-stock Eastern upper class."*

Yet the ambiguities of language, and its relationship to racial "stock" and social standing, extend back as far as the early days of the revolutionary period. According to an eyewitness account by George Washington's friend the Marquis de Chastellux, there was much talk of a new official language in which the business of the newly emancipated colonies could be conducted. One active suggestion was for the use of Hebrew, and as Chastellux put it:

> The proposal was, that it should be taught in the schools and made use of in all public acts. We may imagine that this project went no farther, but we conclude from the mere suggestion that the Americans could not express in a more energetic manner their aversion to the English.

Interestingly, Charles Astor Bristed records that the Continental Congress also discussed the possibility of adopting Greek as the American language; the proposal being eventually rejected on the ground that "it would be more convenient for us to keep the language as it is, and make the English speak Greek." This must be the earliest example of America trying to be Greece to the British Rome, and serves as a good illustration of what Sir Stephen Spender in another context has called "Love-Hate Relations." A committee of the Continental Congress, as early as 1778, recommended that "the language of the United States" be employed in all replies or answers to the French minister. Though it remained the national language, in other words, English was rebaptized as American wherever possible and became a proper subject for cultural nationalist debate. As late as 1795, the House of Representatives narrowly defeated a motion that all its documents and proceedings be printed also in German. The tie vote was cast by the Speaker, one Friedrich Muhlenberg.

It was in this context that Noah Webster evolved his plan for a distinct grammar of American English. He conceived this idea in 1783, feeling it essential to nationhood that the tongue of the rejected "mother country" be superseded. In one of his favorite pamphlets it was asserted that "America is an independent empire, and ought to assume a national character." Appealing to the New York legislature to allow him copyright for his *American Spelling and Grammar*, he described the book patriotically as "designed particularly for the youth in the American Empire."

Most of these efforts to dilute or qualify the place of English were unsuccessful, and as the thirteen colonies began to expand across the entire North American continent, it was English they took with them across the mountains. Of course, there were habits of speech and developments of slang and pronunciation which made the American accent or accents identifiable anywhere in the world, but these were variations on an English theme. Nineteenth-century travelers and visitors from Britain never tired of making fun of these barbarisms. Mrs. Frances Trollope and Charles Dickens both observed what can be still be observed today—the tendency of Americans to speak in a more pompous and convoluted fashion, especially on official or decorous occasions, than their reputation for informality or ease would warrant. (G. K. Chesterton would later write a poem mocking the American fondness for abbreviation and economy—the substitution of "elevator" for "lift," say, or "apartment" for "flat." We could now add "transportation" for "transport.") Captain Marryat, who came to the United States with the announced purpose of "doing serious injury to the cause of democracy," was also enabled to rouse many an easy laugh among his more polished and superior readers across the foam.

All the subsequent revivals of the language question have been connected either to political Anglophobia, to immigration, to American "expansionism," to the battle for "Anglo-Saxondom," or to some combination of these. It is significant that Theodore Roosevelt, whose attachment to alliance with Britain was chiefly a function of his expansionist ideology, tried to carry on Webster's imperial work by issuing an executive order in 1906. The order concerned "Simplified Spelling" and mandated the Government Printing Office to employ three hundred new usages such as, most famously, the word "thru." For many years, the defense of Simplified Spelling was the emblem of the anti-British patriots in American society. The staunchest defender and practitioner of the scheme was the bristling Colonel Robert McCormick, whose *Chicago Tribune* was for decades the beating heart of Anglophobia. It was also a loud and persistent voice for "anti-imperialist" American imperialism; isolationist in point of Europe and raucously interventionist in point of the Pacific and the Caribbean. It later became the mouthpiece of the "neutral" America First campaign, and was the bane of the suave young men who were sent to staff the British propaganda and information departments. Its general ethos could be summarized in the celebrated Chicago mayor "Big Bill" Thompson, who swore to punch King George V "in the snoot" if he ever dared set foot in that democratic bailiwick. Not even the stoutest speechifier at the Watertoast dinner in *Martin Chuzzlewit* (" 'Bring forth that lion!' said the young Columbian. 'Alone, I dare him! I taunt that lion' ") could match him. The *Tribune* did not abandon the Simplified Spelling dogma until 1955, long after it had been ridiculed and neglected in general.

In 1923, another McCormick, Representative Washington Jay McCormick of Montana, introduced a bill into the House which would have made "the American Language" the official language of the United States. In *The Nation* he offered a glimpse of the

blend of literary and national emotions which went to make up the
energy of the language question:

> It was only when Cooper, Irving, Mark Twain, Whitman and
> O. Henry dropped the Order of the Garter and began to write
> American that their wings of immortality sprouted. Had Noah
> Webster, instead of styling his monumental work the Amer-
> ican Dictionary of the English Language, written a Dictionary
> of the American Language, he would have become a founder
> instead of a compiler. Let our writers drop their top-coats,
> spats and swagger-sticks, and assume occasionally their buck-
> skin, moccasins and tomahawks.

Twain would have derived hilarious relish from that last sentence,
as would H. L. Mencken. But the preceding ones make very plain
the resentment of England *for*, and moreover the subliminal identification of England *with*, the images and stereotypes of class and
class superiority. The notion of the American as rough-hewn and
honest, and of the Englishman as a drawling, affected, effete snob,
is an essential part of Anglo-American love-hate relations, and has
not been quite extinguished even today.

McCormick's bill failed to catch any legislative tide, but in the
same year an Illinois legislator named Frank Ryan managed to have
a very similar one enacted by the state legislature. In its preamble,
which might have been drafted by the *Chicago Tribune*, there was
an emphasis not just upon class but upon race:

> *Whereas*, since the creation of the American Republic there
> have been certain Tory elements in our country who have
> never become reconciled to our republican institutions and
> have ever clung to the tradition of King and Empire; and
> *Whereas*, the assumed dominance of this Tory element—in
> the social, business and political life of America—tends to
> force the other racial units, in self-defense, to organize on
> racial lines . . .

There followed a mandate for American-as-she-is-spoke. These initiatives, which of course were sponsored by men who had never echoed Twain for his anti-imperialism even if they praised him for his authentic Americanism, also occurred at a time when mass immigration was not a fighting matter, and when the need for "Anglo-Saxon" or "white" solidarity was to that extent correspondingly less. They also occurred during a period of reaction against foreign entanglement, when "isolationism" was chiefly directed at the sort of British influence bragged about by Sir Gilbert Parker. Two widely separated counterexamples may help to illustrate the ironies of this aspect of the relationship.

In the same year, 1890, as those Shakespearean starlings took wing over Central Park, William Dean Howells's character Basil March, in the novel *A Hazard of New Fortunes*, found that the East Side of New York was not at all, or rather no longer, to his taste. He noticed:

> What must strike every observer returning to the city after a prolonged absence: the numerical subordination of the dominant race . . . The small eyes, the high cheeks, the broad noses, the puff lips, the bare cue-filletted skulls of Russians, Poles, Czechs, Chinese, the furtive glitter of Italians, the blond dullness of Germans, the cold quiet of Scandinavians.

This was fairly comprehensive, and also fairly typical of its kind and time. Only a few years later, in *The American Scene*, Henry James registered the disgust of "a sensitive citizen" on viewing the teeming sheds at Ellis Island and feeling the indignity of being thus compelled "to share the sanctity of his *American* consciousness, the intimacy of his *American* patriotism, with the inconceivable alien" (italics mine). On the Lower East Side he detected "the hard glitter of Israel." More than this, he winced at the accents and vernaculars employed, and described the Yiddish cafés as "the torture rooms of the living idiom." This had already become his major preoccupation when he contemplated the arrival of new migrants. An America which had spent much of the nineteenth century trying to originate and copyright an individually *American* style in speech and writing now found itself defending the purity of *English* and the allied concept of manners and mores that English implied. Two years before he published *The American Scene*, James had given a graduation address to the young ladies of Bryn Mawr College. Entitled "The Question of Our Speech," it argued for both "a coherent culture" and "a tone standard." That the two ideas were inseparable in James's mind, and inextricable from other and related considerations, is not to be doubted:

> The *vox Americana* is for the spectator one of the stumbling blocks of our continent. It has been, among the organs of the schooled and newspapered races, perceptibly the most abandoned to its fate.

It's noticeable that James alludes to "races" rather than classes in this connection. Not that the idea of class distinction is altogether absent from the discourse:

> To the American common school, to the American newspaper, and to the American Dutchman and Dago, as the voice of the people describes them, we have simply handed over our property—not exactly bound hand and foot, I admit, like Andromeda awaiting her Perseus, but at least distracted, dishevelled, despoiled, diverted of that beautiful and becoming drapery of native atmosphere and circumstances which had, from far back, made, on its behalf, for practical protection, for a due tenderness of interest.

Who ever said that James chewed more than he bit off? In a few sentences, he has derogated the new immigrants, displaced to the shoulders of "the people" the vulgarisms with which he slyly describes them, and cloaked both of these two subconscious appeals in the apparel of chivalry, while upholding the purity of the tongue!

Within a few years, all of this was to strike James as having been in the nature of a rehearsal. Not only did he feel English, in reaction to the mongrelization and vulgarization of America, but he actually *was* English. In a little-known essay written just after the onset of the Great War, and published by the Central Committee for National Patriotic Organisations in London, he addressed himself to "The Question of the Mind." He had had to confront, so he wrote,

> the fact that the social characteristics, the elements of race and history, the native and acquired values, the whole "psychological" mystery marking the people of Great Britain, were so abruptly thrust into the critical smelting-pot for a citizen of another country, a country up to the present speaking formally neutral, who had spent long years of his life on English soil and in English air.

In prose which must have baffled the hearty patriots who were nonetheless always gratified to publish a committed neutral, James worked himself round to the idea of a British "genius"; a will and intelligence and spirit that existed almost unknown to its possessors—"the genius that had somehow kept acting and impressing just in proportion as so few pains were taken about it." The answer lay, thought James, in something he termed the British *incorrigibility*:

> To grasp even in so absurdly delayed a manner the perception that *there* was one's golden key made the whole certitude come on with a rush. It was incredible and impossible that a people should be so incorrigible unless they were very strong—no people without a great margin could for any period at all afford to be; and with that *constatation* everything was clear. It didn't matter if they were strong because good-natured, or good-natured because strong: the point was to that extraordinary tune in what they could afford.

To an astonishing degree, this analysis ministered to the English self-image, to the long-cherished idea of a people polite and slow to anger, yet formidable when roused; a people who did not start wars but who could finish them; a people who lost every battle but the last. Kipling (of whom James had once said: "almost nothing civilized save steam and patriotism . . . and *such* an uninteresting mind") strove more crudely to touch the same nerve in his gruesome poem "When the English Began to Hate," published at about the same time:

> It was not part of their blood
> It came to them very late
> With long arrears to make good
> When the English began to hate.

He even made the extraordinary claim:

> It was not preached to the crowd
> It was not taught by the state
> No man spoke it aloud
> When the English began to hate.

Which would have come as a surprise to the Central Committee for National Patriotic Organisations, among others, who joined with the government and the Church of England and Rudyard Kipling in spreading every kind of hatred of things and people German. Still, James was in love with a "genius" not a policy. He evidently felt the incompleteness of his position, and decided to become a subject of His Majesty. On the day on which he did so, after formally renouncing his American passport and incurring much bitter criticism from "back home," James proudly announced: "*Civis Britannicus Sum.*" Here was a Latin tribute, and a Roman gesture.

The second example concerns Winston Churchill (who had met James in Kent in early 1915 and rather snubbed him, as well as offended him by persistent use of slang). Almost thirty years later, Churchill was engaged in the most desperate struggle of his life, this time to convince the United States to rescue not just the British Empire but Britain herself. He failed in the first and succeeded in the second and was prepared to pay any price to secure American support and sympathy. On more than one occasion, he proposed joint citizenship between Britain and the United States, a common currency, a common trading area, and a common use by American and British forces of British bases and facilities worldwide. None of this was surprising for a man in his political extremity. What was surprising was his willingness to surrender the English language itself in order to cement the new concordat.

In the 1920s, a Cambridge academic named C. K. Ogden had evolved the idea of "Basic English." This reduced the language to 850 necessary words, with some allowance made for the import of neologisms and new coinages in specialized areas such as science and technology. (It is almost certain from internal evidence that George Orwell derived his bleak and arid invention of "Newspeak" from this source.) One might have thought that Churchill would be revolted to the core by such a proposition, but he saw it as a means of further dissolving the British and American peoples into one another. He first mentioned it at a summit meeting with Roosevelt in Quebec in August 1943. In April 1944, having heard nothing from Washington, he returned to the theme, writing to Roosevelt:

> My conviction is that Basic English will then prove to be a great boon to mankind in the future and a powerful support to the influence of the Anglo-Saxon people in world affairs.

Having apparently received the impression from their Quebec meeting that Roosevelt was taken by the idea, Churchill had appointed no less a person than Leo Amery to chair a Cabinet committee on Basic. Amery, one of the most stout imperialists in the British government, was then Secretary of State for Burma. He had been a close friend and correspondent of Rudyard Kipling, and had in 1940 summoned the magnificent words of Oliver Cromwell dismissing the Long Parliament in order to urge the resignation of the discredited Chamberlain front bench. It is hard to think of a man less likely to acquiesce in the reduction of English to 850 words. Roosevelt seems to have been less enthused by the scheme than either Churchill or Amery. He did not reply for several weeks, and was rather flippant when he did so, even teasing the great man on his strongest point and strongest subject:

> Incidentally, I wonder what the course of history would have been if in May 1940 you had been able to offer the British people only "blood, work, eye water and face water," which I understand is the best that Basic English can do with five famous words.

Meanwhile, he mandated Cordell Hull to look into the question, to sound out some experts and to talk to Congress. At least in the published letters, nothing more is to be found on the matter. Hull, as Secretary of State, was known as the leading exponent of Woodrow Wilson's style of pious internationalism. He appears to have let the project expire in committee, since his few notes on it express little more than distaste.

It is mistaken to imagine that these controversies about the proper relation of language to ethnicity belong only to the past. As late as the election campaign of 1988, there was a noticeable recrudescence of themes that had been familiar in Woodrow Wilson's time. The racial and religious composition of the United States is again a very crucial and strongly felt issue, with attitudes toward it probably running far deeper than the political class cares to admit. Not only did the Republican victory in that election make skillful use of what might be called *Mayflower* imagery in the presentation of George Bush and his family, but the opinion makers found themselves surprised by the success of the most blatant elements in that appeal. Governor Michael Dukakis's evocation of the Emma

Lazarus myth and the immigrant version of the American dream was a failure to an extent that astonished his advisers. Not all of this could be attributed to the subliminal influence of black-white hostility which also surfaced in the campaign under the more restrained and tasteful (and suggestive) rubric of "crime and the underclass." Television advertisements featuring a notorious black criminal named Willie Horton also showed Michael Dukakis without a shave and looking distinctly swarthy.

Commentators who declared themselves either surprised or depressed by the reserve strength of the nativist instinct in 1988 could with profit have paid more attention to a proposition that succeeded in getting on the ballot in seventeen states. With variations in wording and provision, all these propositions called for English to be the official language, and all of them passed. This was a response to the newest and perhaps the most important wave of recent immigration, legal and illegal, which has brought millions of Asian and Hispanic settlers to the cities of the United States.

Certain features of this immigration made it different in kind and degree from its predecessors. Most of the new arrivals were from states and cultures to which they still possessed a loyalty—very unlike the Ukrainian Jew or even the Irishman of the 1890s. Most were able to retain touch with their countries of origin, and were not abandoning all connection with a heartless and persecuting homeland. None were white. None were Protestant.

These considerations had not escaped the framers of the "English only" proposition, or the national lobby that was organized to promulgate it. Entitled innocuously but interestingly "U.S. English," this establishment grouping in Washington had been founded by the former California senator S. I. Hayakawa and a Michigan ophthalmologist named John Tanton. Its advisory board reflected the genteel aspect of the English question, being adorned by such reassuring figures as Walter Cronkite and Alistair Cooke, Saul Bellow and Bruno Bettelheim, Norman Podhoretz as an intellectual makeweight, and such lesser functionaries of the government of the tongue as Arnold Schwarzenegger and Walter Annenberg.

Ostensibly, the U.S. English lobby sought to make English, the existing lingua franca of business, tourism, entertainment, and air traffic control, into the national language. It appeared to offer all newcomers the chance to learn it. However, it transpired to have another purpose in mind.

It had been noticeable that the Washington offices of U.S. English were the same as those for FAIR, the Federation for American Immigration Reform, which campaigned for very much tighter borders. But only upon an investigation by James Crawford, author of a study of bilingual education, did some other, more traditional connections and filiations become evident.

U.S. English, it emerged, was a project of "U.S. Inc.," a tax-exempt body which underwrote a number of other groups, such as the Center for Immigration Studies, Americans for Border Control, and Californians for Population Stabilization. There was no mistaking the timbre of this joint output, which had little to do with the teaching of "the Queen's English" except as this bore upon the connection between that English and certain inherited conceptions of race and tribal security. Dr. John Tanton, the originating author and patron of this cluster of groups and initiatives, was himself in no doubt that "the question of bilingualism grows out of U.S. immigration policy."

So much might have seemed to be obvious, at least until Dr. Tanton wrote a paper which, phrased in the poor and affected English which is often found among the language's more ostentatious upholders, created a crisis for his hitherto blue-chip WASP and Jewish campaign. As he coarsely put it:

> "*Gobernar es poblar*" translates as "to govern is to populate."
> In this society, will the present majority peaceably hand over
> its political power to a group that is simply more fertile? Can
> *homo contraceptivus* compete with *homo progenitiva* if bor-
> ders aren't controlled?

Having rather clumsily Latinized or Romanized his argument, Tanton moved to a more demotic style. He warned sternly of such alarming cultural imports as "the tradition of the *mordida* (bribe), the lack of involvement in public affairs," and Roman Catholicism with its tendency to "pitch out the separation of church and state." He continued to skirt around these aspects of the problem—the most conspicuous opponents of church-state separation in the 1980s having been fundamentalist Protestants—making an excursion through allegedly low "educability" before returning with relish to his main theme, which was, as ever, sex and fertility:

> Perhaps this is the first instance in which those with their pants up are going to get caught by those with their pants down. As whites see their power and control over their lives declining, will they simply go quietly into the night. Or will there be an explosion?

This piece of inadvertence—the shift to "white" as the key word speaks volumes in the extract above, as well as showing the secondary significance of ideas like "culture" and "language"—led to the resignation of many of the U.S. English board members, among them Walter Cronkite and the neoconservative Hispanic Linda Chavez. It also led to closer scrutiny of the network of which Dr. Tanton was the convenor. The chairman of the Florida English campaign, for example, had advocated the elimination of emergency telephone services in Spanish in order to supply what he called "an incentive" to the learning of the tongue of Shakespeare and Dickens. His Dade County equivalent had warned that "the United States is not a mongrel nation." Rusty Butler, an aide to Senator Steven Symms of Idaho, had forwarded the senator's call for an English-language amendment to the Constitution by saying that "the language issue could feed and guide terrorism in the U.S." Finally, it was discovered that among the donors to Dr. Tanton's network was the Pioneer Fund, established in the unpropitious year of 1937 to proselytize for what it then called "applied genetics in present-day Germany."

All of these rather dank connections had something inevitable about them, redolent of the old paranoid connection between immigration and subversion as well as between immigration and racial/religious purity. More interesting was the group for which Dr. Tanton had prepared his revealing paper. It was a private organization calling itself WITAN. The title, which mystified many reporters, is taken from the dim past of Anglo-Saxondom, when the Witenagemot, or conclave of wise men, would meet under the oak tree to consider the good of the folk. It was instructive to learn that, at the root of an apparently open but complex national argument about language and identity, there lay the imagined counsels of an obscure post-Roman tribal synod, attempting to impose Anglo-Saxon attitudes upon the most variegated and pluralist society in history.

But, like the migration of Shakespearean birds, Anglo-Saxon attitudes are able in the United States, in some sense, to cut with the grain. The multiple influence of history, literature, language, and kinship is very strong, and has in the past and the present run deeper than ad hoc British attempts to manipulate it for political purposes.

These opposed and separated instances help form the parentheses within which, in this century, the British and the Americans have existed in one another's imaginations. At one pole, the WASP identity can only confirm and reassure itself by an almost excessive reliance on England and things English. At the other, the British elite makes an instinctive but shrewd determination that its own survival necessitates a metamorphosis of the "Anglo-Saxon" into the "Anglo-American," with the American element grudgingly admitted to predominate. In between came the eclipse of British power by the United States, the consequent decline of Anglophobia, and the instatement of Anglophilia as a matter of fashion rather than of class or political affiliation. The residue of Anglo-Saxondom lives on in the debate over immigration, now rekindled for a new generation. But in the numerous and popular newspaper columns which presume to advise Americans on matters of pronunciation, etymology, and lexicography, it is the *Oxford English Dictionary* that is the final court of appeal. Even at this great remove from the original "Swarming of the English," the subtle and latent connections between race, social standing, sophistication, education, and even religion remain traceable. Though they are often represented innocuously as something merely "cultural," these same latent connections are an endowment from a prolonged engagement with empire, war, and nationalism.

[6]

From Love to Hate and Back Again

Bombastic though he was, Sir Gilbert Parker had been right to say that the Monroe Doctrine, that first stirring of an American imperium, would have been unthinkable without the British fleet. But of course his tribute was a consciously one-sided one. While they could, the British fought tenaciously against the expansion of the United States across North America. But they also had an interest in limiting the penetration of other European imperial powers when it came to South America. This is, in effect, the paradox expressed by Canning when he boasted of having "called the New World into existence in order to redress the failure of the Old." Canning may have phrased this in such a way as to flatter the Americans, but he had another agenda in mind. True, he favored the recognition of new self-governing Republics in formerly Spanish America, if only because, as he put it, British investment interests in Colombia and Mexico were so considerable as to exceed "mere commercial speculations." Still, he showed another kind of calculation in a document that was unknown until H. W. V. Temperley uncovered it in the British Museum in the early part of this century:

The other and perhaps still more powerful motive is my apprehension of the ambition and ascendancy of the U.S.A. It is obviously the policy of that Government to connect itself with all the powers of America in a general Transatlantic League, of which it would have the sole discretion. I need only say how inconvenient such an ascendancy may be in time of peace and how formidable in case of war.

Just as Canning was a hypocrite when it came to overseas possessions and rivals for them, so was President Monroe's Secretary of State, the celebrated John Quincy Adams. He also tried to fight on two fronts, consolidating the American state as a continental power and excluding foreign intervention from its periphery. In other words, both London and Washington (not for the first time) thought they were being clever at the expense of the other. Richard van Alstyne puts it neatly in his history of the Monroe Doctrine moment:

> Adams made no headway against Britain in his notions of preemptive right over North America. And it is one of the great ironies of history that, while he was trying to aggrandise the United States in the Northwest at her (Britain's) expense, he was gambling on her protection against the intervention of the continental powers in Latin America.

This odd combination of rivalry and alliance, collusion and suspicion, was to be the pattern of Anglo-American relations for many years—until the entente of 1898 in fact—and in some reminiscent forms even after that. Take the matter of Cuba. Canning was convinced that Adams and Monroe coveted the island. He also thought that the French had designs on it. The French suspected that the British wanted Cuba for themselves. Adams felt that if the United States did not preponderate in Cuba, it would fall into the clutches of Britain or France. As is usually the case when empires compete, each side was amply justified in its suspicions. Adams actually wanted Cuba to become a state of the Union. We know from the memoirs of Chateaubriand, then French Foreign Minister, that France was also casting languorous glances in that direction.

Viewed in this perspective, the Monroe Doctrine was really an early compromise with European imperialism rather than a repudiation of it. Both sides thought they had been cleverer: Adams got Monroe to drop a naïve amendment stating that the United States had "no intention of acquiring any portion of the Spanish possessions for ourselves," while Canning wrote to a colleague just one year after the Doctrine's promulgation to say: "The deed is done, the nail is driven, Spanish America is free; and if we do not mismanage our affairs sadly, *she is English.*"

In point of fact, the British did mismanage their affairs very sadly. Hoping to keep the long-sought route to China for themselves, they struggled long and hard to deny the Pacific Northwest to the nascent United States. Canning wrote to Lord Liverpool in 1826 concerning the possibility of a concession in this area:

> Think what a task it will be to justify this transaction to Parliament, if upon this transaction we rest our justification for abandoning the whole NW Coast of America to the Yankees. *I feel the shame of such a statement burning on my face by anticipation.*

The Yankees shall not have America! Even Temperley, Canning's great chronicler and admirer, italicized that last sentence.

Whenever they could afford to try, the British opposed the consolidation of the United States as a continental power. And whenever they could not inhibit the extension of American power into Mexico, the isthmus, and beyond, they tried to take a share in it. This policy was reflected in American tactics and attitudes. Victor Kiernan puts it deftly when he says, of the period before the Civil War: "In short, while America picked up imperial manners from Britain beyond the seas, beyond the mountains it was hurried into imitation of them."

The name of Adams recurs in this narrative because it was John

Quincy Adams who operated the balance between rivalry and collusion in Anglo-American relations, first as Secretary of State and then as President, and because it was his son, Charles Francis Adams, who became Lincoln's envoy to Britain during the Civil War. It is from Charles's son, Henry, that we have a seminal account not just of Anglo-American relations but of the swing of the pendulum between Anglophilia and Anglophobia and of the alterations in imperial context which dictated the rhythm of this love-hate relationship.

Young Henry had been most impressed by England on his very first visit in 1858. Like Kipling starting in California and working eastward, Adams made his landfall in Liverpool and traveled by degrees to the capital:

> Then came the journey up to London through Birmingham and the Black District, another lesson, which needed much more to be rightly felt. The plunge into darkness lurid with flames; the sense of unknown horror in this weird gloom which then existed nowhere else, and never had existed before, except in volcanic craters; the violent contrast between this dense, smoky, impenetrable darkness, and the soft green charm that one glided into as one emerged—the revelation of an unknown society of the pit—made a boy uncomfortable, though he had no idea that Karl Marx was standing there waiting for him, and that sooner or later the process of education would have to deal with Karl Marx much more than with Professor Bowen of Harvard College or his Satanic free-trade majesty John Stuart Mill.

In later years, American visitors to England did not find that their first impression was of the country's huge economic and industrial strength. But as early as 1858, that was still a commanding fact to an American. Adams reacted as a Greek islander might have done on first seeing Rome. "The most insolent structures in the world," said Henry Adams, "were the Royal Exchange and the Bank of England."

The insolence showed itself in innumerable ways, one of which was the encouragement of Southern expansionism in the United States. As the ally and patron of the cotton industry, and the former patron of the slave trade, Great Britain's Establishment had a hundred and one ties of affection and emotion with the Southerners, and an equal and opposite repulsion for the tradesmen and financiers of the North. The very idea of the Southern gentleman— along the lines of caricature that Woodrow Wilson later etched— was an *English* simulacrum of the landed gentry and the colonial planter combined.

Something of this sense—of superiority assumed by the British and inferiority felt by the Americans—seemed to communicate itself with renewed force to Adams when he returned to London in 1861, one month after the outbreak of the "War Between the States." His task was to act as his father's private secretary, and as he sadly described the situation in the third person: "In the mission attached to Mr. Adams in 1861, the only rag of legitimacy or order was the private secretary, whose stature was not sufficient to impose awe on the Court and Parliament of Great Britain." He was not to be disappointed by this premonition. The "Court and Parliament of Great Britain" still looked upon the United States as an upstart nation, and derived no little *Schadenfreude* from the contemplation of America's difficulties:

For a hundred years the chief effort of his family had aimed at bringing the Government of England into intelligent co-operation with the aims and interests of America. His father was about to make a new effort, and this time the chance of success was promising. The slave States had been the chief apparent obstacle to good understanding. As for the private secretary himself, he was, like all Bostonians, instinctively English. He could not conceive the idea of a hostile England.

He was soon to do so. On May 13, 1861, the British government "recognized the belligerency of the Confederacy," which is to say, it adopted a position of feigned neutrality. According to Gladstone, this meant that Lord Palmerston "desired the severance [of the Confederacy] as a diminution of a dangerous power, but prudently held his tongue." Lord John Russell, at the Foreign Office, received envoys from the rebel states as if they had already established their title. In this, perhaps, there was an ironic echo of his own comment two years earlier, when he had angrily rebuked the American General Harney for occupying the Pacific coastal island of San Juan. "It is of the nature of the U.S. citizens," Lord John had sneered, "to push themselves where they have no right to go, and it is of the nature of the U.S. government not to venture to disavow acts they cannot have the face to approve." On that occasion, the dispute had been composed in traditional manner by sending the Prince of Wales to the White House in order to assuage President Buchanan's lust for royal notice. But the Civil War allowed no such mollifying maneuver, and Abraham Lincoln was in any case rather indifferent to monarchy, and it was the British who consistently "failed to disavow acts" they did not "have the face to approve."

The relevant pages of *The Education* show Adams half appalled and half admiring at repeated demonstrations of British hypocrisy and double and treble dealing. When two Confederate agents, Mason and Slidell, were taken off the British mail boat *Trent* by the Northern warship *San Jacinto*, the British coolly threatened to make this a *casus belli*, and sent reinforcements to Canada while openly discussing an invasion through Maine. This was to react rather fiercely, perhaps, to the Union doing what Nelson had once done. At any rate, it forced Lincoln to back down and set up a chorus of anti-Union growls in the British Tory press. Henry Adams himself was savagely denounced by Delane in *The Times*, and life in the clubs and drawing rooms of London was made barely supportable to him.

Freud once wrote about "the narcissism of small differences," pointing out how the bitterest quarrels often arise between people and groups with strongly marked external similarities, and that it is these similarities that excite the quarrel. Something like this happens quite frequently in Anglo-American relations, and it certainly seems to have exerted itself both on the British upper class and on Henry Adams. From instinctive Boston Englishman at one moment, he moved to a position where he observed:

> Familiar as the whole tribe of Adamses had been for three generations with the impenetrable stupidity of the British mind, and weary of the long struggle to teach it its own interests, the fourth generation still could not quite persuade itself that this new British stupidity was natural.

There, if ever, is an Old World sentiment masquerading as a New World one—the permanent ambivalence which later found expression in Adams's letters and in the writings of Henry James. Chivvied in Mayfair, Adams discovered (temporarily) honest virtues in men like Richard Cobden and John Bright and the Yorkshireman William E. Forster, whose sturdy, unaffected, rough-hewn nature became a source of consolation. "Anarchists" though they were regarded by what Adams terms "the so-called Established orders," they were a great prop and stay to the American legation.

While the future Admiral Mahan was on blockade duty off the coast of the Confederacy, Laird's yard at Liverpool was constructing vessels for the rebel side to employ against him. The best-known of these, the *Alabama*, completed around the time of the *Trent* incident, was to send over fifty Union ships to the bottom while the pretense of neutrality went on. "Lord Russell's replies to Mr. Adams's notes were discourteous in their indifference, and, to an irritable young private secretary of twenty-four, were insolent in their disregard of truth." "Insolent"—like the Royal Exchange and the Bank of England. Adams had further to endure, after the second battle of Bull Run, hearing one Cabinet minister gaily remark to another at a Palace reception: "So the Federals have got another hiding!" He had to put up with Thackeray's maudlin diatribe in favor of chivalry and Southern womanhood, delivered in lachry-mose tones at a reception at Sir Henry Holland's, and the anti-Lincoln oaths of his former idol Carlyle. All this, and the daily gloatings of *The Times* as the Union cause bled and suffered. Small wonder that he "wanted nothing so much as to wipe England off the Earth. Never could any good come from that besotted race!"

As Lincoln and Seward began to establish a kind of mastery over the situation, with the Emancipation Proclamation and with su-perior generalship, the British policy declined in proportion. Which is to say that it moved from the sham of neutrality to active partisanship for the Confederacy. The decision was signaled by crocodile tears for the mounting casualty lists on both sides and pious talk about international intervention to bring about a "set-tlement." On September 17, 1862, Russell wrote to Palmerston:

> Whether the Federal army is destroyed or not, it is clear that it is driven back to Washington and has made no progress as such in subduing the insurgent States. Such being the case, I agree with you that the time is come for offering mediation to the United States Government with a view to the recog-nition of the independence of the Confederates. I agree fur-ther that in case of failure, we ought ourselves to recognise the Southern States as an independent State.

Behind the formalities of this initiative there lurked rather more than diplomatic judgment, as a later paragraph made clear:

> We ought to make ourselves safe in Canada, not by sending more troops there, but by concentrating those we have in a few defensible posts before the winter sets in.

The fact that Palmerston was uncharacteristically cautious in his reply did little to dull the rage of Adams, who was to be even more shocked, in his chapter sarcastically entitled "Political Morality," by the behavior of Mr. Gladstone. This paragon of the English

virtues made a speech in Newcastle, prompted by his own professed concern for "the risk of violent impatience in the cotton-
towns of Lancashire," in which he made a show of yielding to the
utilitarian principle of "facts":

> We may have our own opinions about slavery; we may be for
> or against the South; but there is no doubt that Jefferson Davis
> and other leaders of the South have made an army; they are
> making, it appears, a navy; and they have made, what is more
> than either, they have made a nation.

Robert E. Lee had incontestably made an army, but the Confederate navy was made in England, and well Mr. Gladstone knew
it. The future "Grand Old Man" even gave his imprimatur to a
backstairs deal with Napoleon III, whereby the patron of Maxi-
milian made "a proposition which had no sense except as a bribe
for Palmerston to replace America, from pole to pole, in her old
dependence on Europe, and to replace England in her old sovereignty of the seas, if Palmerston would support France in
Mexico." That, allowing for Adams's archaic use of "replace" to
mean "restore" or "return," was putting it neatly. In 1896, Gladstone himself was to publish an apology for his partiality, regretting
"such an utterance from a Cabinet Minister of a power allied in
blood and language." Of course, by those definitions both South
and North had been so allied, but by 1896 that could be forgotten
and, as we have seen, by 1896 the ties of "blood and language"
were coming back into the height of fashion.

The *Schadenfreude* was soon to be an American quality. As Grant
and Sherman brought the superior economic and military sinews
of the North into play (as Adams's nemesis Karl Marx had foreseen
they would), the British began to make themselves more agreeable.
Vicksburg and Gettysburg became great names, and Adams recorded exultingly: "During the July days, Londoners were stupid
with unbelief. They were learning from the Yankees how to fight."
This lesson was also driven home in diplomacy. Lord John Russell

was told in terms by Adams Sr. that if the two warships being completed for the Confederates in Liverpool were allowed to follow the *Alabama*, there would be war. Russell, after an infinity of hemming and hawing, told the Admiralty: "It is of the utmost importance and urgency that the ironclads building at Birkenhead should not go to America to break the blockade."

With this letter, Britain in effect gave up trying to forestall, weaken, or abort the consolidation of "America" as a continental union. Adams was free to resume at least one of his pursuits, which was a love affair with the English and with the idea of Anglo-American rapprochement—the roles of mentor and student, senior and junior partner, being reversed.

Trite though it may be to describe Adams's emotions about England as symptomatic of a love-hate relationship, that is what they were. His increasing familiarity with the country, often expressed in terms of contempt, also contained a rather languidly expressed commitment to its well-being. On his first sight of the country in 1858, he was awed by Eaton Hall

> as Thackeray or Dickens would have felt in the presence of a Duke. The very name of Grosvenor struck a note of grandeur. The long suite of lofty, gilded rooms with their gilded furniture; the portraits; the terraces; the gardens; the landscape— the sense of superiority in the England of the fifties, actually set the rich nobleman apart, above Americans and shop-keepers.

Leaving England's shores at the end of the American Civil War, he found that it was only London, with its homes and hansom cabs, that he missed.

> He felt no sensation whatever in the atmosphere of the British peerage, but mainly an habitual dislike to most of the people who frequented their country houses; he had become English to the point of sharing their petty social divisions, their dislikes

and prejudices against each other; he took England no longer with the awe of American youth, but with the habit of an old and rather worn suit of clothes.

Some of this may have been written for effect—after all, he had shown some earlier acquaintance with English manners by the mere fact of being "a Bostonian." And it seems clear that on his return to America, he used English reserve and superiority as a sort of protective carapace against the surrounding vulgarity. Post-Lincoln America was a disappointment to Adams; a decided disappointment with its corruption, vulgarity, and place seeking. The word "gilded," used by Adams to express the summit of English refinement, became appropriated by Mark Twain to describe the gross grandeur of the emerging American century. In Washington, Adams surrounded himself with an English-style set, seeking refuge from the brittle New World in the affectations of the Old (and thus making his large individual contribution to a pose which can still be observed among Americans of a certain type).

After his wife's suicide in particular, Adams's home took on the appearance of an Englishman's bachelor retreat inhabited by an avuncular ogre. He kept up a circle of polished, cynical, worldly, snobbish, well-connected friends. He sponsored a series of "nieces-in-wish," most of whom were charming and accomplished in their way and most of whom married English lords in deference to the new imperatives of the day. Martha Cameron, daughter of neighbors on Lafayette Square, wed the Hon. Ronald Lindsay, younger son of the Earl of Crawford and Balcarres. Then there were the "three Marys" who adorned his famous noonday breakfast receptions. Mary Leiter became Lady Curzon, Mary Endicott married Joseph Chamberlain, and Mary Grant became Mrs. William Oswald Charlton, thus furnishing Adams with every kind of British entrée. Of his grown-up companions, the preferred trio were John Hay, an Anglicized American, Henry Cabot Lodge, virtually an Americanized Englishman, and Cecil Spring-Rice, an English diplomat who formed extensive attachments in America. These three men were a considerable reinforcement to Theodore Roosevelt, who was a frequent guest at the house and who reciprocated with invitations to the Executive Mansion across the way. He, too, shared the foible of thinking in threes and called Hay, Lodge, and Adams "the Three Musketeers of Culture."

Less amenable to frivolity, and less keen on reclusive pursuits, was Henry's brother Brooks Adams. He considered himself to be of the elect rather than of the elite and espoused a sternly determinist worldview. Brooks was very fond of terms like "decadence" and had a strict cyclical view of the rise and fall of great powers. One of his fixed determinations was that England was in eclipse, and that by exploiting this fact the United States could achieve destiny. Where Henry Adams was Anglophile, albeit at times despairing of his love, Brooks was almost Anglophobic. He would have scorned the idea that there was any emotion in this attitude; for him it was a predestinate fact that Britain had sunk into apathy and impotence, and thus deserved to be stripped of her preeminence. Sometimes, this dogmatism could be interesting, and often got as far as a kind of vulgar Marxism. In analyzing why the British Establishment had never quite made up its mind to support the Confederacy outright, he boldly opined:

> Hitherto, speaking broadly, the landed gentry had predominated, but, if the franchise were to be extended widely, none could tell whither power might migrate. Certainly, it would not remain with those who had enjoyed it. Therefore the aristocracy assuming that if the South should prevail the enfranchisement of the proletariat might be indefinitely postponed, the proletariat accepting it as axiom that their fortunes were bound up with the fortunes of the North.

There is an echo, at least, of what Henry Adams had noticed when Gladstone spoke of "violent impatience in the cotton-towns of Lancashire," where English workers sacrificed to side with the Union in spite of the short-term influence of the cotton interests.

In his books *The Law of Civilization and Decay* and *America's Economic Supremacy* (both published by the newly transatlanticized firm of Macmillan), Brooks Adams struck the same chord with relentless monotony. In an extraordinary essay, with the giveaway title of "Natural Selection in Literature," he illustrated the decline of England by contrasting the manliness and martial nobility of Sir Walter Scott with the miserable hesitation and scruple of Charles Dickens. Of the latter he said, pityingly, that "the nearest approach to an attempt at the heroic in behalf of any of his lovers, was the street brawl between Nicholas Nickleby and Sir Mulberry Hawk." He scorned Dickens because that author "seldom undertook to describe the gentleman, the soldier, or the adventurer, and when he did, he unconsciously caricatured them because he knew those temperaments only by their antagonism to his own." (We can see in this the ancestry of today's school of muscular American criticism, directed at writers like E. M. Forster or Joseph Heller and surging from the pens of Joseph Epstein and Norman Podhoretz. In *The Law of Civilization and Decay*, Brooks Adams announced that "one of the first signs of advancing civilizations is the fall in the value of women in men's eyes.") Adams took signs of femininity and sloth as symptomatic of a declining imperial will. Of the Boer War and its early reverses for the Crown he wrote:

A year ago Great Britain attacked a few thousand obscure peasants in Central Africa. To the bewilderment of mankind her armies were defeated, her troops fled in rout, her choicest regiments surrendered. London was plunged in dismay; for the first time in her history the Kingdom seemed to lose confidence in herself, and leaned upon the Colonies. Then the world, actuated by one common instinct, closed upon the enfeebled giant.

Brooks Adams was indulging his weakness for generalization here, but he was right about the dependence upon American finance that the Boer War created in English war-making circles. He quoted *The Economist* as pointing out that while "in 1891 the Bank of England could draw gold from New York" in forced settlement, it was now forced to borrow not only American capital but American gold as well. It was not, then, the "insolent" institution Henry Adams had seen in 1858.

Brooks did not waste time, as his brother was wont to do, in composing elegies for a departed English glory. Having decided that "England is relatively losing vitality, that the focus of energy and wealth is shifting and that, therefore, a period of instability is impending," he went on confidently to say:

> Should this supposition be true, no event could be more momentous to America; for, if the western continent is gaining at the expense of the eastern, the United States must shortly bear the burden England has done, must assume the responsibilities and perform the tasks which have within human memory fallen to the share of England, and must be equipped accordingly.

"Burden" again. The last point was addressed, as was most of what Brooks Adams wrote, to Roosevelt and Mahan. Like them, he held the view both that America should combine with England and that America should supersede or transcend England. "Should an Anglo-Saxon coalition be made, and succeed," he wrote in *The Spanish War*, "it would alter profoundly the equilibrium of the world. . . . Probably human society would then be absolutely dominated by a vast combination of peoples whose right wing would rest upon the British Isles." In a final flourish, he predicted that the oceans could thereby be dominated "*much as the Romans encompassed the Mediterranean.*" For this purpose, naturally, the Philippines, "rich, coal-bearing and with fine harbors, seem a predestined base for the United States." But even as he preached collaboration, for the practical reason that "England and the United States combined could easily maintain a fleet which would make them supreme at sea; while as rivals they might be ruined," he wrote, in *England's Decadence in the West Indies*, that "the British Empire in the Western tropics is disintegrating." And this prospect meant "*expansion for America, and corresponding decline for England*" (italics mine). This was the element in the grand design that Chamberlain failed to notice and Kipling failed to hymn. It contains, also, a presentiment of the later writing of Arnold Toynbee and James Burnham.

Anglicized though they were in their different ways, the Adams brothers were extremely un-English in their attachment to determinist, "scientific" philosophy. They were also very inconsistent about it, especially as regarded England herself. Returning to London in the hinge year of 1898, Henry Adams noted "at each turn how the great city grew smaller as it doubled in size; cheaper as it quadrupled its wealth; less influential as its empire widened; less dignified as it tried to be civil." This seemed rather like a transference of his feelings about America, which had, as he showed in his novel *Democracy*, revolted him in just this way. He also wrote, in *The Education*, that to him the Boer War was "almost a personal outrage" and that if the British ever tried to treat Canada as they had treated the Boers, the United States would be obliged to intervene. Yet his letters tell a different story. To his brother Brooks, in one of the private exchanges of theirs which never seem to have omitted an attack on Jewry, he wrote that "the impossible has happened and the Boers have shown their incapacity to run the machine by running it off the track. This is the first strong evidence I have seen *that the English are in the right*." Moreover, he wrote that the lessons of the Spanish-American War were "staggering for Europe. To Germany they seem to me almost a *coup de grâce*. They give England enormous confidence . . . Chamberlain's foreign policy will doubtless take the conscious direction of a war which is indispensable to its ends."

Neither Adams could quite decide what to think about Wilhelmine Germany, the prime supporter of the Boers. At times, they thought the growth of the Kaiser's power had "in twenty years

effected what Adamses had tried for two hundred years in vain—
frightened England into America's arms." Later, Brooks was to
write of how America was drawn into the First World War "by the
resistless attraction of the British economic system." So much for
determinism. But they agreed on the rough symbiosis achieved by
John Hay's adroit diplomacy in London and Washington. Henry
Adams, who took the view in retrospect that "every step" taken
by his ancestors "had the object of bringing England into an American system," now wrote immodestly:

> As he sat at Hay's table, listening to any member of the British
> Cabinet, for all were alike now, discuss the Philippines as a
> question of balance of power in the East, he could see that
> the family work of a hundred and fifty years fell at once into
> the grand perspective of true empire building, which Hay's
> work set off with artistic skill.

How this sat with his private view—that "the Anglo-American alliance is almost inevitable. The idiocy and tomfoolery of the Kaiser
Willy have given an impulse to the Anglo-American business which
seems already beyond control. You know what an Anglo-American
alliance means to gold bugs, and what an ocean of corruption we
shall sail into"—is for his admirers to say. It does seem certain,
though, that, like Mahan, Adams regarded war and expansion as
an insurance against the sickly virus of socialism. Adams considered
the growth of this idea to be inevitable, detestable, and avoidable,
depending on whom he might be addressing. He had no love for
Jews or capitalists, but, as he said, he preferred them to the masses.
This was perhaps a poor return for the solidarity of Cobden and
Bright. But men of that stamp were not to be included in the plans
for a great new world empire of Anglo-Saxondom.

An Adams had been prominent in every phase of the Anglo-
American evolution: in the revolution against George III and the
proclamation of a Continental Congress and Constitution; in the
expansion and consolidation of the United States (in alternate con-

cert and conflict with Britain); in the Civil War and in the adoption by the Union of the "expansionist" dreams once nourished by the South. The ambivalence of Henry Adams about the alliance of 1898 had to do with residual suspicion of British "stupidity" and unease about the Anglo-German war which he could often see was coming.

In the decision about America's side in that conflict, a decision which many Americans believe to have been the first and last loss of innocence, the Adams "set" was also to find itself heavily engaged. One of its members, Sir Cecil Spring-Rice, provides a convenient and fairly exact register of the fluctuations in temperature and interest that eventuated in what American critics called "Mr. Wilson's war," but which was really the next and most violent stage in the Romanization of the United States via the British connection.

Spring-Rice had a knack and talent for friendship and an easy way with Americans. He was also rather a deft and rapid worker. In August 1886, as a young Foreign Office clerk, he was returning from America by sea and made an effort to be agreeable to a politician who was making the same voyage. As he wrote to his brother: "I came over with Roosevelt, who has been standing for the mayoralty of New York against H. George and who is supposed to be the boss Republican young man." By November, Roosevelt was writing to Spring-Rice from Brown's Hotel in Mayfair, accepting an invitation to dine at the Savile Club. On December 2 of the same year, when Roosevelt married Edith Kermit Carow at St. George's, Hanover Square, Spring-Rice was best man. Roosevelt's sister, Mrs. Cowles, wrote in a letter: "Dear Springy was so delightful and like himself when I went to put on Edith's veil. I warned Theodore to start immediately for the church as it was a foggy day, and they were intensely preoccupied in a discussion over the population of an island in the Southern Pacific."

Probably bad news for the Hawaiians, if they had but known it. In the same month, "Springy" applied to exchange posts with a secretary at the British legation in Washington. Until the 1890s, the United States neither appointed nor received "ambassadors" as such, and some of Spring-Rice's superiors felt he was making a mistake. One of them, Sir Lionel Sackville-West (later Lord Sackville), wrote to him in puzzlement, saying:

> I hope you may get your exchange, though why choose Washington which is out of all politics? Of course it is interesting in a way, and West's a charming chief. But still it seems so off the line.

There, in a phrase or two, was the traditional British mandarin's continued refusal to get the point of the United States. Spring-Rice was perhaps better off for this indifference, and freer to pursue his acquaintance and inclination than he would have been at a European embassy. *The Education of Henry Adams*, recalling Springy's time in Washington between 1887 and 1895, noticed:

> Whatever one's preference in politics might be, one's house was bound to the Republican interest when sandwiched between Senator Cameron, John Hay and Cabot Lodge, with Theodore Roosevelt equally at home in them all, and Cecil Spring-Rice to unite them by impartial variety.

Springy, in fact, was the glass of fashion and the mold of form for generations of British diplomats who have come after him and sought, with varying degrees of success, to get on a similar Washington footing. He had the right sort of eccentricities (of which chronic untidiness was the most endearing), the right sort of lightly worn Balliol classical education, and the right poise between distinction and democracy in his manners. He made tremendous headway with the then just-emerging breed known as the Washington hostess; getting himself practically adopted as the perfect bachelor by Mrs. Cameron and Mrs. Lodge. The British have sent some tailor's dummies, some overwrought charmers, and some sycophants to Washington since then; none of them the equal of Springy because all of them swam in the tepid stream of the "special relationship." When Spring-Rice was first in Washington, there was no such thing. England was still puissant, and still looked upon with great suspicion.

Canadian officials were impounding American fishing boats for poaching. American opinion of the British handling of Irish Home Rule was distinctly jaundiced. It took remarkably little to arouse anti-British feeling in the growing United States electorate. That electorate's choice of Cleveland in 1893 was a blow to Springy, who wrote gloomily to his brother:

> For England the Republican administration is the best; for though unpleasant to the last degree, it was capable and certain under Harrison; under Cleveland it may be anything— and Cleveland is bound to show that he was *not* elected by British gold, by being as disagreeable to us as possible.

As if to spite Springy, there was a prompt partisan tussle over Hawaii, with the Democrats withdrawing their protectorate over the islands and the Republicans shouting that if the United States did not annex, Great Britain would move to fill the vacuum. But he was right about Cleveland, though the crucial metal was silver and not gold.

Seeking to draw upon the reservoir of anti-British sentiment, and in general "to busy giddy minds with foreign quarrels," Cleveland made a tremendous issue of the dispute between Britain and Venezuela over the placing of the latter country's boundary. This, although it involved him in the possibility of a direct confrontation with the unsmiling regime of Lord Salisbury, had the advantage of domestic popularity. "It is time we act for ourselves and not be consulting England," cried the aspirant Congressman William Jennings Bryan of Nebraska, who was to make the call for "free silver" his own. A timely invocation of the Monroe Doctrine, in which until that time he had shown little interest, was an excellent way for Cleveland to put himself at the head of this powerful movement, and to attach to himself all the populist resentment engendered by the British banks and British gold. During the contest over silver repeal, Senator Francis Cockrell of Missouri had asked the dangerous question: "Shall we bow the knee to England?" Once this question had been asked, it took a tougher politician than Cleveland to risk giving the impression that the answer was "yes." The free-silver faction, ranging from William "Coin" Harvey to the Nevada Republican William Stewart, actually welcomed the idea of war in their rhetoric; Harvey so far forgetting himself as to say that war with England would be "the most just war ever waged by man."

The British, slightly to their own surprise, announced in early 1895 that they were prepared to arbitrate the line of the Venezuelan border. In a foretaste of the mentality that would in time leapfrog Anglophobia and result directly in the safer idea of a Spanish-American War, the Democrats and Republicans combined to say that this was not good enough. Henry Cabot Lodge wrote a pamphlet on the relevance of the Monroe Doctrine, and Attorney General Richard Olney, he of the suppression of the Pullman strike, took up the populist cry with a brief that said: "Today, the United States is practically sovereign on this continent, and its fiat is law upon the subjects to which it confines its interposition." This kind of talk—the revenge for British arrogance in 1862—got him the Secretaryship of State. The fact that London waited for a long and contemptuous time before replying to the demarche did him no harm. War fever infected both parties, both houses, and most newspapers. The Hay-Adams circle were, as usual, not sure whether they quite liked this saber-flourishing and mobocracy. After Cleveland had told Congress on December 17, 1895, that he was prepared to fight England over the border with Venezuela, arousing the wildest passions thereby, Henry Adams put it down to "the bitterness excited by the silver struggle," and John Hay spoke meaningfully of the President's being in "a disturbed state of mind." Spring-Rice took Kipling in person to see the deliberations of Congress at this time, which impressed him as sordid and dangerous both, and, as we saw, shook him powerfully with the horror of a possible war between the two cousinly powers.

It would have been ghastly and fascinating to see what might have happened next. What actually happened next was a telegram from Kaiser Wilhelm of Germany to Paul Kruger, praising him for repelling a British raid on the Transvaal. At that message, which was transmitted three weeks after Cleveland's minatory address to Congress, Lord Salisbury made shift to forget about the Venezuelan boundary and to advocate conciliation all round. The danger had passed, but it left America in possession of a new and more strenuous claim to apply the Monroe Doctrine without scruple, and it left the British with a strong sensation that here was a formidable enemy not to make.

Just as Kipling seems to have decided "never again," so does Spring-Rice. Posted shortly afterward to the highly relevant embassy at Berlin, he kept up his Washington friendships and his American correspondence. His relief—that American belligerence was now transferred to Spain—was palpable. As he wrote to Hay, after Admiral Dewey's walkover in the Philippines:

We have just received the glorious news from Manila. How curious it is—the continuity of history, the struggle that began 400 years ago of which we are seeing the last chapter. How the historians criticise Cromwell for siding against Spain! It was the divine instinct ingrained in the race which has brought us to where we are.

That was on May 7, 1898, and one can only guess at the emotion which made Springy reach for the unaccustomed symbol of Cromwell. To Henry Cabot Lodge on July 8, he was so unctuous as to be practically servile:

I can't tell you with what pleasure I see that Hawaii is at length to be annexed. The pleasure is selfish and has in one sense nothing to do with the real or permanent advantage to

America which I believe will result from the step. I think that there can be no doubt that there is an intention (and a natural one) to depose English civilization (I mean yours as much and more than mine) from the Pacific. The new order of things which is to replace it may be better; but it isn't ours, it is absolutely and wholly different from ours, and we have the right and duty to defend what we most certainly have fairly won on the American, Australian and Chinese coasts. I don't believe that England, the island, is strong enough, or will remain comparatively strong enough to defend English civilization alone—and I have no sympathy whatever with the people who believe that English institutions, literature, language and greatness are courtiers at the throne of London. I believe they are common possessions, to be defended, as they were won, in common—and to be enjoyed in common too. And I welcome any step which America takes outside her continent because it tends to the increase of the common good.

I need not say how excited we all are at the very welcome proof you have given that people who talk English can still fight.

Springy's last compliment was quite rich, given that Lodge had shown every sign of advancing his political career, not three years earlier, to prove that America could still fight *England*. The urgency of Spring-Rice's friendliness is probably explained in a letter he wrote to his old companion Roosevelt at about this time, giving the Berlin perspective upon Manifest Destiny:

I have been very much interested in watching the view taken here about Cuba. As far as I can judge, the feeling in official circles is as follows. To begin with, there is the feud that every official German has with America, which is regarded as a huge machine for teaching Germans English and make [sic] them Republican.

Spring-Rice did not return to the United States until 1913, when he did so as His Britannic Majesty's ambassador. Woodrow Wilson had been elected, more or less as a consequence of the split between Springy's old friend Roosevelt and his less intimate acquaintance Taft. Once again, those Englishmen who desired closer and warmer relations with America were confronted by ever more promiscuous interpretations of the Monroe Doctrine. There was a lingering dispute over the Panama Canal and the rights of its users, where the British felt that the United States was acting high-handedly. And the United States was determined to overrule European opinion about Mexico, then in the throes of revolutionary turmoil after the end of the long rule of Porfirio Díaz. Wilson managed to get British support for the second policy by making well-timed concessions on the first. The British jurist Lord Montrose, for example, consistently took Roosevelt's interpretation of the Canadian-Alaskan border dispute; helping to settle it in a manner which put the new alliance with America above sentimental considerations of the "Old Dominion." The Hay-Pauncefote Treaty on the Panama Canal saw the British abandon the claim of equal privilege in Panama that they had felt able to insist upon at the time of the Clayton-Bulwer Treaty of 1850. Henceforth, the United States was recognized as possessing the right to "construct, maintain and control" the Canal, and the British reserved their right only to oppose discrimination in rates: the issue which Wilson composed.

Most striking of all was the issue of Venezuela. In late 1902, and in order to impress on the Venezuelans the necessity of paying their debts, Britain joined with Germany and Italy in blockading and bombarding the Venezuelan coast. This time, there was no anti-British fervor in the United States to rival that of 1895. But, sensitive to the Monroe Doctrine, the British government withdrew its claims, officially regretted the collusion with Germany, and declared an end to the use of force. Roosevelt later claimed that he had been readying Admiral Dewey and the fleet to dissuade the Kaiser. Kipling wrote a poem, "The Rowers," which breathed contempt for any alliance with "the Goth and the shameless Hun."

With a number of false starts and failures of synchronicity, then, a general pattern of collaboration was emerging. Britain would give the United States a more or less free hand in Central America and the Caribbean; allowing Roosevelt, for instance, to amputate the national territory of Colombia in order to Americanize the Panama Canal Zone and indeed to create Panama in the first place. This blind eye to "the big stick" permitted the British Admiralty to recall its naval squadron from Bermuda and to leave only a skeletal presence in the West Indies—thus vindicating the predictions of Mahan and Brooks Adams. In general, British priorities were being reordered to deal with Germany, and her alliance with America against lesser breeds everywhere else allowed her to hope that America might come to see Europe through British eyes as well.

In coaxing this perception into life, Spring-Rice had to be rather silky. The golden opportunities of the *Lusitania* and the Zimmermann Telegram lay in the future; in the meantime he confronted a public opinion that was generally hostile to embroilment in a European quarrel between crowned heads. Moreover, of the minority who did take a partisan view, not all by any means took a pro-British one. In 1913, more than 8 million of America's 105 million inhabitants either had been born in Germany or had at least one German parent. And there were 4.5 million Irish-Americans as well, most of whom had no love for England. Neither of these national minorities fell within Woodrow Wilson's definition of the "sordid and hapless elements," the sweepings of Eastern and Southern Europe, and both had substantial political representations and a lively and popular press.

Springy's first task was to get the Mexican difficulty out of the way. American official and demotic opinion inclined (not without justification) to the view that the British had recognized the Huerta regime, which came to power over the dead body of Díaz's successor, Madero, because of the great interests held by the Pearson-Cowdray family. Spring-Rice rather confirmed this in an ingratiating letter to his friend Henry Cabot Lodge in August 1914:

[Sir Edward] Grey was pressed by all the financial people to do something, and so spoke privately to [U.S. Ambassador] Page to ask him to find out what were the views of the US as to this policy and if they were inclined to adopt it. I subsequently wrote to [William Jennings] Bryan [Secretary of State], telling him that the press was publishing alarming news about Mexico, and that British subjects might very well suffer if the U.S.G. took violent measures. (The Greasers can no more distinguish between a Britisher and an American than between a crocodile and an alligator.)

This was the Mexican power, supine before foreigners, against which Britain would shortly warn America in the drama of the Zimmermann Telegram. Meanwhile, Springy wrote to Roosevelt anxious to renew old solidarities:

Oh, T.R., how I wish I could see you. I nearly wept in Rock Creek Park at the rock. I could *hear* you—the flowers are indeed beautiful now. How lovely it all is.

Few envoys could hope to enjoy this kind of intimacy, and even if not all the Adams circle could be counted on all the time, they were generally a staunch phalanx of allies in the interventionist and English cause. Meanwhile, Wilson had repealed the offending Panama tolls and thereby recruited British support for the upstart Pancho Villa. In the March before the outbreak of war in Europe, Spring-Rice found an unintentionally apt metaphor for the situation:

There are not nearly so many attacks against Great Britain as there used to be, although we are reminded that the young American eagle lined his nest with the mane of the British Lion.

Indeed. Once war had begun in August 1914, Spring-Rice immediately began to draw the lines of battle. These involved the precise identification of two objectives—American public opinion and American sea power. Considerations of race, nation, and class soon became salient. Having quoted his friend Roosevelt to the effect that:

> England's consistent friendliness towards us for decades past, and Germany's attitude during the Spanish War and in South Africa, have combined to produce a friendliness in the U.S. for England as against Germany and a general apprehension of German designs,

Spring-Rice continued, to Sir Edward Grey at the Foreign Office, in a less optimistic frame of mind:

> This seems the feeling of the native American; but there are other elements, and the influence of the Germans and especially the German Jews is very great, and in parts of the country is supreme. We must not count on American sympathy as assured to us. *A very little incident might change it,* and there are the cleverest people in the world at work with large sums at their back who will let no opportunity pass to do us mischief. [Italics mine.]

This letter, with its slightly John Buchan-ish undertone, showed the tone of British self-pity that was to recur throughout the conflict. It seemed very bad form, to Spring-Rice, that the Germans had any rights on the high seas at all. As he went on:

> Another matter is the question of the transfer of the flag to the Hamburg Amerika ships. It is not a very pleasant business. The Company is practically a German government affair. The ships are used for Government purposes, the Emperor himself is a large share-holder, and so is the great banking house of Kuhn & Loeb of New York. A member of that house has been

appointed to a very responsible post in NY, though only just
naturalized.

Decidedly unpleasant, that the King's cousin, who had been an
honored guest at Cowes on his yacht during Admiral Mahan's
triumphant visit, should presume so far. The renunciation of German titles by the British royal family, the transformation of Saxe-
Coburg-Gotha into Windsor and Battenberg into Mountbatten, lay
ahead. So did a comparable and related anti-Hun hysteria in America. For now, Springy and others had served notice that those "only
just naturalized," such as Mr. Warburg of the Federal Reserve,
who had been a business partner to Mr. McAdoo, Secretary of the
Treasury and son-in-law to President Wilson, were not really kith
and kin in the proper sense at all.

A few months later Spring-Rice was writing peevishly to his old
friend Sir Valentine Chirol. On this occasion, he felt that it was
the American toiler who was letting down the side, by giving an
ear to Wilson's canting (as it turned out) about "strict neutrality:"

> George Trevelyan had an admirable study in his *Bright* on
> the attitude of our working classes to the North during the
> cotton famine. I wish that the Americans would take a similar
> view of their obligations. They signed the Hague Treaty. That
> Treaty has been shamefully and repeatedly violated. They
> never protested and have not once raised their voice against
> these violations or on behalf of the weak and suppressed.
> When the Jews in Romania were touched they howled loud
> enough, because the Jews in New York had votes. When Jew
> bagmen were turned out of Russia, they broke off their treaty
> with the one country which had uniformly been friendly to
> them in the hour of their greatest need.

Here, Springy sounds more like Sapper than Buchan. His diatribes
against the eternally troublesome Hebrew (who would care about
him when he could thrill to the King of the Belgians?) are of a
certain recognizable type and period. His invocation of Bright is

less usual and more suggestive. Was there, perhaps, a residual conscience at work? The British Establishment had scorned and pelted Bright and his plebeian supporters for their support of the Union side. Now they saw them as the great model of selfless and ethical conduct; almost as an example for an ungrateful America to emulate. Spring-Rice chose to forget the role of Palmerston and Gladstone and Russell in forwarding secession and slavery in the American Civil War. He also forgot the terms in which Bright had upheld the Union cause. On March 26, 1863, young Henry Adams had attended, as part of his education, a workers' meeting at St. James's Hall, London. There he heard Bright denounce the surreptitious and cynical British policy, recording the speech himself in these terms:

> "Privilege thinks it has a great interest in the American contest" he began in his massive, deliberate tones; ". . . and every morning with blatant voice, it comes into our streets and curses the American Republic. Privilege has beheld an afflicting spectacle for many years past. It has beheld thirty million of men happy and prosperous, without emperors—without king (*cheers*)—without the surroundings of a court (*renewed cheers*)—without nobles, except such as are made by eminence in intellect and virtue—without State bishops and State priests, those vendors of the love that works salvation (*cheers*)—without great armies and great navies—without a great debt and great taxes—and Privilege has shuddered at what might happen to old Europe if this great experiment should succeed."
>
> An ingenious man, with an inventive mind, might have managed, in the same number of lines, to offend more Englishmen than Bright struck in this sentence; but he must have betrayed artifice and hurt his oratory . . .

Springy, if he had ever read his old and dear friend's memoir (he often addressed him in correspondence as "Uncle Henry"), must have been impervious to the irony.

The Churchill Cult

Edward Lutyens
Biscuit Factory edifice

How and why is it that the name and prestige of Sir Winston Churchill are so easily appropriated by Americans of the kind I described in the Introduction: Americans who are generally identified with privilege and conservatism to an extent that Churchill himself never was?

The Churchill cult in the United States, as currently practiced, makes its association with such aspects of American life practically inevitable. The figure of the grand old man is the *summa* of "special relationship" politics and emotions. Invested with the awesome grandeur and integrity of the 1940 resistance to Hitler, and gifted as few before or since with the power to make historic phrases, Churchill is morally irrefragable in American discourse, and can be quoted even more safely than Lincoln in that he was never a member of any American faction.

Given the universality of his standing and appeal, Churchill is an icon of which jealous use is made by the political and military conservatives to whom the "special relationship" is a potent source of reinforcement. But he also occupies an unrivaled place in the common stock of reference, ranging from the mock-heroic to the downright kitsch.

On the western reach of Massachusetts Avenue in Washington, D.C., hard by the Naval Observatory, which houses the vice presidential mansion, there stands an imposing bronze statue of Sir Winston, cigar in hand, making his instantly recognizable gesture of victory. (He is rooted to the turf outside the attractively proportioned residence built by Sir Edwin Lutyens, designer of New Delhi, rather than the adjacent biscuit-factory-style edifice which houses the public parts of Britain's largest overseas mission.) On as many mornings as not, the cigar-holding hand of the sculpture has a bouquet or a posy placed in it, though no one, according to local lore, has ever seen the flowers being placed there. There is no reason to disbelieve the British embassy staff, who deny responsibility for these garlands and tributes. They insist that the floral salute is a spontaneous thing, the tradition of the neighbors and inhabitants. This is a prosperous and political suburb of the town, with multiple "special relationship" connections, and there seems no harm in believing that the Washington Establishment regards the statue as its personal property.

Can the same be said of the Country Club Plaza in Kansas City? Here, in the center of the shopping area, there stands an enormous bronze of Sir Winston and his wife, Clementine. It is entitled *Married Love*, and it inescapably reminds one of what happened to the Graham Sutherland portrait which Churchill did not like. ("It makes me look stupid, which I ain't," he said, before ordering it to be fed into the family boiler.) Adjacent to the statue is a speaker which, if requested by the press of a button, will emit a version of the "blood, toil, tears, and sweat" peroration. The likeness is based on a smaller sculpture by Oscar Nemon. It is the joint conception of a dentist named Joseph Jacobs and a local real estate operator called Miller Nichols, heir to the shopping center itself, who agreed some years ago that the youth of Kansas City were in need of "symbolism" to encourage "traditional values." Kansas City, no great foe of traditional values, already possessed one of their exemplars in the form of the Hallmark greeting-card company. This pervasive organization, which markets the children-and-pets motif across the continental United States in times of anniversary, nuptial, and bereavement, had already established a lien on the

Churchill cult in the 1950s, when it successfully promoted a tour of the grand old man's watercolor paintings.

Examples of the high and low manifestations of the cult can be found in the most improbable places. In New Orleans, the least English of all American cities, tourists threading their way to the river in order to take a Cajun-style cruise to the battle sites of the War of 1812 must pass an immense statue of Churchill hard by the waterfront, at the approach to a monstrous Hilton Hotel whose suites are named Windsor, Newbury, Rosebery. It might be too much to say that this statue eclipses the gilded Joan of Arc sculpture a few blocks away, but it is certainly on something like an equal footing.

In the public realm, there is an almost unappeasable demand for Churchillian invocation. The decline of direct Soviet-American confrontation has slightly lessened the intensity of the Munich analogy, which is the most salient form in which Churchillism lives on. But any issue of principle, or any confrontation with a lesser power than Russia, can also bring the "lessons of Munich" tripping off a speaker's tongue. Very few occasions upon which the call for strength and resolution is made can be counted as free of this garnish, and they are a staple of "special relationship" summits as well.

Oddly enough, the second principal strain of Churchillism has to do with the gentrification of political weakness. An easy resort to a Churchillism can be a safe indication that the speaker is in a tight corner. A politician detected in lying, bullying, or antisocial conduct is unusually apt to reach for his glossary of bulldoggery.

Examples of the first kind were especially easy to come by in the early years of the Reagan epoch, and of the second kind as those years drew to their close. Shortly after taking office, Ronald Reagan gave instructions that a portrait of Churchill be hung at the center of the White House "situation room." The intention was to invest the crusade against the then "Evil Empire" with the moral aura of Dunkirk and the Blitz. Caspar Weinberger, later knighted by the Queen for his services to the "special relationship," and the chief designer of the military half of this crusade, was and is the possessor of a large personal library of Churchilliana. He seldom exempted the great man from his speeches on strategy, and is a frequent attender at Churchill dinners and Churchill commemorative occasions. When the time for his retirement came, he was given a *vale* by President Reagan in which the Leader of the Free World said: "I've occasionally called Cap 'my Disraeli.' But as I think of him and the service he's given the nation in the cause of freedom and peace, more than anyone else it's Churchill who comes to mind." Borrowing freely from Churchill's rhetoric, Reagan cited him on the call of "great causes, beyond space and time, which, whether we like it or not, spell duty." When there was a doubt about the feasibility or the desirability of the notorious "Star Wars" contrivance, and when this doubt began to make itself felt in the Pentagon, enthusiasts for the scheme framed and mounted a Churchillism and gave it to Mr. Weinberger to hang in his office. It read: "Never give in, never, never, never, never—in things great or small, large or petty." (This rather unsafe injunction, made by Churchill to the schoolboys of Harrow on one of his few return visits to an academy he had thoroughly disliked, was also taken as the motto of G. Gordon Liddy, most unrepentant of the Watergate convicts, during his post-prison book tour.)

Although Harold Wilson once gave his critics a laugh by saying of Britain that "our frontiers are on the Himalayas," and although Sir Anthony Eden had his moment of tragicomedy in the Suez Canal Zone having waited too long in Churchill's anteroom, and although Margaret Thatcher proved able in a pinch to move a fleet to victory in the South Atlantic, Winston Churchill was the last British Prime Minister who really possessed an Imperial General Staff and who really enjoyed a panoptic grasp of affairs. This, in alliance with his high oratorical style and his generally conservative growl, makes him an ideal fetish object for American "hawks." One thing more is necessary for this speechwriter's heaven to be complete. Churchill is no longer alive. And his greatest purpose, the maintenance of British world power, in which he expended all his mighty breath, is safely whimsical and antique. He is therefore meet to be celebrated by the political descendants of American conservatism, which in his lifetime oscillated between collecting on the British war debt and upholding the banner of "America First."

Thus, among the members of the Churchill Society, a group of buffs who meet for weekends of patriotic oratory in the cities of the South and the Midwest, were to be found in 1988 John Lehman, Ronald Reagan's Secretary of the Navy, and Sam Nunn, the Georgian chairman of the Senate Armed Services Committee. Among conservative columnists, who form a kind of corps of unacknowledged legislators in public life, George Will, William F. Buckley, and William Safire have very frequent recourse to admonitory or hortatory Churchillisms. A computer survey of Mr. Safire's columns found that he made reference to Churchill once in every four articles on average. The same survey unearthed 1,200 allusions to Churchill in leading American newspapers between April and December in 1984, a period selected at random.

The extent and degree to which Churchill has been absorbed by the American political culture (for modern American politicians and editorialists do not make references or allusions to historical figures unless they have some clear assurance about their "name recognition") may also be gauged in another way. Churchill is the resort of choice for a politician who is on the ropes. Gordon Liddy, as we saw, used him as an exculpatory inspiration. So did his boss, in a celebrated television interview in April 1988. Former President Richard Nixon, invited to ruminate on the workings of fate, recalled:

> 1972, as you know, was a very big year. A lot of things were going on. Winston Churchill once wrote that strong leaders usually do the big things well, but they foul up on small things, and then the small things become big. I should have read that before Watergate happened.

This wry gift did not desert the disgraced Nixon when he turned to the election then in progress:

> Winston Churchill has said that there's no part of the education of a politician is more indispensable than the fighting of elections. George Bush has had a very good education in that respect. Coming back from the defeat in Iowa, he has wiped out the opposition, and he's developed that inner strength and toughness that was certainly not there beforehand.

Both of these statements were greeted respectfully. At the time of the Iran-contra scandal, Admiral John Poindexter quoted Winston Churchill to the effect that, in wartime, truth is so precious that it must be safeguarded by "a bodyguard of lies." The United States was not at war at that time, but the admiral was seconding an aperçu offered by George Shultz, who had said exactly the same thing a few months previously about the administration's "disinformation campaign" concerning Libya. While recuperating after his suicide attempt and before the congressional investigation of the Iran-contra network that had precipitated it, Robert McFarlane said: "I suppose it's a pretentious thing to say, but I have to think about people who have overcome apparent near-catastrophic difficulty, from Jefferson to Churchill." When Senator John Tower's nomination as Secretary of Defense was foundering, more on his alleged inebriation than on his political shortcomings, his supporters protested that Churchill had thrived on a diet of alcohol. In early 1990, when Vice President Dan Quayle was continuing to warn of the Russian threat and to stress the need for a larger Star Wars budget, he gave it out that he had been impressed by William Manchester's biography of Churchill, and was therefore wary of another Munich. His literary preference until this time had been for Tom Clancy.

In all these instances, the use of Churchill is totemic and is supposed to bring a reverent and attentive response. A glance at

obviously

the references above, which is a mere sample from the relatively recent past, is enough to illustrate the point. Scarcely less arresting than the image of Caspar Weinberger as Disraeli (*when* did Reagan first call him that?) is the notion of Churchill the solvent of Watergate, Churchill the moral and political tutor of George Bush, Churchill the posthumous licensee of a mercenary foreign policy.

One way of viewing the Churchill cult is to see it as the residue of a half-forgotten transition whereby the strategic majority of the American Establishment crossed over from isolationism to interventionism. In many ways, Winston Churchill was the human bridge across which this transition was made. But not until the very end of his career was he, or could he be, praised for his contribution to this crucial evolution.

Churchill's first contact with American affairs was a distinctly tangential one, though it has a bearing on the critical year of 1898. A few years before that historic "expansionist" moment, the young scion of an English nobleman and an American heiress found himself chafing for lack of what John Hay would shortly call "a splendid little war." As a young officer, tired of listening to old campaigners, he wrote:

> All my money had been spent on polo parties, and as I could not afford to hunt, I searched the world for some scene of adventure or excitement. The global peace in which mankind had for so many years languished was broken only in one quarter of the globe.

That quarter was Cuba, long a place of arms between the European and American powers. Churchill took ship there in 1895, to observe how the Spanish Empire was faring against the rebels and to lend the Spanish occupiers a hand. Having had some tinge of romantic sympathy with the insurgents, he was surprised to find that the Spanish officers regarded the war not as a mere colonial affair but as a contest for the integrity of Spain itself. Translating this conviction back into the colonial language most easily available to him, Churchill recorded: "They felt about Cuba, it seemed, just as we felt about Ireland. This impressed me much." Shortly after reaching this conclusion, he got his wish. "The thirtieth of November was my 21st birthday, and on that day for the first time I heard shots fired in anger, and heard bullets strike flesh or whistle through the air."

He came out of Cuba unscathed and soon afterward found that "the danger—as the subaltern regarded it—which in those days seemed so real of Liberal and democratic governments making war impossible" was, as ever, an illusion. Making perhaps the same subliminal connection as Admiral Mahan was later to make, he took part in the South African war even as American soldiery was engaging itself on San Juan Hill and at Manila Bay, and in 1899 was taken prisoner by the Boers during the wreck of an armored train. He made a spectacular escape from captivity, which helped propel him forward both as a journalist and as a politician. In 1900, like any new celebrity, he embarked on a lecture tour of the United States, making an imperialist case for the Chamberlain government and meeting with a decidedly mixed response. Of the American audiences who came to hear him, "a great many of them thought that the Boers were in the right, and the Irish everywhere showed themselves actively hostile."

None of these experiences was the equal, for the young Churchill, of an encounter with the moving spirit of the Anti-Imperialist League, whose eloquence was already being overborne by the flashier poetry of Rudyard Kipling:

My opening lecture in New York was under the auspices of no less a personage than "Mark Twain" himself. I was thrilled by this famous companion of my youth. He was now very old and snow-white, and combined with a noble air a most delightful style of conversation. Of course we argued about the war. After some exchanges I found myself beaten back to the citadel, "My country right or wrong." "Ah," said the old gentleman. "When the poor country is fighting for its life, I agree. But this was not your case."

Twain then inscribed one of his own books to young Churchill, remarking pithily on the flyleaf: "To do good is noble; to teach others to do good is nobler, and no trouble."

Churchill would spend much of the next half century trying to enlist the aid of the United States for a British Empire which, whether right or wrong, was passing its zenith. He sought to do so in ways which, while they would incur a debt to America, would nonetheless preserve British and imperial freedom of action. His final failure to do this is set out in Chapter 8. But in the course of the struggle, he helped both directly and indirectly to unlock the imperial potential of the United States.

He played a pivotal role in the great drama of the *Lusitania*, which more than any other single incident prepared United States public opinion for a war on the terrain of old Europe. On May 7, 1915, this British Cunard liner of 30,000 tons was hit by a single torpedo from the German submarine U-20, commanded by Kapitänleutnant Walter Schwieger. Of those 1,195 civilians who perished in the chilly waters off southern Ireland, 140 were American citizens.

Anybody who had made the least study of the Spanish-American War knew that it had "started," for all public and political purposes, with the blowing up of the USS *Maine* in Havana harbor. In spite of the fact that the Spanish authorities gave Havana's best cemetery in perpetuity for the burial of the dead, looked after the injured, and proposed a joint Spanish-American inquiry into the calamity, all conciliation was rejected. Compensation and an acceptance of responsibility, as well as political concessions, were demanded. The demand was backed up by an extraordinary public hysteria, in which the words "Remember the Maine!" became a loyalty oath and a war cry combined. As Geoffrey Perret recounts in his history *A Country Made by War*: "There was no escaping it. Even the journal of sober-minded New England literati, the *Atlantic Monthly*, succumbed, putting Old Glory on its cover." Congress eagerly voted President McKinley all the powers necessary for war. Not until 1976 did the U.S. Navy admit that the *Maine* had exploded because of a fire.

Any student of psychological warfare and American politics would therefore understand at once the importance of a single dramatic atrocity. As it happened, the British Admiralty in 1915 possessed a department operating under the direct command of Winston Churchill. It was called "Room Forty," and its job was that of intelligence and deception.

As with the *Maine*, the evidence of the cause of the disaster had to be rearranged. The *Lusitania* had broken up and sunk in an extremely short time, after being hit by only one torpedo. It therefore had to be found that more than one torpedo had struck her. This task was performed by a pantomime court of inquiry headed by Lord Mersey. It had then to be denied that the *Lusitania* was carrying any munitions of war. This denial was made repeatedly and strenuously by every organ of the British government. In fact, unknown to the civilians who had booked passage on her, the ship had been carrying 1,248 cases of shells, six million rounds of ammunition, and eighteen cases of percussion fuses. These were part of J. P. Morgan's contribution to the Western Front, financed discreetly by Morgan Grenfell.

Given that both elements in the official story were outright lies, it has to be asked how such a valuable cargo came to be put in jeopardy. Later scholars have been able to view evidence that was unavailable to public opinion at the time—public opinion at the time having been falsely told that the German barbarians had struck a *Lusitania* medal to reward the crew for drowning civilians.

In his pathbreaking book *Room Forty*, which is a standard history of British Naval Intelligence during the First World War, Patrick Beesly makes a highly scrupulous forensic analysis of the *Lusitania* affair. As a former serving Naval Intelligence officer and staunch patriot, he finds his own conclusion as unwelcome as it is inescapable. U-20 was known to be in the same waters as the *Lusitania* and had sunk several vessels in that area in the preceding days. Yet Winston Churchill's Admiralty conveyed no warning to the ship, and none of the customary evasive precautions, already well established, was put into operation. Escort vessels were actually deployed *away* from the scene of danger. After elucidating all this, Beesly points out that negligence—the only alternative explanation—would have had to be kept up studiedly for ten whole days. This places a greater strain on credulity than can be borne. Beesly was also impressed by the fact that the relevant files "went missing" from the British Admiralty archives just as he began his inquiries. His eventual finding is the more convincing, perhaps, to a post-*Maine* and post-Tonkin Gulf generation, and more persuasive for being distasteful to him:

> For my part, unless and until fresh information comes to light, I am reluctantly driven to the conclusion that there *was* a conspiracy deliberately to put the *Lusitania* at risk in the hope that even an abortive attack on her would bring the United States into war. Such a conspiracy could not have been put into effect without Winston Churchill's express permission and approval.

If we take conspiracy here to have its adult and realistic rather than its paranoid meaning—in other words, "a secret agreement for prearranged ends"—we can see that Beesly makes an excellent case. He establishes a motive and a causative chain where more strain and artifice are required to believe in coincidence than in the "agreement."

In elucidating Churchill's own frame of mind, it is instructive to leap forward a quarter of a century to July 15, 1941, when the British were again striving to end American neutrality. Admiral Little, then head of the British Admiralty delegation in Washington, wrote to Admiral Pound, the First Sea Lord, saying that "the brightest hope for getting America into the war lies in the escorting arrangements to Iceland, and let us hope the Germans will not be slow in attacking them. Otherwise I think it would be best for us to organise an attack by our own submarines and preferably on the escort!" Churchill himself, who had quit the Admiralty to become Prime Minister, told Pound at a time when the *Bismarck*'s consort *Prinz Eugen* was being tracked in the Atlantic: "It would be better for instance that she should be located by a US ship as this might tempt her to fire on that ship, then providing the incident for which the US government would be so grateful." When they spoke or joked in confidence, the veterans of the British Admiralty certainly seemed to have what might be called a *Lusitania* mentality

Having acted with flamboyance at a critical juncture in the enlargement of the Great War, Churchill went on to try to enlist the United States in the prolongation of it. As a boy taken to Remembrance Day services in England (which invariably featured Churchillian inspiration), I was at first puzzled by the fact that some war memorials were inscribed with the names of the fallen in "The Great War 1914–1918" and others with the identical inscription except for "1919" as the closing date. The notion that hostilities ended at the memorable eleventh hour of the eleventh day of the eleventh month in 1918 is so convenient and so solemnized that its untruth is often overlooked.

In fact, British and American troops—together with the forces of many other nations—continued to make war after the Armistice was signed. They were fighting in Russia against the Bolshevik regime, ostensibly because it had made a separate peace with Germany but also to prevent the spread of revolution in Europe and Asia. The policy of military intervention was preeminently a British policy, and within the British government it was preeminently the policy of Winston Churchill.

Determined to continue the wartime alliance of convenience with the United States, the British government made efforts to persuade the ever-squeamish Woodrow Wilson to commit American forces to the strategy of armed containment. Arthur Balfour secured a promise from Wilson's aide Colonel House that the

United States would aid the "White" General Aleksei Kaledin, with the aid distributed through British and French outlets to preserve what would now be called "deniability." There were some interesting misgivings expressed about the necessity of cooperating with Japan, which had also taken advantage of the Revolution and the Civil War to land troops at Vladivostok. Spring-Rice, in Washington, expected Secretary of State Robert Lansing to object to this show of expansion by a power usually regarded with suspicion. But no, said Lansing, the Americans should not deny to Japan a right that the United States had claimed in Mexico and might need to claim again. Imperial thinking was becoming easier—Lansing was more sanguine than Lord Curzon, the former viceroy with the dollar-princess wife. He had misgivings about playing the Japanese card, because the use of yellow men against Russians would "enormously enhance the prestige of Asiatics against Europeans, and would consequently react upon the attitude of Indians towards the British."

Churchill's plan had been to set up a government based in Siberia under the control of Admiral Aleksandr Kolchak. Kolchak was a Czarist diehard with a fondness for absolutism in the running of his own affairs, but Churchill and his military nominee in the area, General Alfred Knox, considered him the mainstay of their policy. This led to a quarrel between Knox and Major General William S. Graves, who commanded the American Expeditionary Force in Siberia and found himself under what was in effect British command. He did not like the company that he and his troops were keeping. "I doubt," he wrote in his candid memoir of what he called the American "adventure" in Siberia, "if history will show any country in the world during the last fifty years where murder could be committed so safely, and with less danger of punishment, than in Siberia during the regime of Admiral Kolchak." General Graves was in no doubt as to the source of this unwise and morally questionable policy. He noted grimly in his book that Winston Churchill had admitted, in the House of Commons, that the Kolchak regime was a puppet. He had said: "The British government called it into being, for our own aid, at a time when necessity demanded it." To General Graves, this was a clear violation of the letter and the spirit of Woodrow Wilson's Fourteen Points and meant that Churchill had deceived the American forces in telling them that their mission was to safeguard dumps of Allied supplies or to rescue demobilized Czech prisoners of war—the two principal excuses on offer at the time. For his scruples, he received a great deal of calumny from the British:

> The Chief of Staff told me, after my return from the Far East, that I would never know half the pressure the British brought in Washington to have me relieved. I have other information equally reliable that they did not stop until they reached the President.

The British commander, Knox, actually wrote to Graves saying that the Americans were aiding the Communists not only objectively but also subjectively. "There is a widespread propaganda," he said slyly, "to the effect that your countrymen are pro-Bolshevik. I think in the context of Allied solidarity, and of the safety of Allied detachments, you should try to contradict this." One of Knox's subordinates, Colonel John Ward, also protested that "out of sixty liaison officers and translators" with the American staff, "over fifty were Russian Jews." To this Graves replied that he never inquired whether a soldier was Jewish or not but that

> Colonel Ward knew that Jews were anathema to the autocracy of Russia, the particular party he was supporting, and by this false statement he was trying to curry favor with his associates in Siberia. Colonel Ward's chapter on American Forces in Siberia is filled with mis-statements of alleged facts and occurrences, all of which showed a bitterness of feeling and resentment against our troops.

I have previously stated enough to show that this bitterness and resentment was due to the fact that I would not permit the British to dictate to me what I should do.

Another American eyewitness to this fascinating and forgotten episode in warfare was Ralph Albertson, an American journalist who was at that time coordinating the relief efforts of the YMCA. His book *Fighting Without a War* was published in 1920, after he had been the last American to leave Archangel. He related his story from the "grunt" point of view, conveying extreme distaste for the way in which Churchill's policy had downgraded American soldiers. The average soldier was uncertain even of the purpose of the war:

> His officers could not tell him. They had never been told. They wanted to know. What they did know was that at every town, in every position, on every piece of work, in every detail of responsibility, an English officer stood over them telling them what to do.

Albertson found the doughboys very exercised by the absence of the Stars and Stripes from the scene of operations. He described a Christmas service in Shenkursk where, though "Americans predominated in numbers," "a British chaplain read the service, concluding naturally with 'God Save the King.' As we filed out an American private was heard to remark: 'Who ever heard of the Star-Spangled Banner anyhow?' " Albertson disliked the British habit of referring routinely to Russian civilians as "swine," and he was astounded by the tone of their propaganda, which was obsessed with boasts about the British Empire as well as

> the charitableness of British royalty, and lately the severity of terms demanded of Germany. Great piles of sheets of old war pictures with Russian captions were scattered broadcast upon a war-bored population, and Russian editions of a transparently over-censored news communiqué which told who

dined with the King, who got the Order of the Garter, who was responsible for the Great War, how bad the Bolsheviks are, and how the great international game of cricket is getting on . . .

This brief but intense military fiasco, which marked the first time in history that anybody had tried to invade Russia from the north, is memorable for other reasons. It was yet a further tentative step by American power into the quarrels of old Europe. It was the first official declaration by the United States that it regarded Communism as an enemy in general, and Russia as an enemy in particular (in this respect making a good match with the anti-Bolshevik and anti-immigrant convulsions going on simultaneously in America itself).

If today you visit the White Chapel Cemetery in Detroit, Michigan, you can see the Polar Bear Monument, erected in memory of those who lost their lives in the American expedition to Russia. The ambivalence of the survivors about the war they had fought is expressed by the inscription, which is from Stephen Decatur but which oddly recalls Churchill's 1900 exchange with Mark Twain: "Our country! In her intercourse with foreign nations, may she always be in the right; but our country, right or wrong." This unknown monument to unknown soldiers predates the celebrated Vietnam Memorial by sixty years, and greatly exceeds it in the ambiguity and irony which it expresses. In the fighting of undeclared wars against godless Communism, Winston Churchill was America's mentor almost thirty years before his "Iron Curtain" speech.

In the revulsion from foreign entanglement that overtook the United States after Versailles, Winston Churchill was a figure almost of demonology. The revulsion itself was a compound of petty isolationism, of anti-war sentiment, of anti-imperialist principle, and of ordinary self-interest. Its most eloquent and principled spokesman was Senator William Borah of Idaho, a former Shakespearean actor who emerged as the conscience of "Americanism."

Borah was able to touch a number of chords in his dramatic and finally successful campaign against Wilson and the League of Nations. The Irish-Americans were still seething about the British repression of the Easter Rising in 1916, and demanded to know why Ireland was not included in the grand Wilsonian design of "self-determination" for the smaller nations. Supporters of the Monroe Doctrine argued that a League of Nations would dilute American freedom of action in the expansionist cause. Others, taking a more sanctified liberal line, invoked Thomas Jefferson's lapidary warning against "entangling alliances."

Borah opened his campaign, in the first of three great senatorial interventions, on September 5, 1919. His subject was the perfidy of Winston Churchill in the matter of Russia. The speech could be the pattern for every later dissenting statement on undeclared wars and political adventures through Senator William Fulbright to our own day:

> Mr. President, we are not at war with Russia; Congress has not declared war against the Russian government or the Russian people. The people of the United States do not desire to be at war with Russia. . . . Whatever is being done in that country in the way of armed intervention is without constitutional authority. . . . Our boys are being sacrificed to satisfy the sinister ambition of other powers.

Turning to the villain of the piece, Senator Borah swiftly identified "a member of the English government and the head of one of its departments" as the author of the tragic policy:

> When Churchill speaks of it he defines it in his speech as being a policy based on military intervention to put down a certain force in Russia and establish a government satisfactory to the allied powers. It is plainly a policy of military intervention, first to establish a government such as we think a proper government for those people, and secondly to bring

about a situation where Japan will secure further interests in Siberia. This is the plan in all its concealed but hideous truth, and every boy who dies in Russia is a sacrifice to the unlawful and intolerable scheme.

Having made the obligatory reference to "boys" and extended himself so far as to describe "the imperialistic maw of a despotic power," Borah cited a recent Churchill speech which had said:

The uplift of Russia from her present situation will be the first duty of the League of Nations, and it is a vital interest of the allied powers. . . . The League of Nations is on its trial in regard to Russia. If the League of Nations cannot save Russia, Russia in her agony will destroy the League of Nations.

"This," thundered Borah to the chamber, "is not original with Mr. Churchill. That is precisely the principle and the policy announced by Metternich in 1822." There was much more in the same, actually rather sub-Churchillian vein.

A few weeks later, on November 19, 1919, Senator Borah gave an epic speech opposing the confirmation of the Versailles Treaty and the endorsement of the League of Nations Covenant. The speech is credited with having catalyzed every kind of misgiving about Wilson's foreign policy and to have led to that policy's defeat and eclipse. The Vice President, Thomas Marshall, sent Borah a note after the debate which said that "even a mummy on a pedestal could not remain silent after such a speech." The acting British ambassador, Viscount Grey, who had stood in after the death of Spring-Rice, said gallantly that he had "watched this debate most carefully and in all my experience I have never heard a debate on a higher plane than that conducted by Senator Borah." Actually, the viscount was muttering polite obsequies over Spring-Rice's hopes and, for the time being at least, his lifetime's aspiration.

As anti-British reaction set in more decidedly, there were to be two further rebuffs to the Churchillian conception of Anglo-

American relations. The first of these was at the Washington Dis-
armament Conference, where a debt-ridden British delegation was
compelled to listen in astonishment while a foreign power dictated
terms about the size of the British fleet. The conference, also held
at the instigation of Senator Borah, was convened in November
1921. Secretary of State Charles Hughes put forward a moratorium
on the further construction of warships, proposing an eventual ratio
of 5, 5, and 3 as between America, Britain, and Japan. He was so
bold as to give the names of twenty-three warships that the Royal
Navy would have to put out of commission.

A second and related move was the exertion of American pressure
to break off the Anglo-Japanese naval treaty. Colonel House notwithstanding, the United States had come to suspect Japanese
intentions and to suspect the British of nurturing these. By seeking
to limit the size and capacity of the British fleet, while simultaneously isolating Japan, Hughes and others were indirectly con-
summating the Mahan scheme of a graduated American maritime
supremacy, following British footsteps and challenging the Yellow
Peril but doing so in such a way as to gain eventual primacy. In
all of these graduated steps—the rejection of Versailles and the
League, the limiting of the power of the British Admiralty, and
the attempted dissolution of Anglo-Japanese ties—the United
States was striking at the figure of Winston Churchill, who embodied all these causes in their most John Bullish interpretation.

It also went without saying that the German-Americans, however
newly circumspect they had become about their identity, hated
Churchill and that the Irish-Americans had not forgotten his long
attachment to the Unionist cause. These considerations, allied to
the general reaction, made it easier to present the British as ungrateful and rather cynical. In the 1920s, Navy Department war-
fighting contingency plans called for "preparedness" in a struggle
against England at sea. "Preparedness"—the very term coined by
the wartime Anglophiles in order to coax the United States into
war on the British side. Admiral H. M. P. House, who had been
a member of the American naval staff at the Versailles conference,

called for open discussion of the possibility of war with Britain and Japan. He urged the construction of a United States navy equal to "any other two navies in the world." And the suspicion was mutual. Churchill feared that the United States had designs upon the British Empire and upon the system of Imperial Preference. In July 1927, in his capacity as Chancellor of the Exchequer, he told his Cabinet colleagues:

> No doubt it is quite right in the interest of peace to go on talking about war with the United States being "unthinkable." But everyone knows that this is not true. However foolish and disastrous such a war would be . . . we do not wish to put ourselves in the power of the United States. We cannot tell what they might do if at some future date they were in a position to give us orders about our policy, say, in India or Egypt or Canada, or any other great matter behind which their electioneering forces were marshalled.

Churchill in this period was the champion of the gold standard and the imperial system, and fiercely opposed any rival hegemony from any quarter. His alarmism and obduracy—especially about Indian independence—reduced his usefulness as a warning voice against Nazi ambition, because he was suspected of demagogy and warmongering. If this was true, as it was, even in the British Conservative Party, it was much more true in the American heartlands. When Churchill later strove to engage the United States in war once again, he had to overcome the accumulated mass of distrust that he had earned on his own behalf in much less noble causes.

The particular story of that great battle—to overcome the isolationism and neutralism that he had helped to encourage—is told in the next chapter. It is ironic that the final precipitation of America into the Second World War came as the result, not of Churchill's exhortations, but of an assault from the Japanese empire against which Senator Borah had been warning.

[8]

FDR's Victory; Churchill's Defeat

Reviewing the American reaction to the aftermath of the First
World War, Professor Selig Adler identified a predominant
strain of what he called "disillusionist" thinking. Many in the British
Establishment were slow to appreciate the depth and extent of this
phenomenon. When Lloyd George boasted in 1921 that "the people who govern America are our people. They are our kith and
kin. The other breeds are not on top," he was uttering a serious
foolishness. The United States might well value its claim to an
English bloodline, and had certainly not turned pacifist or squeam-
ish (as the war in Nicaragua was to demonstrate with particular
vividness in 1927). But the idea that it had been "played for a
sucker" by the British until 1918 was almost an orthodox belief.
"Isolationism," which is a weaker term for "disillusionism" and a
rather misleading version of it, took the form not of a retreat into
a fortress America but of an extreme reluctance to engage once
more in a European war. There were several strains in this isolationism, many of them powerfully strengthened by Churchill himself, and his battle against them was of necessity an uphill one.

For the general public, it was probably the hearings of the Nye
Committee that did most to materialize suspicion about "entangling
alliances." Named for its astute and cunning chairman, Senator
Gerald P. Nye of North Dakota, the committee held a rather in-

discriminate investigation into the role of fat cats in First World War profiteering, the mendacity of bankers, and the "Daddy Warbucks" method of cartelization. The easy populist term for this concert of interest and profit between imperial Britain and domestic American robber baronage was "economic royalism"—a handy encapsulation that further implied the idea of a British and monarchic upper crust. Even Roosevelt became fond of this useful term.

More fastidious isolationists could turn to Charles A. Beard, doyen of American historians, who also had a considerable journalistic audience. Beard was hagridden by the experience of 1914–18, and felt that the United States had been eased into war in order to recover the enormous and promiscuous loans she had made to the Allies. He spoke of the corrupting effects this had had on the American polity and inveighed against the "Atlas load" of "moneylending and huckstering abroad." The British, in other words, were to pay dearly for having had J. P. Morgan as their wartime broker and patron.

On the right, of course, was the America First movement with its tinge of chauvinist and Fascist sympathy. The young Charles Lindbergh had watched his father run for the governorship of Minnesota in 1918 on a platform which decried the effects of "Mr. Wilson's war" and had seen how crowds could be stirred. Still, the generally nativist timbre of the America First propaganda did not prevent some liberals, including some distinguished future Establishment Anglophiles such as Kingman Brewster and Blair Clark, from enlisting in its undiscriminating ranks.

Among liberals, there was a quasi-isolationist culture which could be justified in terms of anti-imperialist and anti-war feeling. This, too, had a "Never again" tone to it. Bruce Bliven of *The New Republic* was not atypical when he wrote, in 1939:

I remember when a country that did not want to go to war was tricked and bullied and persuaded into doing so . . . and so I feel, as I watch the motion picture of events unreeling on the screen of time, that I have seen it all before. This is where I came in.

It was the singular achievement of Churchill and Roosevelt between them to overcome this widespread mentality. Roosevelt's genius lay in seeing the opportunity for America that was presented by the rivalry between the European empires and fascism. The Neutrality Act of 1937 more or less secured him the best of both worlds in future negotiations with the British. The Act effectively prohibited economic entanglement with any belligerent in any war and thus preempted the use of the American flag as an insurer or collector of debt. But it did permit the President to make exceptions at his own discretion *if the goods were paid for in advance and if they left America in foreign vessels.*

Certain naïve objections were made to this combination of policy options, known to the idealistic as the "cash and carry" exemption. The *New York Herald Tribune* wittily described the Act as "an Act to Preserve the United States from Intervention in the War of 1917–1918." This was quite near the bull's-eye, but not as near as Senator Borah, who commented high-mindedly: "We seek to avoid all risks, all danger, but we make certain to get all the profits." He spoke, perhaps, more perceptively than he knew.

After the war, Churchill was to say: "No lover ever studied the whims of his mistress as I did those of President Roosevelt." Roosevelt was perfectly ready to be seduced, but only on certain conditions, for which he was quite prepared to ration his favors. Inscribed in the Churchill-Roosevelt wartime correspondence is the germination of United States postwar supremacy and of the inheritance of conditions and responsibilities that would challenge and undermine that supremacy. In his *English History, 1914–1945,* A. J. P. Taylor made the judgment that "of the great men at the top, Roosevelt was the only one who knew what he was doing: he made the United States the greatest power in the world at virtually no cost." This opinion might have to be qualified over the longer term, but the record of the correspondence shows the Romanization of America at the point of its zenith.

The exchange of letters and cables and afterthoughts between these two men is an incomparable trove. It affords an unprecedented occasion for the study of Anglo-American relations at their critical point—the point of definitive, unarguable replacement by the United States of Great Britain as the supreme maritime, military, and economic power on the globe. It is also a highly revealing emotional dialogue and a minor but distinct literary accomplishment. Those who read and reread it with care can scan almost the entire register of differences, from the stylistic to the diplomatic, which had been on view before and which have been salient since. Above all, the archive of correspondence is the authentic corrective to the romantic gloss laid on the subject by later memoirs and narratives. The great contributor to this romantic or idyllic version was in fact Churchill himself. Setting a tone which has informed all British official and semi-official history since 1945, he wrote to Dwight Eisenhower in March 1953 about his own *History of the Second World War*, saying:

> I am most anxious that nothing should be published which might seem to others to threaten our current relations in our public duties or impair the sympathy and understanding which exist between our two countries. I have therefore gone over the book again in the last few months and have taken great pains to ensure that it contains nothing which might imply that there was in those days any controversy or lack of confidence between us.

His anxiety, which may have been occasioned by the imminent publication of the State Department papers on the Malta and Yalta conferences, was understandable. In fact, almost from the declaration of war against Nazi Germany, Churchill was engaged in a sort of "Second Front," to protect the British Empire, against his putative ally. The letters, which were not published in full until 1984, make this plainer than even the most daring revisionist historians had previously suggested.

The first thing to notice is that, contrary to a widespread impression, the exchange of letters was actually initiated by Roosevelt. This may seem a slight thing but was not. For a President to write to a British minister (Churchill was still at the Admiralty on September 11, 1939, when the first letter arrived) was unusual and would have been unusual even if one country had not been a belligerent and the other a neutral. Roosevelt had been Woodrow Wilson's Assistant Secretary of the Navy during the First World War and kept up an interest in matters nautical. He had, we know, read Admiral Mahan with great care. He began thus:

> My dear Churchill,
> It is because you and I occupied similar positions in the World War that I want you to know how glad I am that you are back again in the Admiralty. Your problems are, I realize, complicated by new factors but the essential is not very different. What I want you and the Prime Minister to know is that I shall at all times welcome it if you will keep me in touch personally with anything you want me to know about. You can always send sealed letters through your pouch or my pouch.

This was the sort of communication which would have, had it been leaked, maddened the American isolationists beyond words. So, if they had known the details, would the first "incident" that arose for discussion between the two men.

In an eerie reminiscence of 1915, a naval attaché in Berlin reported a conversation in which Nazi Grand Admiral Erich Raeder warned that the American merchant vessel *Iroquois* would be sunk by the British in order to implicate Germany. The nearest seaport to the position of the *Iroquois* in early October 1939 was Queenstown, off which the *Lusitania* had been torpedoed. Churchill cabled Roosevelt that "U-boat danger inconceivable in these broad waters. Only method can be time-bomb planted at Queenstown. We think this not impossible." Nothing eventuated, but perhaps the shades of Room Forty gibbered a bit.

The next incident was more tangible. In December 1939, three British cruisers bottled up the Nazi pocket battleship *Graf Spee* in the Uruguayan port of Montevideo, where her captain ordered her scuttled. The battle had violated the nonbelligerency zone set up by the United States and the Latin American nations at Panama shortly before. Thus the first British naval victory of World War II was met by a Monroe Doctrine protest from the State Department.

But, by May 15, 1940, Churchill was Prime Minister and made it his first order of business to send Roosevelt a long message. Using the pseudonym "Former Naval Person," which he was to retain for the course of the war, he appealed for the very thing—an American declaration of nonbelligerency—which had so offended the British when proclaimed by Woodrow Wilson. He also appealed for the sending of aid on a "cash and carry" basis, stressing, with what his editor, Professor Warren Kimball, called "a tone of desperation," that "we shall go on paying dollars for as long as we can, but I should like to feel reasonably sure that when we can pay no more, you will give us the stuff all the same." Churchill also requested "the visit of a United States squadron to Irish ports, which might well be prolonged." This plea, which aimed to forestall German exploitation of Irish neutrality, was brushed off in Roosevelt's reply. No American politician would ever again repeat Wilson's mistake of ignoring Irish susceptibilities in favor of British interests. But he looked forward to negotiating with the Canadian Arthur Purvis, head of the British Purchasing Mission in the United States.

There was another hint of the teachings of Admiral Mahan in a message Roosevelt sent to the French Prime Minister, Paul Reynaud, on June 13, 1940. This cable, which was wrongly interpreted by Churchill as a pledge to enter the war, ended with the sentence: "Naval Power in world affairs still carries the lessons of history, as Admiral Darlan well knows." But Roosevelt's firm grasp of Mahan's classic and its lessons became evident on August 13 of that year, when he wrote that some fifty superannuated destroyers, together with motor torpedo boats and planes, could be made available for the defense of Britain only on this condition:

> if the American people and the Congress frankly recognized that in return therefor the national defense and security of the United States would be enhanced. For that reason it would be necessary, in the event that it proves possible to release the materiel above mentioned, that the British Government find itself able and willing to take the two following steps:
>
> 1. Assurance on the part of the Prime Minister that in the event that the waters of Great Britain become untenable for British ships of war, the latter would not be turned over to the Germans or sunk, but would be sent to other parts of the Empire for continued defense of the Empire.
> 2. An agreement on the part of Great Britain that the British Government would authorize the use of Newfoundland, Bermuda, the Bahamas, Jamaica, St. Lucia, Trinidad and British Guiana as naval and air bases by the United States in the event of an attack on the American hemisphere by any non-American nation; and in the meantime the United States to have the right to establish such bases and to use them for training and exercise purposes with the understanding that the land necessary for the above could be acquired by the United States through purchase or through a 99-year lease.

Churchill's reply contained gratitude and protest in about equal measure. He was particularly anxious that Roosevelt did not publish the details of the agreement in the form adumbrated. Here was a dilemma: Roosevelt feared anti-British reaction from the isolationists in the 1940 election if it did *not* look as if America was profiting by the deal, and Churchill feared anti-American reaction in Britain if it did. Churchill was especially touchy about discussing contingency plans for the disposal of the British fleet in the event of conquest or surrender—two eventualities he was at pains to rule out in public. He artfully employed phrases like "beyond a peradventure" and "instrumentalities," which were borrowed from Woodrow Wilson. He also distrusted the suggestion that the fleet be sent to Canada, which seemed too blatant an invitation to its annexation by the United States Navy. But he finally gave the required assurance, adding with a characteristic growl that "these hypothetical contingencies seem more likely to concern the German fleet or what is left of it than our own."

At this early stage, both men habitually referred to "the British Empire" in their exchange of communications, a style which was to be amended considerably as events wore on. The first sign of it came in a draft letter from Churchill in November 1940, which anticipated Fulton, Missouri, by some years and looked forward to a postwar world in which

> peace comes from power behind law and government, and not from disarmament and anarchy. Power in the hands of these two great liberal nations, with the free nations of the British Commonwealth and the American Republics associated in some way with them so as to ensure that that power is not abused, offers the only stable prospect of peace. It is clear that we shall be able to build nothing for many years out of the youth of Europe, which has been educated in Nazi and Communist doctrines.

Clearly the word "liberal" and the word "Empire" did not sort well together. In the message as finally sent the following month after discussion in Cabinet, paragraph one refers to "the British Commonwealth of Nations" though paragraph four describes the first half of 1940 as "a period of disaster for the Allies and for the

Empire." No less of interest was the way in which the message illustrated the difference in standing between the two countries compared with 1914:

> While we will do our utmost and shrink from no proper sacrifice to make payments across the exchange, I believe that you will agree that it would be wrong in principle and mutually disadvantageous in effect if, at the height of this struggle, Great Britain were to be divested of all saleable assets so that after victory was won with our Blood, civilisation saved and time gained for the United States to be fully armed against all eventualities, we should stand stripped to the bone.

Churchill's epistolary style was never suppliant, and it always sought to appeal both to pride and to self-interest in its recipient. Great effort and reflection went into the composition of these cables and letters, which were seldom crude or hasty in their manner despite the laconic breeziness of many of Roosevelt's replies. Roosevelt, indeed, failed to reply to Churchill's message of congratulation on his 1940 election victory, perhaps because Wendell Willkie had been making demagogic use of early Churchillian attacks on the "socialist" New Deal and Churchill had not disowned the remarks employed. This did not prevent Churchill from beginning to refer to Roosevelt in almost religious tones, once thanking him for "this very present help in time of trouble" and once directing him gratefully to look up 2 Corinthians 6:2. The letter quoted above, moving from the question of natural justice to the matter of realism, went on to point out that a Britain "stripped to the bone"

> would be unable after the war to purchase the large balance of imports from the United States over and above the volume of our exports which is agreeable to your tariffs and domestic economy. Not only should we in Great Britain suffer cruel

privations but widespread unemployment in the United States would follow the curtailment of American exporting power.

This was an abrupt shift to Keynesianism from a former champion of the gold standard. Not that gold ceased to figure in Anglo-American relations. In a later communication, Churchill struck out a reference to "a sheriff collecting the last assets of a helpless debtor." This was his immediate response to the American proposal to load an American warship with thirty million pounds' worth of South African gold and carry it to the United States for insurance on British debt. In the context of this plan (which was eventually carried out) Churchill preferred to allude to "the Dominions." In the case of the West Indies bases under the proposed Lend-Lease exchange, he at first objected to some of the American terms—such as the provision for British subjects arrested there to be tried in American courts—but in the end gave in, noting in a March 1941 memo that "the strategic value of these Islands or bases is incomparably greater to the United States than to Great Britain. They were in fact chiefly valuable to us as a means of attacking the United States." Another vindication of Mahan. As soon as May 1941, he was again having to allay American fears of British imperialism, by promising that any move to seize the Azores from Portugal would be for the duration of the war only.

In compensation for these indignities, it could be felt and seen that American neutrality was eroding fast. Not until 1974 was it officially acknowledged that the German battleship *Bismarck*, sunk in May 1941, had actually been spotted by an American flier named Ensign Leonard B. Smith, who had been flying as a copilot in combat for some weeks before doing the Royal Navy this historic favor and who had thus made nonsense of the Neutrality Act. (He more than made up for Tyler Kent, a code clerk in Joseph Kennedy's American embassy, who had until mid-1940 been leaking Churchill-Roosevelt cables to fellow isolationists and to pro-Axis consulates.)

But the imperial theme never ceased to recur. In June 1941,

Churchill felt bound to reassure Roosevelt about troop movements in the Middle East, saying "we have no political interests at all in Syria, except to win the war." A few days later, he was offering the United States a bomber base at Bathurst in Gambia on the same terms as those concluded in the West Indies, but, it seems, without consulting any Gambians. The next month, Adolf Berle minuted Roosevelt from the State Department that Britain had designs on Syria and the Balkans, too, and intended "to channelize the trade and economics of this area through London when the war is over." Again, there was a determination not to repeat Woodrow Wilson's humiliation over "secret treaties."

This determination was made exceedingly plain to Churchill at the Atlantic Conference, held at Placentia Bay, Newfoundland, at one of the new American bases being readied on former "Dominion" soil. Churchill had actually solicited the meeting, but got slightly more than he had bargained for when it eventually took place.

A noticeable absence from the Atlantic Conference, and indeed from most of Churchill's pleading and argument at this time, was that of the theme of blood. Anglo-Saxon consanguinity and tradition were a staple of British output on the American propaganda market, but did not figure very greatly, if at all, in public diplomacy. In his own public efforts, Roosevelt was just as inclined to stress France as an ally (she was, after all, in theory America's oldest) as he was Britain. And there was no repeat of anti-Germanism—in fact, until quite late in 1941, pro-German forces in America were active and confident. (The fate of German-Americans in 1917 was to be reserved, in even more bitter and concentrated form, for Japanese-Americans after 1941.)

The final draft of the Atlantic Charter excluded proposed State Department phrasing about the undesirability of closed and protective economic systems, but included an endorsement of the principle of self-determination. These two issues continued to nag at Churchill whatever the general fortunes of war might be. Having bid adieu to Roosevelt (in the name of "His Majesty's Government and the British Commonwealth" this time), Churchill found himself upon his return to London faced with a demand from Cordell Hull, imposing stern control over British reexport of Lend-Lease goods. This was an aid to American firms who might wish to try their hand in territories hitherto barred to them by Imperial Preference. A short while afterward, at the International Wheat Meeting in Washington, the United States pushed hard for fixed prices and production controls, which broke the Imperial Preference system in the case of Australia and Canada. Since the Neutrality Acts were in the process of being amended to allow American merchant ships to be armed and to enter zones of war, there was little the British side could do but complain.

This phase came to an abrupt end on December 7, 1941, with the attack on Pearl Harbor. For his next three cables to Churchill, announcing Congress's declaration of war and speaking about "the same boat," Roosevelt employed the word "Empire." Churchill, according to Sir Arthur Bryant, told the War Cabinet that the time for soft talk with America was past. "Oh! That is the way we talked to her while we were wooing her; now that she is in the harem we talk to her quite differently!" This, it turned out, was a mere emotional interlude on both sides.

Unconsciously inaugurating a long period of Conservative suspicion about American designs on the Empire, Churchill wrote to Roosevelt on January 14, 1942, asking for a guarantee that there were no plans to transfer sovereignty in British possessions in the West Indies. Artlessly, he suggested the appeasement of his colonial-minded backbenchers "possibly in reply to an inspired question at a Press Conference." Next month came the first note of self-pity—Churchill canceled an intemperate reply to a message to Roosevelt in which the latter had urged him to accept the abandonment of Imperial Preference as the price of Lend-Lease. Again there were mutterings from the Tory backbenchers, one of which mutters got as far as the unsent cable but had lodged in numerous British minds along the way:

As I told you I consider situation is completely altered by entry of the United States into the war. This makes us no

longer a consultant receiving help from a generous sympathizer, but two comrades fighting for life side by side. In this
connection it must be remembered that for a large part of 27
months we carried on the struggle single-handed . . .

Two days later, in the cable that *was* sent, Churchill dropped this
catty reminder but did say:

I found Cabinet at its second meeting on this subject even
more resolved against trading the principle of Imperial Preference as consideration for Lease-Lend [sic]. I have always
been opposed or lukewarm to Imperial Preference but the
issue did not turn on the fiscal aspect . . . The great majority
of the Cabinet felt that if we bargained the principle of Imperial Preference for the sake of Lease-Lend we should have
accepted *an intervention in the domestic affairs of the British
Empire,* and that this would lead to dangerous debates in
Parliament as well as to further outbreak of the German propaganda of the kind you read to me on the second night of
my visit about *the United States breaking up the British Empire and reducing us to the level of territory of the Union.*
[Italics mine.]

Two weeks later, the Master Lend-Lease Agreement was signed,
with the nondiscriminating Article VII included and Imperial Preference set aside. In the context of Preference, Churchill could
hardly avoid the use of the term Empire, though the notion of that
Empire having "domestic affairs" must have struck American readers as a bit farfetched. (The notion of the British being reduced
"to the level of territory of the Union" could probably, even given
the emotional circumstances, have been more tactfully put.) In the
course of the discussion, Roosevelt had sought briefly to be emollient and had chosen a revealing example by writing:

It seems to me the proposed note leaves a clear implication that Empire preference and, say, agreements between ourselves and the Philippines are excluded before we sit down at the table.

When Churchill read that butter-wouldn't-melt reference to "say, . . . the Philippines," did he recall his conversation with Mark Twain about imperial scrounging four decades before? It's probable that he did not, because Roosevelt's message arrived on February 11, 1942, and on February 10, 1942, Churchill was frantically engaged in cabling Wavell about the unthinkable prospect of the loss of Singapore. The call to Wavell might have frozen even Kipling's blood:

> There must at this stage be no thought of saving the troops or sparing the population. The battle must be fought to the bitter end at all costs . . . Commanders and senior officers should die with their troops. The honour of the British Empire and of the British Army is at stake. I rely on you to show no mercy to weakness in any form. With the Russians fighting as they are and the Americans so stubborn at Luzon, the whole reputation of our country and our race is involved.

Similar considerations were involved in the long resistance which Churchill put up to Roosevelt's persistent nudges about Indian independence. Churchill had gone so far as to leave Stanley Baldwin's "Shadow Cabinet" ten years earlier on this question, protesting at even the mildest flirtation by Tories with a move to eventual freedom for India. He was unlikely to vary this stand to please an American Democrat. Whenever the argument about self-determination came up, he was able to adapt his general opposition to make it sound like wartime exigency. At different times he argued that Britain could not break its trust with the Muslims, with the Untouchables, and with the princes, or at least not in time of war. In the immediate aftermath of the Singapore debacle,

Roosevelt nonetheless strove to keep the question on the agenda. He even rather archly suggested a trial confederation for India, on the model of the thirteen colonies. If the analogy lacked force, the repeated application of pressure did not. Churchill even told Harry Hopkins that he was ready to resign on the point, rather than concede to his fellow Old Harrovian Jawaharlal Nehru. On May 31, 1942, Churchill cabled Hopkins expressing concern at the movements of Roosevelt's commissioner in Delhi, Louis Johnson:

> There are rumors that the President will invite Pandit Nehru to the United States. I hope there is no truth in this and that anyway the President will consult me beforehand. We do not at all relish the prospect of Johnson's return to India. The Viceroy is also much perturbed at the prospect. We are fighting to defend this vast mass of helpless Indians from imminent invasion.

A few weeks later, on July 30, Churchill was fending off America's favorite Asian politician in the same tones. "We do not agree," he cabled to Roosevelt, "with Chiang Kai Shek's estimate of the Indian situation. The Congress Party in no way represents India." Two weeks after that, he cabled again, saying:

> I take it amiss Chiang should seek to make difficulties between us and should interfere in matters about which he has proved himself most ill-informed which affect our Sovereign rights. Decision to intern Gandhi was taken by executive of Twelve, at which only one European was present.

In a not too subtle allusion to Chiang's feline wife, who was known to have made an impression on Roosevelt, Churchill added: "The style of his message prompts me to say *Cherchez la femme.*"

That same month, August 1942, saw the first American success in replacing the British in the Middle East. Roosevelt had earlier suggested that the Americans operate the Trans-Persian Railroad, which the British had originally constructed. Averell Harriman, a man not unfamiliar with the railroad business (and the man who, under the title of "Defense Expediter," was Roosevelt's real envoy in London), prevailed on Churchill to agree that the line would be better if retooled and operated by the United States. When General Brooke objected that this would make British forces in Persia completely dependent on America, Churchill breezily responded: "In whose hands could we be better dependent?" He was later to distrust the use made by the United States of this, another of the many "openings" dictated by wartime pressure. But at that stage, with American tanks bolstering the British presence at Tobruk, Churchill was inclined to be sunny. He described himself in cables as Roosevelt's "loyal Lieutenant," "asking only to put my viewpoint plainly before you," and employed this same characterization (rather different from the reverse imagery of master and mistress) in talking with Harriman. But he was always insistent on full acknowledgment where he could get it. He disliked Roosevelt's presentation of the landings in North Africa as an all-American affair and suggested changing "Egyptian campaign" to "British campaign in Egypt" in the presidential press release on the subject in October 1942. This was modest enough in view of events at El Alamein.

Meanwhile, the maritime position of the United Kingdom was deteriorating catastrophically, and leading to an ever-greater dependence upon the United States. By way of his friend and colleague Oliver Lyttelton, on October 31, 1942, Churchill implored Roosevelt to bear the new situation in mind:

We must ask for a fair share of the merchant shipping and of the escort vessels. All our labour and capacity is engaged in the war effort. We have had to sacrifice 100,000 tons of merchant shipbuilding in order to get more corvettes, and we cannot hope to produce more than 1,100,000 British gross tons of new merchant ships in the calendar year 1943. We have lost enormously in ships used in the common interest,

and we trust to you to give us a fair and just assignment of
your new vast construction to sail under our own flag.

On the very next day, so intense was Churchill's attention to every
aspect of the relationship with Roosevelt, he wrote again. This
time, the subject was another historical irony: General Jan Smuts,
who had fought against Churchill in the Boer War, was now Prime
Minister of South Africa. In this capacity, he had succeeded in
bringing his country into the war on England's side (not without
stern opposition from the pro-Nazi Afrikaner militants who were
later to create official apartheid). Churchill hoped that an invitation
to Smuts might be procured to visit the United States:

> He has of course great responsibilities in South Africa where
> his personality has held the fort. I hope however he may be
> persuaded to go. There are things he could say to the Amer-
> ican people about the British Empire or Commonwealth of
> Nations which we could not say ourselves with equal accep-
> tance. Naturally people are much hurt over here by the Luce-
> Willkie line.

Thus Churchill, former hammer of the Boers, recommended his
old foe as an antidote to the "anticolonialism" professed for its own
reasons by the American right.

A continuous feature of the Churchill-Roosevelt correspondence
is Churchill's extraordinary sensitivity to tone and nuance. In November 1942, he wrote to the President saying: "We have had a
letter from General Hartle stating that under directive from the
United States War Department ('Any construction in excess of the
requirements for a force of 427,000 must be accomplished entirely
by your own labour and with your own materials and that Lend-
Lease materials cannot be furnished in these instances'). This has
caused us very great concern." The matter in dispute here was the
disposition of forces for a landing in Europe, but Churchill disliked
very much to find things out in this way, rather than to have them

conveyed first for his approval, and never let slip an opportunity to assert British amour propre. It was an unfailing source of hurt to him that he could never persuade Roosevelt to visit Britain during the war, and though he pretended to understand that there were physical difficulties in the way of the journey, he cannot have been surprised to be told, in December 1942, that "England must be out for me for political reasons." Roosevelt never forgot the reserve strength of anti-British and "anticolonial" feeling, and always sought to forestall any gibes about "Britain's quarrel."

On the anniversary of Pearl Harbor that same month, Churchill's commemorative message spoke only of "the British Commonwealth of Nations."

Having stressed his own American parentage wherever possible, Churchill did the same for Harold Macmillan as 1942 drew to its close. Recommending him as a personal representative on Eisenhower's staff, he asked Roosevelt for leave to publish the appointment and added: "He is animated by the friendliest feelings towards the United States and his mother hails from Kentucky." In fact, Macmillan, whose name was routinely misspelled in the cable traffic, had a mother born in Spencer, Indiana. But the chance to stress bloodlines was one which Churchill never missed.

In February 1943, after the Casablanca Conference, Churchill sent Roosevelt a long, ruminative letter headed "Morning Thoughts." Only one paragraph of this is reproduced in his memoirs. The whole and original version makes plainer his preoccupation with a post-victory settlement that would give Great Britain at least an equal footing with its wartime senior partner. When he spoke of the differences in proportion, he did so with the greatest circumspection. In a future United Nations, he wrote:

Great Britain will certainly do her utmost to organise a coalition of resistance to any act of aggression committed by any power; it is believed that the United States will cooperate with her and even possibly take the lead of the world, on account of her numbers and strength, in the good work of preventing such tendencies to aggression before they break into open war.

Toward the end of the "Morning Thoughts," Churchill wrote: "At the same time one must not ignore the difficulties which the United States Constitution interposes against prolonged European commitments." It is not clear whether Churchill actually believed that there was a constitutional impediment to such commitments, or whether he wished that there was a term set to the American presence in Europe, or whether he had simply been impressed by the strength of the isolationists in Congress even in wartime. The slip is intriguing, especially for a man who prided himself on a command of American politics.

Questions of precedence, particularly in North Africa, alternated with moments of warmth throughout 1943. In March, Roosevelt took up the question of bloodlines again, sending Churchill a photograph of the American general Sylvester Churchill, who had died in 1862, and pointing out a resemblance. In his later memoirs, Churchill confirmed that the general was indeed descended from the Dorsetshire Churchills and gave a family tree by way of illustration. It may also have pleased Churchill to receive a cable from Roosevelt later that month discussing rumors of a Nazi invasion of Spain and saying that in that contingency "the Combined Staffs should immediately study methods of re-establishing the Duke of Wellington's war of a number of years ago." The vagueness of the historic attribution here was made up for by an invocation of England's glory.

If this allusion was unintentional in recalling historic antagonism between Britain and France, it was one of the few communications from Washington that did not specifically complain about French intransigence. Throughout 1943, Roosevelt's detestation of de Gaulle continued to mount, as did his pressure on Churchill to disown the leader of the Free French. On May 21, 1943, to oblige Roosevelt, Churchill even cabled his War Cabinet to propose the withdrawal of British support for de Gaulle: a proposal that was finally shelved *sine die*. In this and other quarrels with the French leader, most of which took place at American instigation, were the seeds of much postwar rancor. Churchill's "America First" prejudices extended as far as support for Roosevelt in the matter of Dakar, the French West African port which he hoped to secure for the United States after the war. De Gaulle never forgave the British for their uncritical Atlanticism, and exacted a high price for it when the option of Europe became, too late, an attractive one for the postwar British Establishment.

Visiting Washington at the end of May 1943, Churchill sent Roosevelt a memorandum which extended and developed the themes of his earlier "Morning Thoughts." The core of the memorandum was an astonishing proposal for a quasi-merger between "the British Commonwealth" (as he called it on this occasion) and the United States:

He [Churchill] would like the citizens of each without losing their present nationality to be able to come and settle and trade with freedom and equal rights in the territories of the other. There might even be a common passport or a special form of passport or visa. There might even be some common form of citizenship, under which citizens of the United States and of the British Commonwealth might enjoy voting privileges after residential qualification and be eligible for public office in the territories of the other . . .

Churchill also proposed an extension of the "destroyers for bases" agreement under Lend-Lease whereby in the postwar world "the United States should have the use of such bases in British territory as she might find necessary for her own defense, for a strong United States was a vital interest of the British Commonwealth, and vice-versa." Turning to the Pacific, there were "British islands and harbours" there. "If he had anything to do with the direction of public affairs after the war, he would certainly advocate that the

United States had the use of those that they might require for bases."

Present at the luncheon where these thoughts were propounded were Vice President Henry Wallace, Secretary of War Henry Stimson, and Under Secretary of State Sumner Welles. They might not have guessed that within a few years the United States would indeed have the use of British and British-controlled soil, and would have this use, moreover, without any romantic nonsense about reciprocal citizenship.

The next month, in fact, Roosevelt attempted to arrange a meeting with Stalin without Churchill's knowledge or participation. The editors of the correspondence note that he "flatly lied" by later telling Churchill that such a meeting was Stalin's idea. Churchill worried that any "big two" rapprochement would be at Britain's expense, and expressed himself bitterly on June 25, 1943, this time mentioning the Empire:

> You must excuse me expressing myself with the frankness that our friendship and the gravity of the issue warrant. I do not underrate the use that enemy propaganda would make of a meeting between the heads of Soviet Russia and the United States at this juncture with the British Commonwealth and Empire excluded . . . Nevertheless, whatever you decide, I shall sustain to the best of my ability here.

By way of mollification for his deceit, Roosevelt made a proposal for a later meeting of himself, Stalin, and Churchill in Quebec, which he referred to soothingly as "General Wolfe's stronghold." The two men were also able to extract some camaraderie from, of all things, the notorious Stalinist motion picture *Mission to Moscow*. (In this film, based on the mendacious book by Ambassador Joseph Davies, Churchill had been played by Dudley Malone, who had with Roosevelt been an Assistant Secretary in the Woodrow Wilson administration.) But these national and personal pleasantries did not suffice to disguise the growing divergence of interests in various theaters from the Mediterranean to the Far East, where

General Stilwell showed increased vexation at Britain's preference for fighting to restore her empire.

In September 1943, Churchill visited the United States again and, on receiving an honorary degree from Harvard, reiterated his proposal for "common citizenship" between the United States and the United Kingdom. It may be significant that at this time he was out of sympathy with the Labor governments of Australia and New Zealand, both of whom (perhaps with memories of Churchill and Gallipoli) were slightly refractory about the indefinite provision of troops. His continuous rhetoric about "the English-speaking peoples" in fact concealed an inclination to place America above the white dominions; "English-speaking" being always a synonym for "English by blood" in any case. His emphasis on this common tie was a conditioned response to the Anglophobia of many American field commanders. General George Marshall had become convinced that British policy in the Middle East and Asia was colonial in inspiration, and thus that it shirked the frontal assault upon Germany and Japan that was necessary to shorten the war. Churchill's occasionally opportunist proposals, such as a plan to recover Malaya and Singapore, were so nearly designed to confirm American suspicions, and so unmilitary in themselves, that they met with opposition even from British Chiefs of Staff. The differences crystallized around the appointment of Lord Mountbatten to the position of "Supreme Commander, South East Asia." Churchill felt moved to contact Roosevelt in October 1943 and to protest:

> Some of the United States papers seem to have begun attacking Mountbatten bitterly, and he has been affected by accounts telegraphed here describing him as "The British Princeling and Glamour Boy who has ousted the proved veteran MacArthur from his rightful sphere . . . or words to that effect.

These semi-social and semi-colonial resentments, very common in the American press of that time, formed a permanent counterpoint to invocations of cousinhood or brotherhood, and were probably inseparable from them. The same mixed feeling of superiority and inferiority was aptly hit off a few weeks later, when five United States senators denounced Roosevelt for failing to uphold American interests. Referring self-pityingly to the United States as "a global sucker," the five pressed for trade advantages to be exerted in repayment for American aid. The group was by no means composed of backwoodsmen or hicks, and was senior and bipartisan, consisting of Richard Russell, Democrat of Georgia; Albert Chandler, Democrat of Kentucky; James Mead, Democrat of New York; Owen Brewster, Republican of Maine; and Henry Cabot Lodge, Republican of Massachusetts. The last name, in particular, exemplified the American tradition of anti-British, but Anglicized, ultra-conservatism.

Churchill's response, which was addressed in the first instance to Harry Hopkins, allowed him to release a number of long-pent-up resentments. The Five Senators, he wrote, had it all wrong:

> Complaints are made about the bases lent by Britain to the United States in the West Indies in 1940 in return for the fifty destroyers. These fifty destroyers, though very old, were most helpful at the critical time to us who were fighting alone against Germany and Italy, but no human being could pretend that the destroyers were in any way an equivalent for the immense strategic advantages conceded in seven islands vital to the United States.

This was, to say the least, a different tone from the one adopted by Churchill when the original "destroyers for bases" agreement was signed. Responding to the charge made by the senators that the British were "Out-Smarting their American Allies everywhere," he replied that "we have nowhere 'taken over' territory alone except in Italian East Africa which we liberated alone. In the Solomons we never withdrew our administrators. They worked on secretly throughout the Japanese occupation and the natives responded most loyally." Employing the standard rhetoric of solidarity, he deplored such charges being made at a time "when the blood and treasure of our two races is poured out." It was not clear which two races were meant, since the usual tocsin sounded was to the effect that the English and Americans were *one*. But the slip was perhaps an apt one, given that the pressure of the five senators was to lead Roosevelt to set up the Foreign Economic Administration and was to prefigure even wider disagreements about the future of reconquered colonies.

Prosaic reality was pressing in from every side in this month (which saw the presentation by Churchill to Roosevelt of the Kipling poems). Churchill had to fend off a "friendly suggestion" from Roosevelt that Brigadier General William Donovan, legendary director of the OSS, should be placed in command of resistance work in the Balkans, a region of historic British predominance. Next month, November 1943, Churchill was hurt to discover that Roosevelt was again attempting to deal with Stalin behind his back in the run-up to the Cairo and Tehran summits. His cable began:

> There seems to have been a most unfortunate misunderstanding.

And it ended:

> I was very glad to hear also from Ambassador Clark Kerr that you contemplate going on November 26th to Teheran. I rather wish you had been able to let me know direct.

At preparatory talks in Moscow among the Foreign Ministers, Anthony Eden had acted as spokesman for the Anglo-American alliance. This was, in the words of the editor of the Churchill-Roosevelt correspondence, "the last time during World War II that the Americans would accept anything less than the role of senior partner with Britain." At the subsequent meeting in Tehran, once and future site of the ascendancy of America over Britain, Churchill was deprived of his ambition to be chairman of the conference; an ambition he had forwarded by citing his seniority in age, his alphabetical precedence, and the greater historic standing of the British Empire over the two young superpowers. Rebuffed in this claim, and told that Roosevelt and Stalin would meet privately, Churchill sarcastically told Averell Harriman that he was "glad to obey orders." The summit was also significant in that it definitively overruled Churchill's preference for continued operations in the British-dominated Aegean and Mediterranean, and concentrated all efforts on the "Second Front" in mainland Europe. Next month, in December, Roosevelt rubbed in the new relationship by brusquely opposing Churchill's plan to restore King George to the throne of Greece.

The year 1944 opened with a renewal of ill-feeling over India. Admiral William Leahy had written to Roosevelt saying:

> It has become evident that differences between the interests and objectives of the United States and Great Britain in Southeast Asia raise serious objections to the continuance of the New Delhi Committee. Much of the territory in which military operations in that theater of the war are to be conducted consists of portions of the British Empire now under Japanese occupation. British interests and objectives in that area are, therefore, both military and political, while those of the United States are concerned with the defeat of Japan. . . . The State Department has consistently taken the position of opposing any integration of our propaganda program for the India-Burma region with the program of the British.

This may have been righteous and hypocritical in respect of presumed American altruism, but it was accurate in respect of Britain, which made no secret of its intention to restore "the King-Emperor" wherever and whenever possible. (As so often in this story, it appears that the imperial motives of others are always easier to discern.) Roosevelt acted on the letter of Leahy's message, contacting Churchill and recommending the scrapping of the New

Delhi Committee. He added a veiled threat in his own handwriting, saying that discontinuation of the committee would obviate the need for him to make "a trip to India to sort it out." Churchill could have wanted few things less than a presidential visit to India.

Admiral Leahy also urged Roosevelt to pursue a policy at odds with the British in the matter of Western Europe. In spite of the fact that it was on the British flank in the plans for the invasion of Normandy, the prize of northwestern Germany with the ports of Hamburg and Bremen was felt in Washington to be worth the military risk. "Although the occupation of the northern area will render our military problem more difficult initially," wrote Leahy to the President, "the long-term political and military advantages to the United States are of such importance that we should not accept the recommendation of the British chiefs of staff."

As 1944 drew on, the word "political" increasingly took precedence over the word "military" in the discussion of Anglo-American commitments. On the American home front, the Five Senators were still active, touring American bases overseas and returning home to denounce what they termed "giveaway" programs. They wanted raw materials as well as bases in exchange for Lend-Lease, and they understood that the crucial raw material was oil. Responding to these and other pressures, Roosevelt called for high-level Anglo-American talks on oil, placing such key words as "transportation rights," "concession rights," and "price and marketing policies" on the agenda. This drew a furious response from Lord Halifax at the Washington embassy, who exclaimed that the Americans "were treating us shockingly, and that they were being as cavalier as U.J." Since U.J. in cable parlance meant "Uncle Joe," one has a measure of British pique.

Churchill understood instinctively that this meant an American challenge to the British position. He wrote to Roosevelt in February 1944, saying:

There is apprehension in some quarters here that the United States has a desire to deprive us of our oil assets in the Middle East on which, among other things, the whole supply of our navy depends. This sensitiveness has of course been greatly aggravated by the Five Senators.

This, as it turned out, was only the harbinger of future rivalry. Roosevelt's reply was unexpectedly tough:

You point to the apprehension on your side that the United States desires to deprive you of oil assets in the Middle East. On the other hand, I am disturbed about the rumor that the British wish to horn in on Saudi Arabian oil reserves.

He insisted on going ahead with the Cabinet-level oil discussions. At the same time, he took the side of Under Secretary of State Edward Stettinius against Treasury Secretary Henry Morgenthau on the restriction of British dollar balances in America. Both Stettinius and Morgenthau favored reducing and restricting British balances, but Morgenthau felt the question could be postponed until after the war. Stettinius vigorously disagreed, telling Roosevelt that "if the financial side of the war is run in such a way as to keep British balances at or about $1 billion, we thereby reduce our chance to achieve the basic economic policy we want and need." Roosevelt expressed his usual view that "the domestic aspect of this situation was great enough to be controlling": his invariable and unanswerable practice when conveying news of this sort to Churchill. The same consideration applied to the simultaneous cancellation of Lend-Lease agreements which benefited the British economy rather than the war effort. Many of these, such as Caribbean sugar purchases, also involved jostling over colonial possessions.

Oil, currency, colonies, and trade: it was difficult not to discern a pattern of American maneuver aimed at an ever-wider "Open Door." Certainly, that conception was self-consciously present in the minds of men like Stettinius. And it appears to have dawned on an increasingly gloomy Churchill, who, writing to Roosevelt with his reservations about Middle East oil talks on February 24, 1944, said sadly:

> Your telegram dismisses all these points and if you will allow me to say so seemed to convey your decision on these matters.

By way of reply a mere five days later, Churchill received one of the most astonishing communications of the entire correspondence. It took the form of a memorandum, commissioned by Roosevelt, from Major General Patrick Hurley. Hurley was an ambitious soldier-diplomat who acted as presidential "fact-finder" in the Middle East. Although he was a staunch Republican, his memo described the enemies of United States policy as "greedy minorities, monopolies, aggression and imperialism." In its rhetoric, the memo is the most classic expression of American antiimperial imperialism since Mahan. As Hurley put it:

> The imperialism of Germany, Japan, Italy, France, Belgium, Portugal and the Netherlands will, we hope, end or be radically revised by this war. British imperialism seems to have acquired new life. This appearance, however, is illusory. What appears to be a new life of British imperialism is the result of the infusion, into its emaciated form, of the blood of productivity and liberty from a free nation through lend-lease. British imperialism is being defended today by the blood of the soldiers of the most democratic nation on earth.

Glancing backward for a moment, Hurley defined Woodrow Wilson's policy in the First World War as "designed 'to make the world safe for democracy' and to sustain Britain as a first class world power. Sustaining Britain as a first class world power has for many years been the cornerstone of America's foreign policy." Hurley added, with another echo from Mahan, that "I have long believed and have many times stated publicly that the ultimate destiny of the English-speaking peoples is a single destiny." However, he

asserted, "an effort to establish true freedom among the less favored
nations, so many of which are under the present shadow of imperialism, *will almost inevitably run counter to the policy of sustaining Britain as a first class world power.*" (Italics mine.)

Turning to the business in hand, which was Iran, Hurley urged
Roosevelt to disassociate entirely from British policy there. "Many
Iranian officials believe that American troops are in Iran on the
invitation and for the purpose of serving as an instrumentality of
Britain." That this was harmful to American objectives seemed clear
to Hurley, who added:

> In addition to this the United Kingdom Commercial Cor-
> poration which was first engaged in preclusive purchasing in
> Iran has since been selling American lend-lease supplies to
> civilians and to the Government of Iran. Lastly through our
> lend-lease supplies, paid for by the American taxpayer, the
> United Kingdom Commercial Corporation has been attempt-
> ing and, to a considerable degree, succeeding in establishing
> a complete trade monopoly in Iran. . . . The Iranians believe
> that the post-war monopoly plans of the United Kingdom
> Commercial Corporation now have the support of the United
> States government.

Urging the rival claims of the United States Commercial Corporation, Hurley pointed out that there would soon "be a great rush
on the part of American businessmen to get oil, mineral and other
concessions in Iran. I suggest that the State Department, with the
assistance of the other agencies of our government, should be prepared to advise the Government of Iran definitely concerning the
character and other qualifications of every applicant for a concession."

Among those American businesses trying to get concessions in
Iran was the Sinclair Oil Company, with which General Hurley
had an exceedingly close personal and business relationship.
Churchill's reply, which was three whole months in coming, could

hardly have been more contemptuous had he known of this connection, which he did not. One can almost see the angry cigar smoke wreathing the riposte:

> The General seems to have some ideas about British imperialism which I confess make me rub my eyes. He makes out, for example, that there is an irrepressible conflict between imperialism and democracy. I make bold, however, to suggest that British imperialism has spread and is spreading democracy more widely than any other system of government since the beginning of time.

No inverted commas for "imperialism"; no euphemisms about "Commonwealth of Nations"; this was *Ur*-Churchill refusing to apologize for Empire. He may or may not have snorted at Roosevelt's promise, made in the meantime on March 3, 1944: "Please do accept my assurances that we are not making sheep's eyes at your oil fields in Iraq or Iran." And he must have been outraged by Hurley's mention of German and Italian imperialism in the same breath as British. Something of the resentment he felt at this period is to be found in a deleted passage from one of his cables. The matter under debate was the transfer by Roosevelt of captured Italian ships to the Soviet navy, but the hurt nerve of amour propre obviously ran deeper than that:

> Considering Great Britain has suffered at least twenty times the naval losses of your fleet in the Mediterranean and has been fighting the Italians since June 1940, we had hoped to be consulted or at least informed beforehand.

The day after he decided not to send this bitter sentence, Churchill wrote to Roosevelt saying:

> Thank you very much for your assurances about no sheep's eyes at our oil fields at Iran and Iraq. Let me reciprocate by

giving you the fullest assurance that we have no thought of trying to horn in upon your interests or property in Saudi Arabia. My position on this, as in all matters, is that Great Britain seeks no advantage, territorial or otherwise, as the result of the war. On the other hand she will not be deprived of anything which rightly belongs to her after having given her best services to the good cause—at least not so long as your humble servant is entrusted with the conduct of her affairs.

Five days later, in a less sensitive vein, Churchill was again protesting at the proposed reductions of British dollar balances:

Will you allow me to say that the suggestion of reducing our dollar balances, which constitute our sole liquid reserve, to one billion dollars would really not be consistent with equal treatment of Allies or with any conception of equal sacrifice or pooling of resources. We have not shirked our duty or indulged in an easy way of living. We have already spent practically all our convertible foreign assets in the struggle. We alone of the Allies will emerge from the war with great masses of war debts. I do not know what would happen if we were now asked to disperse our last liquid reserves required to meet pressing needs, or how I could put my case to Parliament without it affecting public sentiment in the most painful manner and that at a time when British and American blood will be flowing in broad and equal streams.

Next day, ever equal to the literary demands of wartime, Churchill sent Harry Hopkins a hand-lettered parchment with an inscription to commemorate the death in action of his son Stephen. Movingly taken from the closing scene of *Macbeth*, it evoked the idea of blood and common heritage very aptly:

Your son, my Lord, has paid a soldier's debt;
He only liv'd but till he was a man;
The which no sooner had his prowess confirm'd
In the unshrinking station where he fought,
But like a man he died.

At about this time, Roosevelt made another of his ingratiating references to past British generalship. Discussing his loathing for de Gaulle and his refusal to receive him in Washington, he said that if de Gaulle asked for a meeting, "I will incline my head with complete suavity and with all that is required by the etiquette of the 18th Century. This is farther than the Great Duke would have gone, don't you think so?" Keeping up the joshing atmosphere that prevailed whenever there was no outright *froideur*, the next cable from Churchill referred to trouble with nationalist "wogs" in Egypt. This might or might not have been an implied rebuke to General Hurley's pretended concern for the wretched of the earth under the British yoke. But Roosevelt showed that he was still serious about this, by refusing Churchill's appeal for extra ships to relieve famine in British-controlled India. Throughout 1944, in fact, Churchill continued to give ground to superior force, using his own prestige and the emotional ties of earlier years to delay matters where he could. For example, he always tried to follow Roosevelt's suit—overruling his own Foreign Secretary, Anthony Eden—in derogating de Gaulle. At the time of the Normandy landings he wrote to Roosevelt in almost fawning terms, describing his peremptory treatment of the general and saying, "I have repeatedly told de Gaulle and he acknowledged it without irritation that failing an agreement, I stand with you."

De Gaulle himself had an even clearer memory of this meeting, which he set out in his memoir *Unity*. "Each time we must choose between Europe and the open sea," Churchill told him, "we shall always choose the open sea. Each time I must choose between you and Roosevelt, I shall always choose Roosevelt." This at a time when British forces were fighting their way onto the beaches of Normandy.

Speaking of "open seas," it was in this same month that Roosevelt protested at the British attempt to establish a "sphere of influence" in the Mediterranean and the Balkans. An aspect of this protest concerned American worries that the British were making separate agreements with the Soviet Union in Romania and Greece. One State Department minute told the President: "The British are giving us informal notice that the U.K. expects to follow a strong policy in regard to the Eastern Mediterranean even if it means standing up and making deals with the Soviet Union. This is part and parcel of the British policy of regarding the Mediterranean as a British sea." Meanwhile, the corresponding view in the British Foreign Office was that the U.K. "could not have a free foreign policy in Europe as long as there was an American Supreme Commander responsible to the Combined Chiefs of Staff in Washington." Both confidential opinions were, in their different ways, correct. (So was Churchill's otherwise seemingly irrelevant reminder, at this point, of the fact that Britain had allowed the United States a free hand in South America.)

It was actually in the context of the Monroe Doctrine that the next Anglo-American friction arose. The United States refused to recognize Juan Perón's coup in Argentina in 1944 unless he agreed to suppress pro-Nazi activity in his country. His predictable refusal led the State Department to withdraw the American ambassador; an action considered inadvisable by the British Foreign Office, which bore in mind the importance of Argentine beef to the United Kingdom. Under pressure, and perhaps not unmindful of the recent objections to Britain's independent line in the Balkans, Churchill sent a rather acerbic cable reporting the recall of the British envoy and adding:

This decision has been taken in response to your appeal for a "common stand." There is a good deal of anxiety in the Foreign Office and the War Cabinet. I do not myself see where this policy is leading to nor what we expect to get out of the Argentines by this method. . . . I hope you will not mind my saying, as is my duty, that we ourselves were placed in an invidious position by this American decision, to which we are now asked to conform, being taken without consultation with us. We were faced with a fait accompli.

Rare for Churchill to say anything three times, especially anything critical. He must have felt himself in a position of moral advantage.

If he exploited this position, it was partly on the ground of its rarity. In a really astonishing volte-face, Roosevelt did receive de Gaulle at the White House on July 6, 1944, a matter of weeks after he had bragged to Churchill that "I will not ever have it said by the French or by American or British commentators that I invited him to visit me in Washington." More, he unbent to the general to no little extent, confiding in him his postwar plans for a post-colonial world. According to de Gaulle in his memoirs, the President proposed a "permanent system of intervention" with a chain of American bases occupying what had been French and British possessions in Africa and Asia. By including China and France in his plan, Roosevelt also demonstrated a preference for what he had termed "the United Nations" over Anglo-Americanism. Churchill was highly displeased to hear of all this but was dissuaded from making a demarche.

Later that month he reverted to form, ending a cable by saying that he hoped soon "to be able to report all clear on the British Empire front." He also protested about the Argentine situation once more, reminding Roosevelt: "You would not send your soldiers into battle on the British meat service ration, which is far above what is given to workmen. Your people are eating per head more meat and more poultry than before the war while ours are mostly sharply cut."

As the European and Middle Eastern theaters widened, Churchill seized every chance to stay in the game as at least the senior of the junior partners. In August, discussing the Italian campaign, he told a British staff meeting that "a victory would greatly strengthen our hand in the forthcoming discussions with the Americans." Arguing in Cabinet about the wisdom of creating a specifically Jewish brigade in Palestine—a proposal made by Chaim Weizmann without effect at the outbreak of war—he said: "Remember the object of this is to give pleasure and an expression to rightful sentiments, and that it certainly will be welcomed widely in the United States." The flag of the Jewish brigade, as he wrote to Roosevelt, would be "the Star of David on a white background with two light blue bars. I cannot see why this should not be done." Within a few years, this flag would be a source of rancor between Britain and the United States, but for the moment the concession was seen to be a shrewd one.

A surreal discussion took place at the second Quebec Conference in September 1944, with Roosevelt outdoing Churchill in vengeful feeling and policy toward "the Hun." The Morgenthau plan called for the complete deindustrialization of Germany and the reduction of the German people to permanent agrarian status; the Carthage to the new Rome. Initially, Churchill's response to the plan was to describe it as "unnatural, un-Christian and unnecessary," but he altered his position and signed a joint memorandum which called for the crushing of "Germany into a country primarily agricultural and pastoral in its character," the word "pastoral" being added at Churchill's own prompting. Having made this turnaround to please Roosevelt, he was to see the Morgenthau plan defeated by the combined opposition of Hull and Stimson. Ending this fantastic meeting by giving Roosevelt a copy of his wartime speeches, Churchill inscribed it bizarrely: "To FDR from WSC. A fresh egg from the fruitful hen." The one concrete result of the Quebec meeting was the acceptance, over Admiral King's protests, of British ships to aid the American fleet in the Far East. Roosevelt was not deceived by the timing of this gesture, later telling Morgenthau: "All they want is Singapore back." The next month saw the cancellation of an amphibious landing in formerly British colonial Burma for which Churchill had particularly hoped forces might be spared.

During the now notorious October 1944 meetings between himself and Stalin in Moscow, Churchill helped put the iron in a curtain he was later famously to christen. Consenting to Russian control over the Baltic states of Latvia, Estonia, and Lithuania, and brokering a further exchange of Soviet influence in Poland and Romania for British predominance in Greece, Churchill actually told Stalin that "it was better to express these things in diplomatic terms and not to use the phrase 'dividing into spheres,' because the Americans might be shocked." Averell Harriman, who reported with some accuracy and prescience to Roosevelt on these private meetings, was not exactly shocked. He and the President adopted a "wait and see" policy in the face of this, Churchill's most barefaced attempt to keep Britain a superpower.

This ambition received another check at the less dramatic-sounding International Civil Aviation Conference, held in Chicago at the beginning of December 1944. The British side at this conference having tried to restrict American aviation routes to the Atlantic, Roosevelt quite blatantly threatened a cutoff of Lend-Lease unless the proposal was dropped. To this message Churchill replied:

I was of course very much hurt that this form of pressure should be applied to us, and I hope it will not be thought that the Cabinet was aware of it or influenced by it at the time they agreed to my request. It seems almost to amount to a threat of indirect blockade.

Two days later he added:

The British Empire is asked to put invaluable and irreplaceable bases for air transport all over the world at the disposal of such nations as are capable of using them. This means of course primarily and in bulk placing them at the disposal of the United States.

This showed, though by way of trying to avoid it, that Churchill had got the main point. The same point was made in his appeal in the same cable to be generous.

> You will have the greatest navy in the world. You will have,
> I hope, the greatest air force. You will have the greatest trade.
> You have all the gold.

In a reply drafted by Dean Acheson (which referred to "the British Empire"), Roosevelt more or less told Churchill not to be silly.

Simultaneously, Roosevelt was taking an unsentimental line about the withdrawal of two Chinese nationalist divisions from India. Although the military logic of this was clear, since they were to support Chiang Kai-shek's positions under American command, British anxiety about a further postponement of the recapture of Burma was unconcealed.

In Greece, too, Churchill found that his policy was strenuously opposed by the American administration. Having committed British troops to the victory of one faction in the nascent civil war, he was furious when Admiral King issued an order prohibiting American ships from bringing supplies to British forces in Greece. During the heavy street fighting that followed the British intervention, the American ambassador in Athens at one point refused to allow British troops to drink from the fountain in his garden. Churchill was bewildered by the American attitude, telling Harry Hopkins: "If it can be said in the streets of Athens that the United States are against us, then more British blood will be shed and much more Greek." He thought that the self-evident Communism of the EAM/ELAS leadership would justify his cause in American eyes. But Washington knew that Churchill had concerted his Greek policy with Stalin in advance. It also had little taste for the Greek monarchy. Most of all, however, it viewed with disfavor any autonomous British zone in the Balkans.

Between the meetings at Malta and Yalta in the opening months of 1945, Roosevelt studiously avoided Churchill and even told Stalin not to inform him of his planned movements. He also failed to answer Churchill's repeated pleas that he visit Britain en route to the Black Sea. Additional mortification was provoked by the American decision to sign bilateral aviation agreements with, among other countries, the Irish Republic. Churchill cabled Roosevelt on January 29:

> I have just heard from Dublin that your people are asking the Government of Southern Ireland to sign a bilateral civil aviation agreement. Naturally everyone here is astonished that this should have been started without our being told beforehand.

Hearing nothing for over a month, Churchill renewed the attack, still referring insultingly and incorrectly to "Southern Ireland," but varying this at one point by saying:

> Our special concern with Eire is obvious on political and geographical grounds, and it is indeed much closer than that of the United States with the Argentine.

He received no reply to his demand that the bilateral agreement be annulled.

Meanwhile, no opportunity was lost for American officials to press Britain for economic concessions. Even at the Yalta summit itself, Roosevelt, at the urging of Stettinius, sent Churchill a memo reminding him of Article VII of the Lend-Lease agreement. This article called for an end to discriminatory trade arrangements within the British Empire. Churchill sought to put off any discussion of this, and there ensued a period of what might be termed Fabian tactics, with John Maynard Keynes at the British Treasury fending off American officials who sought what they called "the liberalization of world trade."

In the last few weeks of Roosevelt's life, Churchill seemed to sense a reticence in him. "I hope," he cabled on March 17, "that the rather numerous telegrams I have to send you on so many of our difficult and intertwined affairs are not becoming a bore to you." The reason for this unusually tentative tone may have been Roosevelt's failure to respond to a telegram about the future of Indochina. Roosevelt had hoped to forestall a French recolonization in the area but died before he could answer a message from Churchill, who was disingenuously proposing an Anglo-American alliance to bring about that precise outcome. The great correspondence thus closes on the outer verge of the long-impending calamity of America and post-colonial Vietnam. Given the constant tension, even in wartime, between British "direct rule" imperialism and American expansionism, this is less of an irony than it may appear.

[9]

Churchill's Revenge

By the time the Second World War was over, isolationists of every stripe had been definitively overtaken by events. It might not be too much to say that they had been undone by history. The combination of victory in a good cause and the measureless expansion of opportunities for American power and influence remade the national consensus. The great phrases in which this achievement could be expressed tended to be Churchillian ones—especially since they could now be adapted so readily to the new *Kulturkampf* with the Soviet Union. Those who harbored misgivings about that—whether Robert Taft on the right or Henry Wallace on the left—could be easily stilled by an appeal to the lessons of Munich and a crisp reminder that the "appeasers" had been wrong last time. Had not Neville Chamberlain said, in reply to a suggestion from Roosevelt that there should be an international conference to discuss the dangers of war, that it would be a bad idea because it was "likely to excite the derision of Germany and Italy. They might even use it to postpone conversations with us"? The *tap, tap* of his umbrella has been used to ridicule all those who felt doubts about the nuclear umbrella ever since. In this immense contest, the figure of Churchill has had the status of an icon. The Fulton address confirmed this standing for a generation.

Before reviewing Fulton and its imagery, a word on "isolationism." Although it is a term now employed to diminish the moral standing of those who oppose an imperial foreign policy, and though it has the imputation of small-mindedness and parochialism, it does not have an unambiguous history. In 1848, when the Hungarian patriot Lajos Kossuth toured the United States, he inspired generous sentiments in the minds of many Americans. The simplicity and dignity of his appeal against Russian and Austrian imperialism won support for the idea of Europe's "Captive Nations." President Millard Fillmore, his Secretary of State, Daniel Webster, and the great Henry Clay all seemed in public to endorse this idea. But they were likewise careful to caution Kossuth in private; Webster in particular telling him that the mere suggestion of "intervention" would fall upon "ears as deaf as adders." Henry Clay added consolingly that the liberty of Hungary and other subject countries would be advanced more by an America that kept its "lamp burning brightly on this Western shore, as a light to all nations, than to hazard its utter extinction, amid the ruins of fallen or falling republics in Europe." These last phrases oddly anticipate Emma Lazarus and her verses on the Statue of Liberty and Winston Churchill's wartime quotation from Arthur Hugh Clough's hymnal poem, with its famous line: "But westward, look, the land is bright."

As the Hungarians were to discover anew in 1956, American policy has been a series of oscillations between great causes overseas and the need to avoid quagmires. A world role has necessitated the striking of brave attitudes and the issuing of numerous promissory notes to allies, while the attention of Congress and the public has been easier to engage than to maintain. In 1848, the American partisans of Kossuth described as "isolationist" the refusal of those who paid lip service to Hungary to commit America to force. In 1956, an analogous policy of mere verbal and propaganda support for the Hungarian Revolution was described by its opponents as "appeasement." Kossuth's admirers were slightly inflamed by the intoxicating victory over Mexico in 1848. Those who were in the mood for a crusade in 1956 were similarly resplendent in the prestige of a speech given in Fulton, Missouri.

After having lost his electoral mandate a few months after Roosevelt's death, Churchill was to make one more grand attempt to preserve a full partnership of equals. He journeyed to Fulton on March 5, 1946, and there delivered himself of the last speech upon which he would ever be seriously quoted. A few months earlier, on December 13, 1945, there had been an emotional and angry debate in the House of Commons concerning the terms of the postwar American loan to Britain, which terms were thought by many Members of Parliament to be arrogant and humiliating. One hundred MPs voted against the incoming Labor government for approving the terms of the loan, and an astounding one hundred and sixty-nine abstained, including Churchill himself. But this unprecedented revulsion at the rise of the new Rome could, as Churchill well understood, risk a petty and embittered nationalism. By appealing to the burgeoning sense of American globalism and internationalism, he tried his utmost to preserve and retain the spirit of Anglo-Americanism and of Anglo-Saxondom, too.

Since he had himself signed away Poland and the Baltic states to Stalin, in a meeting which he tried to keep secret from Roosevelt and Harriman, Churchill was gambling for very high stakes when he described the "Iron Curtain" as extending "from Stettin in the Baltic." But a close reading of the speech shows that anti-Soviet solidarity was only its secondary and instrumental purpose. Its main thrust was an appeal for a "special relationship." Having rather arbitrarily traced the evolution of "the rights of man" themselves to the "joint inheritance of the English-speaking world" via Magna Carta and the Declaration of Independence, he struck the clear note that has resonated since:

> Neither the sure prevention of war nor the continuous rise of world organisation will be gained without what I have called the fraternal association of the English-speaking peoples. This means a special relationship between the British Commonwealth *and Empire* and the United States. This is no time for generalities. I venture to be precise. Fraternal association

requires not only the growing friendship and mutual understanding between our two *vast but kindred* systems of society,
but the continuance of the intimate relations between our
military advisors, leading to common study of potential dangers, similarity of weapons and manuals of instruction and
interchange of officers and cadets at colleges. It should carry
with it the continuance of the present facilities for mutual
security by the *joint use* of all naval and air-force bases *in the
possession of either country all over the world*. [Italics mine.]

And again, in closing:

If the population of the English-speaking Commonwealth
be added to that of the United States, with all that such cooperation implies in the air, on the sea and in science and
industry, there will be no quivering, precarious balance of
power to offer its temptation to ambition or adventure.

This element in the speech considerably outweighed the fairly
conventional anti-Soviet invocation, most of which seems to have
been taken directly from James Burnham. The italicized words
make it clear that for Churchill the words "British" and "Empire"
could not be divorced without great pain and difficulty. He was
shrewder than he knew in proposing that anti-Communism came
before anti-imperialism:

Except in the British Commonwealth and in this United
States, where Communism is in its infancy, the Communist
parties or fifth columns constitute a growing challenge and
peril to Christian civilisation.

Quite clearly, it is the words "Iron Curtain" that have been
retained from this long speech, and the context which has been
placed in history's discard. Churchill's listeners were well able to
annex his prestige for what they did care about—the emerging

superpower competition—while politely overlooking his appeal that Britain be considered their serious equal in that competition.

One clue to the astonishing durability of this speech in the American annals may be the otherwise unremarked congruence between Churchill's global generalizations and those of James Burnham. It is easy now to forget the importance of Burnham's writing in the formation of American imperial thinking, but his words were decisive among intellectuals and the literate public in the 1940s and 1950s (David Riesman in *The Lonely Crowd* spoke of "Marx, Mosca, Michels, Pareto, Weber, Veblen or Burnham") and were seminal as regards the American right. Even people who had not themselves read Burnham were swayed by columnists and politicians and academics who had.

Burnham was oddly but powerfully equipped for the task in hand. The son of a British Catholic emigrant to Chicago, he made a partial return to his English roots by becoming a Balliol man and specializing in English literature. He spent the 1930s classically enough: engaging with T. S. Eliot on modernism and aesthetics in the pages of *The Symposium*, polemicizing with the *Partisan Review* crowd, foreseeing the Hitler-Stalin pact, and writing a spirited critique of Leon Trotsky (then his only point of similarity with Churchill, whose own piece on the old revolutionary was published at about the same time in *Great Contemporaries*).

Burnham's biographer, Samuel Francis, makes the excellent point that his ideas, "unlike those of virtually any other major American conservative thinker in this century, were profoundly modernist and at the same time counter-revolutionary." His transition from Marxism to conservatism was most powerfully expressed in *The Managerial Revolution*, which John Kenneth Galbraith ranks with Keynes's *General Theory* and Berle and Means's *The Modern Corporation and Private Property* as one of the three great economic texts of the prewar period. The book was an unquestionable influence on C. Wright Mills (who wrote a long critique of it) and on George Orwell (who also wrote a long critique of it and clearly evolved some of the lineaments of his *1984* from its predictions). When it came out, it was reviewed over three days in *The New York Times* and earned its author a photograph in *Time*. From then on, everything Burnham wrote won him attention. In 1945, for example, he contributed a famous article called "Lenin's Heir" to *Partisan Review*. He employed a form of Platonism to describe how

> the Soviet power, emanating from the integrally totalitarian center, proceed[s] outward by Absorption (the Baltics, Bessarabia, Bukovina, East Poland), Domination (Finland, the Balkans, Mongolia, North China, and tomorrow Germany), Orienting influence (Italy, France, Turkey, Iran, Central and South China) until it is dissipated in the outer material sphere, beyond the Eurasian boundaries, of momentary Appeasement and Infiltration (England, the United States).

This "geopolitical vision" existed in Burnham's mind perhaps more vividly than it did in Stalin's; nevertheless, it was an example of the potency of strategic generalization—a tendency which, with Burnham's help, was utterly to vanquish isolationism as the real ideology of American conservatives.

It is not possible to say with absolute certainty that Churchill read him, but the Prime Minister was a voracious consumer and might well have interested himself in an author with such a following in wartime American opinion. If, for example, he had read *The Managerial Revolution*, published in March 1941, he would have been very much impressed to read the following:

> For the United States to try to draw back into a national shell bounded by the forty-eight states would be fairly rapid political suicide. Suicides are committed by nations as well as by individuals. But there is not the slightest reason to suppose that the United States will accept suicide.

This would have given Churchill satisfaction, since it was precisely what he hoped for and was urging on Roosevelt. A later passage in the same vein might have caused him to grunt a little, since it was precisely what he strove to *stop* Roosevelt from thinking:

> The first great plan in the third stage is for the United States to become what might be called the "receiver" for the disintegrating British Empire. (We are not, of course, interested in the propagandistic terms that are used in current references to this action.) The attempt is to swing the orientation of the Empire from its historical dependence on Europe to dependence on and subordination to the American central area. Success in the case of the English Dominion (Canada) and possessions located in the Americas is already at hand. . . . Along with the United States' receivership plan for the British Empire go still broader aims in connection with the rest of South America, the Far East (including conspicuously the Far Eastern colonies of formerly sovereign European states) and in fact the whole world.

This passage also raises the intriguing possibility that Roosevelt might have been reading 1941's political best-seller. So does the following paragraph:

> It will be seen that I take herein for granted that the United States will be in the war. This, also, is not much of a speculation. By earlier standards of the meaning of war and peace, the United States has been in the second world war almost from its start. . . . Factories making belligerent airplanes in New York or New Jersey or California are as much a part of the total war machine as those located in Coventry or Southampton or Manchester.

Burnham went on to say confidently that "it is plain that the United States will join the war in all respects during 1941," and that this would rapidly make England "secondary." His book is also notable for an early usage in the equation of Fascism with Communism—the employment of the term "fifth column" to describe the Western Communist parties. "Fifth column" had until recently been a descriptive term to denote hidden sympathizers of Franco among the population of besieged Madrid, and covert supporters of Fascism in general.

This latter term, in particular, was taken up by Churchill in his Fulton speech. So were a number of Burnham's apocalyptic flourishes. There is a striking similarity between Churchill at Fulton and Burnham in *The Struggle for the World*, which was published a few months later. This book was the fruit of Burnham's labors at the Office of Strategic Services, forerunner of the CIA, and had actually been partially written as a briefing for the American side at Yalta. (This engagement of Burnham's was not merely a wartime one. According to E. Howard Hunt's memoirs, Burnham was a consultant to the covert action staff of the CIA—the Office of Policy Coordination—"on virtually every subject of interest to our organization." Hunt also described Burnham as "professorial in the best sense of the word. He wore tweed jackets and British shoes and a nice foulard.")

JB

Even France, under the pressure of her huge Fifth Column, is permitted to sabotage a reorientation. France, freed from internal Communists, could be a great friend and bulwark to the United States and Western Civilization in the struggle for the world.

WSC

Again, one cannot imagine a regenerated Europe without a strong France. All my life I have worked for a strong France and I never lost faith in her destiny, even in the darkest hours. I will not lose faith now. However, in a great number of countries, far from the Russian frontiers and throughout the world, Communist Fifth Columns are established and work in complete unity and absolute obedience . . .

JB

In August 1945, communist domination, though not yet fully consolidated, extended in the West to a line from Stettin south to the Dalmatian coast.

WSC

From Stettin in the Baltic to Trieste in the Adriatic, an iron curtain has descended across the Continent.

Burnham, of course, was a near-paranoid writer who detected consistent patterns where Churchill rather sketched grand designs. In 1963, he was to denounce President Kennedy's nuclear test ban treaty, comparing it to Munich and citing A. L. Rowse's book *All Souls and Appeasement*. But, like Churchill, he enjoyed roaming the known world in his utterances. And, like Churchill, he saw the future as an Anglo-American condominium, without, however, any sentimentality about a "special relationship." He took Churchill's Harvard speech and Washington memo of 1943, which had proposed joint American-British citizenship and sovereignty, and extended them into a more systematic proposal. Nor did he shrink from using a term that was still distasteful to Americans.

> The reality is that the only alternative to the Communist World Empire is an American Empire which will be, if not literally world-wide in formal boundaries, capable of exercising decisive world control.

Driven on by his own logic, Burnham continued:

> The supreme policy formulated in this chapter would, I believe, dictate an immediate proposal by the United States to

Great Britain and the British Dominions: common citizenship
and full political union.

Burnham went on to point out that Churchill had proposed a modest version of this idea already, only to be greeted (as Burnham
noticed and as most people have forgotten) with quite strong Anglophobic and anti-American reactions on both sides of the Atlantic.
"We may grant," he added in the light of this, "that the union
could not take place through an altogether spontaneous birth. The
forceps would have to be used, or at least kept at hand. However,
enough of the historical premises hold to make union possible.
Historical origin, language, literature, legal principles, form of government are a single heritage."

Burnham did not hesitate to spell out the implications, and to
forecast what would, in fact, prove to be the decisive obstacle:

> Such a union would mean that Britain, her Dominions and
> the United States would become partners in the imperial
> federation. In the first stages, Britain would necessarily be
> the junior partner. This fact, which follows not merely from
> popular prejudices, but from the reality of power relations,
> is the greatest obstacle to the union. It is harsh to ask so great
> a nation, which for three hundred years led the world, to
> accept a lower place than the first, especially when the claim
> comes from an upstart whose only superior qualification—
> unfortunately, the deciding qualification—is the weight of ma-
> terial might.

But in seeking to mollify this potential British objection, Burnham made a significant proposal that could have been designed to
woo Churchill personally. In order to strengthen the international
front against Communism, he argued, India should be kept within
an Anglo-American orbit with a quasi-independent standing analogous to that of the Philippines. Here, especially with the Filipino
parallel, was the white man's burden being shouldered with a will.

With one year to go before India proclaimed independence, Burnham audaciously argued that continued stewardship would be preferable and that "India's share could be large enough to reconcile her people, perhaps, to some adjustment of their ideal hopes."

With that hefty "perhaps," Burnham's grand structure collapsed about him. But *The Struggle for the World* nonetheless represented a high synthesis of all its predecessors. Less racial than Brooks Adams, less sentimental than Andrew Carnegie, less romantic than Rudyard Kipling, more ruthless than Theodore Roosevelt, more rigorous than Arnold Toynbee, more logical than Winston Churchill, the argument was doomed to be shelved. Or most of it was. With its near-harmony with Churchill, who had after all been prepared even to bastardize the English tongue in the interest of Anglo-American unity, and with its evocation of a global common foe, Burnham's gloss on Fulton provided (and provides) an important substratum of the grammar of the Cold War and the "special relationship." And if his proposal for a grand union of the two nations and their dominions was too frankly imperial and too obviously impractical, his earlier idea of an American empire taking the British Empire into "receivership" was neither.

Since they could neither oppose receivership nor take it kindly, the British managed after an undignified struggle to get much of the worst of both worlds. By the time that Churchill died in 1965, James Burnham's patron and successor William F. Buckley felt able to write of him:

> It is true that at Fulton, Missouri, in 1946, Churchill focussed the attention of the world, as again only he had the power to do, on the deteriorating situation. But he seemed thereafter to have lost the great engine that fired him ten years earlier to force the recognition of reality. . . .
>
> He turned over the leadership of the world to the faltering hands of Americans who were manifestly his inferiors in the understanding of history and the management of human affairs, and contented himself to write dramatically about de-

cisive battles won for freedom on the soil of England centuries
ago. . . .

(Residual Anglo-American solidarity and *pudeur* caused this obituary to be one of the few Buckley columns that were not syn-
dicated.)

This is a nice example of the superiority/inferiority complex of
the "special relationship" at work. Buckley, of course, had as a
youth followed the majority of American conservatives who opposed aid to Britain in 1940. And he had wished for Fulton to
translate into a full-dress "roll-back" of Soviet power in Europe.
For him, as for most imperially minded Americans, Churchill is a
mere thesaurus of quotations for "standing tall," invested with a
literary muscle and moral sinew that the cause in question would
not merit of itself. Here, for example, is a 1987 *National Review*
editorial on United States policy in the Persian Gulf, comparing
either Iran or Iraq (or perhaps both) to the Axis before Munich:

> These Democrats are in a fairy-castle world where defense
> spending is wasteful and foreign policy an indulgence. Win-
> ston Churchill watched Britain sink into that delusion in the
> 1930s: "I have watched this famous island descending incon-
> tinently, fecklessly, the stairway which leads to a dark gulf."
> Defend the Persian Gulf, or descend into Churchill's gulf.
> The former is painful, the latter is worse.

As an envoi, we may consider Clark Clifford's reminiscence of
the train ride to Fulton. Instructed by Harry Truman to make
much of the recently deposed Churchill, Clifford was attentive as
the presidential club car (the *Magellan*, furnished and upholstered
like a gentleman's den) moved across America from Union Station
to its rendezvous at the aptly named Westminster College in Fulton, Missouri. Later to be the confidant of successive Presidents
and Secretaries of State, Clifford played poker with Churchill every
evening and took care not to win too much or too often lest this

arouse bitter jests about Britain's indebtedness. On one such evening, he recalled in an interview with Sidney Blumenthal of *The Washington Post,* the hour was late and Churchill was nursing a scotch. "The fact is," said this rather reduced but still intimidating figure, "that America has now become the hope of the world. Britain has had its day. At one time we had dominions all over the world. . . . But England is gradually drying up. The leadership must be taken over by the United States. You have the country, the people; you have the democratic spirit, the natural resources which England has not. . . . If I were to be born again, I'd want to be born an American."

On the eve of his best-received and best-assimilated American speech, Churchill seems to have given way to resignation. The response to the speech certainly took him up on this implicit surrender. It is another way of illustrating what can be found in other areas of American culture and politics—that the reverence and affection for things English has increased in direct proportion to the overshadowing and relegation of real British power.

[10]

Imperial Receivership

If James Burnham's concept of "receivership" had ever been made explicit, with the British being asked to disburden themselves of empire in a planned and graduated fashion and the United States moving to assume the said burdens with coordination and consent, there might have been some impressive results. The same is true for the recurrent but always ill-timed proposal for a merger of citizenship and sovereignty between the two countries (though the price of Basic English might have been too high to pay). But in the event, the displacement of Britain by America as a world gendarme and guarantor was a chaotic, brutal, and dishonest process. On the British side there were residual commitments to a continued imperial role, and on the American side a repressed reluctance to actually *seem* to be seeking one.

As a consequence, the history of receivership is a mixed history of improvisation, secret diplomacy, covert action, inter-Establishment jealousy, and military disaster. There was, under the affectation of Anglo-American solidarity, a continuation of the old politics by other means. Elements of this mutual suspicion, though seldom stressed, endure to this day. They arise from the original lack of synchronicity and from the British habit of only giving up where they had to. As a result, the United States very often was compelled to pick up where a sudden British scuttle had left off, and very often that scuttle was in a country or region where the British had insisted on sole consideration until the last moment. This had two undesirable results. It ministered to the American sense of a painful duty selflessly shouldered—a parody of Kipling's original appeal over the Philippines—and it meant that the United States very often inherited the direct instruments and attitudes of the British style of rule.

This disordered transition actually began while Roosevelt was on his deathbed, at the supposed high noon of the Anglo-American "special relationship." The first steps toward America's least happy entanglement were taken in 1944–45 as a result of British policy in Vietnam. As in the precedent case of Russia in 1918, the moving spirit was Winston Churchill.

Actually, the American involvement in Indochina represented a posthumous victory of Churchill over Roosevelt. Although Churchill had largely gone along with Roosevelt's attempts to undermine de Gaulle politically, he had never shown any enthusiasm for Roosevelt's opposition to the French Union, as its empire was grandly called. On general principles of solidarity with the principle of empire, he had held out for the maintenance and the restoration of European rule in Asia wherever and whenever possible. He was particularly satisfied when, at Potsdam on July 23, 1945, the decision was taken to place southern French Indochina under the command of the British. The rapid Japanese collapse in the following month meant that the British, in the ironic shape of the 20th Indian Division of the Fourteenth Army, became the masters of Saigon *et ses environs*. The commander, Major General Douglas Gracey, was one of those British generals—like Dyer of Amritsar, Scobie of Athens, and Percival of Cork and Singapore—who are not made much of in English school history books but who make history all the same.

According to Bernard Fall, Roosevelt's dislike of the French empire was intense. "His preoccupation amounted almost to a fixation." He once told Cordell Hull that "France has had the country [Vietnam] for nearly one hundred years, and the people are worse off than they were in the beginning. France has milked it for one hundred years. The people of Indo-China deserve something better than that." He put the latter sentiment in formal terms to the State Department, ordering that, war exigency or no war exigency, "no French troops whatever should be used in operations in Indo-China." And before his death he told the Chiefs of Staff that he "favored anything that was against the Japanese, so long as the United States is not aligned with the French." It is worth noting that Sir Anthony Eden himself told Roosevelt that his wartime proposal for "trusteeship" of colonial states was "rather hard on the French." He meant, by analogy, hard on the British, but his words could have come back to haunt him if statesmen were ever to be haunted in that way. Eden also saw, at least when it suited him to do so, that "Roosevelt's dislike of colonialism, while it was a principle with him, was not the less cherished for its possible advantages." How true, and how Kiplingesque in its hypocritical want of insight. Roosevelt was no less shrewd about British "principle" in the matter, commenting after Yalta of his trusteeship proposal that "the British didn't like it. It might bust up their Empire, because if the Indo-Chinese were to work together and eventually get their independence, the Burmese might do the same thing." How true, and how Teddy Rooseveltesque in its apparent altruism.

This crux, or something very like it, must have been in General Gracey's mind as, with Indian troops, he oversaw South Vietnam between September 1945 and March 1946. He may have sensed that, with Roosevelt gone, American "anticolonialism" would slacken. If he did, he would have been matching the sentiments of that great anti-imperialist Major General Patrick Hurley, whom we met in the tussle with Churchill over Iran in 1944 and who, oil company representative though he may have been, could still pen an excellent memo. As he had written to Truman:

I had been definitely directed verbally by President Roosevelt in regard to his policy in Indo-China . . . Lord Louis Mountbatten is using American Lend-Lease supplies and our

American resources to invade Indo-China to defeat what we believe to be the American policy and to re-establish French Imperialism. . . . The move of the Imperialistic powers to use American resources and enable them to move with force into Indo-China is not for the main purpose of participating in the war against Japan.

Hurley here employed *precisely* the same objection—to the use by Britain of Lend-Lease material for political ends—as he had in Iran. He also made the same bold use of the term "imperialism." Truman's response was more guarded than Roosevelt's. It was in 1945, in fact, that the idea of an informal partition of Vietnam was beginning to suggest itself. (This drew on the long-meditated British reaction to any colonial problem.) The ironic aspect of this partition, in the light of future events, was that it gave North Vietnam to China—at least to China in the person of Chiang Kai-shek.

If it had been a matter of parceling out Indochina in the wake of a Japanese surrender, there might conceivably have been something for everybody. But the Vietminh forces, who had actually borne the heat and burden of the day against the Japanese and who had been pained witnesses to Vichy French collaboration with the "Co-Prosperity Sphere," wished to take a hand in their own country's affairs. This was the ingredient in which Roosevelt had, no doubt for his own reasons, believed. To General Gracey, it occurred as more in the nature of a law and order problem; so much so that he rearmed Japanese POWs to combat the Vietminh and other independence forces.

An Englishman reading the record of that time has occasion to feel the sudden lurch that an ancient spectator of Euripides might experience. In December 1945, communiqués report British and Indian forces "patrolling against harassing opposition" in Bien Hoa and Thu Dan Mot. One of their commanders, Brigadier C. H. B. ("Roddy") Rodham, directed: "It is therefore perfectly legitimate to look upon *all* locals anywhere near where a shot has been fired as enemies, and treacherous ones at that, and treat them accordingly." This last stand of the fighting Raj is the thread of Ariadne: the connecting line between the British debacle in India and the American catastrophe in Vietnam. "We have done our best for the French," General Gracey said to the U.S. journalist Harold Isaacs. "It is up to them to carry on." Up to a point, he might well have added if he had possessed Euripides' advantages.

"Anticolonial" protest was of two kinds, especially when it became known that, as Harold Isaacs reported of the Japanese POWs deployed by Gracey, "the British were delighted with the discipline shown by their late enemy and were often warmly admiring, in the best playing-field tradition, of their fine military qualities. It was all very comradely." The first reaction came from Pandit Nehru during his 1946 visit to the United States, where he told *The New York Times*:

> We have watched British intervention there with growing anger, shame and helplessness, that Indian troops should be used for doing Britain's dirty work against our friends who are fighting the same fight as we.

The second came from General Douglas MacArthur, who was in one sense Mountbatten's and Gracey's commanding officer:

> If there is anything that makes my blood boil, it is to see our allies in Indo-China deploying Japanese troops to reconquer the little people we promised to liberate. It is the most ignoble kind of betrayal.

By then, General Gracey had allowed the French *colons* to mount a coup in Saigon—the notorious putsch of September 23, 1945—and to take more or less unrestricted vengeance on the Vietminh. He also permitted the return of the French High Commissioner, Vice Admiral Thierry d'Argenlieu, a former Carmelite monk dedicated to the dream of the *mission civilisatrice* and said by one of his aides to possess "the most brilliant mind of the twelfth century." Not since Professor Jean Izoulet praised Admiral Mahan and wrote of *"l'expropriation des 'races incompétentes'"* had French mysticism and British phlegm been brought into such improbable alignment. The most sturdy defense of General Gracey's actions was written by Dennis Duncanson, an English academic and member of the British Advisory Mission to Vietnam, who said that the objectives of the occupation were to "ensure public order temporarily against the consequences of war until the surrendering enemy forces were out of the way and the power recognised by the Allies as sovereign, namely France, was in a position to resume its administrative responsibilities." In these euphemistic, colonial phrases one can detect the logic and the illogic which was soon to become the code of the Quiet American. When United States ground troops were at their most committed two decades later, Duncanson emerged as one of their most vocal "special relationship" defenders in England. Vietnam was an element in the "receivership" that not even Burnham had bargained for.

Contrast this with the genesis of the Truman Doctrine, almost a demonstration case of what James Burnham had been intending. On the morning of February 24, 1947, the British chargé d'affaires in Washington gave the formal quietus to Britain's ambition, upheld with such guile and tenacity in the face of American protests (see pages 235–37), to retain a "sphere of influence" in the Balkans. He did this by the simple expedient of being driven to the State Department and telling Secretary George Marshall that His Majesty's government could no longer make good on its commitments to Greece and Turkey. Directly implied in this confession of political and economic exhaustion was the idea that the United States should take up the burden. Under Secretary Dean Acheson lost no time in composing a memorandum which argued that "the British are wholly sincere in this matter and . . . the situation is as critical as they state."

Later on the same day, a Special Committee to Study Assistance to Greece and Turkey was convened at the State Department. In the chair was Loy Henderson, who was later to distinguish himself in Anglo-American operations in Iran. Reviewing the British note, and perhaps considering the oblique question about British sincerity and British consistency that was buried in Acheson's wording, he expressed the view that it "appeared to be in line with recent British moves in getting out of Burma, India and Palestine," adding that "the British government seemed to feel itself unable to maintain its imperial structure on the same scale as in the past." Acting with extreme speed, President Truman gave a joint address to Congress on March 12, 1947, proclaiming the doctrine that bears his name and inscribing the post-Fulton promise that "it must be the policy of the United States to support free peoples who are resisting attempted subjugation by armed minorities or by outside pressures." His accompanying request for millions of dollars in aid to both the Greek and Turkish governments was swiftly approved. By July, the United States embassy in Athens was roundly criticizing those whose concerns, about the restoration of the Greek monarchy, it had itself been putting forward only three years previously. After Fulton, too, they had a new rhetoric to deploy. Those who doubted the wisdom of the policy, said the embassy, were guilty of making "appeasement appeals." This was a deft reversal of the anti-Churchillian policy followed by American diplomats in Greece until that time.

The week of Truman's address to Congress happened to be the week that James Burnham published *The Struggle for the World*, and *Life* magazine alone devoted thirteen pages to the coincidence. *Time* promoted discussion of the book to its "International" section. Reinhold Niebuhr's *Christian Century* was among the few skeptics, saying of Burnham's global argument: "It fits the 'Stop Russia' policy of the Truman Doctrine so exactly that one can hardly read it without thinking, 'Here, whether they realize it or not, is what the Senators and Representatives who voted for the initial move under the new doctrine—the Greek-Turkish aid bill—were really approving as the foreign policy of the United States.'"

If it was true that Burnham had been intellectually influential, it was also true that British capitulation had been very weighty in evoking an instant response from the United States. Many former isolationist and anti-English Republicans joined the Democrats by voting, in effect, to take up where the British had stopped. "The Third World War," ran Burnham's opening sentence to *The Struggle for the World*, "began in April 1944." His reference, which was typically hortatory and extreme, was to a Communist-led mutiny in the Greek armed forces that month. But he perfectly anticipated Truman's language about "armed Communist gangs," and if his sentence had read "Cold War" instead of "Third World War," it would be hard to fault as a historical statement. (Burnham liked the second formulation so much more than the first that when he launched his *National Review* column he entitled it "Third World War" and thus lent a distinct tone and flavor to every conservative Cold War pronouncement from McCarthy to Goldwater and beyond.)

The United States had been angered by Churchill's 1944 instruction to General Scobie (the General Gracey of Athens) to conduct himself "as if you were in a conquered city where a local rebellion is in progress." But by the end of the 1940s, American envoys in Athens had become well used to a proconsular line and style of their own. Especially quick to see the advantages of this aspect of "receivership" was Ambassador John Peurifoy, who openly arbitrated, as if he were governor-general or viceroy, when it came to deciding which conservative statesman was in or out of favor, and who (as King Paul sourly noted) even felt able to give terse instructions to the Palace itself. With his task in Greece accomplished, Peurifoy was sent to occupy the United States embassy in Guatemala City, where he played a decisive part in the overthrow of the government of Jacobo Arbenz. He was later to lose his life in an accident while *en poste* in Indochina, thus becoming one of the first Americans to span three continents in a proconsular capacity—an achievement which would not have been possible had the United States not taken up or inherited so many burdens so soon.

Attempting to put the bravest face on this rather haphazard

undertaking, extending as it did from the squalor and cynicism of the Vietnam intervention to the haste and the U-turn of the British scuttle in Greece and Turkey, the conservative André Visson wrote a celebrated postwar essay called, revealingly enough, *The Athenian Complex*. Designed to allay and compose European misgivings about the rise of American power, it condensed European and especially English reservations as follows:

Accustomed to judge their own civilisation not so much by its scientific and mechanical achievements as by its artistic achievements, they ask: Where are the American cathedrals? Where are the American philosophers, the American Shakespeares, Racines, Goethes and Tolstoys; the American Raphaels, Rembrandts, Gainsboroughs, Cézannes and van Goghs; the American Beethovens, Mozarts, Debussys and Tchaikovskys?

They ask the same questions the Greeks of Athens were asking in the third century B.C., when the rising Roman Empire was imposing its leadership on the peoples living around the Mediterranean. Proud of their artistic monuments, of their magnificent theaters, of their great philosophers, of their perfect artistic taste and intellectual refinement, the Athenians were saying to the Romans . . . You certainly have superiority in military power and you are much wealthier than we are, but all your power and all your wealth cannot take away from us our cultural and intellectual superiority.

Visson made a shrewd point when he observed, a little later:

Of course if the hour for Britain to pass on her great historic mission has struck, the British would definitely prefer to have as successors their younger American relatives rather than intellectual Latins, unbalanced Germans or temperamental Slavs.

It can be said for "receivership" that, painful though it was, it spared Britain the protracted misery endured by Belgium, Holland, France, and Portugal during the course of decolonization. Suez was a textbook case of shambles and humiliation, but at least it was brief and decisive. There was no bloody, drawn-out torture of the Algerian or Angolan variety. This was not just because, as many British commentators believe, the Empire was wound up with relative humanity and dispatch. It was because Britain, unlike her European imperial rivals, had the option of a partial merger with another empire, linked through kinship and alliance in war. (This also meant that Britain stood stupidly aloof from the formative period of Western European Union, but that cost was not to become apparent until much later.) Other European nations were to see their former possessions become drawn into the American orbit, but without the salve of a "special relationship" with the metropolis. Speaking of the Marshall Plan, the conservative Visson said that it expressed the American "willingness to take the 'white man's burden' off the tired British shoulders. It is of vital importance for the British that the Americans succeed in this undertaking. And the British themselves hope that the Americans will succeed in spite of their alarming lack of experience and training." Here again, this is Rome, not Athens, to a new Rome. As Gore Vidal puts it in "At Home in Washington, D.C.": "At the park's edge our entirely own and perfectly unique Henry Adams held court for decades in a house opposite to the Executive Mansion where grandfather and great-grandfather had reigned over a capital that was little more than a village down whose muddy main street ran a shallow creek that was known to some even then as—what else?—the Tiber."

Actually Visson was slightly too orthodox in proposing the idea of an unstrained cousinhood, where the English uncle and the American nephew keep up an affectionate correspondence and the uncle knows that his younger brother's son married "a woman of mixed nationality and uncertain social background. Was she an Irish maid? A German seamstress? A Scandinavian farmer's daughter? An Italian singer? Or perhaps some Slavic girl? The older English brother has never been able to find out. He knows only that this non-Anglo-Saxon mother must be chiefly responsible for the boy's being different from his own children. But, thank God! there is enough English blood." His emphasis on blood makes it tempting to say that Visson was too sanguine. Indeed, he imputed a design or a destiny to a process which was much more ambivalent than he realized or conceded, and he gave it a dignified Graeco-Roman overlay that it did not really deserve. If the British had really wanted a historic hand-over rather than a set of half-sincere concessions and adjustments, then they would or could have added Cyprus, say, to the area of American responsibility when they handed over Greece and Turkey. Instead, they clung jealously to the island as a crown colony and Middle Eastern base, and protracted an unusually complex problem into the life of succeeding generations. A good instance of the general rancor and bad faith with which receivership was conducted is the little-studied case of Guatemala in 1954.

In June 1954, the Eisenhower administration was in the middle of its concerted military, economic, and political campaign to remove the government of Guatemala. American airplanes were bombing the country, regional boycotts of Guatemalan products were being coordinated, and Jacobo Arbenz and his Cabinet were being arraigned as surrogates of Moscow in the hemisphere. The blockade of Guatemala, which had impertinently proposed to nationalize certain properties controlled by the United Fruit Company, was enforced by a rather questionable policy of "stop and search" on the high seas. Not even the State Department was sure that such a tactic was legal. Deputy Under Secretary of State Robert Murphy, a former Roosevelt wartime aide, had enough sense of history to write, in a memo: "Our present action should give stir to the bones of Admiral von Tirpitz, and no doubt the conversation of some German naval officers will relate to our 'good neighbor' policy as *spurlos versenkt* (sunk without trace)."

Murphy correctly surmised that the British would not take kindly to "stop and search." Anthony Eden, then Foreign Secretary and deputy to the reelected Winston Churchill, protested that his government "could not possibly acquiesce in forcible action against British ships on the high seas." Eisenhower's Secretary of State, John Foster Dulles, riposted in the language of Fulton and "rollback." He told Eden that "rules applicable in the past no longer meet the situation and [are] required to be reviewed or flexibly applied." On June 18, 1954, Eden very unwillingly announced that Britain, while rejecting any U.S. right of search, would itself detain British ships suspected of conveying arms to Guatemala. He was privately bitter about this undignified concession, saying that free passage on the high seas "was a proud right which the British had never before given up even in wartime and the Americans never ever said 'thank you.' " Eisenhower's press secretary, Jim Hagerty, confided to his diary that, after all, the United States had fought the War of 1812 on the ostensible question of unmolested neutral shipping. "I don't see how, with our traditional opposition to search and seizure, we could possibly have proposed it, and I don't blame the British for one minute getting rough in their answers."

Later in June, a British-registered freighter named the *Springfiord*, with a British captain, was bombed and partially sunk by a CIA plane operating from General Somoza's Nicaragua with the general's personal approval for the mission. Suspected of carrying petrol for the Arbenz government, the vessel had a cargo no more lethal than coffee and cotton. No public protest was made by the British, who accepted a personal apology delivered to their Washington embassy by "roll-back" enthusiast Frank Wisner of the CIA, along with discreet payment from the Agency of $1.5 million to Lloyd's of London.

Such was the situation on the high seas. At the United Nations, the British were in a yet more awkward position. Henry Cabot Lodge, the U.S. ambassador to the UN, was attempting to isolate Guatemala publicly. Neutral and Latin American states had made the apparently unexceptionable proposal that the Security Council send a team of observers to Central America. Lodge, Eisenhower, and Dulles opposed this idea vehemently, since they sought to keep the Guatemala issue confined to their "sphere of influence," the Organization of American States. They were furious when they heard that Britain and France were thinking of backing the move. "The British," said Eisenhower, bluntly speaking in Monrovian tones, "expect us to give them a free ride and side with them on Cyprus. And yet they won't even support us on Guatemala! Let's give them a lesson."

The "lesson" took two forms. On June 24, it was decided that the United States would veto the proposal if the British supported it. This would have been the first use of the veto by America against an ally since the world body's formation. And on June 25, at a meeting in the White House with Churchill and Eden, Eisenhower talked what he called "cold turkey." There would, he told them, be no further American support for their positions on Cyprus or the Suez Canal Zone unless they ceased to contemplate this disloyalty. (The French, significantly and perhaps fatefully, were told the same thing in respect of Indochina.) Eisenhower's instinct was shrewd. At the time, the Greek government was attempting to raise the matter of the colonial status of the Greek majority in Cyprus, and the British position in Egypt was the target of increasing criticism from the emerging Afro-Asian bloc at the UN. As a result, the British and French abstained on the motion and thereby, given the makeup of the Security Council, ensured its defeat.

This little incident, considerable in its ramifications, perfectly illustrates the point made by Theodore Roosevelt in his 1918 letter to Kipling, where he had said, in referring to an earlier period:

> In those good old days the policies of the United States and Great Britain toward one another, and toward much of the outside world, were sufficiently alike to give a touch of humor to the virtuous honour expressed by each at the kind of conduct of the other which most closely resembled its own.

The period of decolonization and receivership, which saw the United States take over the former position of the Belgians in the Congo, the French in Indochina, the Dutch in Indonesia, and the British in the Mediterranean and the Middle East, was anticipated in all essentials by that rather teasing observation. At times, British and American policy could be concerted, even at some cost to pride, into the semblance of a united front. At other times, a lack of synchronization was evident, or a residual desire to maintain historic British freedom of action. At such times, there was liable to be grumbling about American "imperialism" from the British Establishment and sanctimony about British "colonialism" from the Washington side. The ill-tempered and grudging collusion over Guatemala perfectly captures the essence of a war of words and emotions in which both parties felt justified and both could correctly accuse the other of hypocrisy. Eisenhower may have invoked the Monroe Doctrine in protesting at one British proposal for Guatemala, but what he actually wanted *was* British intervention in Central America on his own terms. The British may have sniffed about Cyprus and Suez being their "internal affair," but again they yearned, not for American abstention, but for American support.

As in the case of the Churchill-Roosevelt correspondence on Iranian and Saudi oil, both nations rightly suspected the other of self-interested designs. (United Fruit lobbyists in Congress had played on this memory artfully, pointing out that British oil assets were being menaced by nationalization in Iran, that American assets in Iran might be "next," and that the habit of nationalization should not be allowed to spread to or from Guatemala. If they could see the connection, so could others.) Iran was to be the alternative scenario in the drama of "receivership."

There is only one uncensored account of the Anglo-American overthrow of the Mossadegh government in Iran in 1953, and it occurs in the memoirs of C. M. ("Monty") Woodhouse, which were published in London in 1982. (*Countercoup*, the account given by his American opposite number, Kermit Roosevelt, was extensively cut and bowdlerized, with even Woodhouse's name excluded and all allusions to British Petroleum removed. Among these excisions was the fact, later confirmed by Miles Copeland, that Kermit Roosevelt had brought James Burnham to Washington to advise on the political and psychological impetus of the coup.) Woodhouse escaped the usual treatment accorded to British intelligence officers turned memoirists because he is a former Conservative Member of Parliament, a family friend of the Churchills, and a man of unstained reputation during his time at "the Firm." During the Second World War he had been a highly successful resistance coordinator in Greece and had watched the birth of the Cold War there with considerable interest.

There is something emblematic in the cooperation of this protégé of Churchill's with Theodore Roosevelt's grandson. It was a classic instance of what was to be a recurring British self-image in counterrevolutionary enterprises that were undertaken with the new senior partner. In other words, the United States supplied the muscle and the British provided the *nous*. (This formulation is sometimes varied to read "their money and our brains.") It also prefigured the general hand-over of British influence in the Middle East to American receivership, a process which was not always to be so smooth and cooperative.

Woodhouse's entry into Iranian history took place at the moment when Mossadegh was threatening to nationalize the Anglo Iranian Oil Company (AIOC), now better known as British Petroleum. A British minister, Richard Stokes, had visited Iran but returned with no concessions and spoke feelingly, if absurdly, about "grass growing in the streets of Abadan," where the AIOC refineries were located. As Woodhouse put it:

> The Americans were more likely to work with us if they saw the problem as one of containing Communism rather than restoring the position of the AIOC. *Although some representatives of American oil companies seemed to be circling like vultures over Iran,* American officials were inclined to be more cooperative. Averell Harriman, a roving Ambassador of

great experience, had been associated with Stokes's negotiating mission. Loy Henderson changed the atmosphere in the US Embassy towards sympathy with the British case. [Italics mine.]

This paragraph is almost a classic of "special relationship" prose. The clause in italics expresses the latent British suspicion and is a clear echo of Churchill's misgivings as expressed to Roosevelt in 1944–45. Averell Harriman appears, the great wartime emollient in Anglo-American diplomacy and himself a relation by marriage of the lion of Fulton. Loy Henderson was the envoy who had eased the transition between British and American hegemony in Greece after the hasty promulgation of the Truman Doctrine. There was, then, even if for differing purposes, a wary communion of interests and a shared bank of expertise and experience.

Returning to London to brief the Foreign Office, Woodhouse found that a pessimistic view was being taken of his ability to mount a destabilization of Mossadegh. "But Eden," as he put it, "left one loophole open. He remarked that an operation such as we contemplated would have no chance without American support." This was exactly what Woodhouse had been hoping to hear, and the election of Eisenhower a few days later was to give him his cue. The new administration had a Dulles at State and a Dulles at the CIA. It was to both departments that Woodhouse took his plan for what "was called, rather too obviously, Operation Boot." He found that doors in Washington opened very readily. He also knew that the idea of British imperialism was not a great selling point, but that the spirit of Fulton was. Therefore:

Not wishing to be accused of trying to use the Americans to pull British chestnuts out of the fire, I decided to emphasise the Communist threat to Iran rather than the need to recover control of the oil industry.

The Anglo-American candidate for the Iranian presidency was, it was agreed in Washington, to be General Fazlullah Zahedi. Woodhouse describes this selection as "ironic," which from one point of view it most certainly was. During the Second World War, Zahedi had been a leading Nazi agent and had been arrested by the British and interned in Palestine. "Now we were all turning to him as the potential savior of Iran from the Soviet bloc." The CIA's director of operations, Frank Wisner, was a staunch proponent of the James Burnham view of the world and had already enlisted a substantial number of ex-Nazis for the purposes of "rolling back" the Iron Curtain. He was an early enthusiast for Operation Boot and for the Zahedi option.

While in America, Woodhouse took the opportunity to look around, and made various imperishable "special relationship" entries in his memoirs. He visited Major Gerry Wines, a wartime colleague and First World War veteran, in Dallas. "Southern hospitality proved even warmer than I had expected. Over a Thanksgiving dinner in a Texas mansion, I reminded Gerry Wines of a more Spartan Thanksgiving we had celebrated in Greece, when he had impressed on me that 'you Limeys think Thanksgiving is the Fourth of July!' " Then came the moment without which no English gentleman's visit to the United States is complete:

> I did my Christmas shopping at Neiman-Marcus, where one of the salesgirls begged me to "just go right on talking— I just love that cute British accent."

And on the way home, he had the moment without which no English gentleman's return from America is complete:

> An American sitting next to me in the plane, who had never been to London before, expressed anxiety about the fogs he had been told about, so I had done my best to reassure him that they were very rare. On the day after our arrival the worst smog of the century descended on London, and lasted

two weeks. I happened to run into my American friend in Claridges while the smog was at its thickest, and offered him my apologies. He assured me that it was the greatest experience of his life, and he would not have missed it for anything.

Dickensian "heritage trails" did not have to be faked in those days.

A medical indisposition on the part of Sir Anthony Eden—one which was to be of great moment in Anglo-American relations a few years later—led Churchill to take over the Foreign Office for a few months and to silence all doubts about Operation Boot. One of the doubts concerned the personality and record of General Zahedi, described by Patrick Dean of British intelligence at a Washington planning meeting as "a bit of a shocker." This classic of "special relationship" talk was merely decorative. On Woodhouse's own account, the whole operation had by then become American-directed. He went off on a tour of the Far East, while on July 19, 1953, Kermit Roosevelt crossed the Iraqi border into Iran and began closing the net and making promises to the Shah. After a nerve-racking false start, which led to the Shah's fleeing the country to Rome, a combination of CIA money, military preparedness, and carefully planned mob demonstrations managed to tip the scale. On August 23, 1953, General Zahedi was able to welcome a restored Pahlavi dynasty and to put relations with Britain and America back on their former footing. "In London," noted Woodhouse, "the shares of the AIOC rose sharply on the Stock Exchange."

Reviewing the situation with the advantage of perspective, Woodhouse observed that it had been conservative ayatollahs who had been of most help in organizing pro-Shah demonstrations. He also recorded the fact that, Stock Exchange notwithstanding, "the AIOC . . . never regained its exclusive position in Iran, but it recovered some of its losses through participation in an international consortium." The nature of that consortium can be guessed at from Woodhouse's minuting of "an immediate grant of 45 million dollars to the new Iranian government" from Washington and also from the fact that Iran applied to join the Baghdad Pact, a British-dominated group of treaty nations, which after the Suez fiasco became the American-dominated Central Treaty Organization (CENTO). In the new oil concession, the renamed "British Petroleum" held 40 percent and Standard Oil of New Jersey, Standard Oil of California, Gulf Oil, Texas Oil, and Socony-Mobil each held 8 percent. This improved the American stake in Iranian oil from nil to 40 percent. As a coda, Woodhouse added: "What we did not foresee was that the Shah would gather new strength and use it so capriciously and tyrannically, nor that the US government and the Foreign Office would fail so abjectly to keep him on a reasonable course." On this uncharacteristic "special relationship" note, the story of Operation Boot draws to a close, except for two ironic footnotes.

Woodhouse, who was a pronounced philhellene from his wartime days, worried that the British were asking for trouble in their refusal to grant freedom to Cyprus. In 1954, he made an approach to Allen Dulles, proposing that CIA influence be brought to bear on Churchill to reconsider the matter. "A few weeks later the reply came back that the President was unwilling to intervene. He thought he had urged quite enough new initiatives on Churchill already, though I could not think what they were." If Woodhouse had known what his friends Allen Dulles and Frank Wisner had been up to in parallel in Guatemala, and of the complicity of Churchill and Eden and of the price of that complicity, he might have been able to solve the mystery of their sudden coolness about the rights of small nations and the need for British decolonization.

Finally, describing a chill that was to set in among the Anglo-American elites, Woodhouse recalls in his memoir:

> We still cooperated in a few unspectacular activities: for instance, we jointly founded and funded the periodical *Encounter* as a vehicle for intellectual propaganda. But the CIA became increasingly preoccupied with power and prestige, and increasingly confident that it no longer needed British expertise so much.

Whether Woodhouse knew it or not, one of the founders of the American Committee for Cultural Freedom was James Burnham, who was recommended to *Encounter* and its editor, Stephen Spender, by Irving Kristol as "a first-rate essayist on cultural matters." Under this rubric, the author of the "receivership" idea was to gain in Anglo-American stature.

Although Woodhouse never worked it out, the Iran and Guatemala operations of 1953 and 1954 (the root of so much later grief in two hemispheres) in many ways form a "pair," at least in the sense suggested to Kipling by Theodore Roosevelt.

This is more than may be said for the other two grand episodes in, respectively, American and British postwar alliance politics. Vietnam and Suez were not just questions of imposing discipline on small and impudent nations like Iran and Guatemala. They represented great power judgments about the possibility of halting or bridling in the one case Vietnamese and in the second case Arab nationalism. In both the formative and the active periods of these two crises, London and Washington behaved much more like imperial rivals than allies, and failed to keep up the habit of collusion which, however reluctant and unequal, had served them well enough in more limited theaters.

As the French position in Vietnam deteriorated toward its humiliation at Dien Bien Phu in 1954, Sir Anthony Eden as Foreign Secretary and Sir Winston Churchill as Prime Minister were attempting to save French face as well as American. Eden wrote, deludedly, that there was a middle path of partition. (The British, of course, always say that in these situations. Even General Gracey, the military author of the Vietnam impasse, had found a natural billet after Saigon as one of the commanders of the army of newly created Pakistan.) Pleadingly, Eden wrote: "There was some indication of a greater willingness in Vietnam to face partition . . . we felt that the distress at amputation might prove more apparent than real."

Absurd though this opinion seems today, at the time it struck John Foster Dulles as a milksop half measure. He wanted a more vigorous operation to save the French position in Vietnam, and he wanted a "united front" of anti-Communist Asian nations to underwrite it. This front was to include Taiwan, which he trusted, but not "neutralist" India, which he did not. Sir Anthony rather belatedly put the case for Indian susceptibilities about exclusion, perhaps feeling more sympathetic than he might have done owing to the fact that Britain had just been excluded by the United States from membership in the ANZUS pact linking America, Australia, and New Zealand. Snubbed over the question of the old "white dominions" and the "New Commonwealth," he had little enough inducement to follow Dulles into Vietnam behind the tattered French tricolor. (If Dulles had hoped to rally Eden to this banner, he contradicted himself in a private conversation with him in London in April 1954, where, in Burnham-like fashion, "Mr. Dulles concluded with pessimistic comments about France. He wondered whether France was not, by a process of historical evolution, inevitably ceasing to be a great power.") Later in the London meeting, Dulles reached for the Churchill-Burnham analogy in its crudest form. Eden recorded:

> I was not convinced by the assertion which Mr. Dulles then made, that the situation in Indo-China was analogous to the Japanese invasion of Manchuria in 1931 and to Hitler's reoccupation of the Rhineland.

Eden was a proven liar, and one should never use any citation from his memoirs and papers without a more authoritative confirmation. In this case, confirmation exists in the form of a letter from Eisenhower to Churchill, dispatched only one week earlier. Churchill may or may not have relished its condescending tone:

> If I may refer again to history; we failed to halt Hirohito, Mussolini and Hitler by not acting in unity and in time. That marked the beginning of many years of stark tragedy and

desperate peril. May it not be that our nations have learned something from that peril?

Since both Churchill and Eden had been prominent among the anti-Munich Tories at the relevant time, they never scrupled to make the comparison themselves. But they were extremely choosy about those whom they would allow to use the Munich analogy against them. Indeed, Eden finally replied to Dulles in tones of genuine exasperation, albeit via a cable to the ambassador in Washington written to be passed on in more diplomatic form:

> Americans may think the time past when they need consider the feelings or difficulties of their allies. It is the conviction that this tendency becomes more pronounced every week that is creating mounting difficulties for anyone in this country who wants to maintain close Anglo-American relations.

No whit abashed, Dulles waited a week before demanding British support for an all-out American bombardment of Vietnam to save the French position at Dien Bien Phu. Eden's comment on this in his memoirs—that "we might well find ourselves involved in the wrong war against the wrong man in the wrong place"—was to become famous in other mouths and versions long after he had departed the political scene.

After consultation with Churchill, accordingly, the British government announced formally that "the best hope of a lasting solution lay in some form of partition." And that British imperial solution was what, at the subsequent meeting in Geneva, the Vietnamese got. Representing as it did the very minimum of each participant's actual desire, partition in Vietnam was to be even less stable than its classic forerunners in Ireland, Palestine, and the Indian subcontinent.

The grudging American acceptance of this outcome was accompanied by two further ironic developments. First, Sir Anthony Eden was denounced all over the United States media and Congress for proposing a "Locarno" alliance of pro-Western states in Asia. Since Locarno had been the name of a failed prewar configuration of countries trying to keep the peace in Europe, it was promptly confused with Munich and Eden had to endure in public what he had already suffered from Dulles in private—the allegation that he favored "appeasement."

Second, as Sir Anthony himself recorded, in careful "special relationship" prose:

> Before leaving England, the Prime Minister and I had read a report from Washington of a meeting between Mr. Dulles and some leading American journalists. According to an account which our Embassy thought reliable, the Secretary of State had declared his conviction that American policy in the Middle East, as well as in Asia, had been badly handicapped by a tendency to support British and French "colonial" views. He was reported to have spoken of his determination to talk bluntly about the Middle East, and of his aim to "shift policies." Sir Winston and I heard nothing of these misgivings during our talks in Washington. Perhaps they were overshadowed by events in Guatemala.

One could hardly condense more of the contradictions of receivership into one paragraph. Balked of his objectives in Indochina, which arose entirely out of a desire to uphold French colonialism, Mr. Dulles rounded on his "colonial" allies, including the ally, Britain, that had restored French colonialism to Indochina in the first place. Britain's Foreign Secretary, commenting on this, makes a sarcastic allusion to an American neo-colonial enterprise in Guatemala, about which, as it happened, neither the British nor the American government found it possible to be frank. Within two years, Eden was to appeal for the indulgence of Dulles and Eisenhower in another colonial enterprise at Suez, urging them, in the words of his own memoirs, to consider the matter of Nasser's Egypt in this light:

The world would have suffered less if Hitler had been resisted on the Rhine, in Austria or in Czechoslovakia, rather than in Poland.

Or, again:

The West has been as slow to read Nasser's *A Philosophy of Revolution* as it was to read Hitler's *Mein Kampf*, with less excuse because it is shorter and not so turgid.

Mr. Dulles and President Eisenhower chose, on this occasion, to find the Munich analogy unpersuasive. Suez is a thrice-told tale, and not worth retelling in any detail except as a reminder of how intense was British Establishment resentment at American neutrality, and how decided was the American Establishment that the British hour in the Middle East was over. The United States did not actually confine itself to neutrality. It strenuously opposed, at the United Nations and elsewhere, the British collusion with France and Israel in the invasion of Egypt. More, it openly stated its doubts that the British in Cyprus and the French in Algeria were really pursuing a justifiable policy. The first occasion when the British used their power of veto in the United Nations was to defeat a resolution on Suez put forward by Mr. Henry Cabot Lodge which would have condemned the Anglo-French ultimatum to Egypt. "It was not Soviet Russia or any Arab state," minuted Eden bitterly, "but the Government of the United States which took the lead in the Assembly against Israel, France and Britain." Vice President Nixon put forward the U.S. government's line in a speech in which he said:

For the first time in history we have shown independence of Anglo-French policies towards Africa and Asia which seemed to us to reflect the colonial tradition. This *declaration of independence* has had an electrifying effect throughout the world. [Italics mine.]

No doubt there was a touch of *Schadenfreude* in the American position, derived from resentment at British high-mindedness and pragmatism over Vietnam. Considering that Eisenhower had extorted British support for *his* covert invasion of Guatemala by suggesting continued American understanding for the British position in Cyprus and the Canal Zone (a riposte that the British Tories could not possibly make in public), the British reciprocal resentment is not hard to imagine. A glance at the London *Times* correspondence columns for the autumn of 1956, or the speeches of Conservative backbenchers in the same period, shows the outpouring of a long-pent-up dislike for, and suspicion of, American global intentions and political morality. Significantly, American tardiness in entering the war against Hitler was an almost universal theme in these effusions.

For a few days in the last weeks of 1956, the wartime analogy seemed less of a strain on credulity than it would normally be. Petrol rationing was imposed in Britain for the first time since the war. And there was another reminder of the vulnerability of the pound sterling to the American Treasury, of the sort that had not been driven home since 1944. British reserves fell $57 million in September, $84 million in October, and $309 million in November, to the point where Harold Macmillan, Chancellor of the Exchequer, had to humiliate himself in the House of Commons. In Cabinet he said that unless there was a change of course in the invasion he had so heartily supported, he "could not anymore be responsible for Her Majesty's Exchequer."

At this point, or somewhere near it, consideration of the "special relationship" began to weigh in Washington at least as heavily as the consideration of "anticolonialism" in the Middle East. The British had announced a humbling cease-fire only a few hours after their brutal and chaotic landings. Their Treasury could hardly be called their own. The whole thing had turned out so much worse than anybody could possibly have predicted. And even Eisenhower, who had been appalled by British duplicity in respect of himself, could not welcome the total collapse of Eden and his government. Conversations between Winthrop Aldrich, the U.S. ambassador in London, and Eisenhower make it plain that the President wanted to save what he could of Tory prestige. Indeed, as Donald Neff puts it in his surpassing history of the Suez affair:

> Although the messages on the secret negotiations between Aldrich and the leadership of the Tory Party remain classified by the government, transcripts of Eisenhower's telephone conversations make it clear that the Conservative leaders and the Eisenhower Administration now began a secret collusion of their own. Its purpose was to keep the Conservative government in power in Britain.

A word, here, on Ambassador Winthrop Aldrich. In his own person, he was the very example of the class and business aspects of the "special relationship." He was also a good instance of its ethnic solidarity. He was the son of Senator Nelson Aldrich of Rhode Island, a nineteenth-century railway and streetcar king. His older sister Abby married John D. Rockefeller in 1901. The family had English governesses (the Misses Tetlow) and owned rather a good chunk of Warwick Neck, near Narragansett Bay. In the Library of Congress to this day you can find a five-volume genealogy of the Aldriches, privately bound and published, which shows their connection to the posterity of George Aldrich, of Derbyshire, England, who left Derby for Dorchester, Massachusetts, in 1631.

Winthrop Aldrich spent most of his maturity managing the Chase Manhattan Bank and supporting the Republican political interest. During the Second World War he worked for British War Relief and was decorated at Buckingham Palace by King George. At the end of the war, he testified before the Senate on the decisive matter of a U.S. loan to Britain, in the words of his Harvard Business School biographer, "because he thought it would speed up the removal of British controls on foreign trade and exchange long before the Bretton Woods agreements could make their effect felt. The administration's case for the loan had been made to Congress on these grounds, and in his testimony Aldrich presented similar arguments relating to the elimination of the sterling area as a result of the loan." This testimony of a conservative banker on behalf of a Democratic administration helped ease the loan past the jealous scrutiny of Republican isolationists such as Robert Taft.

On his arrival as ambassador to the Court of St. James's in 1953, having been a distinguished supporter of Eisenhower's election campaign and weathered a few awkward questions at his confirmation hearing, Aldrich addressed the Pilgrims' Society Dinner and the English-Speaking Union. These routine stops for a new envoy were made more pointful by his traceable lineage and his strong defense, on the latter occasion, of American intervention in both world wars. The British, he said in this last connection, had had to wait too long for America to see its own best interests and principles. An enraged editorial from Colonel McCormick's still isolationist *Chicago Tribune* greeted this opinion, which it said was "the gospel according to Roosevelt and Wall Street and is vicious nonsense." But isolationism was no longer the common sense of Middle America, as Eisenhower was to demonstrate.

Aldrich busied himself chiefly in business and industrial circles while in London, and also found time to move the United States ambassador's official residence from 14 Prince's Gate to the commanding position it now occupies at Winfield House, Regent's Park. This home, which had been gifted to the U.S. government by Barbara Hutton some years before, had been a USAF officers' club during the war and remained in use as such. Aldrich decided that it would make a more fitting home. Thanks to the personal intercession of Sir Winston Churchill, he was able to get a ninety-nine-year lease from the Commissioners of Crown Lands for a rent of five pounds. In return he gave an undertaking that the house would be used only as a diplomatic residence. Mrs. Aldrich and a State Department decorating consultant did the rest, and Winfield House was "warmed" at a dinner dance attended by the new Queen and Prince Philip. As a "special relationship" touch, the Queen herself proposed that the party be held on Washington's birthday.

Aldrich was thus well established in London by the time that Suez
had destroyed the composure of his hosts.

There was no need, in the circumstances, to "destabilize" Sir
Anthony Eden. His attempt to emulate Churchill in making furious
broadcasts and ordering the rash deployment of troops and planes
and ships (an attempt perhaps too long meditated during the years
he had dwelt in Churchill's shadow) had in effect discredited itself.
Moreover, he was chronically ill in mind and body, having at certain
moments almost become the unstable maniac that he had obses-
sively claimed to detect in the figure of Nasser. Most pundits
expected that his long-suffering deputy R. A. Butler would succeed
him. But there was another, more serious candidate in the person
of Harold Macmillan. The sequence of events revealed in the traffic
between Ambassador Aldrich and President Eisenhower is a classic
of "special relationship" vernacular.

On November 19, Ambassador Aldrich met with Harold Macmillan, who showed himself willing to sue for peace with Egypt
along Eisenhower-Dulles lines because the alternative was an oil
crisis and the likely dismissal of the Conservative Party from office.
Aldrich telephoned the President personally. "My guess is correct," he said. "I guessed there was going to be a change. . . .
Harold Macmillan is terribly anxious to see you as soon as possible.
I'll spell that out in the message, too."

Eisenhower thereupon called Herbert Hoover, Jr., Under Secretary of State, and asked him what message might have come from
Grosvenor Square. Hoover told him that "the guess is that the
Cabinet is completely to be reshuffled, and that Eden's going out
because of sickness."

Almost at once, Treasury Secretary George Humphrey telephoned. He also had just talked to Aldrich in London. "I want to
remind you," said Eisenhower, "of our discussion about a remote
possibility. Aldrich says part of it is coming about. There are a lot
of conditions we cannot possibly meet." Humphrey's response was
to remind the President of the domestic political stakes in Britain.
"I hate to have a man stick in there and go to a vote of confidence

and get licked. If they throw him out then we have these socialists to lick."

Humphrey here expressed the usual "apolitical" concerns of the Treasury Department, but he also happened to be a friend of R. A. Butler's and a believer in the conventional wisdom about Butler's likely succession. Next day, November 20, 1956, Eisenhower, Hoover, and Humphrey met again. Eisenhower expressed a preference for Macmillan, saying, "He is a fine, straight man and so far as I am concerned the outstanding one of the British I served with during the war." The question then became one of a "fig leaf" that Ambassador Aldrich had mentioned in his written message. It was agreed that the United States would not help the British government unless it consented to a withdrawal from Suez, but that if a withdrawal was undertaken, economic and political aid could be forthcoming in generous quantities. Eisenhower proposed that Aldrich be instructed in those terms. "We can simply couch our statement along the lines of 'on the assumption stated by Macmillan—that is, that they will announce at once an immediate withdrawal—they can be assured of our sympathetic consultation and help.' Also Macmillan can meet with me on that assumption."

The difficulty here was that Eden was still Prime Minister. How was one of his deputies to be approached in this unorthodox fashion? Once again Ambassador Aldrich was asked his advice on the telephone. Eisenhower was extremely circumspect:

"We have been getting your messages and I want to make an inquiry. You are dealing with at least one person—maybe two or three—on a very personal basis. Is it possible for you, without embarrassment, to get together the two that you mentioned in one of your messages?"

"Yes, one of them I have just been playing bridge with. Perhaps I can stop him."

"I'd rather you talk to both together. You know who I mean? One has the same name as my predecessor at the Columbia

University presidency. The other one was with me in the war."

"I know the one with you in the war . . . oh, yes, now I've got it."

"Could you get them informally and say of course we are interested and sympathetic, and as soon as things happen that we anticipate we can furnish a lot of fig leaves?"

"I certainly can say that."

"Will that be enough to get the boys moving?"

"I think it will be."

"You see, we don't want to be in a position of interfering between those two. But we want to have you personally tell them. They are both good friends."

"Yes, very much so. Have you seen my messages regarding my conversations with them all?"

"Yes, with at least two."

"That is wonderful. I will do this—tomorrow?"

"Yes, first thing in the morning."

"I shall certainly do it. And I will then communicate with you at once. Can do it without the slightest embarrassment."

The day after this conversation, which contains all the essential "special relationship" subtexts—from the mention of a bridge game to the nudging reference to Eisenhower's Columbia predecessor, who was named Nicholas Murray Butler—there was another meeting. Secretary Humphrey spoke presciently:

The British are facing a financial crisis within ten days. I think the sequence of events will be this. The British will start out of Suez in a few days. The British will want to come out here a few days later. This will be the time when we must bargain hard with them. Between those dates we must let King Saud, and even Nasser, know that in starting talks with the British, we have not reversed our stand toward them and that we want an understanding with them prior to the British talks. By

December 3 our arrangements must be in hand because that is the date of the British financial announcement.

Humphrey was off by only one day. It was on December 4 that Macmillan told the House that Great Britain had had to ask for extra time to pay off the interest on past loans. By then, Sir Anthony Eden had departed for "recuperation" in Jamaica. Aldrich called from London to say that, whatever the motivation might be, "his resignation would no doubt deflect from British government onus for Suez policy, of which he of course was principal architect. Such action would perhaps enable Tory Party to remain at helm in Britain and would mend U.K.'s strained relations with its allies and friends." This was a succinct expression of the two aims of Washington in the Suez crisis, aims which were successfully consummated by Macmillan's accession to power shortly afterward. He was to make the restoration of "special relationship" ties his first order of business. As he put it in his feline address to the Pilgrims' Dinner, given in honor of Ambassador Aldrich's retirement in January 1957, and referring to the Suez crisis:

> Faced with this situation, Ambassador Aldrich had a unique opportunity and he took it. To my personal knowledge I can tell you that he played a remarkable and indeed an historic role during those anxious weeks. We owe him a debt which we cannot easily repay, and I like to think that his countrymen will feel that they should be equally grateful for what he has done. This is not the time to reveal the whole story, but I would say this . . . it is largely because of what he did during this period that I look forward with such confidence to complete and successful re-establishment of our relations upon the old level.

One should mention three ironic footnotes of the Suez affair. The first was a pathetic letter from Churchill to Eisenhower, penned by the old man on November 23, 1956:

There is not much left for me to do in this world, and I have neither the wish nor the strength to be involved in the present political stress and turmoil. But I do believe with unfaltering conviction that the theme of the Anglo-American alliance is more important today than at any time since the war. . . . There seems to be growing misunderstanding and frustration on both sides of the Atlantic. If they be allowed to develop, the skies will darken indeed and it is the Soviet Union that will ride the storm. We should leave it to the historians to argue the rights and wrongs of all that has happened during the past years. If we do not take immediate action in harmony, it is no exaggeration to say that we must expect to see the Middle East and the North African coastline under Soviet control and Western Europe placed at the mercy of the Russians.

This Burnhamesque rant, with mere alarmism substituted for globalism, was a sad terminus for a man who had disputed the merits of 1898 with Mark Twain, had exposed the flank of the *Lusitania*, had bent every nerve and sinew to engage the United States in international disputes on the Anglo-Saxon side, and had laid down the moral and rhetorical grammar of the Cold War. The squalor and pettiness of the Suez War were out of proportion to his missive, which fell on deaf ears. Three days after it was written, Herbert Hoover, Jr., commented laconically to Eisenhower:

It might be necessary for us to approach the British and say that it looks as though they are through in the Middle East and ask if they want us to try to pick up their commitments.

Eisenhower thought this a little brusque. He relaxed the Lodge policy at the UN and obligingly came up with the oil shipments and dollar aid that were to make Macmillan's post-Suez life so surprisingly easy. Only after a decent interval did Hoover's thought become the received opinion. Indeed, within a few years Eden was able to console himself that the United States had inherited his mantle:

> Our intervention at least closed the chapter of complacency about the situation in the Middle East. It led to the Eisenhower Doctrine and from that to Anglo-American intervention in the following summer in Jordan and then Lebanon.

This typically wishful and self-justifying conclusion is to some extent shared by a later generation of American power brokers. Henry Kissinger, in his book *Observations*, wrote that he now felt that the United States should have supported the British over Suez. It is difficult to imagine him holding this opinion at the time, whatever the later rewards of it may be in adding to his reputation for "toughness" and loyalty to allies. The Suez War enabled Eisenhower to make the idea of receivership popular not just in the United States but also in Britain, where it came to all but a diehard minority as a welcome if shamefaced relief. It established the Grosvenor Square embassy at the center of London policy making in a way that not even 1941–45 had done. It placed the United States in a position where it could and did build a "special relationship" with Israel while still retaining a certain credit with the Arab League. It positioned American power to succeed British sovereignty in Jordan, Egypt, and the Persian Gulf, and to enhance the standing it had won in Iran in 1953, while still appearing in the international community to be in harmony with the values of the United Nations.

However, the United States refused to learn for itself the lesson it had helped teach the British. Dulles and Eisenhower were right about Suez, but Eden's misgivings were rather more than vindicated in the case of Vietnam. The mere fact that both governments had employed the consecrated rhetoric of Churchillism and appeasement *against* one another was proof of the failure of receivership, and of the survival of more traditional jealousies over "spheres of influence."

The process now became one of ad hoc succession rather than transition. In early 1964 there was a replay of the origins of the Truman Doctrine, when another British diplomat had himself driven round, this time to the Defense Department in Washington, and announced that Her Majesty's government could no longer discharge its treaty obligations in Cyprus unaided. Thus began the long and unsavory association of the United States with the island's intransigent problems. In this, as in most other cases, the Americans inherited British habits and tactics, and very often old British clients, too. One of the mutations involved via the British connection has been the adapting of classic imperial styles for modern, allegedly nonimperial purposes.

In a striking essay, "Imperialism Without Splendor," published in 1982, Fouad Ajami discussed the way in which European concepts of rule and order had been transmitted imperfectly into American conduct. The *Pax Britannica*, he wrote (employing yet another familiar Roman echo), at least "had its stylists, its romantics, its visionaries." Ajami, a Shia Muslim Lebanese with no reason to love the Western dominion in the Arab world, singled out T. E. Lawrence, Gertrude Bell, and H. St. John Philby as instances of those who accepted the "burden" (another felicitous echo) of "encountering the lives of others, of travelling into their poetry and language, of getting under their skin." In contrast, wrote Ajami,

Pax Americana must be judged a dry, uninspiring affair. It has been a quarter of a century since the Americans replaced the Europeans in the Middle East as a result of the Suez War—long enough to establish a tradition, a discourse, a literature showing flashes of brilliance and yes, eccentricity. But none of this has come to pass.

When he wrote this, the most miserable phase of the American engagement with Lebanon was still in the future, and the most calamitous of all its encounters in the region—the entanglement with the Pahlavi dynasty in Iran—was in the recent past. Even so, Ajami perhaps failed to allow for the extreme American reluctance to be seen as a colonial power. The entire enterprise, after all, was supposed to be "value-free"; to be based upon the provision of weapons, neutral advisers and technicians, and the building blocks of centrist political institutions. Not enough, there amid the air conditioning and the commercial attachés, to thrill the blood or to evoke the high romantic note, hit by Jan Morris's *Farewell the Trumpets*, with which Ajami began.

Very often—usually in the aftermath of some reverse or embarrassment overseas—democratic America conducts an inquest. As the Owl of Minerva flaps her wings, congressmen and academics and "country experts" are all commissioned to ask how it started. Whose idea was Vietnam to begin with? Who lost China? Why does Libya matter to us? Should we have known about Shia Islam? Why has the Gulf turned unstable? Where and what is Grenada? These, and many questions like them, are all part of the permanent passing parade in Washington. Meanwhile, American soldiers and officials, convinced of their own impartiality, attempt to compose differences between Jews and Arabs. Denounced as the deadly foe of Islam by Libyans and Iranians, they can also be found in the streets of Peshawar supporting a Muslim crusade in neighboring Afghanistan.

In almost every case, the original commitment arises out of one or another consequence of "receivership." This perception is often occluded because of the American anticolonial inheritance, which meant a shaky dependence upon client regimes rather than upon the historically British method of direct rule. But without the inheritance of British direct rule, the connection would usually not have been made in the first place.

In several cases, inheritance came as the result of a self-consciously anticolonial strategy. With Libya, for example, the United

States sternly opposed postwar British plans for the partition of the country (the addiction is an incorrigible one) between its two provinces of Cyrenaica and Tripolitania. American influence was exerted to have Libya given independence as a unified state. A Foreign Office minute from Hector McNeil, Ernest Bevin's deputy in 1949, stressed that if Libya with its huge military installations was to be kept in the British sphere, this could only be done on an Anglo-American basis. "Our need is great: our case is not good. We must therefore be as naive as possible," he wrote. The British Chiefs of Staff were even more candid in their assessment, written later in the same year:

> Today, we are still a world power, shouldering many and heavy responsibilities. *We believe the privileged position that we, in contrast to the other European nations, enjoy with the United States and the attention that she now pays to our strategic and other opinions*, and to our requirements, is directly due to our hold on the Middle East and all that this involves. [Italics mine.]

Though there were differences about partition versus federation for this former Italian colony (only the radical Arab nationalists wanted a strong unitary state and nobody consulted them), the aim of both London and Washington was the same—a large military base in the country. To that extent, when there was a quarrel between the British and Americans in the spring of 1951, both parties had right on their side. Andrew Lynch, the U.S. Consul General in Tripoli, accused Roger Allen, head of the Africa Department of the Foreign Office, of wishing to subject Libya to "the dead hand of the sterling area." Allen replied that Lynch was a typical American "imperialist," trying to suborn the colony by means of the almighty dollar. It took some time for this dispute to be composed, with Libya admitted to the British sterling area and extensive American bases constructed at Wheelus Field. Three years after independence, a U.S.-Libya agreement signed in 1954 established the United States as the principal aid donor, at a figure which dwarfed the British contribution. After the British had been humbled at Suez, this left the United States in a position of unchallenged primacy, though dependent on the political clientele around King Idris, who had been the mainstay of the British presence. As a result, when Libya underwent a revolution in 1967 it was principally against the United States and its bases that the rancor of Arab nationalism in the country was directed.

The same unevenness of purpose and mutual dislike were evident in what Julian Amery, in his obituary for Harold Macmillan, called "the last Anglo-American war." This now forgotten but significant episode occurred in October 1955. It arose because the Saudi Arabians, secure in the knowledge of American military and commercial indulgence, had occupied the important Buraimi oasis. In the British view, this belonged to the Sultan of Muscat, a princeling to whom they had a long-standing obligation. In due course, the Sultan's troops retook the oasis under the command of British officers, putting American-backed Saudi forces to flight. This was to the enormous displeasure and surprise of John Foster Dulles and Aramco. At one level, a skirmish between British-protected feudalism and American-sponsored multinational capitalism was an instance of mere jostling at the borders. But Sir Evelyn Shuckburgh, private secretary to Sir Anthony Eden and head of Middle Eastern Affairs at the Foreign Office, did not choose to regard it in that light. He made an entry in his diary for November 22, 1955, which, while not in the least perspicacious about the British position in the Arab world, was quite prescient about the American one:

> The fact is that the American oil men have gone into Saudi Arabia with this vast enterprise which utterly submerged the old economy of the country, without assuming any responsibility for the political effects. *It is as if the East India Company had regarded themselves as "just neutrals."*

Here, perhaps, is the clue to Fouad Ajami's lament about an "imperialism without splendor." As a matter of commerce and strategy and anti-Communism and counterrevolution, it borrowed directly from its British antecedent. But it could not, for cultural and historic reasons, pretend to be a *mission civilisatrice*. Sir Evelyn's tone of distaste, his reserve about the vulgar mass and scale of American undertakings, his disdain at the reliance upon sheer cash, his loftiness about the brash interloper, can still be heard in the voices of some British mandarins to this day, at least when they imagine themselves to be among friends.

In other cases, where British withdrawal had been more precipitate, American receivership was correspondingly more smooth. A *locus classicus* here is the case of Pakistan. Until the partition of the subcontinent at independence, the British governor of the North-West Frontier had been Sir Olaf Caroe, a specialist in what might be called Tory geopolitics. Having administered the uttermost point of the Raj, he was anxious that his expertise did not go to waste. In March 1949, he wrote a lengthy "Mr. X" essay in *The Round Table* (which still called itself "a comprehensive review of imperial politics"). The magazine, which breathed with the collective efforts of Rhodes, Milner, and Lothian, proved too small a forum for Sir Olaf's grand design, and the article was expanded into a seminal book, wonderfully entitled *Wells of Power*. It was addressed directly to "the Americans," "as America with her new vision joins a partner full of garnered knowledge but overcome for a little time with weariness."

The proposal was for a "Northern Screen," to include and bolster loyalist Pakistan and to exclude India. The theory was of "a great oval or ellipse" extending from the oil sheikhdoms of the Gulf to the borders of Afghanistan. As Sir Olaf was later to write:

> I went on a tour of the US for the British Foreign Office in 1952 and had talks with State Department officials and others on these lines, and perhaps some of the exchanges we had were not without effect. Indeed, I have more than once

ventured to flatter myself that J. F. Dulles' phrase "the Northern Tier" and his association of the US with the "Baghdad"
countries in Asia were influenced by the thinking in *Wells of
Power*. In that book I called those countries "the Northern
Screen"—the same idea really.

The American decision to equip the Pakistanis with a large armory,
and to take over the British-trained Punjabi military elite, was taken
very soon afterward, and implemented by Major General George
Olmsted, director of the Pentagon's Office of Military Assistance.
(General Olmsted was later to become the registered Washington
lobbyist for General Rafael Trujillo of the Dominican Republic;
another instance of indirect rule.) Sir Olaf Caroe may or may not
have sincerely believed that British "weariness" was something
that would last only "for a little time." As one of the last great
servants of the King-Emperor, however, he evidently saw it as his
duty to pass the torch and found a hand ready to receive it. Forty
years after the publication of his *Round Table* essay, anonymous
United States "advisers" were playing "the Great Game" in Kandahar, Peshawar, and Jalalabad, where once Lord Roberts and
General Elphinstone had carried the flag and the saber. The American version of the game has, as Ajami might point out, yet to
produce its *Kim* or even its G. A. Henty.

American empire, indeed, tends to define itself in terms of strategic jargon rather than grand design and noble mission. "Free
World" rhetoric gives way to talk of "the backyard" of Central
America and the Caribbean, "the arc of crisis" in the Middle East
and northern Asia, "the southern flank" of NATO and the Mediterranean, "the northern tier" of what was once CENTO, and
numerous other analogies of the far-flung, such as "choke points,"
"arteries," and "lifelines." The most famous of these—the "domi-
noes" of Southeast Asia—derives from the period of Anglo-
American jostling for influence in China and Burma and was
actually originated as a term by "Wild Bill" Donovan. In each case,
the debased globalist rhetoric has a British imperial origin.

But as the domino period came to an end, there *was* a brief moment of Lawrence in the embers of empire. The British writer James Fenton, observing the 1975 sack of the American embassy in Saigon, picked up "a framed quotation from Lawrence of Arabia, which read, 'Better to let them do it imperfectly than to do it perfectly yourself, for it is their country, their war, and your time is short.' "

Discordant Intimacy

Walter Lippmann, that ineffable comforter of the Establishment, was well ahead of his time, and well behind it, too, when he wrote in *The New Republic* of December 9, 1916, that the emotion felt by America for France was "the free friendship men give to those whom they meet only in their leisure," while with the British "we have today the discordant intimacy of business partners and family ties." Immediately ahead lay the famous cry of General Pershing as he landed in France: "Lafayette, we are here!"—while only a little further ahead lay the revulsion from Britain and British imperialism that was to follow the duplicity of "the old country's" foreign policy. This revulsion was not to evaporate entirely until the final displacement of British by American power.

For all that, "discordant intimacy" is a useful term for the special relationship. It helps to explain the different forces and classes in England which have, at different times, complemented the ebb and flow of Anglophobia and Anglophilia in America by contrasting attitudes toward the new cousin.

Since in the present day the "special relationship" is so much a matter of elite cooperation and of the invocation of tribal properties such as kinship and tongue, it is at least worth recalling that English affection for the American republic used to be a question of democracy and liberty. Henry Adams noticed this during his time in England when the very idea of the United States was threatened. By that time, Sir Robert Peel—founder of the Conservative Party— had already plundered Tocqueville for his indictment of the horrid "tyranny of the majority" that was supposed to reign in the lawless and uncouth America. His cast of mind transmitted itself through Tory Britain down to Lady Palmerston's 1858 declaration: "We are fast merging into Democracy and Americanism. Sir Hamilton Seymour teaches his children to speak thro' their noses as that is what he thinks they must all come to." Every "fastidious" British objection to America is contained in that one drawling sentence, capturing the association between vulgarity as defined by Arnold and ochlocracy as understood by the Duke of Wellington in his long struggle against "Reform."

On the other hand, as Henry Pelling put it:

> There was much to appeal to all types of British Radical: Benthamites approved of the liberal constitutions of the states; dissenters and free thinkers acclaimed the absence of a religious establishment; land reformers noted with favour the abundance of cheap and undeveloped land; working men found in America a paradise of high wages and social equality.

Even Charles Dickens conceded, at the opening of *Martin Chuzzlewit*, the hold of America upon the imagination of the English poor. And as late as 1889, the great English radical publication *Reynold's Newspaper* wrote that "anything that adds to the power and authority of the United States among the nations of the earth is to the advantage of all mankind." William Clark, Sir Anthony Eden's disillusioned press secretary, once wrote an emollient book on the "special relationship" in which he said that not until the British *Daily Worker* wrote about Russia in the 1930s was any London newspaper as much in thrall to a foreign power as *Reynold's Newspaper* had been to the United States. The comparison is inexact to a fault. On the occasion quoted above, the paper had been intervening in the debate on Irish Home Rule and ridiculing the then fashionable idea that Ireland should be federated to the United Kingdom in the same fashion as Canada. The very notion, it said, should be repudiated by "all good Radicals, whose cue it is to look to the Great Republic for their precedents, and not to the corrupt and snobbish Dominion." The editorial went on, in heroic defiance of paltry colonial half measures, to advocate the annexation of Canada by the United States.

Labor and radical enthusiasm for America underwent a declension as the "expansionist" movement took hold across the water, and as more overt collusion between British and American imperial maneuvering became evident. This tendency was accompanied by the rise of the great trusts and the "robber baron" fortunes, which also diluted pro-American feeling among English workers and artisans and gave them the uneasy feeling that a plutocracy was in the making. There was also an increasing "aristocracy of labor" within the ranks of the organized workers; this aristocracy being expressed on the American side by Samuel Gompers and the AFL, which defended the rights of native, American, white, skilled toilers, and on the British side by the cautious and craft-dominated TUC. In 1915, Ernest Bevin attended Gompers's convention in San Francisco, taking time out on the visit to admire the exhibition of the opening of the Panama Canal. After making his fraternal delegate's speech, which implored American help against the Kaiser, Bevin was given a presentation. It was a heavy gold ring, embossed with the figure of an undraped woman. As he fought to place the gift on Bevin's dockland fingers, Gompers exclaimed: "What's that you got? A bunch of bananas?" Bevin wore the ring through the General Strike, the betrayal of the socialist cause by the Ramsay MacDonald government, and his own tenure as Churchill's Minister of Labor in wartime. As Britain's Foreign Secretary in 1949, he used it as a signet with which to put the British seal on the NATO Treaty in 1949. Labor, too, has its mutated version of the "special relationship."

Even as Ernest Bevin was settling into the role of America's junior but more experienced partner, there were Conservative voices raised plaintively against the unwisdom of the new super-power. These political plaintiffs were much stronger then than is now remembered, and although they approved the idea of an "Anglo-Saxon" world order, they were by no means content with an outright second-rank position. In a collection of essays entitled *What Europe Thinks of America*, which was edited by James Burnham and distinguished by the work of such hands as Raymond Aron, there was outright nervousness about the fitness of America for global command. The British contributor was Julian Amery, whose father had been a close friend of Kipling's and had, at the crucial last minute, humiliated Neville Chamberlain in the House of Commons in 1940. Amery spoke pithily and as follows:

> It was the United States which prevented the reassertion of Dutch power and influence in Indonesia. It was the United States, in the first flush of post-war liberalism, which gave the Viet Minh party in Indo-China their chance. More indirectly, American influence has fostered and nourished the Arab nationalist movements in French North Africa. European leaders have reluctantly to admit that if the Soviet Union is the greater danger to their national and imperial interests, the greatest injuries so far inflicted on them have come from the United States.

Even though Amery was to fill every last ditch between Suez and Rhodesia in the subsequent years, resigning from Margaret Thatcher's front bench over southern Africa in 1979, it is still a surprise to find him being so plainly suspicious of American anti-British imperialism in 1953. Yet the reader who looks up the debates in the Commons and Lords over Suez and Cyprus in the middle and late 1950s will find no shortage of sulfurous anti-American feeling emitted by the British right. It is probably no coincidence that Amery's war service included a stint with Chiang Kai-shek's forces in Chungking. This gave him an intimacy with those Americans like Burnham who also thought of the postwar period as a liberal American "stab in the back."

It is now officially and generally forgotten that there was ever a pro-American left or an anti-American right in Britain. The intense, homogenizing pressure of the Cold War has divided British politicians and intellectuals into the simplified herds of "pro" and "anti" American. Or at least it has done so until recently. The "special relationship" became a renewed topic of controversy in the mid-1980s and is likely to remain one. Nonetheless, the high ground in Britain has been held for some considerable time and for good historical reasons by a party which has admitted and recognized American hegemony, and which regards this admission and recognition as an indispensable part of the political consensus. In early 1989, with a deep division in NATO over the requisite response to Mikhail Gorbachev's *glasnost/perestroika* revolution from above, *The New York Times* described the British response—an almost automatic endorsement in advance of the skeptical position taken by Washington—as "an Anglo-Saxon alliance" of the U.S.A. and U.K. versus the rest. This development would have been unsurprising to any scholar who had followed the internalization, by the strategic majority of the British political class, of the values of the "special relationship." Existing as far as it can above partisan struggle, this consensus and its epigones from *Encounter* to *The Economist* have come to deserve the title "the American Party." Not the least of the virtues of this party is that it does not formally exist.

The phrase "the American Party" belongs to Professor Norman Birnbaum of Georgetown University, who named it in January 1987:

> I once heard a senior official in the State Department explain how the Soviet Union maintained control in Central and Eastern Europe. In the nations it dominated, academics, bureaucrats, officers, managers, politicians and publishers were in continuous contact with Soviet institutions from the beginning of their careers. They remained deeply rooted in their own

countries, of course, but for them dual loyalties were practically instinctive. The explanation seemed convincing, the more so as it is perfectly applicable to our own mode of rule . . . What is striking about Western Europe is the way an American party, very visible in the old world's elites, does our empire's work.

In Britain, went on Professor Birnbaum, there was

a syndrome that may be termed vicarious imperialism. Their own nations have lost world power; the United States offers a substitute imperial homeland. Political advantages accrue to those who can defame adversaries by intimating that "anti-Americanism" (which may range from criticism of Ronald Reagan to a dislike of fast food) is their motive.

Almost exactly a year before, Neal Ascherson had published an essay in London entitled "A Dumb-Bell World," in which he wrote about the unstated assumptions of the "special relationship" in these terms:

Up to about 40 years ago, those who governed the British and told them what to think inhabited a blob-shaped mental world. It comprised the Home Counties, London south of the Park, Westminster and the Inns of Court. Now, after decades of Fulbright grants and academic exchanges, their descendants inhabit a world shaped like a dumb-bell. At one end, the Home Counties, etc., then a long, thin bit, then another blob consisting of Washington, D.C., and some habitable bits of Manhattan and New England.

The rest of the world, outside this "civilised" dumb-bell, is dark and potty. It speaks foreign languages; it suffers rather disgustingly; nobody can spell its statesmen. Dumb-bell people feel as uneasy in Prague as in Glasgow. When they say "Europe" they mean Dorset, Tuscany and Vermont.

Ascherson described this boldly as "Atlantic provincialism." His view of the myopia of "American Party" members about their own countries was nicely counterpointed by Professor Birnbaum's diagnosis of their myopia about America. As they imbibe "the last free drink at the Aspen Institute . . . none of them could endure for more than five minutes the chaos of our multiethnic and pluralistic politics. They prefer not to notice the anti-authoritarianism, the irreverence and the pacifism of many of our people. Their America consists of the clubs, foreign policy conferences and Ivy League Universities at which their masters are pleased to receive them."

Empires need classes, and the virtue of both these complementary essays lay in their recognition of the undiscussed bonding between these two unacknowledged facts. The "special relationship" rests in many respects on mutually sustaining elites in the two countries. Out of a possible plethora, I select three examples: the Rhodes Scholarships, the Council on Foreign Relations, and Ditchley Park.

The Rhodes Scholarships are a form of bonding of the sort often found in the "special relationship"; at once impossible to quantify and very difficult to overstate. If they have played any part in preserving the ideas of Anglo-Saxondom or of vicarious imperialism, at least it can be shown that such was their founder's intention. According to his closest friend and collaborator, W. T. Stead (who later perished with the *Titanic*), Rhodes placed the dream of Anglo-American union far above any other ideal. He was even, if Stead can be believed, willing to see this union accomplished under the American flag rather than not accomplished at all.

Rhodes himself never went that far in print, but in the first of the weird "Seven Wills" in which he made his bequests, did write as follows:

I have felt that at the present day we are actually limiting our children and perhaps bringing into the world half the human beings we might owing to the lack of country for them to inhabit, that if we had retained America there would at the present moment be many millions more of English living. I contend that we are the finest race in the world and that the more of the world we inhabit the better it is for the human race. Just fancy those parts that are at present inhabited by the most despicable of human beings, what an alteration there would be in them if they were brought under Anglo-Saxon influence.

Since Rhodes was one of the few Oxford philosophers who ever had the chance to put his precepts into practice, it is worth giving his noteworthy ambition in full, as he stated it himself. It was:

The extension of British rule throughout the world, the perfecting of a system of emigration from the United Kingdom and of colonisation by British subjects of all lands wherein the means of livelihood are attainable by energy, labor and enterprise, and especially the occupation by British settlers of the entire Continent of Africa, the Holy Land, the valley of the Euphrates, the Islands of Cyprus and Candia, the whole of South America, the islands of the Pacific not heretofore possessed by Great Britain, the whole of the Malay Archipelago, the seaboard of China and Japan, *the ultimate recovery of the United States of America as an integral part of the British Empire.* [Italics mine.]

This document can be read in Rhodes House, Oxford. Rhodes proposed, in ancillary documents and letters, that a form of secret society be formed to prosecute the enormous scheme, which did, after all, allow him to name two countries after himself before he had done. The secret society should be modeled, he thought, on the Society of Jesus. About the "recovery" of the United States for the Empire he was prepared to compromise in a way which he was not in the cases of Cyprus, say, or Malaya. In one of his papers he proposed that the "Imperial Parliament" should sit for five-year periods, alternating between London and Washington.

The scholarship scheme began, of course, in South Africa. It was originally conceived as an entire university, to be built with funds generated, as Rhodes put it with his customary lack of hypocrisy, "out of the Kaffir's stomach." But by 1899, even with the astounding profits from the Kaffir Compound System, forerunner of apartheid, operated by the De Beers diamond mines, such a scheme seemed, if anything, too limited. Those who remember the Anglo-American "understanding" that was developing in that year, under the combined and related pressures of the Philippine and Boer wars, will not be surprised that it was in 1899 that Rhodes mandated a doubling of his scholarships for students from the white British dominions, and added the stipulation that there should also be two for each state in the American Union. (The number of white dominion scholarships was only 60, which has led several of Rhodes's biographers to record that he believed there to be only thirteen American states. A learned contribution from Sir Francis Wylie in *The American Oxonian* for the month of April 1944 shows, however, that Rhodes knew perfectly well that he was allowing for—then— at least 90 scholarships from the United States. In other words, and in imperial terms, he was giving a vast precedence to America.)

In practice, Rhodes's ignorance of the distinction between state and state was to be troublesome to his executors. An amendment made in 1928 by the trustees is worthy of note because it demonstrates the extraordinary influence attained by the Rhodes Scholarship system by that relatively early date. Voting to change the selection procedure by grouping the states into eight "districts" were the members of the Association of American Universities, the Association of Urban Universities, and the Association of American Colleges. The official historian of the Rhodes Scholarships, Frank Aydelotte, also records the active participation in the argument of the presidents and secretaries of the Rockefeller Foundation, the Kahn Fellowship, the Guggenheim Fellowship, the Carnegie Corporation, the Phelps-Stokes Fund, and the General Education

Board. The question of Oxford and America, and the availability of one to the other, was already very important to those who held the purse strings of the vital grant, fellowship, and foundation systems.

"The function of the college in the University of Oxford," wrote Mr. Aydelotte helpfully in his 1946 history, "is in some respects similar to the function of an American Greek-letter fraternity." (He spared us the thought that there might be any Rome looming over this pure Greece.) However, he felt it important to avoid or counter the charge of uncritical Anglophilia. "The fears which were widely expressed when the Rhodes will was made public, that three years at Oxford would make British subjects, or at any rate Anglomaniacs out of our American boys, have proved to be without foundation." Still answering the question that had not been asked, Aydelotte hurried on to say: "The largest single group living abroad are those who have become American missionaries in China, and perhaps no Rhodes Scholars are better placed to serve their country than are these," which was not bad for 1946.

In a concluding burst of the Anglophilia against which he had been warning, Aydelotte counseled against the idea of the German university (and the related idea, perhaps, of hyphenation). "In the two decades before 1900 the United States learned much from the flourishing German universities of the time. Valuable as were the lessons we learned from Germany, they were, so far as concerns undergraduate work, often misleading . . . the undergraduate college of liberal arts does not exist outside of the Anglo-Saxon world."

The notion of a Rhodes bequest to reconquer America now seems entirely absurd. The subliminal influence of the Rhodes Scholarship is rather like the subliminal influence of the etchings in the men's room at the Harvard Club in New York, which happen to be of Peterhouse, Cambridge, Ely and Durham cathedrals and the West Highlands of Scotland. They act as a reinforcement of English taste and manners upon the American condition. Or, in the opinion of some, they provide a sort of reserved and restrained context in which that condition may be considered. Writing on the decline of the "special relationship" in the *American Oxonian* for Fall 1987, the political economist Robert B. Reich (New Hampshire and University College 1968) said of the English in the post-1945 period:

> Here was a people whom Americans could trust: friends and confidants in an unfriendly and confusing world, who provided another perspective, and thus helped America overcome its chronic tendency towards parochialism. Although the evidence is scattered and anecdotal, there is little doubt that during this era American officials often sought the counsel of their British counterparts, and obtained the sort of frank and confidential advice that one can only get from an old and trusted friend whose judgement is deeply valued.

This certainly contains a truth, if the recollections of Senator J. William Fulbright are anything to go by. In his book *The Price of Empire*, the senator describes his boyhood in the Ozark Mountain town of Fayetteville, Arkansas, and the shock of being translated from this context to Oxford:

> I was invited into various clubs and societies . . . The intellectual sophistication of these young Englishmen astonished me. I was embarrassed by my own inadequacy. The literary clubs met once a month to present papers on prominent authors. I was astonished by the intellectual maturity of these seventeen- and eighteen-year-old boys.
>
> R. B. McCallum was the young don who became my tutor. He couldn't have been more sympathetic and understanding. His main criticism of my weekly papers usually was my use of the English language, the parochialism of my language.

So one of the Senate's future foreign policy colossi was schooled to manners on a Rhodes. (His later endowment of Fulbright scholarships, holders of which became snobbishly known as "Halfbrights," did much by accident to promote the Rhodes Scholarships to the treasured position of being venerable by comparison.) Yet when he took his stand on Vietnam, he was to find all the "intellectual sophisticates" of the British Foreign Office giving smooth encouragement to his enemies.

Perhaps unconsciously, Professor Reich replicates in that earlier passage the high ideal of the relationship between a Rhodes Scholar and his severe Oxford "moral tutor." This relationship was caught nicely, even though in the context of Cambridge and in the relationship with a "supervisor," by Norman Podhoretz in his extraordinary memoir *Making It*. Podhoretz simply could not believe that he was at the same college (Clare) where Geoffrey Chaucer had been. Nor could he at first credit the fact that his servant looked upon him as a sort of honorary WASP. As for the "special relationship":

> The intellectual style of my supervisor, a young don all tweeds and mustache and pipe, was the best possible antidote I could have found to the frenetic pursuit of "brilliance" to which I had become habituated at Columbia. . . . Taciturn, hard-headed, common-sensical, scholarly and as English as empiricism itself, he was not in the least moved by those thrilling leaps of "insight" uninhibited by an excess of knowledge; those pseudo-Germanic syntheses undisturbed by mere detail.

These are the kinds of influence that no foreign system, even with the elaborate peddling arrangements available to it in Washington, can ever hope to buy. But it is an open question whether or not the influence has been used, or is usable, in the wholesome ways depicted by Professor Reich. Probably no American administration ever acted with such disregard for British advice and interests as did the Kennedy administration. Yet it contained eleven Rhodes Scholars, including Dean Rusk, who helped in the architecture of the Vietnam disaster. As David Halberstam wrote in his anatomy of the intellectual roots of that war: "In a nation so large and so diverse, there are few ways of quantifying intelligence or success or ability, so those few that exist are immediately magnified; titles become particularly important . . . All Rhodes Scholars become brilliant . . . Doors will open more readily, invitations will arrive, the phone will ring." One can easily imagine Cecil Rhodes as an enthusiastic supporter of the Vietnam War, but where does this leave Professor Reich and his English version of the *mission civilisatrice* to America?

It may be found, perhaps, as part of the soft underlay of the Anglo-American literary culture. Robert Penn Warren, America's first recipient of the English-inspired Poet Laureateship, was a former Rhodes Scholar. A note in the same edition of the *American Oxonian* heading the news of old boys records that "James H. Billington (New Jersey and Balliol '50) has succeeded Daniel J. Boorstin (Oklahoma and Balliol '34), becoming the Nation's thirteenth Librarian of Congress; so we see one Balliol Rhodes Scholar succeeding another in that distinguished office." This is much more the tone in which Rhodes Scholars talk, though they do not always underline the obvious quite so crassly.

They tend to turn up, even so, in areas where the obvious is not neglected. Rhodes Scholars have been very influential in diplomacy—supplying an important prewar and wartime British ambassador to Washington in the shape of Lord Lothian, and an eminent "know your British" deputy chief of mission in London in the shape of Phillip Kaiser during the ticklish bit of the Vietnam War. Carl Albert, Speaker of the House of Representatives, nearly became President on two occasions during the Watergate crisis of the Constitution—the nearest a Rhodes Scholar has attained to the greatest office. Others, according to surveys and breakdowns, choose principally to enter the professions of law and journalism. They turn up at *The New York Times* and in "serious" East Coast magazines such as *Foreign Policy* and *The Atlantic*. Michael Kinsley, a Rhodes Scholar who has edited both *Harper's* and *The New Republic*, was invited to be a guest editor at *The Economist* in 1988 and thus scored a sort of "special relationship" hat trick. Asked by

The Washington Post to describe his motives in leaving Washington for London during an election campaign, he replied cheerfully with the one word "Anglophilia."

Meanwhile, Halberstam's observation has been vindicated by the passage of time. Rhodes Scholarships have become, more than ever, a special certificate in the lottery of a purely American meritocracy. Ivy League colleges—themselves a transplantation of the English ideal—vie for the prestige that attaches to a good record with the Rhodes Selection Committee. Georgetown University rewards its successful Rhodes candidates with $1,000 in credit at Blackwell's bookshop—midway between Balliol and the Bodleian—and a free tuxedo for Union debates and those all-important formal and club dinners. Harvard, in its 1988 fund-raising letter to alumni, made a special point of stressing that it had sired ten Rhodes Scholars in the preceding twelvemonth.

Oxford itself, meanwhile, is going bankrupt. Increasingly, it hires out its bosky gardens and gray cloisters to conferences and summer schools where the cachet of an ancient address can levy funds. Its colleges look for American masters and wardens in order to facilitate the flow of donations across the Atlantic. Its dons and syndics make embarrassed visits to the United States to learn about the arcana of direct mail. Addressing the Oxford-Cambridge Dinner in Washington in 1986, Oxford Vice-Chancellor Sir Patrick Neill was awkward about naming the sum his university required. "This amount we need," he said, "is so staggering that it would be offputting to mention it." That could have been any British Chancellor of the Exchequer, trying to preserve a civilized atmosphere at Bretton Woods. It calls up J. B. Priestley's famous invocation of Britain's uneasy place at the nuclear "top table," where the old country "still sits, nervously fingering a few remaining chips, like a Treasury official playing with two drunk oil millionaires." "Offputting," perhaps, but so is the recognition of the inequality of the "special relationship," which has transformed Rhodes's imperial dream, along with many others, into a poor relation's reverie of staying on terms, of exerting an uplifting influence, while all the while the ancient family name is being parlayed into fast-track résumés and a shiny prospectus.

The Council on Foreign Relations is another of those British-modeled clubland circles which encourage bonding between aspirants in the worlds of government, diplomacy, the academy, journalism, and finance. Its role is to provide a revolving door through which candidate members of future and present establishments may circulate, and a fish tank of talent from which incoming Presidents and Secretaries of State may select. In their excellent book *Imperial Brain Trust*, William Mintner and Lawrence Shoup quote Henry Kissinger as telling the Council's governor, Hamilton Fish Armstrong, "You invented me." This exaggeration—it was Richard Nixon who invented Mr. Kissinger—is still significant. A glance at the Council's membership rolls reveals an A list of the American Establishment, with a distinct East Coast bias perhaps but increasingly catholic in its inclusiveness and with regional clones designed to redress the bias of its founding fathers.

The origins of the Council lie in the "special relationship" and in that part of it which cements British and American military and political objectives. It was on May 30, 1919, in the immediate post-Versailles period, that a group of American and British luminaries met in the Majestic Hotel in Paris to constitute an Anglo-American forum. Its provisional name was the Institute of International Affairs. Moving spirit in the new Institute was Lionel Curtis, a disciple of none other than Cecil Rhodes. Calling on money from the Rhodes Trust, which exemplified the same imperial and Anglo-Saxon precepts as the original Rhodes Scholarships, Curtis was already a veteran of the "Round Table" groups set up in the white British dominions by Lord Milner and Rhodes himself. Again, one finds Philip Kerr (later British ambassador to Washington under the title of Lord Lothian) as Lionel Curtis's partner in the scheme for "organic union" of the Anglo-American empire. There was also a United States Round Table group, and a number of the advisers to Colonel Edward House and President Woodrow Wilson had been prominent in it. Among them, unsurprisingly, were Thomas W. Lamont of the J. P. Morgan bank and Whitney H. Shepardson, who became the secretary of the American branch of the Institute of International Affairs.

The British branch of the IIA, with Lionel Curtis as its secretary, swiftly took on the essential prefix "Royal," under which title it flourishes to this day. Most outsiders know it by its less cumbersome name of Chatham House, and it is by no means unknown to receive a Foreign Office briefing under what are agreeably known as "Chatham House rules"—the surreptitiously, deep-background culture that informs so much of British public life.

The American section did not enjoy, at first, such a quick takeoff or such distinguished patronage. Instead, it decided to fuse with a near-moribund New York City dining club called the Council on Foreign Relations and add an "Inc." to the name as suffix instead of a "Royal" prefix. The honorary president of the Council on Foreign Relations Inc. was Elihu Root, best remembered for his role as administrator of the territories wrested from Spain in 1898, and for good measure an adviser to the Anglophile Andrew Carnegie as well as first president of the Carnegie Endowment for International Peace. His co-president was John W. Davis, Woodrow Wilson's onetime ambassador to Great Britain and chief counsel to J. P. Morgan and Co. The other names of founding office bearers—Wickersham, Cravath—read like a directory of yesterday's and today's Wall Street law firms. By 1922 the Council had begun to publish *Foreign Affairs*, and it was not long before words like "judicious" and "authoritative" began to be applied to the magazine. Its launching was the brainchild of Edwin F. Gay, a Council figure and the first dean of the Harvard Business School, who had written in 1898: "When I think of the British Empire as our inheritance I think simply of the natural right of succession. That ultimate succession is inevitable."

Broadly speaking, the composition and character of the CFR was one of post-Wilsonian internationalism, with a self-conscious emphasis on America's duty to shoulder a global role. It ranged itself

more or less explicitly against the isolationists, and drew strength
from the more forward-looking and adventurous element of the
business community. Isaiah Bowman, who headed the CFR's Research Committee during much of the interwar period, postulated
an American sphere "whose extent is beyond the Arctic Circle in
Alaska, southward to Samoa and east and west from China to the
Philippines to Liberia and Tangier." He added, employing the
inevitable standard of comparison, that "if our territorial holdings
are not so widely distributed as those of Great Britain, our total
economic power and commercial relations are no less extensive."
Bowman, Gay, and others spent much useful time in the Depres-
sion years arguing for an American strategy based on free trade
and the open door.

As with most other groups and factions favoring assertive American internationalism, the CFR's breakthrough moment came during the Second World War, when its War and Peace Study Project
became an accessory to the State Department. From an early stage,
the CFR influence was exerted on the side of intervention. An
ingenious 1940 recommendation to President Roosevelt, for example, urged that he extend the Monroe Doctrine to define Green-
land as a part of the American continent, and thereby forestall the
Nazis from claiming Danish colonies if they occupied Denmark.
At about this time, too, members of the Council created the Century Group, so called because it gathered at the Pall Mall-imitation
Century Association, a gentlemen's club in New York. The members of the Group, who included numerous individuals associated
with the War and Peace Study Project, claimed the credit for
evolving the "destroyers for bases" agreement that marked the
inauguration of Lend-Lease. Certainly it was at their meeting on
July 25, 1940, that the idea was first broached. From this quid pro
quo beginning, the CFR and its related intellectuals began to consider how American global brokerage might be applied in a more
thoroughgoing fashion. Out of these deliberations came the overarching concept of the "Grand Area"—the "Western Hemisphere,
British Empire, and Far East" bloc—which was to become the

central preoccupation of postwar U.S. foreign policy. Out of these deliberations also emerged the American interpretation of the Atlantic Charter. As early as April 1941, the WPSP proposed a general statement of war aims, anticipating Roosevelt's own later admonitions to Churchill in these words:

> If war aims are stated which seem to be concerned solely with Anglo-American imperialism, they will offer little to people in the rest of the world, and will be vulnerable to Nazi counter-promises. Such aims would also strengthen the most reactionary elements in the United States and the British Empire. The interests of other peoples should be stressed, not only those of Europe, but also of Asia, Africa and Latin America. This would have a better propaganda effect.

This might seem to be an early prefiguration of General Patrick Hurley's "Progressive" and "anticolonial" politics in Iran in 1944–45. If so, the effect seems to have been intentional. In May 1942, CFR president Norman Davis, then secretary of the State Department's security subcommittee of the Advisory Committee on Postwar Foreign Policy (cumbersome Foggy Bottom titles did not begin with Dulles), said baldly that in all likelihood "the British Empire as it existed in the past will never reappear and that the United States will have to take its place." Taking a Roman or at least Latin attitude toward the same question was General George V. Strong of the same committee and the same CFR background, who averred that the United States "must cultivate a mental view toward world settlement after this war which will enable us to impose our own terms, amounting perhaps to a *pax Americana*."

In this, yet another evolution from an English-sponsored imperial forum to a full-blown American internationalist think tank, one can also discern the texture of Englishness. The Mintner-Shoup study found that two-thirds of the directors of the CFR were also members of the Century Association and that, no doubt often overlapping, one-fifth were members of the Links Club, the University

Club, or the Metropolitan Club, the last of which is in Washington.
Seventeen percent of the CFR's directors also had a male relative
who was also a Council member. The names Rockefeller, Fish,
McCloy, and others recur with a reassuring predictability. As one
member, John Franklin Campbell, wrote shortly before his death
about the CFR's famous premises on East Sixty-eighth Street, the
Harold Pratt House:

> If you can walk—or be carried—into the Pratt House, it
> usually means that you are a partner in an investment bank
> or law firm with occasional "trouble-shooting" assignments in
> government . . . the Council is stuffy and clubby and parochial
> and elitist, but it is a place where old moneybags and young
> scholars are able to sit down and learn something from each
> other. It is pompous and pretentious but it still draws men
> of affairs out of their counting-houses and into dialogue with
> men of intellect.

It was in this leather-armchair atmosphere that George Kennan
published his famous "containment" essay in *Foreign Affairs* for
July 1947, and that David Rockefeller and Charles Spofford developed a paper, "Reconstruction in Western Europe," that became the blueprint for the Marshall Plan. The British diplomats
and academics and politicians who solicit invitations to the CFR as
junior partners can at least reflect that, as with so many other similar
American sancta, their ancestors were present at its creation. And
of course they can always reciprocate, if they are eminent enough,
with the magic words: "See you at Ditchley."

At Enstone in Oxfordshire stands an eighteenth-century mansion
built in the reign of George I and almost equidistant from the two
other great houses of the county, which are Blenheim (birthplace
of Winston Churchill and seat of the Dukes of Marlborough) and
Heythrop. Its architect was James Gibbs, who also gave us the
Senate House in Cambridge, the Radcliffe Camera in Oxford, and
the London church of St. Martin-in-the-Fields. The spires of Ox-

ford are visible from the upper stories when the weather is clement. For many generations, the house was the property of the Dillon-Lee family, relations of the Earl of Rochester and upholders of a strong royalist tradition. On the death of the seventeenth Viscount Dillon in 1932, family indigence led to the sale of the house to Ronald and Nancy Tree.

Ronald Tree was the acme of Anglo-American gentry, and his memoir, *When the Moon Was High*, is one of the great testaments of American Anglophilia. His North American side originally hailed from Somerset, England, and had in its genealogy an artillery captain killed in Washington's service at Valley Forge and a postal official who wrote a description of the Capitol after the British had burned it in the War of 1812. Tree's father, Arthur, had been sent to Oxford University, where "he rode to hounds more than he read his books, and polo interested him more than Political Science." Decided on a life of ease in England, he married the daughter of the Chicago tycoon Marshall Field. Young Ronald was born on their estate at Ashorne Hill in Warwickshire in 1897, into a marriage that did not last long because of the defection of his mother to Captain David Beatty, British hero of the Boxer Rising and the Sudan campaign and future hero of Jutland.

After a period of post-divorce shuttling between England and America, Ronald Tree was sent to Winchester, writing of it later in the exact tones of the nostalgic old boy and hymning "the green of the playing fields . . . the austerity of the scholar's quadrangle, backing up on one side to the flint and stone walls of the chapel, and the exquisite and rare little medieval chapel in the centre of its cloisters." Here he formed a friendship with George Cecil, "son of Lord Edward Cecil, the Egyptian administrator whose book, *Leisure of an Egyptian Official*, is among the gems of British literature. After her husband's death, his mother married Lord Milner, the great South African administrator." Tree's other friend was Bim Tennant, son of Lord Glenconner and author of one of those aching poems, "Home Thoughts from Laventie," which evoke the spirit of young Englishmen—eventually including himself—who were to be slaughtered in Flanders. Tree also took a part in the First World War after leaving school. He crossed the Atlantic on a liner in the company of Lord Northcliffe, "on his way to the States to begin his propaganda mission to the Americans," and joined the Naval Air Service. Returning to Europe, he fell in love with Nancy Field, widow of his cousin and niece of Nancy Astor. After the couple decided to make their home in England, the Astors "included us in all their famous political parties at Cliveden and St. James's Square." They did not, however, succeed in annexing the Trees to the appeasement-minded politics that characterized these and other soirées. Tree became Joint Master of the Pytchley hounds, the most inbred fox hunt in England. He became a Tory MP for the rural seat of Market Harborough, thus equaling the Astors as an Anglo-American parliamentarian. But he was to become a stout Churchillian on the only issue that mattered, which is why Ditchley Park is so much a part of the fabric of the "special relationship" to this day.

In the same year that he was elected to the House of Commons, Tree acquired Ditchley and its three thousand acres. His account of the acquisition is almost too charming for words, containing as it does every romantic detail, down to the eccentric servitor, that Hollywood might have mandated. Not since the American family took over the haunted mansion in Oscar Wilde's story "The Canterville Ghost," or since Henry Adams took his leave of the old country, has anything been so fitting:

> We were met by an ancient butler, wearing a red wig, designed I believe to conceal his great age. When he found that my wife came from Virginia he fetched a postcard written to him by Lord Dillon in 1870 when, on a visit to America, he had gone down to Virginia to make the acquaintance of his kinsman, General Robert E. Lee.

(Note that, here, even the convention of British aristocratic kinship with the Confederacy is scrupulously observed.) Tree was captivated by Ditchley at first sight, though conventionally appalled by its traditional state of "no baths, no heating, no lighting." But he managed to install modern amenities in the barbarous English countryside, as well as "a spacious servants' hall, a housekeepers' room, a gun room, and so on." With the assistance of Edward Hudson, founder and editor of *Country Life*, he and his spouse also contrived to rescue the garden and terrace from the neglect of the last Lord Dillon. There was even a change of butler. Collins, who had come to Tree from the Life Guards, "became a legendary figure. A man of great judgement, with a tremendous capacity for detail, he would be rung up by people all over England requiring butlers, enquiring if he knew of the right person for the job."

However determined Tree may have been to indulge a Wodehousian impression of Englishness, in practice he was no drone. Even during "the phony war" he was active on the other side of the Atlantic, attempting to beef up the British propaganda effort in New York and Washington, and soliciting Winthrop Aldrich to help in the foundation of British War Relief. He also made a side trip to Canada, to see John Buchan in his capacity as Governor-General and to discuss with him his experience as an aide to Northcliffe in the last war and his advice for the next. This, with some observations about the awful influence of Colonel McCormick and his pro-Nazi isolationists in Marshall Field's Chicago, formed the basis of a report on British war aims and opportunities in America which among other things predicted the election of Roosevelt for a third term.

Tree was at first ungratefully received for his anti-Nazi activism by the stupid majority in his own party. Having joined the forty-four Conservative MPs who voted against Neville Chamberlain in the crucial vote of confidence, he was at once blackballed, at the instigation of a Tory Whip, on his application to join the Royal Yacht Squadron. But these and other pinpricks from reaction were to be forgotten as events progressed.

David Bruce, who had been secretary to his own father-in-law, Andrew Mellon, when the latter was American ambassador to the

Court of St. James's, arrived in London to assume command of the American Red Cross. On the same ship came "Wild Bill" Donovan, soon to be the first head of the Office of Strategic Services, dispatched by Roosevelt to report on British morale and readiness. Together, these and other Americans with strong British connections (or strong Anglophile and anti-Fascist predilections, like Edward R. Murrow) undercut the suspiciously defeatist attitudes being marketed by Ambassador Joseph Kennedy.

In late 1940, Tree was asked by Churchill if he could offer him " 'accommodation at Ditchley for certain weekends'—and I can still recall the mystery and poetry with which he invested the phrase—'when the moon is high.' " The Chiefs of Staff were worried that the Nazis might bomb the Prime Ministerial residence at Chequers. It was agreed that on nights of good visibility the great man would put up at Ditchley. Thus began a series of dinners and long evenings at which much "special relationship" spadework was done. In his memoirs, *As It Happened*, William Paley, founder of CBS, has given us his impressions in the precise tones that still resonate for so many American Anglophiles and devotees of *Masterpiece Theatre*:

> British hospitality is a special genre, unduplicated anywhere else in the world. Although I had visited England many times before, it was on this wartime trip that I became more conscious than ever before of the understated qualities of the British national character, traditions and sophistication. In some of the most formal, stately country homes and castles, owned by the same families for generations, if not hundreds of years, I came across the most splendid furniture, furnishings and paintings, *much of it of museum quality*. [Italics mine.]

"In the best of these houses," he recalls, "everything was arranged in a sort of casual manner, rich but not ostentatious." Ditchley, on his account, was the best of these houses—"the most beautiful home I had seen in England." Of course, the very polish and style Mr. Paley so admired had been made possible at Ditchley by the lavishness of the Marshall Field Chicago retail fortune, which was anything but "understated."

It was at Ditchley that the Churchills and the Harrimans, the Salisburys and the Lothians, mixed. It was at Ditchley that Churchill, asked at dinner: "How *can* we be Allies of the Russians?" replied: "I believe in holding the carnal until the spiritual is free." Here, too, he first watched *Gone with the Wind* and pronounced himself "pulverised by the strength of their feelings and emotions." At Ditchley, Sir John Colville recorded Churchill's delight at the coming of Lend-Lease, adding that "in view of this Bill it will be more difficult for us to resist the American tendency—which Kingsley Wood lamented to me yesterday—to strip us of everything we possess in payment for what we are about to receive." At Ditchley, Churchill, explaining the world situation after dinner, said that "Germany had 60 million on whom she could count; the remainder were at least a drag and potentially a danger. The British Empire had more white inhabitants than that, and if the U.S. were with us—as he seemed in this discourse to assume they actively would be—there would be another 120 millions." Finally, it was at Ditchley that Churchill discussed with Philip Reed, American chairman of the General Electric Company, a joint U.S.-U.K. currency to be put into circulation after the war. Churchill even designed a symbol for this currency, combining the $ and the £, and gave it to Ronald Tree on a postcard.

Tree kept a visitors' book at Ditchley, which reads like a roll of honor for the "special relationship" of that period, and which records such details as the visits of David Bruce, future ambassador, with "his secretary, the exquisite Evangeline Bell, whom he was shortly to marry." And the guest roster today would reflect the same. David Wills, who succeeded to the ownership of the house, gifted it to the Ditchley Foundation, in the words of the official guide, to continue "this tradition of Anglo-American cooperation . . . to become a permanent centre of study and conference to further friendship and understanding between the two peoples." The house is now administered by the Foreign Office, who enhance the Oxonian atmosphere of the establishment by appointing a "Provost," who is customarily a retired diplomat. Discreet, well-provendered weekend conferences are organized, at which editors and "policy intellectuals" from both sides of the Atlantic can meet those who know, or have known, the thrill of wielding actual power. Here the pulse and temperature of the "special relationship" are regularly and earnestly monitored. In the first of the "Ditchley Papers," published in 1963, Provost H. V. Hodson—ex-fellow of All Souls, ex-editor of *The Sunday Times*—solemnly weighed the problems of perception that impeded better Anglo-American *entente*. Through British eyes, he wrote, the United States often seemed to pursue "an undiscriminating anti-imperialist policy," while the Americans in their turn could object that "on the British side the fault seems often to be the opposite one—failure to recognise the realities of the Cold War." This statesmanlike evenhandedness is characteristic of the Ditchley style, which has certainly striven to make America less anti-imperialist and Britain more Cold War-conscious. Since, as Hodson also put it, "the balance of nuclear deterrence is the supreme governor of the Cold War," much time is expended in Ditchley's dining rooms and gardens on the problems of deployment and the political risks of neutralism or "moral equivalence."

In 1986, Ditchley Park and the Woodrow Wilson Foundation came together to consider the "special relationship" from every conceivable angle. The list of contributors to the conference was in the grand tradition of Ronald Tree's visitors' book, with almost all of the twenty-six participants being able to identify themselves with an Oxford, Cambridge, Harvard, Yale, or Rhodes qualification. Some of the biographies were especially eye-catching, expressing something essential about the effortless assumptions of "special relationship" dining and debating clubs. Here are two contiguous ones, chosen at random from the second half of the alphabetical order:

WILLIAM D. ROGERS (LLB, Yale) is senior partner in the Washington law firm of Arnold and Porter. He was Deputy Coordinator of the Alliance for Progress, 1961–5, and Henry Kissinger's Assistant Secretary of State for Latin America and Under Secretary for International Economics until 1977, with a sabbatical at Cambridge, 1982–3. Author of *The Twilight Struggle* and numerous articles, he is currently preoccupied with the restructuring of the debt of Brazil and Venezuela.

LORD ST. BRIDES (BA, Oxford), GCMG, CVO, BME, PC, was educated at Bradfield and Balliol. He was British High Commissioner in Pakistan, 1961–6, and in India, 1968–71; Permanent Under Secretary of State, Commonwealth Office, and Privy Councillor, 1968; and British High Commissioner in Australia, 1971–6. Since becoming a Life Peer in 1977, he has been a Visiting Fellow at the Universities of Chicago, Pennsylvania, and Texas at Austin, and also at Harvard and Stanford. He is working on his South Asian memoirs, to be entitled *Travelling Hopefully*.

These résumés could scarcely be improved upon, exemplifying as they do the identity of interest, the varying definitions of the white man's burden, and the Establishment internationalism that underlie the Anglo-American alliance. Here, in a country house that could feature in any American TV series on British gracious living, and with the participants breathing the same air as was once breathed by Churchill, Harriman, and Hopkins, every conceivable definition of the word "class" is brought to bear on the mutually agreeable consideration of diplomacy, defense, and the elaboration of common interests. No other American ally is able to call so effortlessly on a heritage such as this.

For a final testimony to the power of "scratches on the mind," let me cite Henry Kissinger in his deceptive book *The White House Years*:

The "Special Relationship" is particularly impervious to abstract theories. . . . It reflected the common language and culture of two sister peoples. It owed no little to the superb self-discipline by which Britain succeeded in maintaining political influence after its physical power had waned.

It was an extraordinary relationship because it rested on no legal claim; it was formalized by no document; it was carried forward by succeeding British governments as if no alternative were conceivable. Britain's influence was great precisely because it never insisted upon it; the "Special Relationship" demonstrated the value of intangibles.

Much like Britain's "unwritten constitution" and "invisible exports," the relationship, in other words, provided an uncheckable, untestable charter for the freedom of action of an unelected class. There were always those in the United States—Henry Kissinger not the least of them—who looked with vicarious envy on this power untrammeled by legislative or legal restraint, and who themselves had good cause to esteem the value of intangibles.

[12]

The Bond of Intelligence

The "cousinhood" of intelligence gathering and espionage forms one of the most absorbing subtexts of the "special relationship." It embodies the shared blood and toil of wartime camaraderie, the mutual exchange of secrets (sequestered from all non-Anglo-American eyes), the bonding that results from confronting common enemies, stretching from the Great War to the Cold War. As well as shared language, there is a second order of communication based upon shared codes and ciphers. And there is a special subdivision of fiction, evolved to express the ironies and rivalries that mark the connection between certain addresses in and around Curzon Street in London and certain floors of a complex in Langley, Virginia.

The ethos of this nasty, hermetic little universe was well captured by Miles Copeland in his indiscreet memoir of CIA life, *The Real Spy World*:

> The British "station" is almost identical with that of the CIA, except, perhaps, that it is normally smaller, better covered and better integrated into the embassy to which it is assigned. Also it is poorer, its budget normally being about a third of the budget of its American counterpart. For this reason, it is in most parts of the world a primary duty of the

British station chief to use his superior prestige and cunning to persuade his CIA colleague to join him in joint Anglo-American operations, for which he supplies the brain and the CIA colleague supplies the funds.

"Cousinhood" also provides its own illustration of the Graeco-Roman succession, as conceived by the British, and of the relationship between money and brains which this succession is fondly supposed to exemplify. Finally, it shows with what speed and dispatch the United States appropriated yet another area of British preeminence and converted it to new purposes while retaining British cooperation.

In the first half of the century, British intelligence was principally a machine for involving the United States in war on the British side. The relative underdevelopment of American espionage made this a simple enough task when coordinated with the "right" social and political strata.

Recall the account given by Admiral Sir William Reginald ("Blinker") Hall, head of British Naval Intelligence in the First World War. Here is his jaunty recollection of the first sniff of the Zimmermann Telegram:

> I am not likely to forget that Wednesday morning, 17 January 1917. There was the usual docket of papers to be gone through on my arrival at the office, and Claud Serocold and I were still at work on them when at almost half past ten de Grey came in. He seemed excited. "D.I.D. [Director of Intelligence Division]," he began, "d'you want to bring America into the war?" "Yes, my boy," I replied.

Blinker, of course, had already played an essential part in making the most of the *Lusitania* incident and was supposed to be on watch for precisely this sort of contingency. But between January 17 and Woodrow Wilson's recall of Congress on March 21, 1917, and the United States' declaration of war on April 6, there was a certain amount of work to be done. First, the British had to get hold of the full text of the telegram, which they had not at first possessed. Second, they had to conceal the fact that they already knew the German imperial codes. Third, they had to present what they uncovered in such a way as to convince President Wilson of a *casus belli*. These three objectives were not smoothly compatible. First, the code groups in this instance were incomplete. Second, Arthur Zimmermann, as German Foreign Minister, was cabling his ambassador in Washington with nothing much more than a contingency plan. Everything he proposed to Mexico—the infamous suggestion that that country should "reconquer the lost territory in Texas, New Mexico, and Arizona"—was to be put to President Carranza only if the United States declared war on Germany. Since Carranza had already had the experience of being invaded by President Wilson, it was not proposed that he invade the United States. (Nor, this time at any rate, did the United States invade Mexico. General Pershing, who had been deep into Mexican territory the previous June, was instead sent to confront the Kaiser.)

Zimmermann threatened to spoil the fun by confirming the contents of the telegram as soon as he was asked about it, which was in Berlin on March 2, 1917, three weeks before Wilson recalled Congress. But Blinker Hall had got in ahead of him, sending a cable to his subordinates in Washington which used the customary code name of "Aaron" for Woodrow Wilson and which subtly reordered the priorities of the telegram:

> Germany guarantees assistance to Mexico if they will reconquer Texas, New Mexico, and Arizona; also proposes alliance with Mexico to make war together. Do not use this till Aaron announces it. Premature disclosure fatal. Full details in possession of Aaron. Alone I did it.

The men of Room Forty in the British Admiralty showed a shrewd understanding of the psychological as well as the political dimension, invoking the spirit of the Monroe Doctrine as well as

America's uneasy conscience about Mexico. In the Second World War, they were also to make skilled use of their superiority, acquired in decades of playing the "great game" across vast tracts of the globe. The possession of the Ultra Secret and the Enigma Machine, both of them products of British flair and inventiveness (though both admittedly owing a great deal to the courage and sacrifice of certain Poles and Jews), was parlayed into an exceptional initiating influence, by the United Kingdom, over the foundation and direction of the United States intelligence system. This influence in turn was used to make astonishing interventions in American domestic politics.

As in the case of the First World War, the British were able to make use of well-placed financial and political, as well as journalistic and academic, allies. William Stephenson, "the man called Intrepid," actually began his operations by persuading men like "Wild Bill" Donovan to get on nickname terms with him (for a while, they were "Big Bill" and "Little Bill") and to help in the politics of influence. The retired General Pershing was induced to come out of retirement and to give a speech in favor of the "destroyers for bases" agreement. A series of articles on "German Fifth Column Tactics" was written by Donovan from material supplied by Stephenson and published in the *Chicago Daily News*—then owned by Frank Knox, Secretary of the Navy—and the *New York Herald Tribune*. This was in August 1940. The second time around, though, the theme of German-American "dual loyalty" was not too heavily stressed. And, the second time around, there was no need to invent atrocity stories.

In fact, Stephenson was more careful than his First World War predecessors had been and so were his hosts. When he established British Security Coordination (BSC) in New York in 1940, it operated out of Rockefeller Center under the time-honored cover of a British Passport Control bureau, but was met with a demand for registration from the State Department while a series of stipulations from the rather Anglophobic FBI. J. Edgar Hoover extracted undertakings from Stephenson not to employ Americans, not to have independent agents under his own control, and to cooperate with the FBI at all times.

It does not seem likely that he ever intended to keep these pledges. As a millionaire in his own right, a Canadian citizen, and a personal friend of Winston Churchill's, he was able to command varying degrees of latitude. He was also empowered to deal with the White House directly on matters of such consuming interest as British work on uranium isotopes and electronic code breaking, matters in which the United Kingdom then led the field and the very stuff of which "bargaining chips" are made.

The personnel upon whom Stephenson could call were precisely of the sort that have since been romanced in a thousand indifferent movies. There was Sir Connop Guthrie, a baronet and former Grenadier Guardsman, who headed the Security Division and established himself in the Cunard Building on Broad Street to keep an eye on shipping. There was Sir William Wiseman, another baronet, who had been a confidant of Woodrow Wilson a quarter of a century before and who had remained on Wall Street as a banker. These and other natural Establishment guerrillas helped to circumvent any literal-mindedness about the Neutrality Act as it might touch British economic or military interests. Occasionally, the taste for shortcuts and swashbuckle led to embarrassment as well as to a certain vicarious admiration from offended Americans. Once, in Baltimore, British intelligence hired trucks and went on a sweep of the bars, rounding up Danish sailors who had been accused of deserting a British convoy. Under Secretary of State Sumner Welles recalled after the war that, upon hearing of this,

I promptly notified the British ambassador. Lord Halifax, needless to say, had received no news of the occurrence, let alone any intimation that such action was to be taken. He was aghast at the reaction that might be provoked, even in wartime, if the American public learned of so flagrant a violation of American sovereignty, and one so painfully reminiscent of the British impressments of colonial days.

Yet it was exactly this corner-cutting, red-tape-slicing brio that showed the experience and the confidence of the British secret services vis-à-vis their junior partners, and which furnishes the material of legend in the folklore of the secret world. (In just the same way at another level, Lord Halifax vindicated the national reputation for rigidity in the upper lip when pelted with eggs and tomatoes by isolationist ladies in Detroit. "We do not have," he murmured, "any such surplus in England.")

Isolationists were a special target of Stephenson's operation. He made a particular effort to embarrass Congressman Hamilton Fish, a domestic political enemy of President Roosevelt and a suspiciously enthusiastic backer of America First. Stephenson discovered checks written to him by prominent Germans and caused their provenance to be published in the American press. He intercepted Fish's mail at Congress and was able to show that his staff was abusing the congressional franking privilege to send out isolationist statements from the *Congressional Record* to pro-Nazi organizations. He was able to show that the chief contact of one of Fish's staff, a certain George Viereck, had violated the Foreign Agents Registration Act. When Congressman Fish stood for re-election in November 1944, the voters of the 26th Congressional District in New York were reminded of these facts in a series of well-informed leaflets. In private, British intelligence veterans do not hesitate to take credit for his failure to be reelected.

More in the tradition of Blinker Hall and the Zimmermann Telegram, British intelligence again cut with the grain of the Monroe Doctrine and fabricated a map showing Nazi designs for an empire in Latin America. Passed by Stephenson to Donovan, the map was flourished by Roosevelt at a Navy Day dinner held in the Mayflower Hotel in Washington on October 27, 1941. "The territory of one of these new puppet states," he said, "includes the Republic of Panama and our great lifeline, the Panama Canal."

Stephenson, indeed, took the credit for having built up Donovan into the United States' first real intelligence chieftain. In May 1941 he cabled London that he had been "attempting to persuade Donovan into accepting the job of coordinating all U.S. intelligence." He was later to say that "had it been comprehended . . . to what extent I was supplying our friend with secret information to build up his candidacy for the position I wanted to see him achieve here," there would have been horror and mayhem throughout British intelligence headquarters in London. Thus, when Roosevelt appointed Donovan to the position of "Coordinator of Information" with the rank of Major General, Stephenson was able to say: "If Donovan had not been able to rely upon BSC assistance, his organisation could not have survived. Indeed, it is a fact that, before he had his own operational machinery in working order, which was not until several months after Pearl Harbor, he was entirely dependent upon it."

In their book *Sub Rosa*, Stewart Alsop and Thomas Braden confirm this pardonably boastful claim. The British, they write, "told him how they trained their men, what weapons they had, and how they communicated with the resistance. Breaking the precedent of centuries, they even sent a man over to sit down with Donovan and explain the workings of British espionage."

When H. Montgomery Hyde's hagiographic history of the Stephenson operation was published in the United States in early 1963, it contained a bonus which the English edition had not. This took the form of an introduction by Ian Fleming. There could hardly have been a happier moment for this piece of atmospherics in cementing the British spy connection, just then looking a little tarnished by defections to the other side. In the early days of the Kennedy presidency, Hugh Sidey had told the readers of *Time* magazine that JFK had a list of ten favorite books, on which *From Russia with Love* ranked at number nine (just ahead of *The Red and the Black*). Fleming had been a dinner guest of the Kennedys during the 1960 election campaign. He had also, in his fabled Caribbean retreat, Goldeneye, entertained Sir Anthony Eden as a house guest while the latter recuperated from the bruising inflicted upon him by the breakdown of the "special relationship" over Suez.

Fleming had been an assistant to the director of British Naval Intelligence during the Second World War. In that capacity, he had composed the charter for General Donovan's tenure as Co-ordinator of Information. Ivar Bryce, a deputy of Stephenson's, recalls: "Ian wrote out the charter for the COI at General Donovan's request. . . . He wrote it as a sort of imaginary exercise describing in detail all the arrangements necessary for financing, paying, organizing, controlling, and training a secret service in a country which had never had one before."

In his introduction, Fleming did his best to evoke the classic melding of designer snobbery and the affectation of "class" that were also his fictional stock-in-trade. Describing the "small study in an expensive apartment block bordering the East River" where Stephenson had his abode, Fleming filled in the details:

> Ranged bookcases, a copy of the Annigoni portrait of the Queen, the Cecil Beaton photograph of Churchill, autographed, a straightforward print of General Donovan, two Krieghoffs, comfortably placed boxes of stale cigarettes . . .

Drawing the readers' attention to what was then a secret, he discussed the fact that the model for his M, "Major-General Sir Stewart Menzies, KCB, KCMG, DSO, MC, and member of White's and the St. James's, formerly of Eton and the Life Guards, was head of the Secret Service in the last war—news which will no doubt cause a delighted shiver to run down the spines of many fellow-members of his clubs and of his local hunt." Fleming there set up a model, of the aristocratic and laconic, that is still faithfully imitated in depictions of British intelligence by American pulp writers such as Tom Clancy, and which survives innumerable revelations of its inauthenticity.

Conforming perfectly to service traditions, Fleming went on to describe his own immediate chief, Rear Admiral J. H. Godfrey of Naval Intelligence, as "the most inspired appointment to this office since 'Blinker' Hall." One sees what he must have meant.

In trespassing with such élan on American turf, Stephenson could call upon prototypes of the gifted gentleman amateur who looked upon England's cause as their own. The most audacious of these was the now forgotten Donald Downes, who after the war also became a fiction writer and had one of his cloak-and-dagger yarns filmed by Anthony Asquith. Of English descent, he was a school-teacher on Cape Cod at the outbreak of war, and made repeated attempts to volunteer for secret work during the period of American neutrality; a period of which he felt the shame very keenly. His memoirs, entitled *The Scarlet Thread*, draw their title from a Bible story about the first spy but could equally well have furnished the name of a romance by Rider Haggard, Conan Doyle, A. E. W. Mason, or (the first British spy story author) Rudyard Kipling. Given a rather grudging "Reserve Commission" in G2 American intelligence, he acquired his own cover as a missionary student and set off through Asia and the Middle East to make himself useful. His admiration for the British took a few knocks on the way, but seems to have strengthened from the test:

> In Singapore it was evident that Mr. Churchill, through no error of his and despite his later denials, was indeed destined to preside over the dissolution of the British Empire, at least in the Orient.

Downes decided this after hearing gloomy British pilots in Raffles' bar (which he charmingly miscalled Ruggles); the ideal setting for a visitor seeking colonial angst. Pushing on to British India and Calcutta ("a city so loathsome to western sensibilities that it leaves a sort of scar on the memory tissue"), he found it hard to decide whether he disliked Indian backwardness more than British supremacy. "In Bombay I saw the great Gandhi himself come to visit his British dentist in a green Rolls-Royce on which was mounted a sign in five languages saying 'Boycott British Goods.'" In general, "it was much more difficult to blame the British after sampling

India, than before. But it was obvious that the British Raj was dead."

Voyaging back through the Persian Gulf, Downes met H. St. John Philby, "advisor to the King of Arabia and Ford agent for the Persian Gulf countries." He was fascinated by this encounter with the personification of British Orientalism; survivor of the contest between the India Office Arabists who had backed Ibn Saud and the War Office Arabists who preferred the Hashemites. "I was anxious to know how this thoroughly English scholar and soldier became so estranged from his homeland." He also wondered how he had got on with his rival, T. E. Lawrence, but felt unable to broach the question. Writing in 1953, in praise of Anglo-American solidarity, Downes was accidentally prescient about the phenomenon that, a few years later, was nearly to poison "special relationship" intelligence gathering for good:

> The agent turns with anger and shame against his own government. By 1945 I grew to understand the Philby-Lawrence reaction and to consider such men, and their honor, as casualties of war—for war cares no more for honor, or for decency and honesty, than it does for life.

Back in New York, Downes made contact with Stephenson's office and was duly recruited as having demonstrated the right kind of pluck and interest. He was at once asked the tough question:

> "Do you feel strongly enough on these matters to work for us in your own country? To spy on your own fellow-Americans and report to us?"

He was able to answer in the affirmative, and was told: "Be careful of the FBI, and the Neutrality Act can land you in prison, for in this work you could not register as the agent of a foreign power as the law requires. It would give the whole show away." Downes busied himself at first with the Free World Association, a coalition of politicians from occupied Europe who ranged from Count Carlo Sforza of Italy to Julio Alvarez del Vayo of Republican Spain. (This grouping, which then called on a multiplicity of exiles and refugees who were committed against neutralism, has also since furnished the luster of its name in the general borrowing of anti-Nazi for anti-Communist terminology.) The targets of his operation were those America First circles which might have been infiltrated, knowingly or otherwise, by agents of Hitler. The list maintained by Downes was impressive, ranging from Senators Nye and Wheeler through Charles Lindbergh to the *Chicago Tribune* and "two officials of the export division of General Motors." After much rummaging in this murky world, with a little discreet and illegal help from Colonel Eugene Prince and the Army Counter-Intelligence Corps, Downes completed a report and was paid "the exciting compliment" of being told that "a copy for the PM would leave by bomber-ferry route."

Not long afterward, Pearl Harbor put a stop to isolationism and Downes transferred from Stephenson's office to that of Wild Bill Donovan. His initial employment was with Allen Dulles, whose office in Rockefeller Center was happily situated just one floor above Stephenson's secret bureau, masquerading until then under the Bulldog Drummond-like name of "Rough Diamonds, Ltd." Once within OSS, he found allies such as David Bruce and George Bowden, all of whom would have agreed with him about "the English—always our betters in this field." Together, these men did much sterling work in Washington, subverting the loyalty of diplomatic missions that represented pro-Axis noncombatants like Spain and Portugal. They caught General Franco red-handed as he refueled Nazi submarines with the American oil that had been intended to keep him neutral. But at every step they were inconvenienced by Hoover's FBI, which seems to have numbered a few *Chicago Tribune* readers among its active membership. Any interference, especially in Monroe Doctrine countries, was not just resented but opposed by the Bureau. "Does J. Edgar think he's fighting on Bunker Hill against us Redcoats or has he really heard of Pearl Harbor?" inquired a drawling but infuriated British intelligence officer of Downes at a meeting in New York.

Downes went on to distinguish himself in numerous theaters of the secret war in Europe and North Africa. His admiration for William J. Donovan grew as the struggle intensified, against both the enemy overseas and the red-tape artists at home. But he was under no illusions as to the source upon which America drew in its race to build an espionage network from scratch:

> The USA was a "secret intelligence virgin." Donovan turned to our British allies, the most experienced nation in the world in intelligence matters. He frankly asked their aid and advice and they unreservedly and energetically supplied him with both.

"Unreservedly" is certainly an exaggeration, but it is beyond doubt that wherever the United States needed to lose any kind of virginity in global affairs, the British were on hand with unguents and aphrodisiacs of all kinds. As Robin Winks puts it judiciously in his racy but expert history of American intelligence and the Yale connection, *Cloak and Gown*:

> Later, when Sir William Stephenson and others claimed that they had taught the Americans what they knew, or when those charged with creating a postwar Central Intelligence Agency wished to refute the claim that such an agency might become an American equivalent of the KGB, there was a good bit of talk about the paternity of American intelligence.

Winks has an excellent account of the X-2, XX, or "Double Cross" fraternity, a transplanted group of Americans headed by Norman Holmes Pearson who made up a part-OSS, part-SIS unit in London. Their task was to be the American partners in the handling of Ultra intelligence. Contact with the British was facilitated by David Bruce (as indicated, member of the Mellon family and future ambassador to London), who became overall director of OSS in England. Ticklish questions of status arose at once, and Donald Downes was able to advise on how these might best be handled. He had already advised Donovan:

> Whoever set up this early experiment in counterintelligence must be able to learn from the British, since they were the masters at the game; at the same time, the person must not be slavishly Anglophilic, as many academics tended to be, for he would have to bring a critical eye to the British operation *so that the Americans would remain independent of, and ultimately improve upon, the British system.* Learning, Downes argued, had to be between social equals if OSS were not forever to be the junior partner. A Yale man, an academic, might carry it off, he thought, and certainly ought to if also a Rhodes Scholar (which Downes believed Pearson to be)—though he acknowledged that the British could be quite snobbish about Rhodes Scholars, who were thought of as the best of the colonials and thus eminently teachable, though not necessarily as yet equals. . . . Pearson was encouraged to use English academic terms and, apparently, to inflate his résumé slightly, for most of his British counterparts called him a don, and though he was in fact an instructor still moderately fearful for his tenure, he converted his brief 1938 summer appointment at the University of Colorado into an associate professor on the record and was referred to then and in the literature since as "a Yale professor."

This question of caste was more or less satisfactorily resolved, and Pearson found that after a lapse of time as a "new boy" he was fairly well accepted by the senior common room elite of St. Albans and Bletchley Park. Just as Donald Downes in New York had got to know British agents, mostly temporary, like A. J. Ayer, Christopher Wren (son of the author of *Beau Geste*), and David Ogilvy, so Pearson benefited from the work of Bletchley scholars like

J. H. Plumb, Geoffrey Barraclough, Asa Briggs, and Edward Crankshaw; the sorts of names now found chiefly in the pages of *The New York Review of Books*. Also present were Roy Jenkins and Angus Wilson, and the decipherer of the Minoan and Mycenean inscriptions, Leonard Palmer. Pearson also knew Benjamin Britten and Humphrey Trevelyan. As the American corps of intelligence workers expanded in this English elite atmosphere, it drew in Telford Taylor, William Bundy, and others who were to be important in the postwar world (Bundy as editor of the Council on Foreign Relations review, *Foreign Affairs*, among other things). Taylor observed that most of the North Americans were New Englanders and had some knowledge of Britain, which helped to smooth the path and to alleviate resentments about British reserve on the one hand and the superior quality of American pay and rations on the other.

Nelson Aldrich, descendant of the Rockefellers and nephew of Winthrop Aldrich of Suez fame at the London embassy, had a stab at the social quintessences here in his delightful book *Old Money*:

> It was underground and behind the lines, in World War II's OSS and the Cold War's CIA, that the Old Money class finally came into an inheritance of all the glamor and peril they had been reading about for years in the work of such Old World romancers as John Buchan, Compton Mackenzie and H. C. McNeile, the creator of Bulldog Drummond. The honor roll of the OSS-CIA between 1941 and 1975, by which time age and discouragement had pretty well decimated their ranks, reads like an alumni bulletin of a St. Midas or an Ivy League school: Allen Dulles, Arthur Schlesinger Jr., Tracy Barnes, Thomas Braden, James J. Angleton, Desmond FitzGerald, Archibald Roosevelt, Kermit Roosevelt, Robert Amory, Richard Bissell, Frank Wisner, Richard Helms *et al*.

It is difficult to think of any more harmonious a collusion between unequals, or any more friendly rivalry, than that existing between the American and British "cousins" at this key moment in a just war. In later and more caricatured forms, it has furnished moments of semi-affectionate confusion in several score novels and films: the American doing his damnedest to choke down the school-dinner food in his plummy colleague's Pall Mall Club; the Englishman trying to get a scotch without ice in Georgetown. It is the foundation of James Bond's husky comradeship with Felix Leiter, and of numerous if slightly more awkward episodes in the works of John le Carré. And it was too good to last. By the end of the war, American intelligence chieftains had come to the same conclusion as their political masters—that Britain's cause was one thing and the British Empire another. Even the Anglophile Donald Downes, who had experienced a few end-of-Empire premonitions in his early travels in the Orient, found himself embroiled in OSS-SIS rivalry. While stationed in North Africa, he saw what happened when Lieutenant Colonel William A. Eddy, late of the United States Marine Corps, was placed in charge of OSS and, as a result of a June 1942 spheres-of-influence agreement, in charge of British operatives in Tangier also. Eddy was, according to Winks, "anti-imperial, a view he had settled on when he had taught English at Cairo University; he was also a much-published scholar, author of books on Jonathan Swift and Samuel Butler, a linguist who moved easily amongst the French and the Arabs, and former President of Hobart College in upstate New York: he was used to command. In World War I he had lost a leg, and the stump and attached wooden leg gave him pain in the heat." Read in profile, this irascible peg-legged polymath sounds much more like the image of a crusty British colonial veteran than an American amateur newcomer. And herein lay the difficulty. Eddy soon discovered that, while the Resistance-oriented Special Operations Executive (SOE) people were more than prepared to cooperate in any war-winning enterprise, the SIS and Foreign Office elements "did not believe in the Atlantic Charter at all." He complained to Donovan that, though he, Eddy, was nominally in command, "he actually had to bow to British wishes on most matters because Eisenhower, who was intent on Allied unity, be-

lieved the British more competent." That myth of experience again!
(Recall that it was in this very theater of North Africa that Macmillan
first proposed his "subtle Greeks to coarse Romans" formulation
to Richard Crossman.)

Pursuing Downes's career as a metaphor for the "special relationship," one finds him touching on almost all the themes that
have exemplified and bedeviled the alliance. Class and empire were
the crosses he bore before the enlistment with Stephenson and
then Donovan. American conservatism became his bugbear during
the thick of the conflict itself, when he was repeatedly thwarted
in his effort to aid the anti-Franco forces in Spain and to cancel
what he regarded as the shame of the West's betrayal of the Republic. His associations with "Jews and Communists," as he once
heard them referred to, made him suspect in military and espionage
circles. He became involved in the bitter Anglo-American dispute
over Greece, with Churchill convinced that the United States was
conspiring against him and America deploring the resuscitation of
a "British sphere" in the Near East. Colonel Sir Ronald Wingate
was later to tell Anthony Cave Brown, Donovan's biographer, of
the average British Establishment reaction at this period:

> We had been at war with Germany longer than any other
> power, we had suffered more, we had sacrificed more, and
> in the end we would lose more than any other power. Yet
> here were these God-awful American academics rushing
> about, talking about the Four Freedoms and the Atlantic
> Charter, and criticizing us for doing successfully what they
> would try and fail to do themselves later—restrain the Rus-
> sians. Donovan was very lucky we didn't send a Guards com-
> pany to OSS Cairo.

Depressed with "unlovely British scheming and American ignorance"—a sad judgment on the wily old power and the brash new
one—Downes set off for Washington. On the way home he stopped
in London and saw Norman Holmes Pearson, who he was later to

claim had warned him about Kim Philby. According to Downes in later life, Philby was said by Pearson to be much too interested in reports on Soviet affairs.

After the war Downes published his now forgotten book *The Scarlet Thread*, which had extreme difficulty in finding an American publisher because of its revelations about J. Edgar Hoover's Anglophobia and sabotage of the war effort (Rinehart offered to take the book only if these chapters were cut). So much did the memoir contradict the emerging Hollywood view of wartime heroics that it was largely ignored by reviewers and booksellers. Switching to fiction, he did better, as mentioned above, with *Orders to Kill*, which was successfully filmed by Anthony Asquith. But he was discouraged from completing *Cauldrons Bubble*, begun in 1965, which first examined the role of homosexuality in the makeup of a secret agent.

By then, the balance of forces in the intelligence world had shifted abruptly against the British as teachers and the Americans as students. The appalling revelations about Philby, Burgess, and Maclean not only had compromised the much-vaunted London "Firm" but had done terrific damage to Western intelligence in general and American espionage in particular. The British had to spend—are still spending—much time in winning back American trust. Matters were made several times worse by the realization that Philby and his associates had survived as long as they had *precisely* because of the features—clubbability, class membership, wit, and polish—that were supposed to be so admirable in the British setup. From the time of their defection, such sentimental attachments and symbols were at a definite discount.

Moreover, the command and control of U.S. intelligence had shifted into the hands of much less sentimental people. The Cold War had altered the mental atmosphere of the spy world. As Winks puts it:

Rigid anti-Communists had been prominent in the OSS, especially toward the end, but they had been balanced by doctrinaire and, more important, pragmatic liberals who were, at least, reasonably well read and educated to the meaning of the language they used. So too were the conservatives of the time; they had read their Burke (especially if they were Anglophiles, as many were) and they did not think "liberal" a term of disrepute.

Perhaps, here, Winks is a trifle unfair. James Jesus Angleton, the very model of the new Manichean breed, certainly had a feeling for the language. He it was who recruited Richard Ellmann to the service, posting him to London in wartime and indirectly enabling him to take the long leave in Ireland (authorized by Norman Holmes Pearson) which led to his discovery of the Yeats manuscripts. Angleton himself was a friend and student of T. S. Eliot, once baffling a British television audience by referring to Soviet policy as "a wilderness of mirrors" and thus losing all those who did not recognize the reference to *Gerontion*. But then he had the advantage, possessed by few of his audience, of an education in the English private school system. Born to a father who had served with Pershing in Mexico and who became a well-connected international businessman, young James went to Chartridge Hill House in Buckinghamshire and then, on the advice of no less a person than Edward VIII's chaplain, to Malvern College, where he became a house prefect and an active Boy Scout. Pushing on to Yale, he became noticeable for his English shirts and accent, as well as for inviting Ezra Pound to visit the campus under the auspices of his undergraduate review *Furioso*.

While in London working on the Ultra material, he often called on Eliot and tried his own hand at poetry. He stood at a slight angle to the "Oh So Social" aspect which jesters attached to the upper-crust Bruce and Mellon OSS, but was considered bright and *sortable* by Bruce and brilliant by others. He was the only American cleared for top-secret Ultra when transferred to the Italian theater. It was in Italy that he made his reputation, and in postwar Italy that he saw the battle against Communism eclipsing all other considerations. On several occasions he took the lead in challenging British hegemony, at one point asking Washington directly whether British policy was binding, through Allied Forces HQ, on all American operations. Later, he overruled British objection to the use of so many CIA "front" organizations. The British reservations were expressed tactically—they felt that all anti-Communist forces would eventually be tarnished by the accusation of being stooges—but were not unconnected to the "anticolonial" policy that these fronts tended to follow. Angleton no longer felt the need to defer, and simply asserted that pro-American groupings would get support.

One of the leading anti-Communist intelligence barons of the period, Frank Wisner, expressed the new order of precedence rather bluntly in a conversation with Kim Philby which he must later have regretted. " 'Whenever we want to subvert any place,' he confided, 'we find the British own an island within easy reach.' "

It was the rising of stars like Angleton in the intelligence world that magnetized people like Peter Wright, who were motivated by power worship and pelf. As Wright himself put it, in his unpleasant but occasionally revealing book *Spycatcher*, a trip to Washington to see Angleton could become an occasion for full-scale dual loyalty, if not actually single loyalty:

> The Capitol building was a giant fresco of pink blossom, blue sky and white marble, capped by a shining gold dome. I always loved visiting Washington, especially in the spring. London was so drab; MI5 so class-ridden and penny-pinching. Like many of the younger, post-war recruits to secret intelligence, I felt America was the great hope, the hub of the Western intelligence wheel. I welcomed her ascendancy with open arms.

Not only did many British intelligence officers feel a sense of inferiority when they compared their own resources with those of the Americans after Suez and Cyprus (in both of which episodes, on his own evidence, Wright played sordid colonial roles in assassination plans); they realized that their political masters, too, had accepted American predominance. In his cupidity, Wright even described the Capitol with a "gold dome," which, Roman though it may look, it does not possess.

The chief, in fact the only, interest of Peter Wright's self-serving book, and the principal interest of the British government's campaign to suppress it, is the light it throws on a dingier aspect of the "special relationship." He has vindicated the many satires on this relationship penned by the only dissident in the genre, John le Carré. He may even form part of the model for Clive, the gruesome British intelligence functionary in *The Russia House*, who was "a technology man, not at ease with live sources, a suburban espiocrat of the modern school. He believed that facts were the only kind of information and he despised whoever was not ruled by them. If he liked anything at all in life apart from his own advancement and his silver Mercedes car, which he refused to take out of the garage if it had so much as a scratch on it, then it was hardware and powerful Americans, in that order."

Clive tells his team that "it is a common misapprehension of this Service that we and the Americans are in the same boat. We're not. Not when it comes to strategy. . . . Where strategy is concerned, we are a tiny, ignorant British coracle and they are the *Queen Elizabeth*. It is not our place to tell them how to run their ship."

This is the moral and mental atmosphere that was exposed to view by Wright's later indiscretions. It represents, not a Greek ceding place to Rome while reserving the right to admonish, but a wholesale collapse into the worship of financial and technical "superiority." Woodhouse may have been the "brains" for Kermit Roosevelt in Iran and have put his sophistication to work, and have later developed a conscience about it. But that was when "cousinhood" was in its early days, and still partook of the leftover bravado of wartime cooperation. As to an extent did Angleton, which was what helped him to purvey his mole fantasies and to recruit a cadre of British intelligence officers who were at all events *prepared* to accept American instructions and to act against an elected British government. This was not to be excused by Angleton's obsession with Kim Philby, the man who had been named by his father for a player in Kipling's "great game." As Kipling makes Kim say:

> Something I owe to the soil that grew
> More to the life that fed
> But most to Allah, who gave me two
> Separate sides to my head.

There is charm in the story of the Anglophile Donald Downes, who volunteered at some risk to himself to help Britain fight the Nazis and who was prepared to spy on his own countrymen in the process. There is precious little amusement in the story of Peter Wright, who became a paranoid mercenary and who wanted only to be on the stronger side. In these two contrasting accounts, there is a quirky microcosm of the ironies and jealousies of "cousinhood," and of the abruptly reversed inequalities in the "special relationship" of which it forms such an essential part.

Nuclear Jealousies

In the last decade, nothing has put the "special relationship" under greater domestic strain in Britain than the siting of U.S. nuclear missiles. Even those who in principle might have agreed to the missiles were wounded in their pride to discover that they had been chosen to host them without being invited to do so. George Orwell captured this sort of public feeling in a *Tribune* column he wrote in 1943:

> Even if you steer clear of Piccadilly with its seething swarms of drunks and whores, it is difficult to go anywhere in London without having the feeling that Britain is now Occupied Territory. . . . Before the war there was no popular anti-American feeling in this country. It all dates from the arrival of the American troops, and it is made vastly worse by the tacit agreement never to discuss it in print.

In perfect contrast, the classic manner of the "special relationship" was defended by David Owen in a review article for *The Sunday Times* as recently as April 3, 1988:

> Mrs. Thatcher believes as a matter of principle that she should never display any public irritation with the course of

Anglo-American relations, and who can say that she is wrong? For all the occasional problems with public opinion at home, if the Atlantic Ocean is to be bridged and the intimacy of our relationship maintained, it is not a bad discipline for our friendship that we should differ only in private.

Only a few months before Dr. Owen wrote his complacent, orthodox article, the British government and Cabinet papers for 1957 had become available under the Thirty-Year Rule and were opened for inspection at the Public Record Office. The most revealing documents concerned a near-catastrophic fire in the plutonium production reactor at Windscale, Cumbria, on October 8, 1957. The fire, which spread from uranium fuel to graphite blocks, was a prefiguration of the Chernobyl disaster. But its details are, still, much less widely known than the Chernobyl ones. Although milk distribution from farms two hundred miles from Windscale was halted, and although workers received 150 times the "normal" lifetime dose of radiation, the British Cabinet decided to censor the inquiry report. In fact, the censorship was considered so important that it was supervised by the Prime Minister, Harold Macmillan, himself.

The reason for the censorship of the inquiry, which was carried out by Sir William Penney of the Atomic Energy Authority, was not the usual one of "national security." Sir William was a trusted official scientist who directed the Atomic Weapons Research Establishment at Aldermaston. Sir Frederick Brundrett, chief scientist at the Ministry of Defense, told Macmillan that there were "no security objections" to releasing the report's conclusions in full. Macmillan's reasons for insisting on an a bowdlerized summary were purely political. The year 1957 was a two-summit year for him, involving the post-Suez rapprochement with President Eisenhower. The first of these summits had been on the British-held territory of Bermuda. The second, in Washington, was impending just as the Windscale inquiry was complete. And the inquiry contained criticism of the Windscale management, as well as the clear finding that the accident could have been devastating. Had not Sir John Cockcroft, the scientist who first split the atom, insisted on radiation filters on the Windscale air-discharge stacks, there would have been a catastrophe. A pre-summit paper prepared for Macmillan and first made public in 1988 said clearly that the main objective of British policy was a "common research and development programme with the Americans." It acknowledged that under the Macmillan plan "we should become dependent on the United States for some of the most important of our future weapons," adding that this was "no more than a recognition of the fact that our national security is already dependent on the United States."

The British objective in 1957 was an amendment of the McMahon Act, which had been passed in 1946 and which forbade the United States government from sharing nuclear information and technology with other countries. The Eisenhower administration was prepared to propose amendments to this legislation to make possible renewed American collaboration with its original nuclear partner—Great Britain. The thirty-year cover-up of the Windscale disaster was designed, in the words of the newly released minutes, to avoid providing "ammunition to those in the United States who would in any case oppose the amendments of the McMahon Act."

The preceding year, at a United States Air Force base at Lakenheath in Suffolk, a B-47 Stratojet had crashed on one of the main runways and exploded among the "storage igloos" which housed nuclear warheads. Inside the igloos were three B-6 atom bombs, modeled on the "Fat Man" plutonium weapon. Although the bombs were burned and damaged, it is extremely unlikely that they could have been detonated. But their high-explosive detonators *could* have detonated, with the force of about 10,000 tons of TNT, and this could have spread the deadly plutonium over a huge area. A senior USAF officer later testified that there could have been a "desert" in East Anglia as a result.

The British public did not find out about *this* near-calamity (which, interestingly, had resulted in the rapid evacuation of the base personnel and their families but not of the neighboring villages) until 1979. A series of articles in the *Omaha World-Herald*, rather than any disclosure by government, brought the episode to light. It would not be the first or only time that British citizens were to find the American press more forthcoming than their own authorities when it came to the "special relationship."

There is a direct connection between the two accidents, and also between the two cover-ups. The emplacement of American nuclear bases in Britain, without a vote or a debate in Parliament, was the British quid pro quo for a renewal of nuclear collaboration with the United States. The two decisions, and the evasion and secrecy which surround them, are in effect the same policy and the same *raison d'état*.

Provost Hodson of Ditchley was right to describe the nuclear balance of terror as "the supreme governor of the Cold War." He would have been equally correct in describing it as the supreme governor of the "special relationship." The United Kingdom is the only country in the world with which the United States formally shares nuclear secrets, nuclear weapons, and nuclear technology. In return, the map of Britain is dotted with over one hundred American "military facilities" of varying size and capacity. In a particularly striking instance of the "Greece to their Rome" conceit, it was British research and technology which, employed as a bargaining counter in the Second World War, first empowered the United States with nuclear knowledge and capability. In a no less striking instance of the role reversal involved in the conceit, the British found themselves almost immediately excluded from the nuclear world to which they had introduced their senior partner, and had to fight hard to regain even subordinate status. But it is its continued standing as a nuclear power which, more than any single thing, gives the British government the feeling that it belongs, still, at the "top table" of nations. The fact that this "independence" is predicated upon dependence is, like certain facts about Orwell's wartime Britain, too obvious and too awkward to receive much attention in polite circles. A month before he popularized the phrase at Fulton, Winston Churchill told the House of Commons: "We should not abandon our special relationship with the United States about the atomic bomb."

The ironic and contradictory story begins in 1940, with Rudolf Peierls and Otto Frisch, two refugees from Nazism, demonstrating the explosive possibilities of uranium 235 at Birmingham University. At about the same time, in Cambridge, two French refugee scientists arrived with the world's only known stock of "heavy water." Heavy water was the most efficient "moderator" for a nuclear reactor of the sort envisaged by Peierls and Frisch, whose findings led to the Maud Committee report. In this report, which is overshadowed in later accounts by the immense prestige of the Manhattan Project, the feasibility of nuclear weaponry was adumbrated for the first time. (As a footnote, let it be remembered that the British did not requite their debt to French nuclear science after the war, preferring to concentrate all their effort on the "special relationship" with America. This had political consequences of a high order, as will appear.)

The Churchill-Roosevelt correspondence contains a number of letters about "Tube Alloys," the British code name for research on fission weapons, and these letters are full, in 1941, of warm expressions of esteem and of willingness to share and cooperate. Frederick L. Hovde, who headed the London bureau of the U.S. Office of Scientific Research and Development, was brought in touch with Sir John Anderson, a former governor of Bengal, who as Lord President of the Council was one of the few ministers "in" on Churchill's most closely held military secret.

Churchill's exploitation of this asset was not very judicious. He both overplayed and underplayed his hand, in one of the few areas where Britain enjoyed an advantage over the United States. At the end of 1941, Roosevelt proposed a joint project which would have involved pooling all nuclear material and expertise. This the British declined in what Professor Margaret Gowing, official historian of the British Atomic Energy Authority, describes as "a most superior tone." Conscious of their lead, they preferred mutual exchange of information but not full-blown collaboration. The offer was not to be repeated. Huge American resources were thereupon deployed on nuclear research, and by 1943 the United States was so far in front that it could and did disdain even the sharing of information. Acting particularly on the advice of Vannevar Bush, head of the American Office of Scientific Research and Development, Roosevelt decided to keep nuclear data from the British in order to prevent them from exploiting atomic power commercially after the war. At the Washington summit in May 1943, Churchill protested loudly at this treatment, as he had already done to Harry Hopkins. There are, suggestively, no written minutes of this discussion, but it seems that Roosevelt must have decided pro tem to overrule Bush and his supporters. The decision cannot have been quick or easy, however, since on July 9, 1943, Churchill cabled Roosevelt:

> Since Harry's telegram of 17th June I have been anxiously awaiting further news about TUBE ALLOYS. My experts are standing by and I find it increasingly difficult to explain delay. If difficulties have arisen, I beg you to let me know at once what they are in case we may be able to help in solving them.

At length, at their meeting in Quebec on August 19, 1943, the two men agreed to full collaboration on "Tube Alloys." This allowed Britain to participate in the Manhattan Project and placed uranium stocks under joint control. Both countries agreed not to use the bomb without the consent of the other, and pledged not to introduce any third member to the nuclear club without mutual agreement. The British scientists removed themselves en bloc to the other side of the Atlantic, though the large number of them based at Los Alamos were not permitted to enter the plutonium plants.

The relationship had thus quickly become a senior-junior one, and there is reason to suppose that Roosevelt went a little further in indulging Churchill's amour propre than his scientific advisers would have liked. The evidence here concerns the Hyde Park agreement of September 1944, when the two leaders pledged to continue atomic cooperation after the defeat of Japan. After Roosevelt's death it was discovered that no United States nuclear agency or official knew of the agreement, and the British embassy was awkwardly asked to furnish a copy. The minister at the embassy feared that a post-Roosevelt America would not honor the agreement but would instead seek a nuclear monopoly. In a distinctive choice of metaphor he observed: "The salad is heaped in a bowl permanently smeared with the garlic of suspicion."

The British were perfunctorily consulted about the decision to obliterate Hiroshima and Nagasaki, and gave their expected consent. But just as the Hyde Park agreement had been superseded, so also was a 1945 agreement between Truman and Attlee which in essence restated the same commitment. In July 1946, the McMahon Act made the passing of classified atomic information to *any* other country an offense punishable by death or life imprisonment. This was the Act which Macmillan in 1957 was striving to amend.

British nuclear policy from then on became a desperate and ceaseless search for ways of binding Britain to the United States. Repeated efforts to resume collaboration were thwarted. In 1948, a partial agreement was struck, known appropriately as a "modus vivendi," by which it was agreed that technical *but not military* cooperation would be resumed. In return, the Labor government had to sign away the clause in the 1943 Quebec agreement which required British consent for American use of nuclear weapons. It continued to work away on its own nuclear weapons, deceiving Parliament by concealing the secret expenditures under the heading of (much needed in the late 1940s) "Repairs to Public Buildings."

The explosion of a Soviet nuclear device in 1949 (attributed in many American circles to the treachery of the British atom spy Klaus Fuchs, who had worked at Los Alamos) changed the situation somewhat in Britain's favor. Sooner than they had thought they would, the generals of the U.S. Strategic Air Command needed forward air bases capable of hitting the Soviet Union. The urgency of their concern increased with the onset of the Korean War—the first time that an American President was to threaten the use of nuclear weapons in public. Attlee agreed to the stationing of B-29 bombers at bases in the United Kingdom—again without much consultation of Cabinet or Parliament—and in return again extracted a pledge that they would not be used without British consent. This pledge was deleted from all official documents by Secretary of State Dean Acheson, who spoke of "unachieving" Attlee's short-term success.

However, an uneasy trade-off had been established between American bases in Britain and British access to American nuclear weapons technique. For the next two decades, there was to be a permanent lack of synchronicity and reciprocation. Almost every British Prime Minister was to know the humiliation of accepting an American weapon system and then seeing it canceled for internal American reasons, or reasons of American statecraft with the Soviet Union. Harold Macmillan suffered this with Skybolt, Harold Wilson with Antelope, and Edward Heath with Poseidon. Yet there was no other conceivable access to nuclear technology, and as a result the pretense of an "independent" British nuclear capacity had to be kept up. The reasoning was summarized succinctly by Field Marshal Lord Carver, Chief of the Defense Staff between 1973 and 1976, in an interview in 1988. Why did Britain insist on remaining nuclear?

> The political argument has pretty much remained the same, which is that it makes us appear, or actually be, *or be thought by other people, particularly the United States, to be* an important nation.
>
> The military arguments produced in support of that have varied a great deal over the years, and have constantly had to be adjusted. [Italics mine.]

In the end, this post-imperial dogma has overwhelmed all concerns, whether from Ernest Bevin or Margaret Thatcher, about the subordination of British defense and security to the United

States. It is a long time since Lord Cherwell, Winston Churchill's adviser on these matters, warned: "If we are unable to make the bombs ourselves and have to rely entirely on the United States for this vital weapon we shall sink to the rank of a second-class nation." Sir Henry Tizard, the government's chief scientific adviser, was more realistic. He accepted the change in Britain's circumstances, observing laconically that the idea of concentrating nuclear production in America was greeted "with the kind of horror one would expect if one made a disrespectful remark about the King."

Harold Macmillan did get his 1958 agreement, trading further bases in Scotland for access to the Skybolt missile and (when that was abruptly canceled) the Polaris system. But he never regained the power to influence American decision making, let alone to exercise a veto on first use. In Bermuda on December 21, 1961, he found himself saying to President Kennedy:

> Every time you lift the phone, Mr. President, I think you may say that you intend to go, and I wonder what answer I would give.

When events became critical, as they soon afterward did over Cuba, the British government was to discover that the United States administration had barely time to consult with itself let alone with its allies. And the reaction times have shortened very considerably since Cuba, which by modern standards was actually a slow-motion, aborted naval engagement.

Stanley Kubrick caught the absurd essence of the situation in his classic *Dr. Strangelove*, where a fatuous and ingratiating RAF stereotype, Captain Mandrake, forever enacts the pretense of parity and consultation with his less polished USAF counterpart, General Jack D. Ripper. As scene succeeds scene, the luckless Mandrake discovers exactly what it means to be a Greek in Ripper's Rome. Mandrake moments in the recent past have included British government "surprise" at Richard Nixon's 1973 nuclear alert, and at Ronald Reagan's decision to adopt the "Star Wars" policy in

1984. The latter decision, which involved the denunciation of deterrence theory as "immoral and unstable," was particularly irritating to the Thatcher government, which had endured considerable political risk and difficulty by supporting the "deterrent" deployment of a new generation of American missiles on British soil, thus reawakening the long-torpid controversy over the United States military presence.

The American occupation of British territory, as it is conducted today, would not surprise Orwell overmuch. In 1943, he had complained of the United States forces being a law unto themselves, and of the shifty reluctance of the British authorities to discuss the matter openly:

> An example is the agreement by which American troops in this country are not liable to British courts for offences against British subjects—practically "extraterritorial rights." Not one English person in ten knows of the existence of this agreement; the newspapers barely reported on it and refrained from commenting on it.

Orwell wrote generally in defense of the American wartime presence and deliberately sought to defuse the anti-American potential of such a situation. But decades after the defeat of Hitler and the death of Stalin, it took a Member of Parliament three years to establish how many United States military facilities Britain was actually hosting.

Robert Cryer, M.P., asked in June 1980 how many such bases there were and on June 18 received a written answer giving the figure of 12 bases and an unspecified number of other "facilities." When he pressed the minister, he got a second answer on July 7 raising the total to 51. A still further question produced the reply, on August 8, of three additional named installations. The ones cited on the third time of asking were Brawdy, which is the largest underwater monitoring station in the American Ocean Surveillance Information System; Machrihanish, a nuclear base which headquarters the U.S. Navy Special Forces unit in Europe; and Felixstowe, a port used for the shipment of bombs by the U.S. Air Force. This brought the total to 54. But a private investigation by the defense and intelligence expert Duncan Campbell, published in *The New Statesman* later in the same year, produced a total of 103 military bases and facilities. The Ministry of Defense at length admitted to 75 bases in a statement issued in April 1983. Inquiry revealed that 73 of these had been in existence on the day that Cryer had been told—on his third request—that the total was 54.

Nations considerably less powerful than Great Britain—such as the Philippines and Turkey—enjoy formal arrangements and signed treaties with the United States where bases on their territory are concerned. When modern Greece negotiates with the American Rome, whether the Prime Minister is Constantine Karamanlis or Andreas Papandreou, there are written leases and protocols to govern the arrangement. Whitehall's decision to forgo any formal or ratifiable agreement is a testimony to the hypnotic power of "special relationship" priorities, and to the belief that partnership with the United States, however defined, transcends all other questions. As the USAF commander in Britain had remarked in 1949: "Never before in history has one first-class power gone into another first-class power's country without any agreement."

A revealing instance of the degree to which this implicit undertaking has been internalized came during the House of Commons debate on the American bombing of Libya in April 1986. Alone of Western European and NATO governments, the Thatcher administration had agreed to allow its territory to be used in preparations for the raid. (A later investigation by *Jane's Defence Weekly* showed clearly that here, too, the imperatives were political rather than military, and that the Reagan administration required an ally and accomplice rather than the few remote airfields which could easily have been duplicated by the carrier decks of the U.S. Sixth Fleet.) Defending her decision to allow F-111 aircraft to fly from bases in

Britain to bomb Tripoli, and replying to a storm of criticism from all parties including her own, Mrs. Thatcher said:

> I remind the Hon. Gentleman that the United States has more than 330,000 members of her forces in Europe to defend our liberty. Because they are here, they are subject to terrorist attack. It is inconceivable that they should be refused the right to use the American aircraft and American pilots in the inherent right of self-defence, to defend their own people.

Of the numerous questions arising from this reply, such as the utility or principle of bombing the center of Tripoli in order to avenge a Berlin discotheque, the most salient was asked by David Steel of the Liberal Party: "Did this not," he asked, "mean that the bases were purely American, to be used as President Reagan might direct?"

Mrs. Thatcher had in fact—perhaps inadvertently—run into the deliberate and inevitable ambiguities of the 1948 "modus vivendi." Only three years earlier, discussing the installation of Cruise and Pershing missiles, she had confidently proclaimed:

> The arrangements we have made for the new missiles are the same as those of long ago between Mr. Churchill and Mr. Truman. They are arrangements for joint decision—not merely joint consultation—but joint decision. I am satisfied that these arrangements would be effective. A joint decision on the use of the bases or the missiles would of course be dual control.

This "of course" is exactly what the American side has always striven to avoid. Here again we return to Dean Acheson, whose horror at the naïveté of Truman was well recorded in his memoirs. At the White House meeting in 1950, with the Korean War at its ominous stage of escalation, he discovered that Attlee was trying to "lead Truman onto the flypaper" and exploit the latent but purposely obscure phrasing of the modus vivendi:

> They had, said the President cheerfully, been discussing the atomic weapon and agreed that neither of us would use these weapons without prior consultation with the other. No one spoke.

Acheson meant "modus vivendi" to mean just what it means in the dictionary: "arrangements between disputants pending settlement of debate, arrangements between people(s) who agree to differ." The phrase had been initially put forward by a State Department functionary named Edmund A. Gullion. According to R. G. Hewlett and F. Duncan in their account *Atomic Shield*: "His British and Canadian colleagues demurred, for the term was most often used to describe the relations between adversaries driven by circumstances to get along together." This was Captain Mandrake bleating. Who was going to believe that Britain would declare nuclear war on the U.S.S.R. all by herself? Hewlett and Duncan add dryly: "To himself Gullion thought *modus vivendi* accurate."

By the time Acheson had done with it—"unachieving" Attlee's momentary coup—the understanding was back where it started, except that by then the military bases in Britain were well established. Secretary of Defense James Forrestal had stated the advantages of these in his July 15, 1948, "Summary of Considerations to Send B-29s to England":

1. It would be an action which would underline to the American people how seriously the government of the United States views the current sequence of events.
2. It would give the Air Force experience in this kind of operation; *it would accustom the British to the necessary habits and routines that go into the accommodation of an alien, even though an allied, power.*
3. We have the opportunity *now* of sending these planes, and

once sent they would become somewhat of an accepted fixture, whereas a deterioration of the situation in Europe might lead to a condition of mind under which the British would be compelled to reverse their present attitude. [Italics mine.]

Forrestal was later asked to resign and committed suicide after a severe breakdown, in the course of which he imagined himself to be followed everywhere by Soviet moles. But his reasoning in 1948 was lucid enough to give birth to an unwritten understanding which the majority of British generals and politicians still regard as sacrosanct. Some concessions are made to local feeling—the USAF bases are signposted as RAF in order to please Captain Mandrake—but the tradition of American personnel being immune from the English courts is as strong as it was when Orwell was writing. In 1979, for example, at St. Mawgan in Cornwall, a U.S. marine killed a local youth while driving and the U.S. Navy succeeded in stopping the inquest. After six months it conducted its own court-martial and fined the offender one dollar.

There is something almost perfectly emblematic of the "special relationship" in the idea of the modus vivendi; a hypocritical and unequal agreement which is both covert and uncodified. The British, of course, delight to conduct foreign policy in this way. It reminds their civil servants and diplomats of the highly convenient and untestable "unwritten Constitution." The American official side also often prefers, for purposes of possible congressional scrutiny, to keep things as "informal" as possible. Dean Acheson records that in 1950, the same year that he "unachieved" Attlee's diplomacy, he discovered a State Department and Foreign Office paper that discussed the "special relationship" in cold print.

It was not the origin that bothered me, but the fact that the wretched paper existed . . . Of course a unique relation existed between Britain and America—our common language and history insured that. But unique did not mean affectionate. We had fought England as an enemy as often as we had fought by her side as an ally. . . . Before Pearl Harbor . . . sentiment was reserved for our "oldest ally," France.

Acheson also worried that the paper, if leaked, could expose him to charges of being "the tool of a foreign power":

> So all copies of the paper that could be found were collected and burned, and my colleagues, after a thorough dressing-down for their naïveté, were urged to channel their senti-mental impulses into a forthcoming speech of mine before the Society of Pilgrims, which by tradition was granted dispen-sation for expressions of this sort.

Thus Acheson, a man accused by Senator McCarthy of being a "stuffy, striped-pants, stuffed-shirt, pseudo-Englishman" (which indeed he looked); a man who was once mistaken for Sir Anthony Eden and did not feel insulted; a man who was of recent English stock. A man, furthermore, who had argued with Roosevelt to forgive Britain the 1914–18 war debt, and who had been prominent in the "destroyers for bases" deal in 1940 that in some ways pre-figured the "nuclear bases for shared nuclear expertise" deal of 1948. Acheson was crucial in the "receivership" of the Empire and in the promulgation of the Truman Doctrine. (At that stage he even told Ambassador Oliver Franks that "the old Kipling approach did not work"—and in relation to Iran, too!) In the 1960s he made a famously stinging speech about how Great Britain had "lost an Empire and not yet found a role." He ended his days as a Wash-ington lobbyist for white Rhodesia, thus perfectly taking on the original coloring of an imperialism he had worked both to sustain and to supersede.

His accurate mention of France as America's oldest ally recalls an initial detail and irony of this chapter. After the war, Britain never repaid her debt to the French heavy-water scientists and, indeed, swore not to share any of the fruits of her later collusion with America. General de Gaulle, who returned to the presidency of France one month before Harold Macmillan wheedled a fresh nuclear "understanding" out of President Eisenhower in 1958, never forgot or forgave this slight. It added greatly to the sum of Britain's difficulties when, very belatedly, Britain made an application to join the European Community, which, hitherto secure in the "special relationship," it had scorned.

De Gaulle's first act on returning to the Elysée in 1958 was to summon General Laurie Norstad, the American officer who commanded NATO forces between 1956 and 1963. According to Jean Lacouture's masterly biography of de Gaulle, he asked Norstad how many American weapons were on French soil and where they were stationed. "*Mon général*," replied Norstad, "I cannot tell you that unless we are alone." De Gaulle asked his staff to leave the room, whereupon Norstad said, with some evidence of *pudeur*, what he could not decently say without humiliating his host before witnesses. In other words, he confessed that he was not allowed to tell de Gaulle the answer, nor was de Gaulle "cleared" to hear it. "Well, *mon général*," said de Gaulle by way of reply, "that is the last time, and mark it well, that a French leader will ever hear such an answer."

Margaret Thatcher is adored by many of her supporters for a willingness to stand up to foreigners where British interests are said to be concerned, but it would be quite impossible for her to employ such tones in addressing even a junior American defense official. The Trident decision, one of the most unpopular and certainly the most expensive of her first decade in office, committed the United Kingdom to an infinity of outlay to "modernize" an American-designed system in order to baptize it as British. This decision was taken in effect before she assumed the reins of office, by a series of purchases and commitments which tied British procurement and deployment to the Pentagon. In 1980 it was revealed that the British fleet of four Polaris submarines could not keep up even the credibility of a continuous two-vessel patrol. Refits and other exigencies meant that for as long as two months out of every twelve, the British strike force consisted of *one* superannuated submarine, cruising the depths like a forlorn cetacean and praying that the day for which it was allegedly designed might never come. Not even a multiple-warhead capacity, cloaked in official secrecy, could make this seem like the rule of Britannia. The "modernization" of the Mandrake fleet, it was argued by even the centrist opposition party, would come, if it came at all, just in time for complete obsolescence.

Thus, although the very idea of "massive retaliation" had grown out of the British nuclear White Paper of 1957, and although the idea of a permanent NATO army of the Rhine was also conceived by Churchill as a means of yoking America to Western Europe, the practice of the relationship grew steadily more paltry than the theory. Increasingly, the British defense chiefs were reduced to those handy "islands" so casually mentioned by Frank Wisner. The British evacuated the wretched inhabitants of Diego Garcia and dumped them in Mauritius in order to clear the way for immense Anglo-American installations on the newly desolate island. They opened the "sovereign bases" in Cyprus for the purpose of manned U-2 flights over the Middle East and, after the "loss" of Iran, the Soviet Union. They even turned their own island into a facility for the United States.

The ironic repayment for this island-donating strategy came in 1982, when to the annoyance of much of official Washington the Thatcher government insisted on a fight with Argentina over the Falklands. When compelled to choose between its Latin and its Atlantic ally, the Reagan administration had little option. It was supported, in its slightly reluctant choice, by an American opinion which decisively sided with the London view of the war. Opinion polls found that Americans of German and Scandinavian and even Italian descent preferred the Anglo-Saxon to the Hispanic worldview. General Vernon Walters, the leading exponent of the military junta solution to Latin American questions and the most experienced warrior in the administration, conceded that "the atavistic business of blood and language" had been essential in determining American partiality.

Yet again, in other words, it was post-imperial patterns which imposed themselves. For the British, it was instinctive and automatic to seek the role of closest cousin, and to mortgage such portions of colonial real estate as remained to the maintenance of a vicarious "seat at the top table." This revealing expression, so redolent of the class system which made it sound natural, supplies the clue to the military half.

Unlike de Gaulle, who went on to show reasoned and important and even prescient dissent about Vietnam, NATO, and dollar inflation, the British exchanged a veto for a ditto. The rewards, even counting the political triumph of the Falklands, were not overly impressive. One year after the Union Jack had been rehoisted over Port Stanley, the BBC invited a series of past and present American statesmen to comment on Prime Minister Thatcher's assertion that command of U.S. bases and missiles in Britain was exerted by "dual control." The reply, whether from Robert McNamara, James Schlesinger, Paul Warnke, or Lucius Battle, was the same. Final authority rested and had always rested in Washington.

Leave the penultimate word to Professor Margaret Gowing, official historian of the British Atomic Energy Authority and chief chronicler of the British "independent deterrent":

> For Britain the symbol of Empire has gone but the symbol of the national nuclear deterrent remains.

Leave the very last word to Sir Arthur Hockaday, Deputy Under Secretary at the Ministry of Defense, who was asked in 1987 whether Britain had the serious intention of penetrating Moscow's antiballistic missile (ABM) defenses with her own personal warheads. With perfect gravity, Sir Arthur gave the reply that, after all, the Russians "regarded Moscow as the Jewel in their Crown."

The lust for imperial image in that choice of phrase was merely comical in the British case, but also expressed the less comical fact that Britain, by a combination of early technical and innovative primacy and later political and military dependency, had done much to pass imperial schemes even into the thermonuclear epoch.

Conclusion

When Walter Annenberg grandly commissioned the English historian Michael Grant to elucidate the possible analogies between the fall of Rome and the crisis of the modern Anglo-American system, Grant came up with thirteen "similarities." Perhaps in deference to his patron, he gave little or no consideration to the one analysis that, at the close of the Vietnam War, might have been said to stare him in the face. In the judgment of many reflective historians, Rome as a *republic* was quite simply corroded by Rome as an *empire*. Whether demonstrable or not, this hypothesis surely deserved to be tested against the historic experience of Britain and the United States.

Britain, of course, had few strictly "republican" virtues to transmit to America. (It still doesn't; preferring to trade on the arcana of an *ancien régime* and the related mysteries of post-imperialism.) Such republican and democratic instincts as did manage to cross the Atlantic from east to west did so as contraband: the astonishing and germinal moral energy of Thomas Paine; the Welsh coal miners who fled their grim valleys and whose sad place names still dot the map of Pennsylvania, to which they brought a tradition of industry and organization. But these are preeminently *not* the sorts of image that leap to mind when the word "Brit" is uttered in today's America.

And in searching for the explanation, one is returned again and again to the *kind* of relationship that has existed between the two states and systems. America, founded in self-conscious opposition to the backward, imperial, complacent, hierarchic English, counterposed a certain utopianism of its own to the solid virtues of kingship, social predestination, conquest, and dominion. The luminous documents composed by the Founders and ratified as law in the Greek-named city of Philadelphia all show, in the sort of English that has quite disappeared from official usage, an educated disrespect for standing armies, hereditary privilege, state surveillance of the citizenry, "foreign entanglements," monarchism, and the rest of it.

But, as I have tried to suggest, all these elements of pre-1776 antiquity have been reimported into America *via* the very connection that 1776 was intended to dissolve. It might well be argued that the United States would have chosen empire over republic in any case, taking its precedents and promptings from itself or elsewhere, but in point of fact the real connection was almost always the English one. (Even the original sin of slavery came from that quarter, though it's not the fault of Thomas Paine of Thetford that it was not choked off in 1776.) American rediscovery of the intoxications of a "natural" aristocracy, of an "expansionist" credo, of an affection for the marks and baubles of caste—all this was conveyed from England as directly as the chests of tea that had once ended up in Boston Harbor. And every time that the United States has been on the verge of a decision: to annex the Spanish Empire, to go to war in Europe, to announce the Soviet Union as the official enemy, to acquire new and weighty "burdens" in the Middle East, Africa, and Asia, to embark upon nuclear weapons research, to establish a national nexus of intelligence gathering, there has been a deceptively languid English adviser at the elbow, urging *yes* in tones that neither hector nor beseech but are always somehow beguiling.

The resulting joint mythology has at some points been semi-institutionalized, in the nuclear, military, and naval symbiosis, in the Rhodes Scholarships, in the joint-stock aspect of Wall Street and the City of London, and through an unwritten but well-observed partnership in diplomacy. More important, though, are perhaps the long rhythms and the latent connections, the unquantifiable and instinctive loyalties that go to make up texture and personality. God or the devil is in the details, according to ancient report, and it is in the wrinkles and crevices of the "special relationship" that much of its fascination is to be found.

The literary glass, for example, always returns contradictory reflections but is essential in giving a true register. To take only the matter of empire, where Kipling himself made such a self-conscious effort to make the precepts of his own poetry come true, one can find that changes in the temperature of Anglo-Americanism were often prefigured, recorded, and synthesized by novelists and essayists, with more prescience and insight than by politicians and diplomats. (There are spectacular exceptions to this, as when Dickens wrote as if the United States were basically a joke in poor taste. But even so, when Martin Chuzzlewit flings ripostes about slavery at Americans who jeer at monarchy or empire, Dickens is on to something even if Chuzzlewit is not.)

It did take some time before English writers decided to take America seriously, and one of the first to do so was a man who had no "bloodline" in the Anglo-Saxon sense. Joseph Conrad's *Nostromo*, published in 1904 when joint Anglo-American hegemony looked like a safe bet, registered the favorable wind but also caught other gusts and currents. In his Central American republic of Costaguana, a rather scrupulous and traditional English trader of good family named Charles Gould finds that his colonial holdings are potentially a burden to him. He is wrenched between *noblesse oblige* and the effete patterns of inheritance, and the nuisance of responsibility. But if Gould is ambivalent, his American rescuer and nemesis is not. In California sits the great figure of Holroyd, ready to buy up any exhausted concession or interest if the time is ripe. Of this man Conrad writes that "his massive profile was the profile of a Caesar's head on an old Roman coin." Borrowing from the oldest image of empire for this purpose, Conrad updates Holroyd as a domineering turn-of-the-century WASP robber baron by giving him "the temperament of a Puritan and an insatiable imagination of conquest." Treating Gould not at all like a Greek, he instructs him brusquely in the realities of Costaguana:

> European capital has been flung into it with both hands for years. Not ours, though. . . . We can sit and watch. Of course, some day we shall step in. . . . We are bound to. We shall run the world's business whether the world likes it or not. The world can't help it—and neither can we, I guess.

Conrad's well-chosen imagery here contains the three distinct themes of Roman evocation, the white man's burden ("The world can't help it—and neither can we"), and Manifest Destiny as the natural successor to older, feebler empires. Holroyd talks almost like Rhodes, who was boasting at this very time that he would annex the planets if he could, and rather like Monroe when he muses: "Europe must be kept out of this continent, and for proper interference on our part the time is not yet right, I dare say." As a character, Holroyd hardly appears in the novel, yet in an extraordinary way he *possesses* its action and by the end he and America possess Costaguana, too. With a tip of his hat to Admiral Mahan, the garrulous English clubman Captain Mitchell buttonholes later visitors to recall how "the United States cruiser, *Powhattan*, was the first to salute" the new flag and the new dispensation of the San Tomé mines.

In 1904, when *Nostromo* was published, few English or American elements were making the effort to see beyond the present. In the United States itself, the WASP aesthetic was celebrated that year by the foundation of the National Academy of Arts and Letters. Its membership, like that of all the best London clubs, was restricted— in this case to fifty deserving persons. Among the privileged fifty were John Hay, who had been the confidant of Rhodes and Kipling while *en poste* at the Court of St. James's and who remained a great prop to Henry Adams; William Dean Howells, student of Rome and another admirer of Kipling; and the Reverend Henry van Dyke, professor of English at the recently renamed Princeton University. Van Dyke is now chiefly remembered, if at all, for his view that Sinclair Lewis was too coarse to be awarded the Nobel Prize.

At almost the same time, the father of John Dos Passos wrote a book called *The Anglo-Saxon Century*, in which he called for an open acknowledgment of the cultural and national affinities between the two peoples, and suggested their reunification in a new, benign world empire. Dos Passos senior was a Wall Street lawyer of the classic type, was on easy terms with the vast quantity of English capital then invested in the United States, was very committed to the world of the club and the Ivy League, and wanted only an alliance with England in foreign affairs while, at home, he could employ its patina of slight but definite superiority.

But an immense change was impending. Probably Henry James's *The Question of the Mind* is the last innocent statement of pure Anglophilia in its coincidence of language, manners, ethnic solidarity, and commitment. And it, too, was written very slightly out of synchronization with the events it engaged with. By 1916, the last chance for a nonantagonistic Anglo-Americanism was dissolving or had dissolved. You can't have empire without war, and although war can bring with it great enthusiasm and solidarity, it also brings the reaction to these things. The modern school of American writing, made possible by the war, was quicker to see this than the Stars and Stripes/Union Jack/Red, White, and Blue crowds who cheered Wilson and Teddy Roosevelt and "preparedness." While men like Dos Passos senior had welcomed the import of toxins from old Europe's imperial war making, others like his son received quite a different education from the unlooked-for collision "over there." As Marcus Cunliffe puts it very aptly:

One of two things seemed to have happened in the Great War to the male American writer of the 1920s. Either he enlisted before the arrival of the main American forces (Hemingway, John Dos Passos, e. e. cummings, all in ambulance units) in which case he tended to conclude that the war was a nightmare which ought not to involve him. Or he failed to get overseas, like Scott Fitzgerald, or James T. Farrell's "Studs Lonigan," or the cadet in William Faulkner's *Soldier's Pay*, or Faulkner himself, whose war service was confined to RAF training in Canada. In that case he felt doubly cheated, having known only the backwash of disillusionment. In Dos Passos' *Three Soldiers* (1921), in cummings' *The Enormous Room* (1922), and in some of Hemingway's work, the hero is an American, looking on at a war fought by other people, for slogans which he as a detached observer sees to be sham.

It was above all as a result of the Great War—logical terminus of the Rhodes-Kipling-Roosevelt-Hay worldview—that antibodies to uncritical Englishness and Anglophilia began to incubate. These were initially of two sorts—the humane internationalist variety and the nativist, robustly modern one. In the first category belongs Randolph Bourne, a child of the short-lived "Progressive Era," who at first had thought that the outgrowing of English modes and limitations was not much more than a process of maturity, of evolving toward an authentic culture in the New World. But he was to come to see this as a matter of urgency. Before the outbreak of war, visiting England during the time of George Dangerfield's "strange death" of liberalism, he responded warmly to things like the women's suffrage movement but found that the country itself seemed "very old and weary, as if the demands of the twentieth century were proving entirely too much for its powers, and it was waiting half-cynically and apathetically for some great cataclysm." As he wrote to a friend: "It pains me to think how we have allowed ourselves to be hypnotized by England: we need to see it as the stupid, blundering, hypocritical beast it is." But these rather trite impressions of a country past its zenith were succeeded by a much more cutting and bitter style once England's war had engulfed the

United States. In essays for *The New Republic* and *The Dial*, influential far beyond their small circulations, he argued fiercely against the "cultural humility" of America in the face of reverently imported referees like Matthew Arnold. It was time, Bourne felt, to "express the soul of this hot chaos of America" in a "new American nationalism." The contest with Anglo-Saxon complacency and Victorian values seemed to him to be one and the same, and he hailed the advent of Theodore Dreiser in particular as an author who captured "an America that is in the process of forming." At a time when dissent was being squashed in the press and in the universities (Columbia announced that its purpose was to turn out "thinking bayonets" via a special course on Western civilization), Bourne intensified his prewar position that "the good things in the American temperament and institutions were not English but are the fruit of our superior cosmopolitanism." As the war ground on and became more chauvinistic, he defended a thesis of his own that owed something to William James, who had written that "the pluralist world is more like a federal republic than an empire or a kingdom."

He was therefore engaged on all fronts, not just against the ideas of empire and kingdom (symbolized by Great Britain) but against the ideas of racial and class superiority that would be necessary to rivet these ideas on the United States. Meeting hyphenation head-on, he announced that the despised hyphenates and immigrants were in fact the best insurance against a "tasteless, colorless fluid of conformity." For its pains in publishing Bourne's vision of "Trans-National America," *The Atlantic Monthly* was deluged with accusations of treason. Even its Bostonian editor, Ellery Sedgwick, wrote privately to Bourne to inquire: "What have we to learn of the institution of democracy from the Huns, the Poles, the Slavs?"

Undaunted, Bourne moved further into opposition and in his most celebrated essay, "The War and the Intellectuals," published by *The Seven Arts*, bluntly described the partisans of the war and its glories as "English colonials." His untimely death in 1918 did not prevent him from exerting a formative influence on the "Lost

Generation" of new, young American writers. In the period of worldliness and "realism" that followed the war there were to be further, more demotic sallies against the hegemony of the old WASP literary establishment and the forces that it stood for. This, too, had its effect in lending a distinctive tone to the sorts of reaction against British political influence that were to become widespread.

There was, in the determined un-Englishness of men like Theodore Dreiser and H. L. Mencken and F. Scott Fitzgerald, a certain ethnic resentment, too, of the sort that Bourne might well have found raw. Still, raw as it may have been, it was energetic. "I wonder why you do the climber so well," wrote John O'Hara to Fitzgerald. "Is it the Irish in you?" Fitzgerald replied: "Being born in that atmosphere of crack, wisecrack and countercrack I developed a two-cylinder inferiority complex. So if I was elected King of Scotland tomorrow after graduating from Eton, Magdalen and the Guards, with an embryonic history which linked me to the Plantagenets, I would still be a parvenu. I spent my youth in alternately crawling in front of the kitchen maids and insulting the great." What is striking here is surely the presumed knowledge of English form, and the assumed usage of English imagery, to denote the sufferings of class and to convey the sense of deracination. Jay Gatsby and Nick Carraway are present somewhere in that discontent. Remember also what Fitzgerald wrote to Edmund Wilson from London in 1921. "God damn the continent of Europe . . . It is of merely antiquarian interest." In a quarter of a century at most, he asserted, New York would be "the global capital of culture" because "culture follows money . . . *we will be the Romans of the next generations as the English are now.*"

Irish self-consciousness, never that difficult to arouse, was at any rate slightly easier to express than German self-pity. But H. L. Mencken and Theodore Dreiser, giants in the dawning age of realism and the modern dry-eyed approach, had both undergone stupid persecution by the anti-"hyphenation" forces during the First World War, and had undergone it not for their pro-German sympathies (which were admitted) but for their German identities. Dreiser's novel *The Genius* was the subject of an astonishing series of attacks, all of them baiting him for his origins, and one assault in particular from Stuart Sherman, professor at the University of Illinois, who accused him of depicting characters who were neither Anglo-Saxon nor moral. Attacked by Mencken, who took up the case with a satire called "The Dreiser Bugaboo," Sherman riposted by saying that Mencken, after all, was an admitted admirer of Joseph Conrad. He appended a list of all the bad elements known to him who possessed German names—among them Alfred A. Knopf and Louis Untermeyer. Poor Mencken himself was denounced for exhibiting "a Teutonic-Oriental pessimism and nihilism." After America's formal entry into the war, Professor Sherman issued an official pamphlet belittling German culture and calling for a boycott of Schopenhauer and Nietzsche.

These disordered attacks, combined with vulgar bans on the music of Beethoven and the foolish attempt to call sauerkraut "Liberty Cabbage" and German measles "Liberty Measles," created a durable antipathy which, after the war, was expressed in the highly popular pages of *The Smart Set*. Mencken, who had complained of a much earlier period in his life that American children's comics had taught him "an immense mass of useless information about English history and the English scene, so that to this day I know more about Henry VIII and Lincoln Cathedral than I know about Millard Fillmore or the Mormon Temple," unmasked his batteries quite early. In *The National Letters* in 1920 he ridiculed the old gang who had missed Sinclair Lewis and had stuck fast to the docile, tepid conventions of New England and the American Academy. "One never remembers a character in the novels of these aloof and de-Americanized Americans; one never encounters an idea in their essays; one never carries away a line out of their poetry. It is literature as an academic exercise." And he took his revenge on the period of anti-German xenophobia by crowing with some truth in 1923:

It is, indeed, curious to note that practically every American author who moaned and sobbed for democracy between the years 1914 and 1919 is now extinct. The rest have gone down the chute of the movies.

When Hemingway began publishing fiction, he dedicated it to Mencken, thus showing the extent to which a new style had set in. There was a shadier side to this style, as we now know from Mencken's posthumously published letters and as might have been guessed from his quarrel with Alfred A. Knopf (also a victim during the Great War for having the wrong-sounding name) about Nazism. In brief, Mencken and his publisher fell out over the question of whether Hitler had a point. But this was a deformity in Mencken personally, and even in retrospect seems to have had more to do with a thwarted, soured German-Americanism than with anything like full-blooded Nazi sympathy. It formed part of the levy or tax that was exacted by the legacy of 1914–18 and by the hubris of the British in trading upon American ethnic rancor.

Dreiser went the other way into near-unconditional fellow traveling, and as late as May 1940 wrote: "If England is not a totalitarian state there never was one. It has been for the last three hundred years a landed and primogeniture-legalized and titled and high-financed autocracy. The clerk and labor classes in England have no more opportunity to express themselves democratically than the Germans, the Russians or the Italians." It was stupidity on this scale—very popular at the time on the American left and right as well as in the isolationist Midwest—which, once superseded, led to the revival of pro-British emotion as a consequence of the Second World War. This time, though, the emotional support came with a definite tariff, as Churchill was to find.

It was in fact in reaction to another Dreiser diatribe that George Orwell wrote in June 1944 that "the American imperialists, *advancing to the attack behind a smoke-screen of novelists*, are always on the lookout for any disreputable detail about the British Empire." Orwell had very recently been much irritated by Dreiser's description of the English as "a nation of horse-riding aristocratic snobs" and, living as he did in a battered and rationed London, wasn't having any of it. Yet he spent much of his own time stressing disreputable details about the British Empire, and even at the height of the war defended the nationalists of India and Burma. So it is impressive to remember that there used to be real tension, even at a time of supposedly warm alliance, over things like class and empire. These matters, then, signified still-existing rivalries and drew upon racial and ethnic jealousies that had been well fertilized. Only the decline in the relative weight and strength of England has allowed good temper and nostalgia to become so general.

If there were ever any Greeks in this relationship, they were the dexterous, cynical, or teasing authors who sought, in the post-1945 period, to warn the United States against becoming too Roman, too solemn, and too top-heavy with grim self-imposed "burdens." Allowing for the grand exception of Gore Vidal, a native Hellenist among American proconsuls, most of these authors were Englishmen who either had some personal colonial experience or who could read the signs of pomposity or self-deception. The best-known of these is of course Graham Greene, who has been justly celebrated for an ability to choose the right place and time from Cuba to Vietnam, and who has been repeatedly excluded from the United States by the bafflingly unironic provisions of the McCarran Act. (He exacted a feline post-imperial revenge by coming to Washington once as a diplomatically immune member of the Panamanian delegation at the signing of the Canal Treaty.)

Greene in *The Quiet American* describes a United States embassy in Saigon in the 1950s where "even their lavatories were air-conditioned." He brings us Joe, the Economic Attaché who while patronizing one of his female staff says: "She likes it. None of this stuffy colonialism." In *Ways of Escape* he argued journalistically that the British learned more than the Americans did from Dien Bien Phu; deciding as a result to pull out of Malaya. Anthony Burgess, in the final volume of his Malay trilogy, *The Long Day Wanes*, implies the alternative conclusion that the Americans intended to replace the British in Malaysia also. Syed Omar, the old colonial retainer, needs a new master and goes to the U.S. Information Service building. "This had formerly been the British Residency: the Americans paid a generous rent to the Sultan for its use." Syed Omar is given a van, on which is painted a picture "in the most beautiful Arabic script, called *Suara Amerika* (The Voice of America)." The newspaper of this name has to be delivered to illiterate villagers, who receive Syed Omar with hospitality and who "never tired of laughing at the picture of the eagle shaking claws with the tiger."

Still in Asia, site of so much Anglo-American jealousy in the Churchill-Roosevelt period, we find J. G. Farrell describing the seduction of an old English merchant house by an Anglicized American officer in *The Singapore Grip*, and J. G. Ballard depicting the American takeover of Shanghai from the Japanese *and* the British in *Empire of the Sun*. His choice of the decisive moment has a cornucopia falling from the belly of a B-29:

Tins of Spam, Klim and Nescafe, bars of chocolate and cellophaned packets of Lucky Strike and Chesterfield cigarettes, bundles of *Reader's Digest* and *Life* magazines, *Time* and *Saturday Evening Post.*

All of this a long way from the time when American policy in China was described as that of "Britain's jackal." Forgotten altogether is Kipling's admonition to any fool who might "try to hustle the East."

As Fouad Ajami might have predicted, the American monuments to this episode—the brief period of United States global hegemony—are in political prose rather than in fiction or poetry. But the titles give off something of a farewell to the trumpet—*Ropes of Sand, The Best and the Brightest, All Fall Down, A Bright Shining Lie*. In the sly but important contribution of English letters to the prosaic, preoccupied world of American policy agony is a subtle trace of the remains of a grand alliance. The relationship will persist, of course, as it has to. But the things that give it persistence are the very factors, limiting by their nature, that prevented it from developing in a more even, various, and possibly durable way. The stress upon blood, upon class, upon empire as the chief test of a national will has been depleting. Its returns show a strong tendency to diminish. Whatever shape the world is now assuming, the time when it could have been governed as an Anglo-American condominium is long past—even when one remembers that this fantasy of Rhodes and Kipling was still being deliberated at Fulton in 1946. For the United States, the appropriation of Englishness has become principally a matter of style and taste, of the sort that could easily be superseded in a generation. For the United Kingdom, or the English, the claim to a "special relationship" with a transatlantic superpower has lost much of its force and savor as the axis of the old Atlantic Charter has rusted on the hinge. The world of Churchill and Roosevelt, to say nothing of the world of Mahan and Hay and the Adamses, has become a historical curio.

It turns out that, whether as empire, partnership, or civilizing mission, the two peoples were not destined to be the lords of humankind. Their main inheritance in the coming polycentric century will be the English language—even if as a final irony this is transmitted through American cultural media and artifacts. Meanwhile it will be a splendid thing if, showing that countries can after all learn from history, the United States decided to become less Roman, and the British decided to become more Greek, and both rediscovered republican virtues in a world without conquerors.

Bibliographic Note

1. GREECE TO THEIR ROME

Juvenal's *Satires* have been edited and introduced by Peter Green in such a way as to instruct the nonclassicist and are available in Penguin. For continuous examples of the lost art of Anglophobia, with much good general reflection on the English besides, Edmund Wilson's *Europe Without Baedeker* should be read, as should his reflections in *The Forties*. André Visson's *The Athenian Complex* was written in order to sweeten Europeans for the bitter pill of American hegemony in 1948, and is long out of print, but it did not avoid some of the salient difficulties of the emerging new order especially as they touched upon cultural aspects. The late Sir Ronald Syme gave a wonderful Brademas Lecture entitled *Greeks Invading the Roman Government*, published by the Hellenic College Press in Brookline, Massachusetts, in 1982. Michael Grant's *The Fall of the Roman Empire: A Reappraisal* was written at the instigation of Ambassador Walter Annenberg and published by the Annenberg School Press in 1975. It bears the marks of its conception, and I consider it in a later chapter, but it does set out to address the latent analogies discussed in this one. Garry Wills, who may dispute with Gore Vidal the latter's claim to be America's official historian, was very suggestive about the Roman republican tradition in his *Cincinnatus: George Washington and the Enlightenment*. Of the innumerable books on Harold Macmillan, Alistair Horne's biography in two volumes (1988 and 1989) is certainly the most exhaustive, though it treats all matters affecting the "special relationship" as if they were too important for the gaze of the profane.

2. BRIT KITSCH

This subject is preeminently a matter of taste, and it's therefore worth consulting Harold Nicholson's *Good Behavior: Being a Study of Certain Types of Civility* (1955), which has some quite feline discussion of Anglo-American distinctions. Martin Green's *Transatlantic Patterns: Cultural Comparisons of England with America* (1977) has dated and has a tendency to be solemn but is one of the few attempts to consider the subject entire. Stephen Spender's *Love-Hate Relations* (1974) has a literary bias and deals as far as possible with the safer aspects of the past. Paul Fussell's *Class* (1983) was given the more emollient title of *Caste Masks* when it was published in the United States, thus neatly reinforcing the point he set out to make in the first place. The Friends of Irish Freedom National Bureau of Information long ago closed its door, but some archives possess its most famous pamphlet, published in May 1920 and called *Owen Wister: Advocate of Racial Hatred: An Unpatriotic American Who Seeks to Destroy American Tradition.* Edward Marsh's memoir *A Number of People* (1939) gives the flavor of feeling about the American cousins at least as evinced by the British diplomatic elite between the wars. Marcus Cunliffe's *The Literature of the United States*, first published in 1954 and reissued in an updated form by Penguin in 1986, is a delightful labor of love by an English scholar smitten with America in the proper way. Nelson W. Aldrich's *Old Money: The Mythology of America's Upper Class* (1988) is among other things an object lesson in how to handle and disclose family secrets. It skillfully depicts, even if only as a secondary purpose, the English texture of America's blue bloods.

3. THE BARD OF EMPIRES

The letters between Theodore Roosevelt and Rudyard Kipling can be found in the Library of Congress. Almost all studies of the man and his life and work discount the influence he exerted on American expansionism, or else seem unaware of it. A partial exception is Lord Birkenhead, whose *Rudyard Kipling* (1978) contains much good material on the correspondence with Roosevelt and related matters. Lord Birkenhead was hampered in the publication by the late Elsie Kipling, Mrs. George Bambridge, whose epilogue piece to Charles Carrington's *Rudyard Kipling: His Life and Work* (1955) is nonetheless full of interest. T. S. Eliot's introduction to *A Choice of Kipling Verse* (1941) preserves the conservative decencies without too much panache. In John Gross's collection of essays *Rudyard Kipling: The Man, His Work and His World* (1972), there are especially fine contributions from Leon Edel, Philip French, and Nirad Chaudhuri. Angus Wilson's *The Strange Ride of Rudyard Kipling* (1977) is a highly enjoyable book which often stresses Kipling's interest in America while never synthesizing said interest into any general discussion. Kingsley Amis's *Rudyard Kipling* (1975 and 1986) is a witty defense of the author from the familiar charges of racism, sexism, imperialism, etc.

4. BLOOD RELATIONS

Michael Hunt's *Ideology and United States Foreign Policy* (1987) and *The Making of a Special Relationship* (1983) are excellent in their tracing of the "British effect" on American diplomatic discourse. Ruth Brandon's short history, *The Dollar Princesses* (1980), gives excellent gossip and anecdotes about the commingling of the respective upper crusts at the *fin de siècle*. E. Digby Baltzell's *The Protestant Establishment* is an indispensable starting point for all students of the subject. *The Rising American Empire* by Richard W. Van Alstyne (1960) fully deserves the admission of indebtedness that it drew from Victor Kiernan in his *America: The New Imperialism* (1981), which is in its turn a trove of research, analysis, and suggestive comparison. The best way to study Mahan is to read him in the original, beginning with *The Influence of Sea Power upon History, 1660–1783*, which is his classic statement. But in order to appreciate his thinking on the potential of empire and the pros and cons of an explicit Anglo-Saxonism, one should also read *The Panama Canal and Sea Power in the Pacific*, with its chapter "The Importance of the Canal to Anglo-Saxon Influence." His article "Possibility of an Anglo-American Reunion" in the *North American Review* for November 1894 is also of great interest, as is his *Lessons of the War with Spain* (1898, 1899). *Types of Naval Officers* (1893) and *The Story of the War in South Africa, 1899–1900* (1900) show his deep attachment to English models of seafaring and soldiering. *Le Salut de la Race Blanche et l'Empire des Mers*, edited by Jean Izoulet (1906), is a real imperial curio that breathes the spirit of its time. W. D. Puleston's *Mahan: The Life and Work of Captain A. T. Mahan* (1939), with its loving preface by Duff Cooper, supplies numerous clues to Mahan's contemporary importance. M. B. Young's *The Rhetoric of Empire: American China Policy 1895–1901* (1968) shows the close coincidence between British and American justifications of conquest. For those who want to read the important but now forgotten Reverend Josiah Strong in the original, his once famous *Our Country* may be found in *Readings in American History*, edited by Oscar Handlin (1957).

5 · VOX AMERICANA

Woodrow Wilson's *A History of the American People* (1901 and 1902) is one of the essential texts of Anglophilia in its mode of historical expression and its social and racial assumptions. *The Columbia Literary History of the United States*, edited by Emory Elliott (1988), is a trove of actual and potential filiations between the two languages and literatures. H. L. Mencken's *The American Language* is amusing and instructive about both the assumptions of Englishness and some of the attempts at challenging these. *Grammar and Good Taste: Reforming the American Language* by Dennis E. Baron (1982) helps illustrate the connection between style and class. Thomas F. Gossett's *Race: The History of an Idea in America* (1963) helps illuminate the ever-intriguing subject of WASPdom. On the political front, Henry Pelling's *America and the British Left* (1956) shows unintentionally that the current form of the "special relationship" rests upon the defeat of radical forces in both countries, which used to enjoy a forgotten "special relationship" of their own. Of the myriad books which treat England's efforts to engage America as a brotherly power in the First World War, I have found Walter Karp's *The Politics of War* (1979) very helpful. *Northcliffe: An Intimate Biography* by Hamilton Fyfe (1969) shows how some part of the trick was worked. Henry James's *England at War: An Essay. The Question of the Mind* can be found, as far as I know, only in the Library of Congress. Stanley Morison's "Personality and Diplomacy in Anglo-American Relations," which deals with the noncultural side of the war bargain, may be found in *Essays Presented to Sir Lewis Namier*, edited by Richard Pares and A. J. P. Taylor (1956).

6. FROM LOVE TO HATE AND BACK AGAIN

America's Economic Supremacy by Brooks Adams was published by Macmillan in 1900 and is very helpful in recalling some part of the spirit of that age. Macmillan also brought out a posthumous volume, edited by Brooks, of the work of Henry Adams. In 1919 this consisted of *The Tendency of History, A Letter to Teachers of American History*, and *The Rule of Phase Applied to History*, with a long preface by Brooks. Reprinted as *The Tendency of History* in 1928, it appeared with the preface removed. *Henry Adams and Brooks Adams: The Education of Two American Historians* by Timothy Paul Donovan (1961) is very good on the contrasts between the two and on the farouche ideas of the lesser-known one. *Henry Adams and His Friends: A Collection of His Unpublished Letters*, edited by Harold Dean Cater (1947), shows the importance of the aside in the consideration of a mind, and has some distressing evidence of prejudice. Stephen Gwynne's *The Letters and Friendships of Sir Cecil Spring-Rice* (1929) is more lenient in that he omits from the letters some of Spring-Rice's more self-righteous remarks about American wartime neutrality.

7. THE CHURCHILL CULT

The Churchill bibliography is too vast to be attempted here, but in its lesser-known aspects can be augmented slightly. For Churchill's devious role in the war of intervention, *America's Siberian Adventure 1918–1920* by Major General William S. Graves (1931) is an eye-opener. So is *Fighting Without a War: An Account of Military Intervention in North Russia* by Ralph Albertson (1920). *Room Forty: British Naval Intelligence 1914–1918* by Patrick Beesly (1982) is one in what threatens to become a British genre of intelligence histories that put the assumptions of their authors into conflict with the demands of truthfulness and see veracity win. Churchill's *My Early Life* is a bombastic account of just that, and is astonishingly unreflective about the United States in view of his later reputation for prescience. On the odd years of Churchill's career in the 1920s and 1930s, Captain Stephen Roskill's *Naval Policy between the Wars* (1968) is a careful but nonetheless startling account of imperial antagonism. In their otherwise highly orthodox and mid-Atlantic book *An Ocean Apart* (1988) David Dimbleby and David Reynolds also deal with this period of Anglo-American estrangement. Brian McKercher, in "Wealth, Power and the New International Order: Britain and the American Challenge in the 1920s" (*Diplomatic History*, Fall 1988), fills in considerable background. "The World War and the Cold War," John Bagguley's essay in *Containment and Revolution* (1967), argues well about the relationship of the one to the other.

8. FDR's Victory; Churchill's Defeat

Here again, the bibliography is more titanic than gigantic. The three volumes of *Churchill and Roosevelt: The Complete Correspondence* (1984) are a tremendous record and have put us all in the debt of their editor, Warren F. Kimball. The titles, *Alliance Emerging, Alliance Forged,* and *Alliance Declining,* are artificial in point of their periodization and slightly misleading in that they show a continuous friction and decline throughout. They still merit the term "indispensable" and have exhaustive accompanying notes and references. Warren Kimball's essay "Lend-Lease and the Open Door: The Temptation of British Opulence 1937–42" (*Political Science Quarterly*, July 1971) rehearses some of the themes that are to be found in the *Correspondence*. *Special Relationships: America in Peace and War* by Sir John Wheeler-Bennett (1975) is a wonderful account, often unintentionally hilarious, of the class aspect of the "special relationship" and of the advantages of breeding in maintaining it. *As It Happened*, by William Paley (1979), shows the susceptibility of certain Americans to that sort of approach. In both cases, the apogee is that of the supposed high noon of wartime collaboration.

9. Churchill's Revenge

On James Burnham, that now neglected figure, the literature is smaller than it should be. His *The Struggle for the World* (1947) bears re-reading, as does George Orwell's critique of it in his *Collected Essays* (1969). Samuel T. Francis's *Power and History* (1984) is an admiring account of Burnham's ideas and influence. A special issue of the *National Review*, published on the occasion of Burnham's death on September 11, 1987, lets some important cats out of the bag.

10. Imperial Receivership

Ian S. MacDonald's collection of documents and readings, *Anglo-American Relations Since the Second World War* (1974), is something to keep by you as you read D. Cameron Watt's *Succeeding John Bull: America in Britain's Place*,

1900–1975 (1985) and *Imperialism at Bay* by William Roger Louis (1978). The latter book, as its title implies, is more prepared to call things by their unambiguous names. *Rise to Globalism: American Foreign Policy 1938–80*, by Stephen Ambrose, also gives an idea of the scale of the process. For some of the lesser-known examples of receivership that I have discussed, *Bitter Fruit* by Stephen Kinzer and Stephen Schlesinger (1982) is a brilliant account of the events in Guatemala, while *Something Ventured* the memoirs of C. M. Woodhouse (1983), contains a deceptively laconic account of the Anglo-American intervention in Iran. George Rosie's *The British in Vietnam* (1970) comes as a surprise to most people. Selig Harrison's articles in *The New Republic* for August 1959 ("Case History of a Mistake") were extraordinarily farsighted about policy in Pakistan and Afghanistan and very illuminating about the British role in the hand-over of power.

11. DISCORDANT INTIMACY

The Special Relationship: Anglo-American Relations Since 1945, edited by William Roger Louis and Hedley Bull (1987), is a very representative collection of Atlanticist wisdom culled from the think tanks of both countries. *The American Rhodes Scholarships: A Review of the First Forty Years* by Frank Aydelotte (1946) is a solemn but informative account, taking the scholarships at their own valuation. Max Beloff contributed a heretical essay entitled "The Special Relationship: An Anglo-American Myth" to the volume *A Century of Conflict: Essays Presented to A. J. P. Taylor*, edited by Martin Gilbert (1966). Dean Acheson's *Present at the Creation* (1970) gives the game away at several points. *Imperial Brain Trust*, by William Mintner and Laurence Shoup (1977), took advantage of a brief self-critical moment in American foreign policy discussion to shine the spotlight on the Council on Foreign Relations. Ronald Tree's memoir *When the Moon Was High* (1975) is another classic of American Anglophilia in a wartime setting. *The Isolationist Impulse: Its Twentieth Century Reaction* by Selig Adler (1957) shows the contrasting influence exerted in America by suspicion of British motives. *Less Than Kin: A Study of Anglo-American Relations* by William Clark (1957) presents the issue from the point of view of a Downing Street flack but does so with some humor and honesty. Sir Harold Nicholson's W. P. Ker Lecture, *The Future of the English-Speaking World* (1948), wavers interestingly between caution and optimism. *Problems in Anglo-American Relations* by H. V. Hodson (Ditchley Paper No. 1, 1963, Ditchley Park Foundation) is a straightforward conservative tract, full of worry about American disapproval of the British. Sir Evelyn Shuckburgh's *Descent to Suez* (1986) is straightforwardly conservative but written by a Foreign Office mandarin who worried that the Americans might be taking Britain too much for granted. Richard Neustadt's memoir on how Washington should handle the British Labor Party, pirated by *New Left Review* in its issue of

September–October 1968, is a perfect example of the private language of manipulation employed by "special relationship" professionals.

12. THE BOND OF INTELLIGENCE

Robin Winks's *Cloak and Gown: Scholars in the Secret War, 1939–1961* (1987) concerns neither God nor man but espionage at Yale, and wittily shows how the ethos of the English club and common room, as applied to intelligence, was applied in America. Donald Downes's *The Scarlet Thread* (1953) is essential for its intuitions about Anglo-Americanism. Nigel West's *The Friends: Britain's Post-War Secret Intelligence Operations* (1988) is part of the culture of the semi-official leak whereby most English people find out what little it is thought fit for them to know. *My Silent War* by Kim Philby (1968) was written before *glasnost* but has some amusing Washington anecdotes. *The Quiet Canadian* by H. Montgomery Hyde is a near-pure hagiography of William Stephenson but contains some handy indiscretions. *The Real Spy World* by Miles Copeland (1974) is oxymoronic in title but realistic about the "special relationship." (Mr. Copeland also contributed a revealing essay on James Burnham to the *National Review* memorial issue mentioned above.) Peter Wright's self-serving but suggestive *Spycatcher* (1987) should be read only in conjunction with David Leigh's *The Wilson Plot* (1988), which has more reliable and extensive information. One day, *British Security Coordination: An Account of Secret Activities in the Western Hemisphere, 1940–45* will be published, or will become available in the Public Record Office. The material for a revised history of the "special relationship," however, has a way of falling foul of the Official Secrets Act.

13. NUCLEAR JEALOUSIES

The Cabinet papers for the Macmillan years are slowly becoming available at the Public Record Office in London. Meanwhile, Dr. Margaret Gowing's *Independence and Deterrence: Britain and Atomic Energy* (1974) is an outstanding account of the political aspects of the Atlantic nuclear alliance. (She also contributed an excellent essay to the Louis-Bull "special relationship" anthology cited in the bibliography for Chapter 11.) R. G. Hewlett and F. Duncan's *A History of the U.S. Atomic Energy Commission* is a necessary and logical counterpart. *The Unsinkable Aircraft Carrier* by Duncan Campbell (1984) is a fine piece of investigation which should shame the Parliament and press that needed to leave such a task to a lone individual. *The Forrestal Diaries: The Inner History of the Cold War*, edited by William Millis (1951), shows the panicky and improvised way in which major long-term decisions were (and by extension are) taken in this field.

Index